D1199415

The Grand Fleet

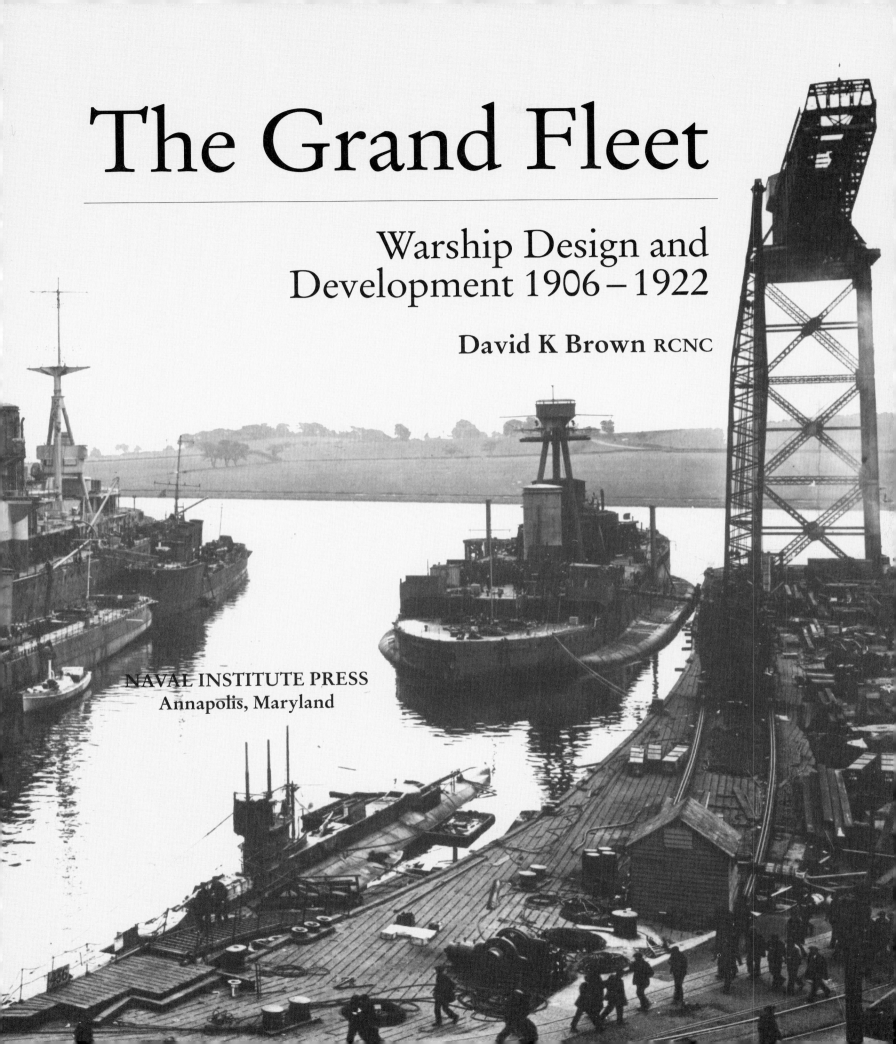

The Grand Fleet

Warship Design and Development 1906–1922

David K Brown RCNC

NAVAL INSTITUTE PRESS
Annapolis, Maryland

Frontispiece

This photograph of John Brown's yard in July 1916 shows many of the ship types described in the book. Next to the building slip is the battlecruiser *Repulse* with the destroyers *Romola* and *Peregrine* (astern) alongside. The submarine *E 35* is on the other side of the basin with the monitor *Erebus* behind, under the 200-ton crane ready to receive her 15in turret. (Imperial War Museum: SP11)

First published in Great Britain in 1999 by Chatham Publishing, 61 Frith Street, London W1V 5TA

Published and distributed in the United States of America and Canada by the Naval Institute Press, Beach Hall, 291 Wood Road, Annapolis, Maryland 21402-5035

A Library of Congress Catalog Card No. is available on request.

ISBN 1-55750-315-X

This edition authorized for sale only in the United States of America, its territories and possessions, and Canada.

Manufactured in Great Britain

Contents

Foreword and Acknowledgements

Part I: Pre-War Developments

Introduction		10
One	Preparations for War	16
Two	Attack and Defence: Pre-War Trials	26

Part II: Pre-War Designs

Three	Battleships	36
Four	Cruisers	55
Five	Destroyers and Early Naval Aviation	68
Six	Submarines	78

Part III: Wartime Experience and Design

Seven	Major Vessels	88
Eight	Wartime Destroyers and Aviation Vessels	106
Nine	Wartime Submarines	124
Ten	Smaller Vessels and Shipbuilding	136
Eleven	Action Damage and the Experience of War	155
Twelve	Warship Design from the Armistice to Washington	172
Thirteen	The Achievement: the Right Ships and the Right Fleet	188

Appendices

1.	Views on the All-Big-Gun Battleship	192
2.	Thornycroft and Yarrow 'Specials' of the First World War	194
3.	Riveting	197
4.	The Stability of a Flooded Ship	199
5.	Second Moment of Area and Moment of Inertia	200

Review of Principal Sources	201
Glossary and Abbreviations	203
Index	205

Foreword and Acknowledgements

THE AIM of this book is to review the design and construction of British warships and their machinery up to and during the First World War, together with the immediate post-war years when lessons of the war were studied, concluding with the Washington Treaty. The technology of guns and their fire control, of torpedoes etc, will be considered only in sufficient depth to recognise their impact on the overall design of the ships. Some of the story is well known and will be dealt with briefly but there are many topics which are less familiar and will be treated in more depth. Where possible, designs which were not built will be described in some detail as they often form the 'missing link' between well-known classes. In particular, attention will be paid to the battleships and cruisers designed just prior to the First World War when ideas were changing rapidly.

By the time *Dreadnought* was designed, naval architecture was a well-developed technology, with scientific backing for most aspects and soundly-based empirical solutions available where direct calculation was not possible. Stability was well understood, though there was some uncertainty over its link with rolling, while the two Froudes had developed procedures for model testing of hulls and propellers, supported by trials, which worked well in most cases and gave the RN an important lead. The structural design method initiated by Rankine and Reed and applied by White had been verified by Biles' trials on the *Wolf*.[1] The design process was not, however, an automatic one and there was plenty of scope for individual styles, perhaps most apparent in the arrangement of armour. Thicker plates were all of the well-proven Krupp Cemented (KC) material but materials for thinner plates varied and the arrangements, confirmed by trials, differed widely. The design methods in use differed little from those which I was taught as a student and used as a young assistant. Only the introduction of the computer made major change possible

Submarine design developed quite quickly and by 1914 the RN's large fleet included a considerable number of overseas boats. From 1913 onwards, the many problems of carrying and operating aircraft at sea were solved, giving the RN in the *Argus* of 1918 the only true aircraft carrier of the war. It is convenient and nearly correct to attribute ships built before the war to Sir Phillip Watts and those during the war to Sir Eustace Tennyson d'Eyncourt. Both were great gentlemen in the traditional sense and great designers.

It was, however, the age of the Marine Engineer. Turbines were novel and there was keen competition between Parsons designs and those of the American Curtis company for which John Brown held the UK licence. Turbines benefited greatly – as did propeller efficiency – from the introduction of gearing just before the war. The use of oil firing presented many difficulties which were gradually overcome. British engineers led the way in all these aspects but, surprisingly, they continued to use large tube boilers long after the benefits of the small tube boiler became apparent, penalising RN ships in weight and space.

The Engineers-in-Chief

Engineer Vice-Admiral Sir John Durston	1903-07
Engineer Vice-Admiral Sir Henry Oram	1907-17
Engineer Vice-Admiral Sir George Goodwin	1917-22
Engineer Vice-Admiral Sir Robert Dixon	1922-28

There is a widespread, but unjustified, belief that funds for the Navy were almost unlimited in the run-up to war. In fact, successive governments were dedicated to economy or to spending in other areas. The way in which available funds were used to achieve a balanced fleet is an important theme.

This book cannot be a history of the shipbuilding industry but tribute must be paid to the very numerous shipyards and their supporting industries, large and small, which built the enormous fleet of the First World War. Minesweeping and anti-submarine warfare needed a very large number of small ships, largely built by shipyards without warship experience. I have included a small selection of plans from the magnificent collection held in the National Maritime Museum and have chosen the smaller ships since they are less well known – and also reproduce better!

It will be suggested that British ship and machinery designers produced ships which stood up well to the first major war for a century. Understandably, the British saw the German Navy as the main rival before the war but it was the industrial skill and might of the USA which would lead by the end of the era.

1. D K Brown, *Warrior to Dreadnought* (London 1997), pp184-5

Acknowledgements

One must make special mention of John Campbell who up to his death in 1998 was such a help on armament matters to so many writers. I must then thank George Moore who read all the drafts and provided many useful ideas and I McCallum for drawing my attention to the importance of shells and their fuses. John Roberts has been most helpful with illustrations. Others who contributed include L Ahlberg, J Brooks, J D Brown, J Coates, K McBride, A Holbrook, G Hudson, I Johnston, R Morris, G Penn, P Pugh, J Shears, T Shaw, R Todd, J Wraight and last but not least, the Chatham editorial team.

The photographs were largely selected from the author's collection. That this is so comprehensive owes much to successive secretaries of the Naval Photograph Club of which the author is Vice President. The original source is acknowledged where known but many are unknown and I apologise for any unwitting use of someone's material. My thanks are also due to the naval secretary of the World Ship Society for permission to use their photographs.

PART I:
Pre-War Developments

Introduction

THE SUCCESS of naval staffs and constructors in developing the ships and fleets which fought the war can be judged from two viewpoints. Firstly, it may be asked if they used existing knowledge wisely in support of their perceived naval objectives and, secondly, if with hindsight either the aims or the means used could have been better. In judging success, national objectives and the resources available must be considered. From the building of the *Dreadnought* in 1905 to the outbreak of war the size of most categories of ship increased greatly as did their numbers.

Numbers of ships 1907-18

Category	Sep 1907	Sep 1914	Nov 1918
Dreadnoughts	1	25	33
Old battleships	61	40	31
Battlecruisers	-	9	9
Cruisers	60	122	96
Destroyers & TB	147	334	618
Torpedo Gunboats	18	18	13
Sloops, patrol, M/S	10	10	294
Submarines	29	75	164
Aircraft carriers*	-	1	13
Monitors	-	-	36
Total inc. misc	390	639	1750

*Including seaplane carriers

A general view of the Grand Fleet at Scapa Flow. The majority of them were designed under Phillip Watts. In the foreground is *Neptune*, with (left to right) *Thunderer, Royal Sovereign, Canada, Erin, Royal Oak, Iron Duke, Orion, Marlborough, Australia, Monarch, St Vincent* and *New Zealand*. (Author's collection)

Aims

The Royal Navy had the traditional objectives of a sea command navy. Jellicoe, first as C-in-C and then First Sea Lord spelt these out.

- To secure the use of the seas for British ships and preventing their use by the enemy.
- To bring economic pressure on the enemy country.
- To prevent invasion of the homeland.[1]

To some extent, the potential to carry out these tasks was seen as a deterrent to war.

Germany's aims were less clear. Tirpitz originally intended to build a fleet of such a size that, though still inferior to the RN, it would pose such a threat, concentrated in the North Sea, that Britain's Imperial ambitions would be constrained. There was a second duty; to keep the Baltic a German Lake. This was sometimes over-stated to win political support at home.[2]

The threat posed by such a hostile fleet and changes forced by new technology led to a re-evaluation of British planning and strategy. In 1908-09 there was a re-appraisal of the traditional 'Two Power Standard' under which the RN had a 10 per cent superiority over the combined strength of the next two largest fleets. The second foreign naval power was now the USA and war with that country was seen as unthinkable.[3] A more realistic standard was seen as a Royal Navy 60 per cent bigger than Germany's, the next largest navy and poten-

The pre-dreadnought battleship *Zealandia*, the first ship to dock at Rosyth, on 28 March 1916. (Author)

tially hostile, and this was finally agreed by Parliament in March 1912.[4]

British strategic thinking gradually adapted to the new threat. In 1903 approval was given to build a new Dockyard at Rosyth at an estimated cost of £3 million for 'works' and £250,000 for machinery, spread over 10 years. The site was 1184 acres and the main basin would be 52½ acres, large enough for eleven battleships (twenty-two doubled-up). The site was purchased during 1904-05 and Easton Gibbs & Co appointed as contractors. By the outbreak of war it was only useable to a limited extent though the work was to complete more or less on schedule. Fisher was a leading opponent, as he thought the North Sea would be out of bounds to big ships and there was already a surplus of Dockyard facilities. The increasing threat from the torpedo, particularly when launched from submarines, was recognised and the old strategy of close blockade of enemy ports was abandoned in favour of a distant blockade, sealing the exits from the North Sea.

It seemed inevitable that conflict between the two navies in the North Sea would lead to one or more major battles. The successive wars between Japan and first China, then Russia, and the Spanish-American War all seemed to show that a decisive battle would occur. The immediate German aim could be seen to be reducing the British superiority by attrition, by the use of mines and torpedoes, and by the defeat of an isolated squadron. The fear of the latter lead, inevitably, to central control of a concentrated fleet, but Admiral William May found in exercises that central control of a very large fleet was difficult as smoke would obscure the view of the C-in-C and flag signals would be hard to see.[5] On the other hand, divisional control was even more difficult and could be dangerous, leading to the possible defeat of an isolated squadron.

A fleet could only develop its full firepower when deployed in a single line and it was expected that the two fleets would fall in in parallel lines until one was defeated. Such a battle, in which the range was changing slowly, if at all, made elaborate fire control systems seem unnecessary.

The majority of naval officers hoped for and expected a decisive British victory but a few senior officers, probably including Fisher, may have realised that this dream was unlikely to be realised. The German fleet, inferior in

1. Admiral J Jellicoe, *The Grand Fleet 1914-1916* (London 1919), Ch 2.

2. P M Kennedy, *The Rise and Fall of British Naval Mastery* (London 1976).

3. An earlier study had shown that a war with the USA could not be won. As a result, the Jamaica dockyard was closed and reductions made elsewhere. The number of ships on the North American and West Indies station was greatly reduced.

4. J T Sumida, *In Defence of Naval Supremacy* (Winchester, Mass. 1989), pp190-1.

5. A Gordon, *The Rules of the Game* (London 1996) – quoting 'Notes on Tactical Exercises 1909–1911', MoD Library Eb012, p355.

The *Queen Elizabeth* class battleship *Barham* fitting out at John Browns. Note the big crane needed to install the main armament of eight 15in guns. (Author's collection)

6. In the mathematical theory of games the aim of avoiding defeat is known as 'minimax regret'.

7. I am indebted to Andrew Lambert for this line of thought.

8. G Bennett, *Charley B* (London 1968), Ch 7.

9. P Pugh, *The Cost of Seapower* (London 1986).

10. Some of this large percentage increase was due to starting from a low base.

11. Sumida, *In Defence of Naval Supremacy*, p60.

12. Bennett, *Charlie B*, Ch 11.

13. Then defined as a numerical superiority of 10 per cent over the combined capital forces of the next two navies.

Total Defence Budgets 1906-1914.

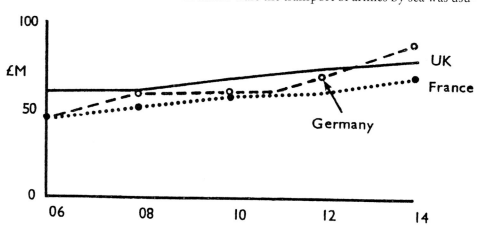

numbers, would almost certainly seek to escape rather than fight to the end. Therefore, the British aim would be to avoid defeat rather than seek victory.[6] Though Fisher was often to proclaim his choice of C-in-C as the new Nelson to win a new Trafalgar, it is more likely that he saw the cautious Jellicoe as a man who would play safe.[7]

Even the mere possibility of a major battle made it essential to out-build the potential enemy in capital ships, leaving little in the way of funds for other categories. Percy Scott and then Fisher were increasingly proclaiming that the day of the big ship was over and the future lay with the submarine, but as Keyes pointed out whilst Commodore, Submarines, the weaknesses of the RN submarine force were largely due to Fisher's decisions to concentrate on coastal boats and the restrictions of the Vickers contract!

In earlier wars the transport of armies by sea was usu-

ally much quicker than movement over dreadful roads but, by 1914, rail systems gave the advantage to the Central Powers. This was slowly appreciated when the War Staff considered some of the Navy's amateur ideas for landings on the North German coast. Sealing the exits from the North Sea stopped German trade and also protected most British merchant ships from attack, but it did also leave the east coast and coastal shipping open to attack and even invasion. Attempts to protect the east coast towns from bombardment would bring the Grand Fleet into waters where it was most vulnerable to submarines and mines. Rosyth only became effective in 1916 and the other Dockyards were ill placed to support North Sea operations, while overseas, the RN had a large number of coaling and signal stations.

This short introduction paints too clear a picture of naval intentions. The Naval Staff was in its infancy and war plans were in the head of the First Sea Lord – Fisher.[8]

Resources

Sea power must always be based on economic power although the converse may also apply. During the nineteenth century the United Kingdom became the leading European industrial power and just maintained that position until the outbreak of war.[9] Germany was, however, catching up fast; between 1898 and 1914 her industrial production rose by 85 per cent,[10] compared with only 40 per cent for the United Kingdom, leaving the two nations level. In the vital aspect of steel production, Germany already produced more than twice as much –

17 million tons – as Britain, which, however, still retained a big lead in shipbuilding capacity.

Financially, the twentieth century began badly for Great Britain: the Boer War was very expensive and, even though the Conservative government greatly increased taxation, only about one-third of the war expenditure was paid out of income. The government fell in December 1905 and in the election which followed was replaced by a Liberal government dedicated to social security – the beginning of the Welfare State – and cutting defence costs.

In 1902, under Lord Selborne (Conservative, First Lord), it had been planned to build seven battleships or First Class cruisers each year up to 1906-07 but this was cut to four under Earl Cawdor in 1905-06. A high point of £41 million in naval spending had been reached in 1904-05 but this was reduced considerably in following years (see table), partly because of Fisher's policy of scrapping older ships and partly because the shock of *Dreadnought* had stopped most other powers from ordering new battleships. The new Government did not challenge the proposed Estimate for 1906-07 but the following year they asked for a further reduction to two battleships with a third only if disarmament talks at the Hague failed – as they did.

The argument over the 1908-09 Estimates was far fiercer; the Admiralty asked for a £2 million increase which was rejected by the Cabinet. Following protests from the naval Board members, the Admiralty were allowed half the increase they had asked for, enabling the building programme to go ahead at the cost of refit work and expenditure on practice ammunition. For the three years 1906-09 Estimates were held at a level some 15 per cent below their peak partly because battleship and big cruiser building fell below even the Cawdor figure.[11] This could be justified by delays in the German programme, friendship with France and the destruction of the Russian fleet. But things were about to change.

By the end of 1908 Germany had begun nine Dreadnought battleships or battlecruisers whilst Britain was only marginally ahead with ten such ships. Britain still benefited from faster building times, particularly in the Royal Dockyards, with an average building time of 27 months (ten ships) compared with 35.9 months in Germany (nine ships). Consequently, in January 1909, the Sea Lords asked the new First Lord, Reginald McKenna, for eight capital ships in the 1909-10 Programme. McKenna proposed six but the majority of the Cabinet would only agree to four. After a bitter debate, it was agreed in February that four ships should be laid down under the normal Programme and that a further four 'contingency' ships would be laid down if necessary. There was a furious press campaign under the slogan 'We want eight and we won't wait', and finally, in July, the Government announced that the contingency ships would be built in response to Dreadnought building by Italy and Austria, which threatened the British

Pre-war Naval Estimates (£ million)

Year	Total £M	Vote 8+9*	Battleship	B'cruiser	Cruiser	Destroyer	Submarine
1905-06	37	19	1	3	-	5	11
1906-07	35	18	3	-	-	2	8
1907-08	33	16	3	-	1	5	12
1908-09	34	17	1	1	6	16	9
1909-10	36	20	6	2	6	20	6
1910-11	43	24	4	1	5	23	6
1911-12	45	25	4	-	4	20	6
1912-13	47	27	4	-	8	20	9
1913-14	52	30	5	-	8	15	11

* Cost of new construction including guns.

position in the Mediterranean. However, there were already objections by Admiral Beresford and others that the Admiralty were building an unbalanced fleet with the Dreadnought force unsupported by cruisers, destroyers and auxiliaries, a point which will be discussed in the final chapter.[12]

The financial year 1909-10 was particularly difficult as spending under the Old Age Pensions Act was rising fast whilst the scope for savings such as those on naval stores were exhausted. The Budget with its greatly raised taxes was rejected by the House of Lords in November 1909 but the election of January 1910 brought the Liberals back to power and the Budget was passed in April.

The Prime Minister (Asquith) had re-affirmed the 'Two Power Standard'[13] in November 1908 but the old threat of France and Russia had been replaced as second and third navies by Germany and the USA. The change to 160 per cent of the German fleet was proposed in April 1909 and announced to Parliament in March 1912. In fact, there was very little difference between the

Patrol boat *P 17*, an attempt to produce a small, cheap destroyer type for escort work. Note the low freeboard and the 4in gun on the superstructure.

Increase in Number of Principal
Categories of Warships

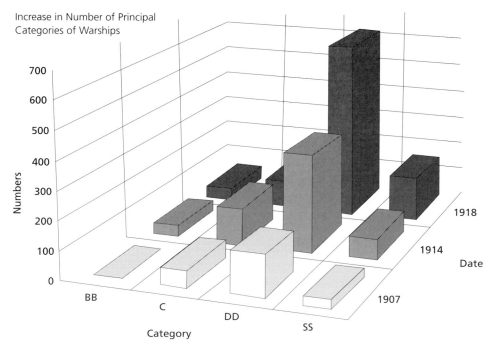

Proportions of spend by
category 1906 – 1914

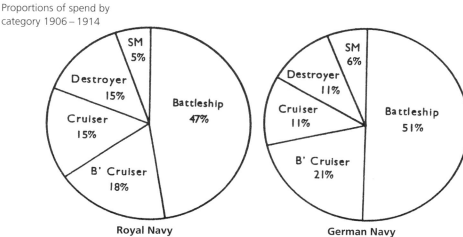

Royal Navy   **German Navy**

New Construction Estimates
1906 – 1914

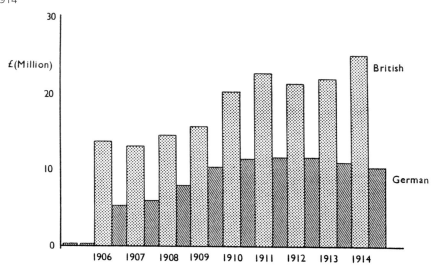

numbers derived from either standard in the years from 1909-10 to the outbreak of war. By 1913 it was intended to have eight Dreadnoughts in the Mediterranean whilst maintaining a 50 per cent superiority over Germany in home waters.

In the early years of the century, Great Britain was spending more on the services than Germany but this position was soon reversed. However, a much larger proportion of the German budget was spent on the army since the navy was always a secondary consideration and the RN was therefore consistently able to out-build them. The diagram below compares the funds devoted by each navy to new construction and figures are given in the tables at the end of this chapter. The make-up of such figures will differ and the diagram should be seen as a rough guide only.

The cumulative total number of ships launched year by year from 1906 to the end of 1914 for each navy is shown in the graphs opposite and the figures are in the notes. The Pie Charts (opposite) attempt to show how the new construction funds were split between ship types by the rival navies. The proportions differ only slightly with both concentrating on capital ships; 65 per cent by the RN, 72 per cent by Germany. It is interesting that neither navy was spending much on submarines.

Germany was building as many capital ships as was possible, limited both by funding and by heavy gun production at Krupps. The British response in capital ships was close to the planned ratio of 1.6:1 and absorbed so much of her resources that there was little to spare for trade protection, minesweeping etc. Any shift of funds would mean fewer capital ships and the margin was narrow. The table below compares the cost of various categories of ship *c*1910-11 and the trade-off ratio between battleships and other vessels.

Comparative costs

Type	Ship	Cost (£x1000)	Relative	Ships/ BB
Battleship	*K George V*	1950	100	1
Cruiser	*Chatham*	350	18	5.5
Destroyer	*Acheron*	88	4.5	22
Submarine	'D' class	89	4.5	22
Minesweeper	'Flower' class	60	3	33

Value of money

In the years leading up to the war there was little inflation or deflation and costs can be compared directly. Once war started, inflation was rapid and cost figures rose quickly. The table below shows the Board of Trade Index of Retail Prices (RPI) based on a value of 100 in 1900. This is far from a perfect measure of inflation in warship building but is the only one available and probably not far out.

Date	RPI	Date	RPI
1905	98	1914	117
1906	101	1915	114
1907	106	1916	186
1908	103	1917	243
1909	104	1918	267
1910	109	1919	296
1911	109	1920	358
1912	115	1921	230
1913	116	1922	185
		1923	185

The relevance of the price index to ship costs is shown in the cost per ton of battlecruisers (Chapter 4) which when adjusted for the index at launch date are fairly constant.

What is a Good Design – and a Good Fleet?

To discuss the question – 'What is a "Good" Design' – is not easy. This question and its answer are seen very differently by different professions and at different times. A narrow definition of naval architecture may lead a few constructors to see an economic and technically sound response to a staff requirement as 'good'. (Not the author's view.) The historian is liable to view the success of a design through the wrong end of the telescope, placing too much emphasis on its later years when the ship is obsolescent, worn out and used for tasks and facing weapons very different from those for which it was designed.

The good design must show to advantage in its operational effectiveness and minimum through-life cost based on appropriate technology in all areas. It should be versatile in capability as built and adaptable to new tasks during its life. A good design will usually be the starting point for a series of designs. The bigger question of what is a good fleet is even more difficult To some extent, the same qualities that make a good ship must also be displayed by a good fleet – effectiveness, economy and versatility.

RN Estimates Vote 8 – Shipbuilding

Date	Dockyard	£ (Million) Materials	Contract	Total
1906	2.4	2.8	8.6	13.8
1907	2.5	3.6	7.6	13.1
1908	2.9	4.2	7.7	14.8
1909	3.1	4.4	8.3	15.8
1910	3.4	4.6	12.4	20.4
1911	3.5	5.0	14.4	22.9
1912	3.5	5.1	13.1	21.7
1913	4.1	5.9	12.2	22.2
1914	4.0	7.1	14.3	25.4

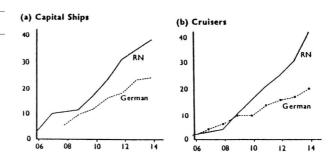

(a) Capital Ships (b) Cruisers

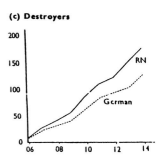

(c) Destroyers

Cumulative totals in various categories

Note **Dockyard** covers salaries and wages with a few other minor items

Materials covers timber, metal, coal, rope, canvas, electrical freight, rent, gas, etc.

Contracts The breakdown for a typical year (1903-4) was

	£K
Propelling machinery	3439
Auxiliary machinery	168
Hulls	3671
Purchase	12
Repairs	722
Inspection	70
Guns	1354
Machinery	188
Reserve Merchant Cruisers	79
Total	9571

German new construction and armaments

Date	Amount Voted £(Million)	Battleships	Ships Large Cruisers	Small Cruisers	Destroyers
1906-7	5.2	2	1	2	12
7-8	5.9	2	1	2	12
8-9	7.8	3	1	2	12
9-10	10.2	3	1	2	12
10-11	11.4	3	1	2	12
11-12	11.7	3	1	2	12
12-13	11.5	1	1	2	12
13-14	11.0	2	2	2	12
14-15	10.3	1	1	2	12

Note: It should not be assumed that these figures can be directly compared with those given for the RN since the breakdown of the above figures is not known.

C 4, a successful coastal submarine. In 1914 the RN had nearly as many submarines as the next two navies put together. (Imperial War Museum: Q41207)

One | Preparations for War

Sir Phillip Watts

Sir Phillip Watts, Director of Naval Construction 1902-12, under whom most ships built before the war were designed. (RCNC)

PHILLIP WATTS rose through the traditional route for a DNC. He was born in 1846 at Portsmouth where his father was a senior shipwright officer. As an apprentice he was outstanding and sent to the School of Naval Architecture at South Kensington. His first post was at Pembroke and he then went on to Haslar where, working under William Froude, he developed a lasting interest in hydrodynamics.[1] He designed the first anti-rolling tanks which were installed in the *Inflexible* where he met Fisher, then her captain, during trials of the tanks in 1872.[2] He played a leading part in the design of the torpedo ram, *Polyphemus*, overcoming numerous technical problems on stability, drainage and ventilation peculiar to this strange ship.

In 1885 he went to work for Armstrongs as part of the complicated deal which brought White back to the Admiralty, where he was responsible for many successful designs. When it became obvious in 1901 that White could continue no longer, Watts wrote to Fisher reminding him of his old promise to make him DNC.

Years later, Lloyd Woollard, writing in the RCNC Journal, said:

> He was a man of the world, who lived in a fine house on the Chelsea Embankment; he was fond of riding and usually took his exercise in that way in the park before setting out for the office which he reached about 1130. He remained in the office until nearly 8 in the evening, though he did not expect his staff to stay late; one shorthand typist sufficed.[3]

When he took over, the *King Edward VII* class design had been completed by the battleship section and it was endorsed jointly by White and Watts.

'Find and catch, hit first and fast and go on hitting whilst resisting enemy attack'[4]

Finding

Finding the enemy was greatly aided by the invention of wireless (radio). From the Crimean War onwards, cable telegraphy had made possible the transmission of information concerning the position of both friendly and enemy ships and of orders to deal with the situation, although cable messages were slow and could only be used for strategic communications. Wireless would have a far greater effect on tactics. Germany had put a great deal of effort into establishing a cable network but their overseas stations were quickly eliminated when war broke out.

The first trials of wireless took place at the end of the nineteenth century and it was first used operationally during the South African War in 1900 and much more extensively during the Russo-Japanese War. Thanks to the combination of Marconi and Captain Jackson the RN kept in the van of progress and by 1905 all ships larger than destroyers had been equipped.[5] Only a year later these sets were replaced by improved models and in 1907 modern destroyers received them.[6] Long-range radio links were gradually replacing cable transmission.

The USN had equipment as good as or superior to that of the RN but the latter had organised their communication procedures better. It is a frequent mistake to think of early wireless as providing instant transmission of messages. From the bridge it had to go to the signal office, be coded, transmitted and then go through the reverse procedure aboard the receiving ship. For a message to travel from bridge to bridge, 20 minutes would often be needed.[7] Most navies had experimented with jamming but without a great deal of success (however, messages did not always get through even without jamming). Early wireless installations had little effect on ship design except for the provision of even higher topmasts. There would only be one set per ship and this made no serious demands on space or power.

Catching

Once located, the enemy ship or fleet had to be caught, demanding superiority in speed. High speed is always expensive and its tactical value is limited unless one side has a very considerable advantage, say 4kts or more. The RN still benefited from the Froudes' pioneer work on model testing of both hull forms and of propellers. Most

1. Froude was to tell the Royal Commission of 1872 of the School and Watts – 'I only know its fruits, in the fact that a gentleman who is acting as one of my assistants in my investigations, and who was educated there has evidently been extremely well taught and is not only well up in the mathematics of naval architecture but in the common sense of the questions dealt with . . .'.

2. It is said that at this time Fisher promised to make Watts DNC when he became First Sea Lord.

3. D K Brown, *A Century of Naval Construction* (London 1983), p94.

4. Whilst this does not seem to be a direct quote from Admiral Fisher, it conveys the essence of his aphorisms on the quality of warships.

5. There are good grounds for claiming that Jackson rather than Marconi was the inventor of wireless. B Kent, *Signal!* (Clanfield 1993), pp26-7.

6. Vice-Admiral Sir Arthur Hezlet, *The Electron and Sea Power* (London 1975), Ch 3; G Bennett, *Naval Battles of the First World War* (London 1968), Ch 10.

7. Kent, *Signal!*, Ch 5 and 6. This author says that simple manoeuvring signals took about 20 minutes in 1914, reduced to 3 minutes by 1916. More complicated signals would take longer.

8. This represented 46,000 individual runs in the Torquay tank and 194,000 at Haslar: D K Brown. 'R E Froude and the Shape of Warships', *Journal of Naval Science*, Vol 13, No 3 (1987).

9. Today, one would think that too much attention was paid to range of stability rather than down flooding angle (see Glossary).

Battleship design

major navies had access to a ship tank by the turn of the century but model testing was not an exact science. Correction factors based on comparison of ship trials with model tests were important and the RN's data bank was far more extensive than that of any other navy, giving it a major advantage in this area. By 1919, when Edmund Froude retired, he and his father had tested models representing 33 classes of battleships, 46 of cruisers, 61 of destroyers and 14 of submarines.[8]

Even the best of hull forms needs a lot of power at high speed. Turbine machinery, discussed later, provided more power from a given space and weight than did a triple-expansion engine and, even more important, the turbine could run reliably for long periods at full power. It is convenient to represent the variation of power (shp) with speed (V) as – $shp \propto V^n$

Values of n at Top Speed

Battleship	4
Cruiser	5-6
Destroyer	4.5

At cruising speed n is about 3 for all ships.

It is tempting – and often correct – to lengthen the ship to reduce the power needed. However, length is expensive as it will usually increase the stresses on the structure and, in a capital ship, will add to the extent of the armoured citadel.

The tools of ship design were well established by the late nineteenth century. Values of strength and stability parameters could be calculated and judged for acceptability in the light of experience.[9] As discussed above, a suitable form could be developed and the power needed for the required speed could be estimated fairly accurately (a few exceptions will be mentioned later). However, each design is an individual act of creation and the skill of the designer lies in the way in which he uses these tools.

There are two basic criteria to be observed in the design of any floating vessel. The first is Archimedes' principle – Weight = Buoyancy – which is automatically satisfied since if the weight is increased, the ship will sink deeper into the water until the buoyancy is sufficient. There would then be the usual, circular arguments such as that the displacement could not be known until the machinery weight was known but the machinery size and hence its weight depended on the displacement. The second criterion is more difficult; space available is equal to or greater than space required. The difficulty lies in the meaning of 'space'; for a start, is the critical aspect volume, area or simply length? (It can be any one – or more.) Then position, both absolute and relative to other spaces, will be important as can be shape.

For ships of generally similar style there was a well

The Grand Fleet at sea with four *Orion* class battleships in the foreground. In the distance are the US Navy battleships which joined the Grand Fleet in 1917 as the 6th Battle Squadron. (Author's collection)

William Froude pioneered the technique of model testing to improve hull forms, giving the RN a valuable lead. (RINA)

Weight groups as a percentage[12]

Ship	Equipt	Armnt	Machy	Fuel	Armour	Hull
Q Elizabeth	3	16.5	14.5	2.5	31	32.5
Iron Duke	3	16	10	3.5	32	33.5
Tiger	3	12.5	21	3	27	34.5
Renown	2.5	12.5	21	3.5	21.5	39
Courageous	3.5	12	16	4	18.5	46
Lt Cruiser	6	5.5	22	7.5	8.5	51
TBD	4.5	4	35	15	-	41.5
P Boat	6	2.5	35	9	-	48
Sloop	8	2	25	15	-	50
Erebus	4.5	14.5	9	3	26	43

known, and fairly reliable,[10] short cut in estimating weight. It was assumed that the weight of the armament was the same percentage of the load displacement as in the previous ship.[11] If the ship was to have a novel type of gun whose weight was unknown (as in the *Queen Elizabeth*'s 15in), an approximate figure would be scaled from an earlier mount. Typically, the armament weight would be 16-18 per cent of the displacement for a battleship. Use of this approach implied that the space requirement varied in the same way as weight from that of the previous ship.

Naval architects tend to differentiate between ships in which considerations of weight dominate the design and those dominated by space or layout. It has usually been assumed, wrongly, that the battleship with its heavy

load of turrets and armour was the ultimate weight-dominated design but the following passage shows that it was upper-deck layout which controlled the design, which in turn explains, if not excuses, the tortured layout of the 12in-gun Dreadnoughts.

A paper prepared by Jellicoe (DNO) with contributions from Phillip Watts, summarised in Appendix 1, reads:

> The effects of blast from high velocity guns impose a minimum limit of distance between guns and thus fix the space to be occupied by the armament . . . while considerations of weight alone might allow more guns, those of space forbid any large increase in numbers, if they are to be used with effect, unless the ship is lengthened abnormally, so as to space them well apart.[13]

This is a much more significant statement than may appear at first sight, as it confirms that DNC did not see battleship design as dominated by weight but by layout. (In this passage 'space' is represented by upper deck length.)

It would seem that the initial step in satisfying the space requirement of the design was to sketch the upper deck layout which arranged the required armament in satisfactory positions and enabled other essential features to be squeezed in as, for example, in the options considered by the *Dreadnought* Committee. DNC Department had a small modelmaking section and a

10. See, however, the problems caused by this approach in the 6in monitors (Chapter 10).

11. The definition of load displacement varied slightly but was usually with the ship fully laden but with only half the fuel – a rough representation of action state.

12. d'Eyncourt papers, DEY 37. National Maritime Museum

13. HM Ships *Dreadnought* and *Invincible*. Tweedmouth Papers, MoD Library. Strictly Secret 25 copies.

14. Since shipbuilders knew this too, they tendered at a constant price per ton. One would expect bigger ships to cost a little less per ton, a self-fulfilling prophecy.

15. D K Brown, *Warrior to Dreadnought* (London 1997). The diagram on p189 shows the blast curve used in the design of *Dreadnought*.

16. With new designs almost every year scaling would be a very accurate process. At least one ship of each class would be 'weighed', *ie* every item worked into the ship would be weighed individually and its position recorded so that the weight and centre of each group could be compared with the estimate and those for future classes refined if necessary.

17. E L Attwood, *Warships – A Text Book* (London 1910), p157.

No 1 tank at Haslar, built by William's son Edmund and opened in 1887. Every surface ship was tested there until recently – it is now an office for accountants. (Admiralty Experiment Works)

simple model would be made at an early stage – Lords of the Admiralty could not read drawings. There was great political pressure to keep the size of individual ships as small as possible since cost per ton was remarkably constant and hence displacement was a reliable guide to tender price.[14]

The other items to be fitted in on the upper deck were the increasing amount of fire control equipment, masts, funnels and boats (Chapter 3). Boats were still important, as battleships would normally be moored offshore rather than come alongside and boats were needed for liberty men. Furthermore, the bigger steam boats were seen as having a role as Second Class torpedo-boats or as small gunboats. There is no doubt that the earlier Dreadnoughts (and battlecruisers) had such a cramped layout that their fighting capability was affected because control tops were in the smoke plume etc. This could have been remedied if the ship had been made a little longer but it is expensive to increase the length of a battleship. The power for top speed would go up little, if at all, since the finer form would offset the increase in displacement but the cruising power would go up and more fuel would be needed. Most importantly, if the separation of the end turrets was increased, the weight of armour would go up considerably and armour was expensive in itself (£92 per ton), whilst the cost of lengthening the ship would be even greater.

Blast effect was the critical factor in layout, and it was accepted that 30lbs/ft^2 was the greatest pressure which could be tolerated.[15] The DNO (Jellicoe) insisted that the main turrets should have an open sighting hood in the roof which precluded the use of superfiring turrets which would have made the layout easier. Open, manned spaces such as bridges, control tops etc, also had to be clear of the blast limits. Fire control was still a new concept at the time of the *Dreadnought* and the effect of hot, dirty funnel gases was not appreciated since the 'fighting tops' of earlier ships were generally below the smoke plume. Jellicoe chaired a working party on boat handling in *Dreadnought* and decided to put the principal mast between the funnels so that it could support the main boat derrick. This put the control top in the smoke plume; the mast got so hot that access was difficult and smoke obscured the sights in the top. There was a secondary control top on the short second mast which was also almost useless.

Once a size and layout had been accepted it was a simple matter to scale up[16] the weights of the hull, equipment etc, from previous ships while the power requirement and hence machinery weight could be estimated from Froude's Iso K book of tabulated resistance data and his parallel data on propeller performance. If, as seems likely, the displacement was fixed at an early stage, some adjustment would have to be made to bring all the weights into agreement with the buoyancy at the intended waterline. There are strong indications that the weight of armour was the main parameter used to

William Froude's propeller dynamometer, used for all propeller tests up to the *Manxman* class of the late 1930s. Despite its agricultural appearance it worked very well, using leather bootlaces as driving bands. (Admiralty Experiment Works)

achieve this balance and that the extent and thickness of armour would be varied as necessary. This may have been an almost subconscious action; the design team pressing strongly for more or less armour when correction to the overall displacement was needed. The displacement derived from the chosen layout would be compared with that derived from the armament weight percentage as a check; serious disagreement was only likely if there was an error.

Attwood, who was head of the battleship section for many years, wrote of an earlier design, the *Duncan*, that because of the higher speed, 'the weight available for protection would only allow a 7in belt to be worked'.[17] It is likely that similar thinking influenced the choice of thin armour in battlecruisers.

Machinery development

Engineer officers

Until 1903 seagoing naval engineers did not have commissions and were technically civilians in uniform. In March of that year they were given naval titles but were not executive officers, could not command a ship and did not wear the executive curl on their sleeve. Some old and new titles were:

Chief Inspector of Machinery	Engineer Rear-Admiral
Inspector of Machinery	Engineer Captain
Fleet Engineer	Engineer Commander
Staff Engineers, Chief Engineer and Engineers	Engineer Lieutenant

Machinery controls aboard a Dreadnought battleship, possibly *Orion*, showing regulating valves and pressure gauges. (*JNE*)

In December 1902 the Admiralty announced what became known as the Selbourne-Fisher scheme by which all officers for the Executive, Engineer and Royal Marines should form a common entry at 12-13, separating as sub-lieutenants at age 20. It was implied that all would have an equal opportunity to reach flag rank. Engineers would be distinguished by (E) following their rank and by a purple stripe and would have the executive curl.[18] Only in December 1914 were the older type of Engineer officer given the same uniform details.

Turbines

The Parsons turbines fitted in *Dreadnought* and other early British turbine ships proved generally satisfactory but there were rival designs from other countries. Parsons' early turbines were of the 'reaction' design in which the blades were so shaped that each pair of adjoining blades acted as a nozzle. Steam expanded in passing through this nozzle when the changes of pressure 'reacted' on the blades, turning the rotor.[19] The action of the 'impulse' turbine, patented in Sweden by de Laval (1889) and in the USA by Curtis (1896) was different;[20] steam expanded through fixed nozzles where its pressure reduced as its velocity increased. The high-speed steam then impinged on the blades of a rotor, very much in the way of a water wheel. In both types there would usually be several stages of blading.

In May 1905 the USN ordered three cruisers with dif-

fering machinery: *Birmingham* with triple-expansion (piston speed 1200 ft/min max.), *Salem* with Curtis turbines and *Chester* with Parsons'.[21] The design speed was 24kts with 24,000hp. Speeds achieved on a 4-hour trial were:[22]

Birmingham	24.3kts
Chester	26.5kts
Salem	25.9kts

The general conclusions were that the reciprocating engines were more economical than Parsons up to 20kts and better than Curtis to 21kts. The Parsons had a moderately greater overload capacity than the Curtis but both turbines were much better than the reciprocating engines and were also much more reliable. Shortly afterwards, John Brown took out a licence to build Curtis turbines. It was thought that the advantage of the Curtis turbine lay in its use of superheated steam, the less severe tolerance in fitting parts[23] and a simplified engine-room layout. A turbine engine-room was a good deal cleaner than one with reciprocating engines but there were still steam and oil leaks. It was noted that forced lubrication had greatly improved the reliability of the reciprocating engines.

In this country, a set of Brown-Curtis turbines was built on shore at Clydebank and the trials were observed by officers from the E-in-C. As a result, these turbines were fitted in the destroyer *Brisk* in 1909 and in the cruiser *Bristol* in 1910. *Bristol* had two separate engine-rooms each driving a single shaft as opposed to the four-shaft arrangement in Parsons-engined ships. The designed performance was 25kts with 22,000shp but on trial she achieved 26.84kts with 24,227shp. The arrangement of pipes and valves was said to be much simpler than in a Parsons layout. The following year saw the cruiser *Yarmouth* receive Brown-Curtis machinery as did five destroyers of the *Acheron* class.[24] By the time the war ended Brown-Curtis turbines were installed in more than 250 destroyers, 22 cruisers, 7 capital ships and 12 'K' class submarines. Parsons were to fight back with a combination impulse-reaction design giving about 7 per cent greater efficiency.

The introduction of oil fuel

Though most accounts of this period mention the introduction of oil fuel, few spell out the advantages and none describe the problems which the Royal Navy's engineers had to overcome in leading the way.[25] There were obvious advantages such as ease of embarkation and stowage, supply to the boilers (and hence reduction in the number of stokers) but the disadvantages of limited supply, high cost and, initially, poorer evaporation seemed more important. Furthermore, coal bunkers formed an important element in the protection schemes of many ships.[26] Two aspects which would today be seen as among the advantages of oil were, initially, quite the opposite; the greater calorific value of oil, 19,000BTU/lb compared with 14,500BTU/lb for the best Welsh coal, could not be realised due to incomplete combustion which led to early oil-burning ships being very smoky. Up to the late 1890s the Navy was content to carry out a few experiments and monitor developments elsewhere.

By 1898 the Great Eastern Railway was achieving some success using Holden burners and an experimental installation was fitted in the destroyer *Surly* using both Holden and Rusden & Eeles burners. Trials in 1898-99 were very disappointing as only about 50 per cent of the full evaporation could be obtained before dense clouds of black smoke were formed and the evaporation per pound of fuel was only 8.8lbs, compared with 10.7lbs using coal. Further trials in 1901 with improved burners from both companies were only a little more successful.

However, greater priority was given to development and a number of boilers were installed within Devonport Dockyard for trials of combustion equipment.[27] During 1902 tests were carried out with the same types of burner as those in *Surly* and these were modified to give better combustion. Better results were achieved and three ships were modified to burn oil in some of their boilers. The battleships *Mars* and *Hannibal* had two of their eight boilers converted whilst another burnt oil in conjunction with coal. The cruiser *Bedford* had her forward boilers, about a quarter of the total, modified for oil burning.

During 1902 further trials were carried out in *Surly* with both the Kermode and the Orde systems of burning. The former used heated, compressed air to spray the fuel and was reasonable successful giving an evaporation of 12.2lbs of water per pound of oil at 91 per cent full power. The Orde system, using superheated steam to vaporise and spray the oil, was less successful.

In the same year a small experimental plant was constructed in the Haslar Gunboat yard,[28] next to Froude's ship tank.[29] There was an experimental brick furnace and two small water tube boilers.[30] The mixing of air with the oil spray was greatly improved using a slotted cone nozzle and high rates of combustion were possible with excellent economy and without clouds of smoke. By 1903, the training of engineer officers and ratings was extended to cover oil burning.

Also in 1903, two boilers of the battleship *Sultan* were converted to burn oil with various types of coal, including bituminous and anthracite. As a result, the experimental oil-only boilers in *Mars*, *Hannibal* and *Bedford* were altered to mixed fuel. There were more trials at Haslar[31] which were not very successful and a modified Kermode system was tried in *Surly* which was rather better but these were abandoned with the success of the simpler 'pressure' system. In this the oil was forced through a special nozzle, without the complication of steam or compressed air, and mixed with air from the slotted cone. This was tried in *Surly* in 1902 and in her sister, *Spiteful*, the following year. Further tests in *Sultan* and at Devonport went well and in 1904 it was decided to fit all battleships and cruisers to burn oil as an auxiliary to coal and the 1905 destroyers were designed for oil only. Secret patents were taken out by J Melrose on behalf of the Admiralty covering the main features of the system.[32] Five new boilers were installed at Haslar and when they were operational the Devonport test site was closed.[33] Trials in *Surly* and *Sultan* continued.

Between September 1904 and January 1905 *Spiteful* using oil only was compared with her coal-burning sister *Peterel*; some of the results are shown below.

More importantly, *Spiteful* needed only three men in the boiler room against six for *Peterel*. A closed-trunk system of forced draught, tried both ashore and in *Surly* during 1905, was found less convenient than the closed stokehold system since the sprayers and cones were less

18. When I joined Devonport Dockyard in 1949 the Engineer Manager was an Engineer Rear-Admiral and he claimed to be the last Engineer in the Navy! The youngsters were just officers with a dash of (E) behind.

19. D Griffiths, *Steam at Sea* (London 1997), Ch 11.

20. Rateau patented an impulse turbine in France whilst Zoelly in 1899 patented a combined turbine in Germany.

21. E C Smith, *A Short History of Naval and Marine Engineering* (Cambridge 1937), p290.

22. These speeds were presumably measured by log and may not have been very reliable.

23. In particular, the blade clearances were not as critical as in the Parsons, reaction design. K T Rowland, *Steam at Sea* (Newton Abbot 1970), Ch 6.

24. By Yarrows and John Brown.

25. My thanks are due to successive editors of the *Journal of Naval Engineering* for providing material on which this section is based.

26. Two feet of coal were equivalent to 1in of steel and full bunkers, even if flooded, preserved much of the buoyancy and stability (Attwood).

27. A Normand boiler (as in *Blonde*), a Belleville and cylindrical, together with two more cylindrical boilers from *Bonaventure*.

28. Best known as the Admiralty Fuel Experimental Station (AFES).

29. Admiralty Experiment Works (AEW).

30. Pinnace type; one White-Forster, one Mumford.

31. Clarkson & Chapel and May burning systems.

32. James Melrose, Chief Inspector of Machinery, assisted by Engineer Commander George Fryer.

33. Babcock & Wilcox, Yarrow large tube, Belleville, Yarrow small tube and Thornycroft small tube.

Comparison of *Spiteful* and *Peterel*

Trial	*Spiteful*		*Peterel*	
	Speed (kts)	Tons oil/hr	Speed (kts)	Tons coal/hr
Two boilers. Max power obtainable by ship's staff	22.4	2.17	20.6	2.262
Portsmouth-Plymouth, Two boilers	21.8	2.52	19.5	2.47
Round Isle of Wight, two boilers	22.3	2.7	21.4	2.5
As above, one boiler, tubes not swept	18.9	1.28	19.0	1.97

accessible. *Mars* and *Hannibal* were changed – again – from steam spraying to the pressure system and several other ships were fitted in the same way to burn oil over coal with satisfactory results.[34] Three engineer officers were appointed to the fleet in November 1905 for 'special duties in connection with oil fuel'.

The first of the 1905 coastal destroyers, known as the 'oily wads', completed in 1906 and tests of their boilers went well, the average evaporation being 14.58lbs of water per pound of oil. Once at sea, a number of teething problems became apparent, notably rapid burning of the air cones. There was also excessive smoke when lighting up with cold oil. Work at Haslar, backed by trials in *Surly*, gradually overcame these problems. The first oiling at sea under way took place in 1906, the battleship *Victorious* towing a tanker, the tow rope supporting the oil hose.[35]

Improvements in the fittings for oil burning enabled those ships fitted for mixed fuel to burn oil only though, when doing so, power was limited to 60 per cent. Development continued and the first formal instructions for using oil fuel were issued in February 1908, revised in August 1910. There were still minor problems; that of the transfer of thick, cold oil from railway trucks was remedied by bleeding compressed air into the tank. Fire-fighting was tried in 1908 with the conclusion that plenty of sea water was the best answer. Experiments were carried out to determine the conditions under which oil floating on the sea could be ignited. There was a boiler explosion in *Britannia* on 29 April 1908 whilst she was burning oil over coal, but tests at Haslar showed that the cause was lack of water and that oil burning in itself had nothing to do with it.

Rather reluctantly, the sixteen *Beagle* class destroyers of the 1908 programme were ordered as coal burners since there was insufficient oil available at supply depots. Their evaporation rate was only 9.8lbs of water per pound of coal compared with 14.6-15.2 achieved by oil-burning ships. Oil was now accepted and the three special duty officers were removed at the end of 1908. By 1911 there were sufficient bunkering ports to meet the likely needs of the fleet.

In 1908 it was decided that the maximum viscosity which could be accepted was 10,000 seconds measured at 32°F on a Redwood viscometer so that oil could be pumped when cold. A new air tube tried in *TB 1*[36] in 1909 proved satisfactory and its use was extended, becoming universal in 1911. In 1910 the C-in-C Home Fleet asked that all restrictions on the use of oil be removed as:

> . . . as oil can be more easily and rapidly replenished (but with little labour) than coal, and its extended use economises the coal and so saves the large amount of time and labour entailed in firing and coal trimming at sea and in coaling in harbour. The use of oil fuel also materially reduces the smoke when burning coal, and

its continuous use practically eliminates the dense smoke formed when first putting on oil fuel and when suddenly increasing speed.

For destroyers, the use of oil greatly increased the power developed from a given size of boiler room and fuel consumption was much less. The coal-burning *Beagle* is compared with the oil-burning *Defender* of the same power and similar capability in the following table.

Comparison of *Beagle* (coal) and *Defender* (oil)

	Beagle Coal	*Defender* Oil
Boiler surface (sq ft)	26,000	19,000
Boiler room weights (tons)	187	142
Boiler room length (ft)	92	61
Total machinery weight (tons)	345	300
Ship length (ft)	270	240
Fuel weight (tons)	225	175
Endurance (actual miles)*	2200 @ 15kts	2600 @ 13kts
Engine and boiler room complement	58	24
Actual speed (kts) (nominal 27)	27.2	28.5
Cost (£)	106,000	83,000

*The *Beagle* was designed for 1500 miles at 15kts and the *Defender* for 2000 miles at 13kts (equivalent to 1500 miles at 15kts).

Aboard *Defender* there was little difficulty in using all the oil compared with the problems of getting at coal in the back of a bunker on *Beagle*. Furthermore, full power was always available and could be maintained in service unlike the unrealistic trials results of coal burners, whilst changes of power when manoeuvring were simple. Oil allowed better control of smoke and of steam output and the boilers could be forced until the fuel was exhausted without wearing out the stokers, while there was little soot or dirt to be removed. The higher powers required for later destroyers such as the *Acasta* class (1911-12) could only be obtained using oil. For 24,500shp they needed boiler rooms 77ft long with 27,000ft² of heating surface.

There were some disadvantages; oil was more expensive and did not provide protection against gunfire, though later it was to form part of torpedo protection systems. Oil stowage on board could not be temporarily increased, as could be done by loading bagged coal. It came from overseas and there were fewer ports at which oil could be obtained. Finally, there was a greater fire hazard.

In 1912 the First Lord (Churchill) set up a 'Royal Commission on Fuel and Engines' under Admiral Fisher to make recommendations on the supply of oil. It was a very distinguished group of naval officers and

34. *Prince George, Argyll, Black Prince, Duke of Edinburgh* and *King Edward VII*.

35. A photograph appears in the advertisement section of *Jane's* 1914.

36. A renumbered coastal destroyer.

37. R F Mackay, *Fisher of Kilverstone* (Oxford 1973), p439.

38. J H Narbeth was one of the secretaries. 'Fifty Years of Naval Progress', *The Shipbuilder* (1927).

39. Arthur C Clarke states his first law 'If a middle-aged scientist or engineer says that something is possible he is probably right. If he says something is impossible he is probably wrong'. If Parsons had said that it was impossible with contemporary materials he would have been right. As so often in engineering progress, the gas turbine depended on better materials.

40. The propeller on a modern frigate might have an efficiency of 0.62 at 435rpm or 0.72 at 210rpm.

41. Smith, *A Short History of Naval and Marine Engineering*, Ch 18.

Beagle, the last coal-burning class of destroyer. There were still parts of the world where supplies of oil were scarce – including the Mediterranean – and this choice was not a sign of reaction. (WSS)

engineers,[37] including Sir Phillip Watts and Sir Henry Oram.[38] They recommended that minimum stocks be held equal to 4 years' peacetime consumption with tankage sufficient for 30 per cent in excess of this. In 1913 it was suggested that the war stock be increased from 3 to 6 months but funding could not be made available.

The word 'engine' in the title of the Commission was inserted at Fisher's insistence as he dreamt of diesel-engined high-speed battleships without funnels, but the diesel technology of the day was unable even to power a destroyer (see Chapter 5). Fisher was even pressing for gas turbines – Sir Charles Parsons was to say 'I do not think the internal combustion engine will ever come in. The internal combustion turbine is an absolute impossibility'.[39]

The Commission's report in November 1912 concluded that oil-firing gave higher speed than coal or mixed firing, increased radius of action, and speedier and easier refuelling. Stoker numbers could be reduced by 55 per cent, steam could be raised more quickly and there would be a saving in shipbuilding cost. This reduction of cost together with a reduction in running costs due to the smaller crew and less maintenance and repair work constituted the main argument for oil. Concealed within these factors were some important technical points; the grate in a hand-fired coal burning boiler could not exceed 7½ft, and hence a large number of boilers were needed. Oil-fired boilers could be up to 30ft long with a considerable reduction in boiler-room size and improvement in subdivision.

The 1910 specification for fuel oil required a flash point of over 200° F and sulphur not more than ¾ per cent which severely limited the number of suppliers but in 1913 these requirements were relaxed to a flash point

of 175° whilst sulphur was to be less than 3 per cent, much increasing the number of potential suppliers. Furthermore, the Government went some way to reducing the risk of dependence on overseas suppliers by buying a 51 per cent share in Anglo-Persian Oil Ltd in 1914.

The final move came with the decision that the fast battleships of the *Queen Elizabeth* class (1912 Programme) should burn only oil. Once again the Royal Navy led the rest of the world in technical development – though, in this case, the lead over the USN was measured in days, comparing the order dates of the *Queen Elizabeth* and the *Oklahoma*! The Russians were early users of oil in the Black Sea, taking advantage its ready availability in that region. The Germans were considerably behind and even their last wartime battleship, *Baden*, had a mixture of oil and coal fired boilers.

Geared turbines

The problem with all the early turbine installations was that turbines needed high rotational speed (rpm) for efficiency whilst propellers performed best at low rpm,[40] the compromise adopted leading to a loss of efficiency in both aspects. Some form of transmission which would enable the turbine to run fast and the propeller slowly was the obvious solution but no such transmission was available. The design of gears to transmit and transform high powers was not easy and such units took time to develop. Parsons had always been aware of the problem and had built a small launch, *Charmian*, with gearing in 1897.[41]

Twelve years later, Parsons bought the cargo ship *Vespasian* for trials. She had been built in 1887 with a single triple-expansion engine working at 145lbs/in². The old engine was refurbished to obtain reliable comparative data and was then replaced by a geared turbine unit, the original boiler, tail shaft and propeller being retained. The high pressure (HP) and low pressure (LP) turbines were side by side, driving a gearbox which reduced the turbine speed of 1700rpm to 74rpm at the propeller. The turbine plant, including gears, weighed 75 tons compared with 100 tons for the reciprocating engine. Top speed increased from 9.5kts to 11kts and there was a reduction in coal consumption of 15 per cent.

The gearing for the *Vespasian* was made by a specialist firm, the Power Plant Company, and seems to have been satisfactory, running for 4 years in her before being transferred to another ship. Parsons found problems in cutting later gears due to the large pitch errors which developed when using available cutting machinery. He eventually developed his own method of cutting which worked well.

In 1911 the Admiralty ordered two destroyers, *Badger* and *Beaver*, with geared HP turbines, each of about 3000shp, the LP turbines driving the shafts directly. The main, double helical wheels had 207 teeth engaging with pinions of nickel steel with 41 and 62 teeth. There was a special coupling for the pinions to allow for the effect of expansion when hot.[42]

These two destroyers had hardly completed when, in 1912, the Admiralty ordered *Leonidas* and *Lucifer* with all geared turbines.[43] Parsons proposed that the LP turbine should run at 1800rpm and the HP at 3000rpm driving the propeller at 380rpm. The anticipated 10 per cent increase in overall efficiency meant that the power could be reduced to 22,500shp instead of 24,500shp in the direct-drive boats for the same speed and hence the total cost could be kept the same. Fuel economy was expected to be 9 per cent better at full power and 26 per cent at low power. The contract price for these two ships was some 5 per cent more than that of most of the

class but was still not the most expensive.[44]

There was friendly debate between Parsons and the Admiralty (S V Goodall) on propeller geometry. It was known that propellers with relatively small blade areas were most efficient at low speeds but at high speeds there would be severe cavitation which would reduce efficiency and a much greater blade area would be better.[45] Unfortunately there was hardly any evidence on which to base the design for an individual ship. Eventually it was decided to make two sets of propellers, one to Parsons' ideas with 54sq ft of area and one to the Admiralty choice of 42.5sq ft, both having the same diameter and pitch. The outbreak of war prevented any elaborate trials but that of *Leonidas* broadly justified the claims of improved efficiency and the Admiralty soon adopted geared turbines for all destroyers. She achieved 30.7kts with 23,135shp on a displacement of 1098 tons – one of the fastest of the class, with least power and amongst the heaviest trials displacement.

Later destroyers – 'M' and 'R' class

During the war it was decided that all future destroyers should have geared turbines (Brown-Curtis preferred) and the geared ships became the 'R' class, which were otherwise very similar to the earlier, ungeared 'M' class. A careful series of comparative trials were carried out between the direct-drive *Norman* with three shafts and geared cruising turbines on the wing shafts and the all-geared, twin shaft *Romola*. At 18kts the *Romola* steamed 8.2nm per ton of oil compared with 7.0nm for *Norman* (15 per cent reduction); at 25kts the distances per ton were 3.88nm and 2.8nm (28 per cent). The importance of these figures can hardly be overstated; at 18kts the 'R' class could steam 775 miles further (ie 43 hours, nearly two days, greater endurance).

Cruisers

Eight light cruisers were ordered under the 1913 Programme and, since the previous *Arethusa* class had failed to reach the desired – but not expected – 30kts, the DNC suggested the use of geared turbines to improve propulsive efficiency. It was decided that the risk of relatively unproven machinery was too great for the whole class but it was agreed to fit geared machinery in two ships, *Calliope* and *Champion*, in different arrangements.

Champion was built by Hawthorn Leslie who proposed a two-shaft arrangement with the port shaft driven by the after engine room. Originally it was intended to use the higher efficiency to reduce the installed boiler power to 37,500hp with only six boilers, thus reducing the length of the forward boiler room by 14ft. The builders later proposed modifications to the boilers which, at a cost of 8 tons would bring the power back to the 40,000shp of the direct-drive ships. Cruising turbines were then introduced adding 32 tons, bringing the design machinery weight to 795 tons turning at 340rpm.

The cruiser *Caroline*'s turbine photographed in 1998. (Author's collection)

Calliope was built in Chatham Dockyard with four shaft machinery of 37,500shp at 480rpm built by Parsons. The first of the direct-drive cruisers, *Caroline*, ran trials in December 1914 and *Champion* a year later. Their trial performance is compared below with unofficial figures for *Calliope*.

Trials figures for *Caroline*, *Champion* and *Calliope*

Ship	Dspt (tons)	shp	Speed (kts)	Fuel tons/day at full power
Caroline	3822	41,020	29 +	550
Champion	3850	41,188	29.5	470
Champion		31,148	28.2	
Calliope	?	30,917	28	420

Note that *Calliope* compares closely with *Champion* at lower power but the former had less installed power and probably could not exceed 28.5kts.[46] This was another clear vindication of the geared turbine and it was used on all later warships as far as was possible. It is remarkable that so many sets of gearing were built in the First World War when most escorts of the second war had to put up with triple-expansion engines.

Thrust blocks

In a direct-drive turbine the steam pressure acting directly on the blades counterbalances most of the thrust in the shaft but in a geared installation this thrust must be taken on a bearing abaft the gearbox. Happily, the solution appeared before the problem became important. An Australian engineer, Michell, had devised a thrust block which depended on pressure lubricated pads.[47] Michell's bearing had a coefficient of friction of about 0.0015 compared with 0.03 for the older, multi-collar block and could carry a pressure of 200-300lbs/in² compared with 50lbs/in² in the older block. It was used first in the cross-channel steamer *Paris* and then in the *Leonidas*. The shafts of the battlecruiser *Hood*, each of which transmitted 36,000shp were 24in in diameter with single-thrust collars 4ft 6in in diameter and 7½in thick. The bearing area of the pads was 1176sq in allowing for a maximum pressure of 200lbs/in² at full speed. Geared drive would hardly have been possible without a thrust bearing of the Michell type,[48] a not uncommon example of a major engineering advance depending on a sub-component.

Hydraulic transmission

The German engineer Dr Föttinger developed a form of hydraulic transmission which was used in a number of German torpedo boats and was also used in the North Sea passenger ship *Königen Luise*. There was a serious proposal to fit transmission of this type in one of the 'C' class cruisers and Goodall was sent to inspect the installation in the *Königen Luise* in June 1914. He noted, with

Caroline's steering gear in 1998. (Author's collection)

interest, that her minelaying sponsons were already in place.[49] The transmission efficiency of the Föttinger gear was said to be about 90 per cent at a 5:1 reduction though it was quiet and reliable.

Boilers

The problem lay mainly in the use of large tube boilers, recommended by the Boiler Committee of 1904.[50] The effect of this decision may be seen in the following comparison of the machinery of the battlecruisers *Tiger* and *Hindenburg*. The German ship had Thornycroft-Schultz boilers based on a British design.

The same point is made in the comparison of the first two designs for *Hood* in February 1916. The version with small tube boilers was 3500 tons lighter and 45ft shorter than the large tube equivalent. This showed how reduction in the size of the boiler rooms made further savings possible in the hull and also reduced the length which needed to be armoured. The report of 1904 believed that the large tube boilers were more reliable and easier to maintain. Even if this was true at the time, and this is by no means certain, it is unlikely that it was true a few years later. Gearing and oil fuel would make further savings possible in later years but, as discussed elsewhere, the E-in-C was very progressive in these aspects and it would have been rash to introduce them earlier for major ships.[51]

42. Science Museum, Marine Engineering catalogue, the starboard gears of *Badger* are held as Inv 1929-670.

43. Ordered from Parsons with hulls from Palmers.

44. £104,200.

45. Cavitation is when water 'boils' in the low-pressure areas on the back (forward side) of a propeller blade. It causes a loss of thrust, damage to the blade and is noisy.

46. A Raven and J Roberts, *British Cruisers of World War II* (London 1980), p44.

47. Smith, *A Short History of Naval and Marine Engineering*, p397.

48. Kingsbury independently developed a similar bearing in the USA.

49. She was sunk on 6 August 1914 having laid the mines which sank the *Amphion*.

50. D K Brown, *Warrior to Dreadnought*, p165.

51. There was discussion over the possibility of all oil fuel for *Tiger* but it was rejected.

Machinery of *Tiger* and *Hindenburg*

Ship	Dspt (tons)	shp	Areas (sq ft) BR	Areas (sq ft) ER	Largest Space (ft³)	M/C wt (tons)	shp/ton
Tiger	28,500	85,000	11,900	6970	76,400	5900	14.4
Hindenburg	26,513	72,000	9480	5110	36,000	3632	19.8

Attack and Defence: Pre-War Trials

Two

IT HAD BEEN a century since the Royal Navy had fought a major battle but, prior to the outbreak of the First World War, there were numerous trials of weapons against ships and these were generally both careful and comprehensive. The earlier trials have been covered in a previous book and need only be summarised.[1]

There are many examples in which design changes are almost simultaneous with the trial, some even before the trial took place. This implies that the change had been decided on in advance and the trial was for confirmation. This is a wise and proper use of trials, particularly as major tests of protection take so long to set up and can only be held at long intervals.

Early trials

The firing against the old battleship *Belleisle* in 1900 was particularly important in the influence it had on later design. The firing ship was the battleship *Majestic* which, at ranges of between 1700 and 1300yds, scored about 30-40 per cent hits. The principal lesson was that high-capacity, Lyddite-filled shells could cause very severe damage. Such shells could be kept out by thin armour and hence light armour was fitted to battleships as an upper belt and as extensions to the main belt, fore and aft.

The trial was also intended to ascertain the risk of wooden fittings catching fire, normal precautions having been taken, possibly inspired by the serious fires in Spanish ships during the war with the USA. Though six small fires were started, they were easily extinguished after firing stopped.[2] It was also noted that fittings should not be mounted on the inside of armour as the impact of a heavy shell would dislodge them, sending them flying dangerously around inside the ship.

The torpedo gunvessel *Landrail* was sunk in October 1906 in trials of the control of fire when several ships were firing simultaneously. Four battleships fired, using inert-filled shell only. The old battleship *Hero* was used for firing trials in 1907 and 1908. Though these trials were primarily of control with two ships firing, live ammunition was used, common shell from the 12in guns, both Lyddite and common from the 9.2in and 6in. The damage caused by high-capacity Lyddite shell from the 9.2in guns was particularly serious.

The old battleship *Edinburgh* after the 1909 firing trials described in this chapter. (Author's collection)

Lessons of the Russo-Japanese War

The RN had a team of observers with the Japanese fleet, led by Captain W C Pakenham, and their reports were studied very carefully and, where lessons were apparent, speedy action was taken. In general, it was thought that the war was old-fashioned, fought by pre-Dreadnought ships lacking fire control.[3] A considerable effort had been made to reduce the fire hazard following the Sino-Japanese and Spanish-American wars and, though fire precautions were reviewed, it was thought that little more was needed, but superstructures were made smaller to reduce the target area. The rapid capsize of several Russian ships was blamed entirely on their excessive tumblehome and the hazards of longitudinal bulkheads on the centre line was ignored despite specific warnings from Pakenham.

The danger of mines was recognised and a considerable effort was put into developing an effective mine-sweeping force (see Chapter 10). It was thought that existing battleships would withstand a single mine explosion unless a magazine exploded and therefore particular attention was given to magazine protection. The poor performance of armour-piercing shells was noted but the RN was about to introduce a new series of shells and it seems to have been thought that these would perform better. Though the lack of success of torpedoes was noted, it was blamed on poor tactics and it was thought that the introduction of gyro course-keeping and of the heater torpedo would greatly enhance the capability of this weapon. In earlier torpedoes the engine was driven by compressed air only, while in the 'heater' torpedo, fuel was sprayed into the air and burnt, much increasing the energy of the gases entering the engine and hence the speed or range of the weapon.

In particular, the Admiralty were convinced that the two main battles had demonstrated the value of the all-big-gun *Dreadnought* and that the 'hail of fire' from batteries of 6in guns inflicted little serious damage. Many critics drew the opposite conclusion but hindsight generally supports the official interpretation.

The *Edinburgh* trials, 1909-10[4]

During these trials the striking velocity of the heavy shells was adjusted to that which would be obtained by 4crh (calibre radius head) shells fired at a range of 6000yds. At this range a 12in shell would travel at 3° to the horizontal and a 6in at 5½° and for the trial the ship was heeled to 10° to represent both shell trajectory and a small angle of roll or heel. However, during most of the trials, *Edinburgh* was rolling through several degrees so the angle of impact is only approximate.

Thin side armour

Two 4in KC plates were erected on the side of the forward superstructure and both these plates and the un-protected superstructure were fired on by 13.5in and 9.2in Lyddite (the Manual is not entirely clear on what shells were used but the description suggests HE); 6in Lyddite was fired at the armour and 12pdr (Lyddite and common) and 3pdr common shell at the superstructure. The smaller shell produced little damage, as did the 6in and 9.2in Lyddite hitting the 4in plate, although the latter did produce some damage in rear of the plate and considerable damage to the deck in front it. The 9.2in fired at the unarmoured superstructure blew large holes in the decks, above and below, and wrecked all fittings in the vicinity.

The 13.5in Lyddite fired at the 4in plate wrecked the bow and deck outboard of the armour and made a hole 3ft x 2½ft in the plate itself, setting it back by up to 27in at the after end. Fragments of the broken plate caused severe damage behind but there was no blast effect inside. The next 13.5in shell was fired at the unprotected superstructure aft, resulting in the whole compartment being wrecked and a section of the side 25ft by 8ft blown out behind. The decks above and below were destroyed and a small fire started. A third 13.5in shell was fired at an undamaged 4in plate and confirmed that armour even as thin as this could greatly reduce the effect of a heavy HE shell.

Effect of heavy HE shell on funnels and boilers

Steam at 25lbs/in² was raised in two boilers directly under the funnel and small fires left burning at the rear of the furnaces. A 13.5in Lyddite shell was fired at the funnel, hitting it 20ft above the boilers. The funnel was brought down with severe but localised damage; the fore and port sides were destroyed but the other sides were little damaged. The armoured gratings were very effective, keeping out most fragments but not the blast, and damage to the furnace and smokebox doors suggested that normal fires would have been blown into the stokeholds. There was considerable damage to steam pipes, valves and to the floor plates, and a dummy stoker was 'killed' by a splinter. The effectiveness of the gratings against the very small fragments of Lyddite shell was surprising. The protection fitted to the uptakes of the contemporary Dreadnought *Neptune* was probably associated with this trial.

Deck protection

Three experimental decks were built behind a ¾in bursting screen. Details were:

K. 2in KNC chilled on 1in mild steel.
L. 1½in KNC on ¾in mild steel.
M. 1½in mild steel on ¾ mild steel.

A 12in APC plugged shell fired against deck K broke up but made a large hole and many fragments got below. A similar shell was deflected on hitting deck L but made a big hole in the deck. Deck M was hit by a 12in CPC

1. D K Brown, *Warrior to Dreadnought*, pp176-8

2. This perhaps missed the point. Small fires are easy to put out when not under attack but when firefighting is interrupted, fires can build up to a major conflagration.

3. D K Brown, 'The Russo-Japanese War. Technical Lessons as Perceived by the RN', *Warship 1996* (1996).

4. Based on the 1915 Gunnery Manual, summarised in D K Brown, 'Attack and Defence 5. Prior to World War I', *Warship 34* (1985).

which was deflected and burst beyond the deck, but again left a large hole in it.

Two more decks were then installed but with very different bursting screens on the side.

G. ¾in mild steel (MS) over ⅝in MS with ¾in screen.
H. ¾in nickel steel over ⅝in nickel steel with a 2in screen.

A page from the Gunnery Manual, 1915, showing the results of one of the trials on the *Edinburgh*.

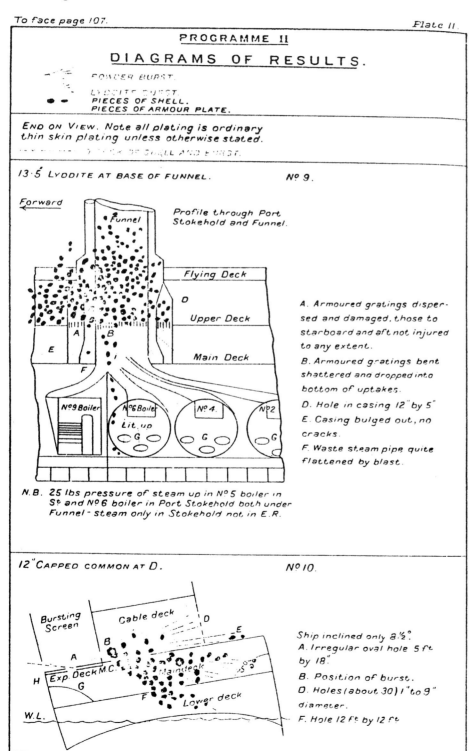

To face page 107.   Plate II.

PROGRAMME II

DIAGRAMS OF RESULTS.

POWDER BURST.
LYDDITE BURST.
PIECES OF SHELL.
PIECES OF ARMOUR PLATE.

END ON VIEW. Note all plating is ordinary thin skin plating unless otherwise stated.

13.5 LYDDITE AT BASE OF FUNNEL.   N⁰ 9.

Forward

Funnel

Profile through Port Stokehold and Funnel.

Flying Deck

D

Upper Deck

Main Deck

N⁰9 Boiler   N⁰6 Boiler   N⁰ 4.   N⁰2
Lit up   G   G   G

A. Armoured gratings dispersed and damaged, those to starboard and aft not injured to any extent.
B. Armoured gratings bent shattered and dropped into bottom of uptakes.
D. Hole in casing 12" by 5"
E. Casing bulged out, no cracks.
F. Waste steam pipe quite flattened by blast.

N.B. 25 lbs pressure of steam up in N⁰5 boiler in St and N⁰6 boiler in Port Stokehold both under Funnel - steam only in Stokehold not in E.R.

12" CAPPED COMMON AT D.   N⁰ 10.

Bursting Screen   Cable deck   D
                                             E
A
Exp Deck M.C.   Main deck
H
G   Lower deck
W.L.

Ship inclined only 8.½°.
A. Irregular oval hole 5 ft by 18".
B. Position of burst.
D. Holes (about 30) 1" to 9" diameter.
F. Hole 12 ft by 12 ft

5035

Both screens were pierced by 6in common shell but the bursts were behind the test deck. Six-inch Lyddite made a hole in the 2in screen but did not damage the deck while a similar shell fired at the ¾in screen burst behind, fragments penetrating the deck. The 2in screen burst a 12in Lyddite shell which caused little damage behind whilst a similar shell against the ¾in screen did burst behind. Six-inch common and Lyddite were fired against the original upper deck, wood over ½in or ¾in steel, the larger fragments of the common shell causing more damage. The value of side protection even only 2in thick was emphasised though it was noted that base-fused shell would have penetrated easily.

The next series of trials were against side and deck protection of the type which might be used on small cruisers.

D. 1¼in KNC over ½in MS.
E. 1in nickel steel over ¾in nickel steel.
F. 1in nickel steel over ¾in MS.

All three had a ¾in screen

A. Was in 2 parts;
   3in side and ⅜in deck
   2½in side and ¾in deck

B. Was intended to study the effect of a shell dropping onto the light upper deck with a protective deck below. It was erected as a bulkhead ¾in forward and ⅜in aft, inside the superstructure and fired on at a small angle.

A variety of 6in common and Lyddite and 12in Lyddite shells were fired at these targets.[5] The overall conclusions were that the chance of penetration of ¾in and ⅜in decks were so nearly equal that the lighter deck should be used with the weight saved put into thicker side armour. Trials of the thicker decks showed the value of higher-quality steel.

Contemporary conclusions

The power of the large, high-capacity, Lyddite-filled shell to cause major damage was re-emphasised, blast effects opening up structure over a wide area. The splinters were generally small (½-ounce average weight) but very numerous and they bounced off any structure hit, giving them an amazing ability to travel round corners. They would break any fittings they hit and cut electric cables and voice pipes as well as causing numerous casualties, but they were too small to penetrate structure. It was noted that though the effects of blast were very serious on normal structure, there was evidence that some slightly stronger structures resisted well. It was therefore thought that vital components, such as funnel casings, could be made blast resistant at little cost.

The splinters of common shell were much larger and therefore penetrated decks and bulkheads to a much greater extent and were not generally deflected from the path of the shell. It was suggested that a combination of

Lyddite and common shell should be used except in attacking heavy armour. The value of even very thin armour in bursting heavy HE shell outside the ship was demonstrated and therefore as much as possible of the ship should be so protected. Armour decks were effective in deflecting shells which hit them directly but, in so doing, pieces of deck would be thrown violently into the space below, so vital equipment should not be placed on the deck below.[6] Internal armour could protect spaces within but only at the expense of spaces outside. Blast-resistant funnel casings were highly desirable and had already been implemented in *Neptune*.

> The experiments demonstrated, what has frequently been shown before, the great value of thin side armour when attacked with high explosive projectiles; but they also demonstrated what, perhaps, what was not fully realised before, viz., that armoured deck plates, of existing thickness, at any rate, do not afford real protection to the vitals of the ship when attacked by heavy high explosive shell unless used in conjunction with thin side armour.

Lessons for ship design followed – side armour to be carried as near the ends as possible and to cover as large an area as possible and that weight was better used in side armour than in a protective deck with an unarmoured side. In small ships the weight available for protection was better applied to the side than the deck.[7] The report also suggested that KNC for decks was not worth the cost, somewhat at variance with the conclusions of the deck protection tests above.

In general, these trials showed that the existing ideas of protection were correct. It is possible that the considerable increase of thin armour at the ends of the *Orion* class battleships (see Chapter 3) were based on early results of these trials, though it is more likely that thinking was moving in that direction anyway. The emphasis on large-capacity HE-filled shells in part reflects the poor performance of British armour-piercing shells, concealing the potential of better shells. The value of the belt of the *Chatham*s and *Arethusa*s was confirmed by this trial. In 1917, the Projectile Committee noted in their report that the lessons of this trial had not been realised.

Empress of India 1913

The firing against this ship on 4 November 1913 was largely to give officers and men experience in firing live ammunition against a real ship as opposed to practice targets and few material lessons were sought or expected. The first firing was by the cruiser *Liverpool* with the target ship held by a single anchor. At a range of about 4750yds she fired sixteen 6in in 1min 58sec scoring seven hits and sixty-six 4in in 3min 7sec for 22 hits. The number of hits against a large, stationary target at close range seems very disappointing but eyewitnesses were impressed, thinking that a light cruiser could inflict serious damage on a battleship caught unawares in poor visibility.[8]

Three battleships then fired in turn

	Rounds	Range (yds)	Hits
Thunderer	40 13.5in	9800	7
Orion	40 13.5in	9800	9-10
King Edward VII	16 12in	8500	5
	18 9.2in	8500	7
	27 6in	8500	5

Four battleships, *King George V*, *Neptune*, *Thunderer* and *Vanguard*, then fired in concentration at 8-10,000yds, firing a total of 95 rounds, mostly old-type common, in 2 minutes for about 22 hits. Very quickly, by 1645hrs the *Empress of India* was badly on fire, with the whole side red hot, and down by the stern. She slowly settled by the stern and capsized, sinking at 1830hrs. It was noted that there was a considerable advantage in firing into the light wind (Force 2-3) as the cordite smoke would be blown clear of the firing ship. Smoke from the target briefly interrupted fire. The fore top of *Empress of India* was clear of smoke and could have maintained control, although it was suggested that a stronger floor for the top was desirable to protect the spotting team. Since the bow of *Empress of India* was always clear of smoke it was thought that a protected emergency control and spotting position in the stem would be valuable and this was, indeed a feature of some battleship designs (1914-15 Programme, see Chapter 3).

The fires were started by *Liverpool*'s Lyddite shells and spread by later hits. One cause of these fires was the wooden decks, which in this old ship were not backed with steel. This was a lesson of the Spanish-American War, well learnt in later British designs. Furthermore, many hatches were blown open giving a good draught to interior fires.

The 1915 Gunnery Manual concluded:

> That the infliction of the first hit is of the utmost importance was fully borne out by this firing. In addition to the feeling of elation in obtaining the first hit and the opposite effect on the enemy, the subsequent immediate development of a large volume of rapid and accurate fire would render it difficult, perhaps, impossible for the opponent to reply.

The need for guns to be continuously ready, particularly in poor visibility, and for steering from the conning tower was emphasised.[9]

Anti-torpedo boat armament

The problem of destroying or at least disabling a torpedo-boat or destroyer before it could launch its torpedo

5. For details, see 1915 Gunnery Manual.

6. It is probable that this influenced the decision to place the protective deck higher in the *Royal Sovereign* class battleships.

7. Note that these decks did not have the deep coal bunkers above of the nineteenth-century cruiser.

8. A preview of the later Solomon Island battles?

9. This seems to contradict the lessons of the Russo-Japanese War where conning towers were useless. Unless the viewing slits were large, commanders could not see, but if they were large, the tower was a splinter trap.

was always difficult and became more difficult as the range of torpedoes increased with the heater and their accuracy improved with gyro course-keeping. The band between maximum effective gun range and that for torpedo firing was small and with destroyer sea speeds approaching 30kts – a mile every two minutes – a gun was needed which could disable with a single hit, but heavier-calibre guns were likely to obtain fewer hits in the time available because of their lower rate of fire.

In 1899 trials were carried out on shore at Shoeburyness against a replica torpedo-boat, complete with a boiler and bunkers. One-pounder shells were ineffective and the 3pdr only on the broadside with a lucky hit in the boiler. Similar tests in 1894 showed that the 3pdr and 6pdr were unlikely to stop a torpedo-boat but that a 12pdr would do so with a single hit.[10] Trials against the old destroyer *Skate* in 1906 confirmed these lessons, but the 4in (25pdr) was found to be very effective, particularly with Lyddite shells.

Trials against the destroyer *Ferret* in 1909-10 showed that a Lyddite filled, 4in shell would make a hole about 29ft x 20ft and common shell 8ft x 5ft in side plating (5lb or 8lb) but the common shell did better when hitting a full coal bunker (but the target was an old and small destroyer). The blast, splinter and, probably, morale effect would all be greater with Lyddite. These trials were carried out with the 4in BL Mk VII and VIII with the much heavier 31lb round, a change apparently unnoticed in Germany which continued with the 22pdr in destroyers. Japan's first destroyer design after the war with Russia, *Umikaze*, designed in 1907 and launched 1910, introduced a 4.7in/40 gun. Pakenham's reports had emphasised the need for heavier destroyer guns and the Japanese obviously agreed.

There were a number of other early trials of gunfire against torpedo craft. Two specially-made rounds of case shot, each containing 100 balls, were tried against *Skate* in 1902, fired from an old 12.5in RML. Though the target was damaged, it was concluded that the maximum range would only be 1200yds and that unacceptable damage would be caused to the rifling of the firing gun. Shrapnel shells were tried both against *Skate* and

later against *Ferret*, without much success, and ricochet shot from both 6in and 4.7in at 1200yds were tried against *Skate*, equally unsucessfully.[11]

Turret roofs

A series of tests were carried out at Shoeburyness in 1907 against two targets representing turret roofs (which comprised some 17 per cent of the horizontal area of a battleship). Both were built with 3in KNC plates but while target 'A' was made up from several small plates, 'B' had two large plates. These were fired on at impact angles of 10° and 15°, the former representing the descent of 12in at 11,400yds, 7.5in at 8400yds and 6in at 7400yds whilst the larger angle allowed for the ship rolling 5°.

The 6in caused no direct damage but sheared many bolts and rivets, an effect more marked with the 7.5in. The 12in shells, particularly the common shell, caused severe damage, mainly to the supporting girders, the bigger plates of target 'B' being less damaged though both allowed splinters to enter. General conclusions were:

- A rope mantlet inside the turret was useful to prevent flying bolts and rivets causing injury.
- Openings in the roof which would admit blast (*eg* sighting hoods) were best eliminated.
- To provide strong supports. (This validated the stronger supports fitted to *Indefatigable*, see Chapter 4.)
- To avoid obstructions on the roof which would cause a shell to detonate instead of glancing off. Light guns should not be mounted on the roof. Such guns were, indeed, removed from the turret roofs in following years.
- Lyddite shell showered neighbouring areas, *eg* bridge, with splinters

A further series of tests were commenced at Shoeburyness in 1913 with 4in plate from various manufacturers. The angle of impact was 20°, made up of 7½° angle of descent, 7½° slope of roof and 5° roll. The

HMS *King George V*. Note the proportion of the deck occupied by turret roofs; some 17 per cent. (Imperial War Museum: Q19556)

shells were 13.5in (1400lb) AP Mk IA filled with salt. Results up to the outbreak of war were:

Plate	Failed above striking velocity
Mild steel	1050ft/sec
KNC plate	1100ft/sec
Vanadium plate	1550ft/sec

Underwater protection and trials

In 1903 the old battleship *Belleisle* was fitted with an elaborate torpedo protection system for trial. Longitudinal bulkheads of 15-25lb plate gave a system of five compartments containing, from the outside – water, cork, coal, air, coal with a total depth of 12ft.[12] A charge of 230lbs of gun cotton was exploded against the hull rupturing all six bulkheads and shifting a boiler 2ft. The result is rather surprising as one would expect the protection to have done better but underwater explosions are notoriously variable in their effect and *Belleisle* seems to have been unlucky.[13]

Following the Russo-Japanese war a trial was carried out on the merchant ship *Ridsdale* which had been fitted with a single thick bulkhead based on what was known of the Russian *Tsessarevitch* which it was believed, incorrectly, had successfully resisted Japanese torpedoes.[14] The trial was successful in withstanding a 230lb charge of guncotton and similar protection was fitted in *Dreadnought*.[15]

Trials with Hood in 1914

The battleship *Hood* (launched 1891) was extensively modified in Portsmouth for these trials with a new longitudinal bulkhead extending for 120ft abreast the machinery. In way of the engine-room a thick 80lb bulkhead was built 7ft outboard of the 17lb engine-room wing bulkhead, fairly similar to the arrangement in the *Queen Elizabeth*. Over the boiler room the inner bulkhead was 80lb and the lighter one was outboard. The original double bottom was retained.

The first trial was carried out in the Beaulieu river on 9 February 1914. A 280lb charge of wet guncotton was exploded 12ft below the surface abreast the middle of the engine-room. The two big watertight compartments forward of the explosion were empty and those abaft were filled with water. The double bottom spaces were all empty. The hole produced by the explosion was 30ft long and 18ft high[16] and damage was most serious in the empty compartments. The light 15lb bulkhead forming the upper part of the double bottom was blown in until it rested on the thick bulkhead, which was severely dished.

In the empty compartments the thick bulkhead was pierced by a fairly large number of fragments of the shell plating, shattered by the explosion. The innermost 17lb bulkhead was slightly distorted and leaked at the

rivets, but the flow of water was well within the capacity of the pumps. It was noted that the horizontal struts connecting the bulkheads had transmitted the blow to the innermost bulkhead and it was decided that for the second experiment these should be cut and rejoined in such a way that they carried tensile loads only. The projectile effect of the shattered shell plating showed that the outer space should be water-filled.

For the second experiment, held at Spithead on 7 May 1914, the double bottom and outer space were water-filled and the inner space, outboard of the 80lb bulkhead, was empty. The 280lb charge made a slightly smaller hole this time but the force was spread in the water-filled compartments, extending the structural damage. The thick bulkhead was only slightly dished and the leakage was again well within the capacity of the pumps. The overall conclusions from these two tests were:

- There should be a thin bulkhead inboard of the thick bulkhead to retain water from inevitable small leaks.
- The bulkheads should be joined by ties, weak in compression (*ie* not struts).
- A thick bulkhead could be made strong enough to prevent the flooding of major compartments.

A conference was held at Portsmouth in September 1914 to consider the results of all trials of underwater protection.[17] The conference noted that it was still unclear which spaces should be full and which empty, though that next to the explosion should certainly be empty to avoid a tamping effect. They also agreed that the space outboard of the thick bulkhead should be liquid-filled in order to slow down flying fragments. Proposals were made for further trials on the optimum arrangement of compartments, the design of the thick bulkheads and the value of venting arrangements but, due to the war, these could not be carried out. *Hood* was sunk on 4 November 1914 to block the southern entrance to Portland harbour where her hull may still be seen on calm days.

In 1914 the British 21in torpedo had a charge of 225lbs and therefore the *Hood* charges were reasonably representative but, before long, charge weights of both British and German torpedoes had doubled.[18] The radius of damage is roughly proportional to the square root of the charge weight. The chance of rupturing a transverse bulkhead distant Dft from the explosion is approximately proportional to the square root of charge weight.[19]

Pre-war shells[20]

At the beginning of the twentieth century the majority of large-calibre projectiles were nose-fused, powder-filled common shell which were very effective in de-

10. Presumably the justification for *Dreadnought's* 12pdr armament.

11. D K Brown, 'Attack and Defence prior to World War I'.

12. D K Brown, 'Attack and Defence Pt III', *Warship 24* (1982). It is quite likely that the temperature was below that at which steel is ductile and that brittle fracture was to blame. Good quality mild steel of the day, as used in *Titanic*, was brittle below about 20° C.

13. The Controller, Admiral May, seems to have decided that torpedo protection would always be impossible; the constructors thought that it showed that success was close.

14. The exact nature of this trial is unclear. The DNC history refers to it as the *Ridsdale* tank.

15. D K Brown, *Warrior to Dreadnought*, p186.

16. This is a big hole for such a charge but in February it is most likely that the steel (including rivets) was in a brittle state.

17. These included some trials on *Terpsichore* in 1913, but no details found.

18. British 21in Mk IV charge 515lbs, German 23.6in, 550lbs.

19. For Second World War torpedoes, filled with Hexanite, there was a 50 per cent chance of a bulkhead failing at $D = 2.25W^{0.422}$ or, roughly, $D = \sqrt{W}$.

20. This section is based on an unpublished manuscript, *The Riddle of the Shells*, by K I McCallum.

stroying lightly-protected structure. Projectiles which were capable of penetrating thick armour (AP) were usually unfilled ('shot') and although forged steel AP were available, these were expensive and many Palliser chilled iron shot remained in service despite the fact that they were useless against cemented armour.

Many attempts were made to produce a true armour-piercing shell which would burst within the target after penetrating thick armour. The difficulty was that such projectiles had to be base-fused, but base fuses, activated by the shock of discharge rather than impact, carried with them the risk of premature explosion. Furthermore, Lyddite-filled shells were particularly liable to premature explosions and for many years the use of Lyddite was forbidden in shells of greater than 8in calibre.

In 1903 Thomas Firth tested their 'Rendable' AP shell which at relatively short range could penetrate armour one calibre in thickness and burst behind. It had a small powder charge which was not very damaging but it was a great advance and was issued in small numbers. The lessons of the Russo-Japanese war were not at all clear[21] and it was generally believed that most of the damage at Tsushima was caused by high capacity, Lyddite-filled shell though it is now thought more likely that the Japanese shells were powder-filled.[22] No shell on either side penetrated thick armour. In the introduction of the 'all-big-gun' *Dreadnought*, Fisher and his advisers saw the powder-filled common and high-capacity HE shell as the principal weapons, supplemented by a few armour-piercing shells to finish off an enemy at shorter range.[23]

Capped shells

In 1906 Hadfield tested the 'Heclon' capped (APC) shell. The soft steel cap pre-stressed the face of the armour before the hardened point of the shell itself made contact, and it was claimed that a 12in APC shell could penetrate 9in KC at 10,000yds and 12in at 6000yds. A year later the same company produced the 'Eron' common pointed capped (CPC) shell. Both these Hadfield shells were forged from 'Era' chrome nickel steel and were fitted with the No 15 fuse, made at Woolwich Arsenal almost certainly under licence from Krupps. From 1908 older shell were gradually withdrawn and replaced by APC and CPC, both powder-filled, together with Lyddite-filled HE shell.[24]

The action of a shell hitting a hardened plate is complicated and differs between capped and uncapped shells. When an uncapped shell (or a 'slow' – under 1750ft/sec – capped shell) hits a hard-faced plate both the point of the shell and the plate round the point of impact will be compressed and driven back in the form of a double cone which will split the body of the shell commencing at the point and working down the shell. The plate becomes dished over about three times the calibre of the shell, spreading the effect of the blow. The hard face will flake

off but will probably have done its job in breaking up the shell so that the plate has to withstand the impact of an unformed collection of broken fragments rather than a penetrating tool. Should the plate still fail, the usual effect is for a cone-shaped piece of plate to be punched out, with a diameter equal to that of the shell at the face and some three times that at the rear.

A cap will spread the shock of impact over the whole head of the shell. Even though the cap is soft, it will still stress the plate so that it is less able to resist when struck by the point itself. Once the point has penetrated the hard face it will still be in the design shape and act as a boring machine in piercing the tough, but softer, back of the plate and drill a hole roughly equal in diameter to that of the shell. The action of the capped shell requires less energy than the punching action of the uncapped shell, giving it a considerable advantage of some 20 per cent in penetrating KC armour.[25]

Penetration at 3000yds

Calibre (in)	MV (ft/sec)	Penetration (in)	
		Capped	Uncapped
12	2500	18	16 (a)
12	2600	16	14 (b)
12	2400	13½	12 (c)
9.2	2800	11½	10 (d)
6	2600	4½	4½

Notes: (a) *Hindustan*, (b) *King Edward VII*, (c) *Majestic*, (d) *King Edward VII*

Early tests of APC were carried out at a normal angle of impact when the cap and shell worked well. However, the fire control revolution led to a great increase in range where oblique impact was almost certain and it was soon found that British shell would break up under those conditions. In particular, APC hitting at 30°, or even less, would break on hitting armour of one calibre in thickness. The main problem seems to have been that the shoulders of the shell casing were too hard and hence brittle and would break under impact. Perforation of 4in KC with 'effect in rear' would be expected with the following striking velocities.

Calibre (in)	Velocity (ft/sec)
12	1700
9.2	1850
7.5	2000

The 1915 Gunnery Manual points out that even thin plate could degrade the effect of Lyddite filled APC; though 12in and 9.2in would detonate behind after piercing a ½in plate at 30° this was not certain with 13.5in or 7.5in. CPC shell, normally powder filled, did rather better in perforating armour at oblique impact.

Penetration of KC plate by CPC at 5000yds and 30° impact.

Gun(in)	Mark	SVel (ft/sec)	Penetration (in)
12	VIII	1719	8.8
	IX	1907	9.7
9.2	X	1826	6.5
	XI	1928	7.0
7.5	I	1640	4.5
	II	1683	4.5
6	VII	1321	2.0
	XI (2 crh)	1502	3.0
	XI (4 crh)	1746	3.5

Note that these results were obtained with salt filled shell.

A 'light' 13.5in CPC shell fired at a 10in KC plate at 20° and striking at 1760ft/sec burst when passing through the plate 'with considerable effect in front and rear'. Six-inch CPC fired against a 3.76in KC plate hitting normally at 1570ft/sec gave all its blast effect to the rear while a similar shell hitting 4in KC at 1600ft/sec at 20° burst in the plate.

Filling

Though the capped armour-piercing shell (APC) had great potential, there were a number of problems which limited performance for many years. The filling of APC was soon changed to Lyddite because of its greater explosive power but this sensitive material would usually explode while the shell was passing through a plate of one calibre thickness, though this explosion might still cause considerable damage behind. The sensitivity of the Lyddite filling concealed the fact that the Krupp-designed fuse often failed to function. An APC shell hitting thin armour would penetrate and burst some distance behind, *eg* a 13.5in shell hitting 4in-thick KC armour would explode 5-18ft behind.

During the Boer War an Explosives Committee of distinguished scientists had been set up to find a safe high explosive for shells. They examined several alternatives to Lyddite including TNT which, it was believed, was being introduced in the German Navy. Though marginally less violent than Lyddite, TNT was comparatively inert and therefore seemed to offer potential as a filling for AP shells. After 1908 the Ordnance Board conducted trials with TNT which gave favourable results, but it could not be adopted because Krupps were unwilling to divulge details of the complex fuse and gain necessary to ensure effective detonation. In view of this the Board decided in 1910 that until a suitable fuse could be devised TNT would not be used. The Board's recommendation that high-capacity Lyddite shells should be tried against an old battleship led to the *Edinburgh* trials discussed earlier. Following these trials

the use of lyddite in APC shells for the 13.5in guns was approved.

In 1914, therefore, the Royal Navy went to war with three main categories of projectile: (1) powder-filled CPC, base fused, which were very effective against unprotected or lightly armoured structure; (2) Lyddite-filled APC (13.5in) designed to explode after penetrating armour but which would usually explode in passing through, and (3) Lyddite-filled HE, nose fused, primarily for shore bombardment, which do not seem to have been as effective as expected.

Cordite and the safety of magazines

In 1886 Vieille in France and Duttenhoffer in Germany developed a propellant from gelatinised nitrocellulose.[26] Two years later Nobel introduced 'Ballistite' with 40-50 per cent nitro-glycerine and the rest nitrocellulose, the nitro-glycerine acting as the solvent. The following year (1889), Frederick Abel and George Dewar at Woolwich Arsenal produced a similar material which they called cordite. It was so similar to ballistite that Nobel sued the government, the case and appeals dragging on till 1895.[27] These legal problems and an explosion at the nitro-glycerine plant at Waltham Abbey slowed the introduction of cordite, which had begun in 1893.

Cordite Mk I consisted of 58 per cent nitro-glycerine, 37 per cent nitrocellulose (guncotton – 13.1 per cent nitrogen) and 5 per cent petroleum jelly. The latter was introduced as a lubricant but it was also a moderately effective stabiliser since its unsaturated hydrocarbons would mop up the decomposition products developed by all but the most pure nitrocellulose. The gases from Mk I were extremely hot and erosive and the resultant excessive wear on gun barrels led to the introduction from 1901 of the first batches of cordite MD, initially for the larger calibre charges.[28] This had a composition of 30 per cent nitro-glycerine, 65 per cent nitrocellulose (guncotton – 13.1 per cent nitrogen) and 5 per cent petroleum jelly which reduced the heat output from 1270 to 1020 calories per gram. There was also a suspicion that Mk I cordite could deteriorate and become unstable though the risk to the ship does not seem to have been appreciated.

Tests and accidents before the First World War

Even in the sailing ship era, great precautions were taken to ensure the safety of the magazine and the introduction of the much more powerful cordite propellant led to a number of trials concerning safe stowage. In 1891-92 experiments were carried out at HMS *Excellent* to test the effect of a shell exploding in an ammunition trunk. A 4.7in shell was exploded in a trunk with two 4.7in cartridges and one shell 2½ft lower down; both the charges exploded but the shell did not. In a second test a 6in shell was exploded above three cartridges and a shell causing two of the cartridges to explode. Further

21. D K Brown, 'The Russo-Japanese War, Technical Lessons as Perceived by the RN'.

22. D K Brown, *Warrior to Dreadnought*, p171.

23. This probably explains why AP shells were tested only at normal impact.

24. Note that there is usually a considerable elapse of time between the introduction of a new equipment and the complete outfitting. This interval is rarely recorded.

25. This passage is based on the 1915 Gunnery Manual but has been shortened and simplified.

26. J Campbell, 'Cordite', *Warship 6* (1978).

27. I McCallum, *The Riddle of the Shells* (unpublished).

28. It would seem that production of Mk I cordite continued for a long time, at least for smaller guns. Some was made in 1916 at Holton Heath. – M R Bowditch. 'Cordite – Poole', MOD PE (1983).

trials were then held with a train of cartridges in a trunk with the upper cartridge detonated electrically. Even with only 2ft 6in spacing between them the 4.7in cartridges (powder or cordite) did not burn but 6in cartridges (powder) needed at least 8ft 6in separation. A 6in cartridge exploding 9ft 6in from a magazine door would wreck it. The lessons recorded were that the trunk must not be directly connected to the magazine and there should be at least 12ft separation between trunk and cartridges.

There was an accidental explosion in the 6in magazine of *Revenge* in 1899 in which it appeared that one QF cartridge exploded spontaneously, setting off the other two cartridges in the case. A similar accident took place in *Fox* in 1906 but only three out of four cartridges exploded. Trials were subsequently carried out ashore which showed the explosion of one cartridge would not necessarily set off all the other cartridges in a case of four and would certainly not affect neighbouring cases. Cordite in closed 100lb cases merely burnt, the lids being blown off, burning out in about 3 seconds.

The tests and the two accidentals convinced the Royal Navy that there would be no disastrous magazine explosions.[29] There was in fact greater concern over the safety of Lyddite shells and for this reason the magazines were sited above the shell rooms. It was, however, recognised that nitrocellulose could decompose leading to spontaneous explosions and that decomposition was most likely if the materials contained impurities. High temperatures speeded decomposition and therefore elaborate cooling machinery was fitted to magazines and records of temperature had to be kept.

The Russo-Japanese War tended to confirm the Navy's views.[30] The Russian battleship *Borodino* sank at Tsushima after a magazine explosion (nitrocellulose propellant), but no details are known.[31] At the Battle of Ulsan on 14 August 1904 the Japanese armoured cruiser *Iwate* suffered an explosion in an upper deck casemate which spread to the casemate below and to the next one aft. The fact that *Iwate*'s 6in cartridges were in brass cases, unlike British ones, may have limited the extent of the explosion. A shell burst in the after turret of the battleship *Fuji* at Tsushima setting fire to three 12in charges. Luckily, the shell burst had blown off most of the roof, allowing venting, and had also fractured a water pipe which helped to put out the fire.

It was thought by the Admiralty that the measures and procedures adopted would much reduce the chance of a small explosion and would prevent a disaster. There were, however, one or two tests which should have caused alarm. Two stacks of 12R cases were erected and the cordite in a lower case ignited. The first stack was of loose cordite (size 3¾) and this exploded, making a crater 26ft wide and 9ft deep (note that this cordite was unconfined other than by the cases). The other stack was of 12in cartridges; only the case ignited burnt, throwing the other cases clear.

This may be the same trial referred to by Sir Hiram Maxim:

> When it was claimed by high officials that English cordite would not detonate, I asserted that it would, providing that the quantity was large enough. I placed 250lbs in a light sheet iron case, and set it off with a powerful fulminator and it exploded exactly like nitroglycerine, making a very deep hole in the ground. This experiment was followed by another, conducted by the Government experts, to disprove what I had asserted. They piled up, I think 2 tons of cordite, on the marshes of Plumstead and simply lighted it at the top. At first it burnt very much like pitch pine shavings, and then commenced to hiss, and flare up; when about a half a ton had been consumed, the remainder went off exactly like dynamite, excavating a hole in the soft earth 15 feet in depth and 24 feet in diameter, and did an immense amount of damage to houses in the vicinity.[32]

Accidents abroad before the War

Ship	Navy	Date	Propellant type	Notes
Maine	US	1898	Powder	Thought at the time to be sabotage[33]
Mikasa	Japan	1905	Cordite	Possibly started accidentally by crew
Aquidaban	Brazil	1906	Cordite	
Iena	France	1907	N'cellulose BN	
Matsushima	Japan	1908	Cordite	Cause unknown
Liberte	France	191	N'cellulose	

There was also an explosion in the Japanese armoured cruiser *Nisshin* (although originally seen as an accident, there was later a confession of sabotage but I am doubtful of all stories of sabotage, and in USS *Kearsage* and *Missouri* in 1904, the details of which unknown. BN – Blanche Nouvelle – was nitrocellulose alone and was favoured by the French, Russian and US navies. The accidents to *Iena* and *Liberte* seems to have confirmed the RN in their view that cordite was safer.

The trials carried out on the safety of propellant and the interpretation of the results of accidents and foreign war experience were carefully conducted and generally comprehensive. Wartime experience, discussed in later showed that these trials etc, had predicted the effects of damage quite accurately. There were, however, two gaps in the trials; there had been no tests of the effect of igniting a large mass of cordite in a confined space – and the Plumstead trial should have sounded a warning – and there had been no trial using a complete turret-trunk-magazine.[34]

29. E L Atwood, *The Modern Warship* (Cambridge 1913). Atwood was then head of the battleship section and is almost complacent in writing of the safety of cordite.

30. D K Brown, 'The Russo-Japanese War; Technical Lessons as perceived by the RN'.

31. An account based on the memory of the sole survivor suggests it may have been a low-order explosion.

32. Letter to the US Secretary of State for the Navy of 17 Jan 1911. Courtesy I McCallum.

33. I S Hansen and D M Wegner, 'Centenary of the Destruction of USS *Maine*', *Naval Engineers' Journal* (March 1988).

34. The old battleship *Renown*, scrapped 1914, could have been used for such a trial or, more realistically, one of the *Canopus* class could have been spared.

PART II:
Pre-War Designs

| # Battleships

A
LMOST ALL serving senior officers of the Royal Navy and the Admiralty were delighted with the success of the *Dreadnought* but her concept was attacked by many retired officers and by writers on naval affairs.[1] Many blamed the Admiralty for initiating a revolution in design which rendered obsolete the RN's numerous fleet of older ships, but it was too late; Pandora's box was open. Fisher and his team were almost certainly correct in their judgement that the revolution was inevitable and that the timing was right with the near-elimination of the Russian fleet temporarily reducing the number of potential enemies. The British lead in turbine machinery also made the change to the *Dreadnought* concept both affordable and timely.

There were still a considerable number of supporters of the 'hail of fire' doctrine, who believed that the rapid fire of a secondary battery would quickly disable an enemy battleship which would then be sunk by 12in AP shell at close range. It was widely claimed that the Russian fleet at Tsushima was disabled in this manner. Examination of the battle does not support this view

and the other big battle in the Yellow Sea, 10 July 1904, even more strongly supports the supremacy of the big gun.[2] Two highly-classified papers, with limited circulation, were prepared, setting out the views of senior staff of the Admiralty. They were probably in the nature of briefing papers so that readers would have the facts readily available to defend the all-big-gun ship. These papers were largely written by Jellicoe, then the Director of Naval Ordnance with contributions by Phillip Watts, DNC, and by the Controller and the conclusions will be summarised below. [3]

These two papers are quoted at length in Appendix 1 since they provide a valid defence against most of the criticisms of the Dreadnought battleship and there was very little opposition within the Admiralty. As range increased, the big gun hit more often and did far more damage when it hit. Most of these arguments also applied to the battlecruiser but there were many who would have preferred the 9.2in gun for that type of ship (see Chapter 4). The balance between quality and quantity will be different in a cruiser from that of the battle line.

Queen Elizabeth seen in Scapa Flow. Note the guns have been removed from the main deck casemates aft as they were flooded too often. The triangular objects on funnels and masts were to confuse the vertical and make rangefinding difficult. However, they were effective only against coincidence rangefinders and were no use against German stereoscopic rangefinders. (Author's collection)

Increase in size

Critics who derided the excessive increase in size and cost of *Dreadnought* were wrong, as she was only slightly bigger and more expensive than her immediate predecessor *Agamemnon*. Sir William White's criticism was more subtle, suggesting that *Dreadnought* was the start of a slippery slope and that there would be a rapid growth in size and cost of future ships. The graph (right) shows he was correct, at least up to a point. The two classes following *Dreadnought* showed only a slight increase in size and a worthwhile reduction in cost. In fact, *Dreadnought* herself was rather expensive, probably due to the long hours of overtime worked – overtime is not only expensive in direct payment but, when used over a long period, productivity falls.

There was a sudden jump in cost for the *Orion* class of the 1909 Programme which introduced the 13.5in gun followed by a steady increase in the next two classes. There was a massive increase with the *Queen Elizabeth* class which had the 15in gun and increased power and speed (it is possible that the change to oil fuel added to cost). The higher cost per ton of the *Royal Sovereigns* of the 1913 Estimates may reflect the beginning of wartime inflation. Though the rise was gradual, costs had increased from about £1.6 million to over £2 million per ship in eight years, a 25 per cent rise.

Guns

The major factor leading to increased size and cost was the bigger gun which in turn led to the requirement for thicker armour over a greater length and for bigger ships both to support the weight and to provide separation from blast effects. The arguments above for the 'all-big-gun ship' apply generally as justification for larger and more powerful guns.[4]

Battleship and battlecruiser main armament

12in Mk X 45 cal: *Dreadnought, Bellerophon* also *Invincible, Indefatigable*

12in Mk XI 50 cal: *St Vincent, Neptune, Colossus*

13.5in Mk 5 (1250lb shell) *Orion, Lion*; (1400lb shell) *King George V, Iron Duke* also *Queen Mary, Tiger*

15in Mk I: *Queen Elizabeth, Royal Sovereign*, also *Renown, Courageous, Hood*

18in Mk I: *Furious*

The 12in Mk X in *Dreadnought* originally had shells with 2crh heads but she changed to 4crh by 1916. Some idea of armour penetration is given in the table below but, as explained in Chapter 11, British shell usually broke up or exploded without penetrating thick armour.[5]

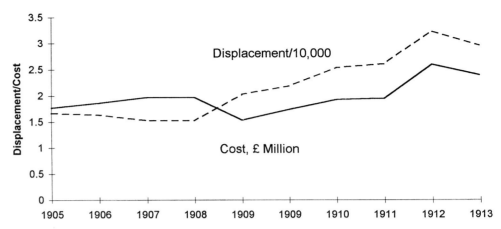

Battleship Displacement and Cost

Armour penetration

Gun (shell weight)	Penetration (ins KC)		Charge weight (lbs)	
	APC	CPC	APC*	CPC**
12in Mk X (850lb)	8	6	26.7	80
12in Mk XI (850lb)	9	8	27.3	80
13.5in (1250lb)	10.6	9	40	117.3
13.5in (1400lb)	11.7	10.7	44.5	117.3
15in (1920lb)	13.4	11.7	60.7	131.9

* Filled Lyddite
** Filled powder

The results for the 12in guns appear to be test results but the angle of impact is not stated. The results for the larger guns are calculated for 30° from normal impact based on normal tests.[6] The bigger shells had far larger bursting charges. The rates of fire did not differ greatly between these big guns. Allowing for spotting, they could fire one round per minute, though it was possible to fire two rounds a minute if necessary.

Upper deck layout

The interaction between blast, masts, boats etc has been explored in detail elsewhere[7] but must be summarised here since, as discussed in Chapter 1, upper deck layout was the starting point of a battleship design. *Dreadnought* had all the features of early fire control systems with a large spotting top on a rigid tripod containing the then new 9ft rangefinder and a pair of Dumaresqs which fed data to Vickers clocks in the Transmitting Station. Considerable attention was paid to protecting the communications between the elements of the control system and the turrets and there was a secondary control position on the signals platform, but this was of little actual value. Unfortunately, the effectiveness of the system was greatly degraded by positioning the mast abaft the forward funnel so that access to

1. D K Brown, *Warrior to Dreadnought*, Ch 11.

2. As for 1.

3. 'The Building Programme of the British Navy'. Tweedmouth Papers, MoD Library. (*Very Secret* – as written – 12 copies printed), 'H M Ships *Dreadnought* and *Invincible*'. (*Strictly Secret*, 25 copies).

4. J Campbell, 'British Naval Guns', *Warship* 17, 18, 19 (1981).

5. Gunnery Manual 1915. MoD Library.

6. Probably unfused, maybe unfilled.

7. J Brooks, 'The Mast and Funnel Question', *Warship 1995* (1995).

Dreadnought upper deck layout

This selection of sketches (by R Perkins) illustrates the problems of upper deck layout in Dreadnought battleships. Blast from the big guns could affect exposed personnel in control positions, at secondary armament and, through the sighting hoods in the turret roofs, gun crews in other turrets, which seemed to rule out superfiring turrets in the early ships. Since increasing the length of the armoured citadel was very expensive, funnels and masts were very cramped and in many ships, the spotting top was in the hot, thick exhaust plume from the funnels. Great importance was also attached to the stowage and easy handling of boats.

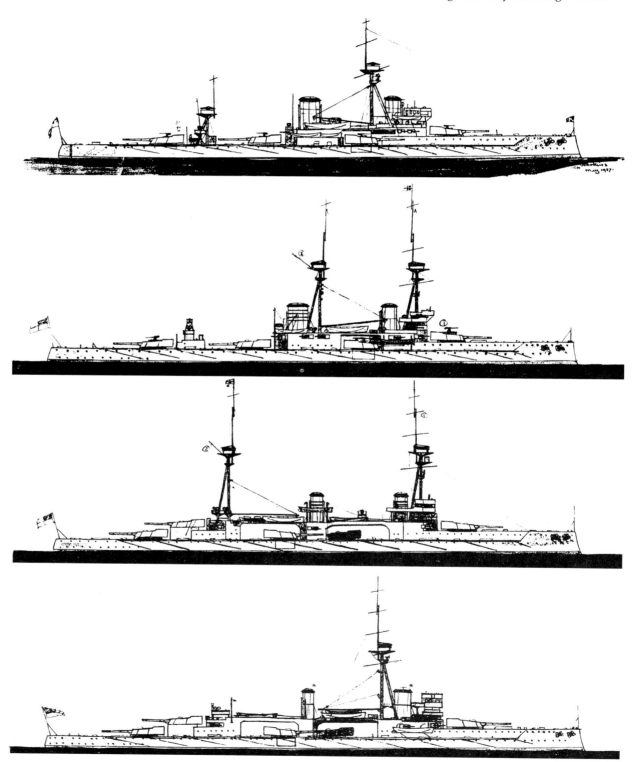

Dreadnought. To some extent, her layout derived from *Agamemnon* with the latter's 9.2in guns replaced with 12in turrets. The mast was placed behind the funnel on Jellicoe's advice to suit boat handling, which often rendered the foretop untenable from heat and fumes.

St Vincent. The layout was much the same as *Dreadnought* but with the foremast ahead of the funnel. The after mast carried the secondary control position and was unsatisfactory.

Neptune. Length was saved by putting the boats on a flying deck over the turrets. Had this been damaged it is likely that the turrets below would have been put out of action. The midships turrets were supposed to be able to fire across the deck but in practice blast damage made this impossible.

Colossus. All the problems of *Neptune* and with the main control top behind the funnel again.

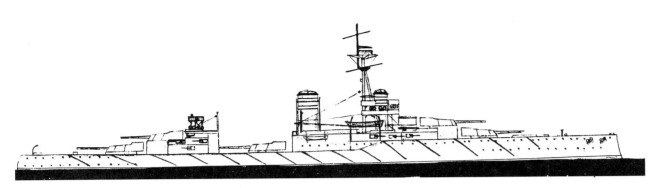

Orion. She was given superfiring turrets to limit the increase in length required by her bigger 13.5in turrets but the upper ones could not fire within about 30° of the axis.

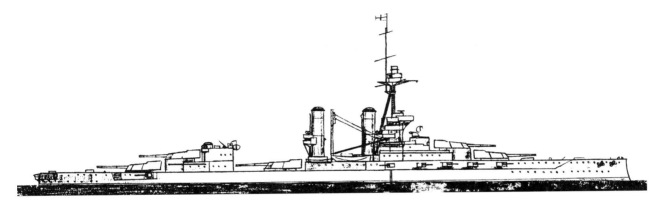

Iron Duke. The increased length required for the secondary battery meant that, at last, there was room for a proper layout of masts and funnels.

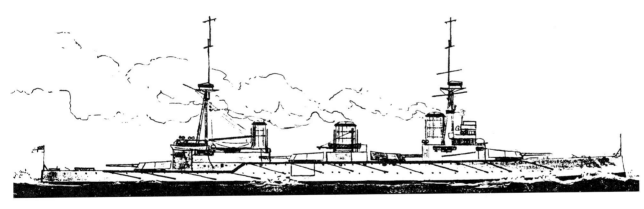

Indefatigable. The increased length compared with the earlier battlecruiser *Invincible* gave some scope for cross-deck firing if the damage to the deck was acceptable.

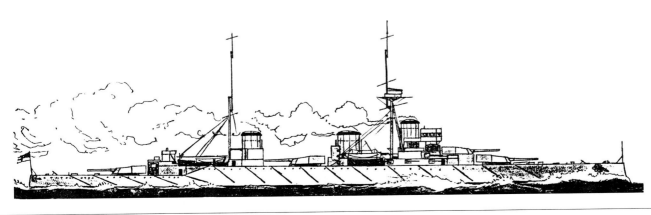

Lion. Hot gases caused enough problems in the battleships with the top behind the funnel but conditions were much worse with the higher power of the battlecruisers. Gases left the funnel at 550° and the arrangement shown had to be rebuilt at a cost of £68,000.

Vanguard. This photo clearly shows the difficulties in arranging the superstructure of Dreadnoughts. The blast from the wing turrets would cause structural damage if fired closer than about 30° from the axis. The foremast and its top is ahead of the funnel (just) but the main mast and its secondary spotting top is in the plume from the forward funnel and was almost useless. *Vanguard* was lost due to an accidental magazine explosion in July 1917 (see Chapter 11). (WSS)

the top was difficult due to heat whilst visibility, particularly with a wind from astern, was bad.

These problems had been realised before she was completed since the generally similar ships of the *Bellerophon* and *St Vincent* classes had a different mast arrangement. The foremast, with spotting top, was forward of the funnels but there was a similar mast and secondary top between the funnels which was again almost useless. The *Invincible* class battlecruisers had a similar foremast with the main abaft all funnels.

Neptune (1908 Programme) had a very strange upper deck layout. The wing turrets were staggered so that they could fire across the deck on either beam but the

length was increased by only 10ft. In order to achieve this the boats were stowed on flying decks over the midship turrets which would be a serious hazard in the event of damage causing the decks to collapse onto the turrets. Similarly, the bridge was positioned above the conning tower which would be obscured if the light bridge collapsed. The after two turrets were superfiring but X turret could not fire within about 30° of the stern because of blast effects on the lower turret through the sighting hoods. The narrow tripod mast forward was ahead of the fore funnel and the main mast well aft. All this effort was largely wasted since it was found that cross-deck firing caused too much damage to the deck

Neptune shows an even more contorted attempt to arrange turrets and superstructure. The midships turrets would cause damage if fired across the deck and were liable to be immobilised if the flying deck over was hit. (Courtesy John Roberts)

for it to be used except in emergency. *Neptune* was the first ship to complete with a director, just below the fore top.

By 1908 the difficulties suffered by all spotting tops were realised and it was suggested by the C-in-C Home Fleet (Sir Francis Bridgeman) that masts were a hazard and that spotting should be carried out from an armoured position on the roof of the conning tower. The advantage of the high spotting top lay first in the greater horizon range, roughly proportional to the square root of the height, but it was argued that in typical North Sea weather it was rarely possible to see the horizon anyway.[8] A well-placed top should also be clear of both funnel smoke and that from fires started in action.

Colossus and *Hercules* (1909 Programme) reverted to a single top arranged as in *Dreadnought* but had a spotting tower, protected by 6in armour, on the roof of the conning tower. The turret arrangement was similar to that of *Neptune* and, even though the bridge was above the conning tower, there was so little space between it, the fore funnel and the mast that heat and smoke problems were inevitable, *Hercules* being the worse since the gases from her Yarrow boilers were hotter. The funnel was raised in 1912 improving conditions on the bridge but making things worse in the top.

The *Orion* class introduced the 13.5in gun and were much bigger ships in consequence. To limit this increase in size, they were given superfiring turrets both fore and aft though the upper turrets could not fire near axial due to blast effects on the lower. The single mast and top was abaft the fore funnel with the usual problems but the extra length enabled the bridge to be abaft the conning tower – at least until it was extended during the war.

The much higher-powered steam plant of the battlecruiser *Lion* made her original tripod mast between the first two funnels quite uninhabitable and she was rebuilt at a cost of £60,000 with a pole mast between the bridge and funnel (see drawing on p.39). Later, this had to be modified into a tripod to carry the weight of a director.

The *King George V* class had the turret arrangement

The breech of the left-hand 13.5in Mk I gun in a twin turret, probably in *Orion*. (Author's collection)

8. This point was considered in the design of the current 'Castle' class OPV and, with better statistics, it was decided that even in North Sea weather, a crow's nest was of value.

Conqueror. B and X turrets were superfiring above A and Y respectively but could not fire anywhere near the axis because blast would enter the lower turret through the sighting hoods (just visible at the fore end of each turret roof). The foremast and spotting top have been placed behind the fore funnel, exposed to smoke, fumes and heat. (WSS)

Centurion. The funnels and masts are now in their proper places, but the sighting hoods remain. (Author's collection)

of the *Orion*s and were designed with a pole mast forward of the funnels. This was changed to a narrow tripod in the last two ships when directors were added and the first two were modified later. The *Iron Duke* class were 25ft longer and completed with a proper tripod. At last, the correct style had been reached and it was followed in the *Queen Elizabeth* and *Royal Sovereign* classes with the midships turret omitted. It is amazing that it took so long to attain a satisfactory arrangement, which was caused by the DNO's insistence on sighting hoods in the roofs of turrets and Jellicoe's obsession with boat-handling arrangements. These unsatisfactory layouts reduced firepower, prejudiced torpedo protection and probably added to cost. As DNO and then as Controller, Jellicoe must accept much of the blame for the unsatisfactory layout of the earlier ships. There is, perhaps, a further contributory factor. In the steady development of a fleet, it is desirable to feed the early lessons from one class into the design of the next but, during the period under discussion, there was a new design every year and a building time of 2½ years meant that the available lessons were two classes removed.

Secondary armament

In Jellicoe's paper justifying the all-big-gun ship he made it clear that there was no value in guns smaller than 12in other than the anti-torpedo boat armament.[9] He also said 'It may be assumed that in future battleships 6-inch guns will not be again mounted singly on the main deck, but if introduced again would like others

of larger calibre be mounted in pairs [twin] turrets and on the upper deck' – though in the same paper it is made clear that there is no space on the upper deck, clear of blast, which could be used for guns. One may note that all German Dreadnoughts mounted a secondary battery of 5.9in guns. There is a paper in the *Tiger* ship's cover which suggests that the German 5.9in battery was intended to destroy the British anti-torpedo boat batteries facilitating their own torpedo attack. By 1909 the increased range of the heater torpedo and the greater size of destroyers appeared to justify a larger secondary gun as, for example, Admiral Mark Kerr's letter of 27 June to Watts.[10] However, he supported the 6in battery on the old, discredited, 'hail of fire' role against enemy battleships as well as a longer-range anti-torpedo boat armament. Kerr claimed he had considerable support from serving officers for these views and he is probably correct in this assertion. The First Lord (McKenna) was impressed and DNC was asked to investigate.

The result was the *Iron Duke*, some 2000 tons bigger than *King George V*, which had a 4in anti-torpedo boat armament. The cost of the earlier class averaged £1.93 million, that of the *Iron Duke*s £2.0 million. The difference was mainly, but not entirely, due to the 6in battery[11] as the later ships had increased torpedo armament and greater fuel stowage. The *Iron Duke*s had to be increased in length by about 25ft to accommodate the bigger battery, even in casemates, and it was so far forward that the casemates were frequently flooded. It will be suggested later that this battery was not only ineffective but also a hazard to the ship.

9. 'HM Ships *Dreadnought & Invincible*'. Tweedmouth Papers, MoD Library. (Written by Jellicoe with input from Watts.)

10. O Parkes, *British Battleships* (London 1956), quoting Admiral Mark Kerr, 'The Navy in my Time'.

11. The *Iron Duke*s had the Mk VII, later battleships Mk XII.

12. J Campbell, *Jutland* (London 1986), p358.

13. Campbell, *Jutland*, p213

Effectiveness of secondary batteries at Jutland

At Jutland, expenditure of secondary ammunition by capital ships was:[12]

	6in	4in
British	850	192

	5.9in	3.5in	6.7in
German	3135	282	95

The hits scored by capital ships were:

On	By British	By German
Battleships	0	9
Cruisers	0	10
Destroyers	4	18

The number of hits on ships which sank can only be estimated (by Campbell) but are of the right order. This leads to a hitting rate of 0.5 per cent for the British batteries and 1.0 per cent for the German. Hits were unlikely as one might expect from hand-worked guns,

close to the waterline and hence with poor visibility. Inertia forces on the heavy and fairly long barrel of the 6in 45cal would make it difficult to train and elevate rapidly, particularly when the ship was pitching and rolling or turning. Fire was normally opened at 7500–8000yds. German accounts say that firing on their destroyers by British battleships was not very effective.[13] One can only wonder if director control, fitted later, would have made a big difference.

The damage caused to capital ships was slight with the exception of one direct hit on the left 15in gun of Y turret in *Warspite* which put it out of action. The cruiser *Calliope* was hit by five 5.9in from *Markgraf* which put two of her 4in guns out of action. The armoured cruiser *Defence* was fired on by the 5.9in of several German ships but the number of hits and the damage caused must be uncertain, as with *Warrior*. Amongst the destroyers, the *Acasta* was hit by two 5.9in from a battlecruiser at about 1820hrs which put her (single) engine-room out of action and she had to be towed back to port, while the *Broke* was badly damaged by nine hits, including one or two 5.9in from *Westfalen* but was able to make her own way home. *Moorsom* and *Onslaught* suffered single hits without serious damage whilst *Onslow* was towed home after three 5.9in hits

Iron Duke is seen early in the war as Jellicoe's flagship of the Grand Fleet. She differed from the *King George V* class by the introduction of a 6in secondary battery, an expensive and potentially hazardous change. (NMM)

from *Lutzow*. *Petard* had four hits from *Westfalen* which slightly reduced her speed and *Porpoise* was hit by two shells from *Posen* or *Oldenburg*. The disabled *Nestor* and *Nomad* were sunk by the 5.9in guns of battleships.

On the German side, the destroyer *V48* was disabled by *Shark* but was then hit by a 6in from the battleship *Valiant*. *G41* had a 6in hit from a battleship on the forecastle and lost speed as a result, while *S51* lost a boiler to a battleship 6in at 1930hrs and *V28* was hit forward, losing speed, at about the same time. All in all, the few hits which were scored caused little damage, but the battleship *Rheinland* suffered two hits from 6in fired by *Black Prince*, one of which caused extensive superficial damage.

There is always an exception; the battleship *Westfalen*'s secondary battery and even her 3.45in guns were extremely well controlled, partly due to skilful use of searchlights. Note that thirty-five rounds of 3.5in were fired in an unsuccessful attempt to sink the disabled destroyer *V4*.

Hazards of secondary batteries

Secondary batteries, distributed along the length of the ship and close to the waterline posed dangers both of flooding and fire/explosion. After the Battle of Jutland, on 1 June 1916 the battlecruiser *Seydlitz* was so low in the water that she was flooding through the gunports but she was on the point of sinking by then. The greatest danger was from the main deck guns mounted aft in *Iron Duke* and *Queen Elizabeth*, which were so close to

the water that flooding occurred in normal steaming and would have gone right under with any underwater damage aft. They were useless and soon removed to the forecastle deck.

The secondary battery could only be given armour of medium thickness, typically 6in, which could be penetrated by main armament projectiles at almost any range. Behind this weak protection there was a considerable amount of ready-use ammunition and more in transit from magazines and shell rooms. The consequences are vividly illustrated by the fire aboard *Malaya* which brought her close to destruction. At 1730hrs a heavy-calibre SAP shell hit the 1in forecastle deck at an angle of 20-25° and burst 7ft later, destroying No 3 starboard 6in gun. The 2in upper deck was forced down several inches and shell fragments wrecked the galley and bakery. It was normal practise to have twelve charges per gun stowed in cases each containing four rounds (it would not be surprising if there were more than twelve rounds per gun in the battery, given the desire for the highest-possible rate of fire). Some of these charges were ignited by shell fragments and others caught fire and burnt without exploding. The whole starboard battery was put out of action and there were 102 casualties. The flash passed down the ammunition hoist into the shell room and was only just prevented from igniting a further ten charges, ready for hoisting. Had these ignited, it is most probable that the 6in magazine would have exploded and, in so doing, set off the forward 15in magazines. There was another small fire aboard the *Colossus* involving 4in charges – four cases

14. D K Brown., 'The Russo-Japanese War, Technical Lessons as Perceived by the RN'.

each containing six charges – but there was no explosion and the fire was soon extinguished.

The battleship *Konig*, under fire from HMS *Iron Duke* at about 1830hrs, had a fire involving a number of 5.9in charges. The fire in the 5.9in casemates of the battle-cruiser *Lutzow* at about 1819hrs seems to have been burning stores and ammunition was not involved.

The loss of the armoured cruisers *Defence* at Jutland and the *Blücher* at Dogger Bank in 1915 showed the danger of flash travelling along ammunition passages. One may also note at Jutland that flame passed down the light cruiser *Southampton*'s hoist to the ammunition passage but was extinguished.

In conclusion, 6in (or 5.9in) secondary batteries aboard capital ships were expensive, unlikely to score hits and their exposed ammunition could endanger the ship. The correct way to protect battleships from destroyer attack was a screen of light cruisers and destroyers. A light 4in battery may well have been desirable to boost morale rather than protect the ship.

Torpedoes

Submerged torpedo tubes were another potentially hazardous feature of battleships of most navies. The introduction of the heater torpedo had greatly increased the speed or range of torpedoes whilst the earlier introduction of gyros had much improved their accuracy. It was thought, wrongly, that these improvements had overcome the problems which had made torpedoes so inef-

fective in the Russo-Japanese War.[14] The British 21in Mk II*** had the following characteristics:

The British 21in Mk II* torpedo**

Speed (kts)	Range (yds)	Running time (mins)
45	4200	3
29	10,750	11

Propagandists for torpedoes would often quote maximum speed combined with the range at the lower speed setting. Belief in the threat of torpedoes was a major factor in pushing the likely range for a gun battle out to 10,000yds, then outside the range of torpedoes. This in turn, led to the heavier and longer-range anti-torpedo boat battery. However, at 10,000yds the running time of a torpedo was 11mins during which the enemy would move an average of 6000yds in an unpredictable direction. The chance of a hit from one or two torpedoes fired from the submerged tubes of a battleship under these conditions was remote, a conclusion fully supported by the results at Jutland.

There were exceptions; the light cruiser *Wiesbaden* probably fired the torpedo which hit *Marlborough* from a submerged tube, with similar objections to those raised above. During the night *Southampton* torpedoed and sank the *Frauenlob* from a submerged tube but at very close range. It was often claimed that a battleship

Malaya. The 6in secondary battery is clearly seen, where a cordite fire during the Battle of Jutland caused 102 casualties. In this late war photograph many of the changes made to all battleships may be seen. The aircraft platforms on B and X turret are the most conspicuous. The remote-controlled searchlights by the funnel can also be seen, as can the director. (Author's collection)

Capital ship torpedoes at Jutland

	British		German	
	Battleships	*Battlecruisers*	*Battleships*	*Battlecruisers*
Torpedo tubes*	84		80	
Number fired	5	8	1	7
Hits	0	0	0	0

*Capital ships of both navies carried 10-16 torpedoes for a British total of 364 21in torpedoes. (18in neglected)

could despatch a disabled opponent using her torpedoes but it was surely more sensible to call up a destroyer for the job.

The hazards of a torpedo armament were of two kinds, the first being the carriage of some 2-3 tons of high explosive, a risk increased in some wartime battle-cruisers with above-water tubes.[15] The second and more serious risk was of flooding in the large spaces needed to operate torpedoes. In *Dreadnought* the torpedo room was the full width of the hold and 24ft long with a door, low down, into the warhead room which was itself again 24ft long. Later ships had even larger spaces, at both ends of the ship. The flooding of *Lutzow* was due in considerable part to the big torpedo flat and leakage from it through a 'watertight' door. As with the 6in secondary battery, the torpedo armament of capital ships was expensive, ineffective and a potential hazard.

Fire control

For a full treatment of the fire control problem one should read Sumida and Brooks.[16] Only a very brief treatment will be given here of the fire control problem and the equipment developed for its solution, the emphasis being on the changes needed in the ships. The first aspect is that the complete system of spotters, rangefinders, calculating machines and, later, the guns had to be connected to each other and these connections were themselves vulnerable. For the first time a battle-ship had a central nervous system and could be 'killed' without being sunk. This was recognised at the time and considerable efforts were made to run the connections under armour wherever possible and to duplicate those which were exposed. However, systems engineering was in its infancy and it is likely that early systems were still vulnerable to battle damage.

The problems of fire control were and remain complex; the guns must be fired at the correct elevation and training angles regardless of the motions of the ship – pitch, roll and yaw as well as deliberate turns. The range must be known and reliable estimates of the enemy's course and speed must be made so that, together with knowledge of one's own course and speed, the position of the enemy when the shell arrives after a flight in excess of 12 seconds, may be calculated. The *Dreadnought* had the initial elements of a system which could produce a solution – a 9ft rangefinder, Dumaresq and the Vickers clock.

By the outbreak of war, the components of the fire-control system had been improved and they were much better integrated. In 1907 a much more powerful and controllable six-cylinder hydraulic engine built by Elswick was installed in the turrets of *Indomitable* and the *Bellerophon*s which enabled the guns to be held continuously on the aiming point and provision was made in the 1908-09 Estimates to fit it in all hydraulically-operated turrets in the fleet. More accurate control valves and, later, swash plate engines improved control of heavy guns still further.

In 1905, Jellicoe advised his successor as DNO (Bacon) to follow up a suggestion by Percy Scott for a trial of 'director firing'. This began in 1907 with the

Bellerophon. Her turrets were laid by a more powerful and sensitive hydraulic plant making continuous aim possible. In 1910 she was used for trials of an early director. In this late-war photo note the training markings on A turret and the flying platform. (see Chapter 8). (Author's collection)

Resolution, probably post-war but little changed other than in smarter paintwork. (Courtesy Julian Mannering)

right-hand gun of each turret of the pre-dreadnought battleship *Africa* and was extended to the other guns in July. A similar system was designed and tried in *Bellerophon* in 1910 and the results were sufficiently good for similar directors to be installed in *Orion, Lion* and later capital ships. The early directors controlled training only and guns were fired at fixed elevation but from *Thunderer* onwards continuous aim for elevation was possible. In 1912, comparative trials between *Thunderer* with a fully-developed director system and *Orion* without, finally demonstrated the value of the director and eight ships were equipped by the outbreak of war, well ahead of any other navy. It has been claimed by Percy Scott that the Admiralty were dragging their heels over the introduction of the director.[17] However, the director and its system was an exceedingly advanced and intricate item of precision engineering and must have strained the industry to its limits. The numbers of skilled workers involved were large; Brooks gives a peak of 360 at Vickers Erith, 107 at Barrow, 800 at Wolseley Motors and 140 installing the systems on board ship.

The later ships had the Dreyer Fire Control Table Mk IV which was much superior to earlier tables. It may be argued that the Pollen table was even better – although much more expensive – but the Dreyer Mk IV should have been adequate for battleships which were likely to fight on near-parallel courses with a slow rate of change of range. It seems likely that the battlecruisers, which were much more likely to fight under conditions of rapid change of range, would have benefitted from the Pollen Argo gear.

Disposition of armour

In the ships up to the *Queen Elizabeth* Sir Phillip Watts followed the armour disposition introduced by Sir William White in *Renown*. The middle deck was the protective deck (reinforced by coal bunkers above),

thickened and sloped down at the side to meet and support the lower edge of the belt. The general style of protection was similar from *Dreadnought* to *Queen Elizabeth* but there were many minor variations in thickness and in extent, both longitudinally and vertically. For this reason, it is difficult to make a good comparative table and that shown below has had to be supplemented by a considerable number of notes.

Belt armour over 4in thick would have been Krupp cemented (KC) and the thinner parts of the belt would probably have been Krupp non-cemented (KNC), of the same steel composition but without the hard, carburised face. Decks were normally high tensile steel (HT); see Chapter 8 for justification. (Decks over 1¾in thick were generally of two thicknesses, rivetted together.)

The lower edge of the main belt was tapered down to 8in in classes prior to the *Royal Sovereign*. The work involved in producing tapered armour was considerable and it seems that extending the thick armour in *Royal Sovereign* may have been a cost saving exercise!

Protection of the ends was altered frequently; not surprisingly since it was hard to decide on the appropri-

15. *Hood* had above-water tubes which may have contributed to her loss in 1941.

16. J T Sumida, *In Defence of Naval Supremacy* (London 1989), J Brooks, 'Fire Control and Capital Design', *War Studies Journal*, Vol 1 No 2 (1996) and 'Fire Control in British Dreadnoughts: a Technical History', Third Conference for New Researchers in Maritime History. Portsmouth, 1995.

17. J Brooks, 'Percy Scott and the Director', *WARSHIP 1995* (1995).

18. Based on R A Burt, *British Battleships of World War I* (Annapolis 1986); K McBride, 'After the *Dreadnought*'. *WARSHIP 1992* and 'Super Dreadnoughts, the *Orion* Battleship Family', *WARSHIP 1993*.

Armour thickness (ins)[18]

| Ship | Belt | | | | Deck | | Barbette | | |
	Main	Upper	Fore	Aft	Flat	Slopes	(ins)	Tons	%
Dreadnought	11	8	6	4	1¾	2¾	11	5000	28
Bellerophon	10	8	7-6	5	1¾	3	9	5389	29
St Vincent	10	8	7-2	2	1½	1¾	9	5500	29
Neptune	10	8	7-2½	2	1¾	1¾	10	5706	29
Colossus	11	8	7-2½	2½	2	2	11	5474	27
Orion	12	8	6-4	2½	1	1	10	6460	29
K George V	12	9-8	6-4	2½	1	1	10	6960	30
Iron Duke	12	9	6-4	6-4	1	1	10	7700	30
Q Elizabeth	13	9-6	6-4	6-4	1¼	1¼	10	8600	32
R Sovereign	13	13	6	6-4	1	2	10	8250	32

ate philosophy. Forward and aft of the end barbettes the hull narrowed rapidly and hence action damage would cause little loss of buoyancy and, more important, of stability. There were few important spaces forward and the steering gear aft would be given separate protection. Flooding forward would lead to some loss of speed and the protection provided was adequate to stop all but the largest splinters from near misses. In addition to the thin end belts, the protective deck was extended fore and aft, usually a little thicker than amidships. (Not shown in table.)

Individual notes

Bellerophon. It is likely that the thinner main belt was accepted after study of the Russo-Japanese War where armour thicker than 6in was not penetrated. The weight saved went into improved torpedo protection. *St Vincent* was generally similar, with a slight increase in the length of the thick belt.

Neptune introduced 1in protection to the uptakes above the middle deck, an idea verified in the *Edinburgh* trials.[19]

Colossus had increased belt thickness but reduced torpedo protection.

Orion had a thicker belt matching her heavier guns and protection to the ends was improved.

King George V had a number of minor increases, particularly to the end bulkheads and this gradual improvement continued in the *Iron Duke* class.

Queen Elizabeth's armour was generally thicker. In particular, the torpedo bulkhead was continuous between the end bulkheads and increased in thickness to 2in. In changing to oil firing, the value of coal bunkers as protection, particularly to the deck, seems to have been forgotten.

Weight breakdown

The *Colossus* Ship's Cover has a breakdown of armour weight which is of interest;

Item	Weight (Tons)	Item	Weight (Tons)
11in belt	1026	8in belt	434
7in belt	150	A barbette	352
P & Q	451	X	341
Y	200	29 Bulkhead	68
42 Bulkhead	26	Aft screen	147
Bolts	32	Main deck	675
Middle deck	805		
Lower deck forward	110	aft	180
Torpedo protection	210	Uptakes	57
Forward CT	125	Aft director tower	12
Lower CT	8	Backing	65
TOTAL	5474		

It is interesting that the main belt only accounts for about one-fifth of the total armour weight. The decks, even though quite thin, account for much more due to their greater area.

Height of deck and stability

In the *Royal Sovereign* '. . . a somewhat reduced metacentric height (GM) was decided upon for these ships with a view to making them steadier gun-platforms than some of the ships with larger GMs' (Sir Eustace Tennyson d'Eyncourt).[20] It was a very marked reduction in GM as shown by inclining experiments.

Comparison of metacentric heights (GM) (ft)

	Valiant Sep 1916	*Royal Oak 1917*	*Ramillies bulged*
Load	5.0	2.0	4.0
Deep	6.5	3.4	4.5
Light		1.14	

The effect of changes in metacentric height on roll behaviour is complicated and it is by no means clear that reduction in GM had much effect on the ships as gunnery platforms. The roll period of a ship is inversely proportional to the square root of the metacentric height, so halving the metacentric height will lead to about a 30 per cent increase in period. The maximum roll angle will not change very much but will occur with the sea abaft the beam instead of forward of the beam in the ship with higher GM. Roll acceleration will be considerably less with the low GM – proportional to the GM. Some idea of the magnitude of these effects is given by the following figures from a computer study of a modern frigate.

Metacentric height and rolling

Metacentric height (ft)	3	5
Max roll angle (Sea State 6)	16°	18°
Angle from bow, worst roll	110°	90°
Max acceleration (deg/sec²)	8	14

D'Eyncourt claimed that the reduction of metacentric height in the *Royal Sovereign* was achieved partly by reducing the beam by 18in and partly by raising the protective deck,[21] giving a higher centre of gravity. This would have had a greater effect on flooded stability than on intact GM, something which was appreciated by d'Eyncourt and his head of battleship design (who was probably E L Atwood) and, for this reason, they decided to raise the protective deck 'to a position well above the level of the deep load line, thus giving more protected freeboard in the damaged condition than in any of our earlier battleships'.[22]

19. See Chapter 2, *Edinburgh* trials.

20. Sir Eustace Tennyson d'Eyncourt. 'Naval Construction During the War', *Trans INA* (1919).

21. I am not convinced that the deck was raised with the intention of lowering GM. These are two separate issues; there was a good case for raising the deck and a different case (which I do not accept) for reducing GM. I do not think d'Eyncourt was telling the full truth; it is hard to distinguish cause and effect.

22. d'Eyncourt as above.

23. W H Garzke and R O Dulin, 'The Bismarck Encounter', *Marine Technology*, Vol 30 No 4 (1993). See also discussion by D K Brown.

24. An extra 1½in of deck would weigh about 1000 tons and there would then be a consequential increase in the size of the ship.

25. Tapered armour was costly and it may be that the uniform 13in plates were actually cheaper.

26. This section is largely based on the reports by Goodall in Washington to the DNC, now in the Public Record Office. They formed the basis for his lecture in Portsmouth, reproduced in *Engineering*, 17 March 1922. Also reports by E L Atwood quoted in N Friedman, *US Battleships* (Annapolis 1985). The remarks on *Baden* are mainly from S V Goodall, 'The ex-German Battleship *Baden*', *Trans INA* (1921). Also from that volume Sir E T d'Eyncourt, 'Notes on some Features of German Warship Construction'.

27. Note that the weights for the US ships are early design estimates and might have increased had the ships been built. *Hood* was nearing completion when Goodall wrote his official paper (May 1918) and her figures were probably largely based on weighed weights, checked by launch displacement.

In the discussion which followed d'Eyncourt's paper, the designer of these 'earlier battleships', Sir Phillip Watts disagreed with d'Eyncourt.

In all of the Dreadnoughts up to the *Royal Sovereign*, the thick protective deck has been placed approximately at the position of the deep load line, because this was considered the best position for it. This deck is the final defence against shell reaching vital parts of the ship by penetrating the armour at, or near, the waterline or by dropping in over the top of the armour. The lower this deck is, the less likely to be struck by flat trajectory fire, and the more likely a dropping shell is to burst by passing through two or three decks before it reaches the protective deck, so that the deck will only be required to keep out the fragments. The new arrangement is not, I contend, nearly as good as that hitherto generally followed.

Needless to say, d'Eyncourt fought back, pointing out that though Watts' ships had been designed with the deck just above the waterline in the load condition, the heavier loading in wartime brought the deck down. This was not too serious in coal-burning ships as the upper bunkers, above the protective deck, did much to preserve both buoyancy and stability but in oil-burning ships, as the *Royal Sovereign*s had become, this was no longer the case. There was an additional thick flat over the magazines to protect them from plunging fire.

With hindsight, it is possible to conclude that both these great men were right in their time. Watts was designing at a time when it was not expected to fire at much over 10,000yds when shells would not fall steeply and the chance of a shell hitting the protective deck was small. Jutland largely confirmed this view (see Chapter 11). D'Eyncourt's point on the protection from upper bunkers is also important. The *Bismarck* of the Second World War generally followed White's style, indeed her armour style was virtually that of the much earlier *Baden*, and performed well in her final, close-range action. While the belt was penetrated, few if any shells could also penetrate the sloped armour behind.[23] Note that the planned sixth ship of the *Queen Elizabeth* class, *Agincourt*, was modified under d'Eyncourt to have a similar armour disposition to the *Royal Sovereign*s.

The design of the *Royal Sovereign* followed the *Edinburgh* firing trials and should have taken more note of the ineffectiveness of protective decks. The 1-2in thickness was inadequate to keep out splinters (without the aid of bunkers, equivalent to some 3in of steel) and should have been increased to at least 3in – but this would have been very heavy.[24] The *Royal Sovereign*s were not hit by shellfire and it is therefore not possible to say how well they would have done. Their main 13in side belt was considerably more extensive than that of the *Queen Elizabeth* which tapered both top and bottom.[25] It seems possible that under the conditions of the First World War, the *Royal Sovereign*s were better protected than the *Queen Elizabeth*s. On the other hand, their low GM or, perhaps more important, their high centre of gravity, was one of factors which made it difficult to modernise them. As shown in the table, the bulges were shaped to raise the metacentre but this would have had less effect under extensive flooding.

The American battleship *Pennsylvania*, an exact contemporary of the *Royal Sovereign*s, adopted a very different style of protection with a deep 13in belt and a 3in deck across the top of it. Other than barbettes, conning tower and uptakes, the rest of the ship was unprotected. She was a somewhat larger ship than her British and German contemporaries which helped to allow for thick armour. Under attack from heavy, high explosive shells, she would have suffered severe damage to the unprotected parts, but whether this would have disabled her is difficult to say. It would depend on the security of main cable runs, particularly gunnery communications, and on the protection of doors, hatches and uptakes. Goodall's reports and those of Atwood, discussed below, suggest that USN ships were not good in these respects.

Some comparisons with foreign designs[26]

Structure

In 1918, Stanley Goodall made a detailed comparison of the hull weights for *Hood* with those for an early study for the US battlecruiser *Lexington* and with BB49 (the *South Dakota* class cancelled in 1922). The comparison was complicated by differences in definition of weight groups but he summarised the main differences in the following table.

American practice lighter	British practice lighter
Transverse framing	Inner bottom
Bulkheads	Protective deck
Strength deck	Stanchions
Framing and plating behind armour	Uptakes and downtakes (US Inclosures)
Ventilation	Paint and cement
Masts	Boat hoisting gear
Electric leads	Doors and hatches

The overall size (Cubic Number = The product of their dimensions) of the three designs[27] was fairly similar so that one may compare the total hull weight directly

Ship	Hull wt (tons)	Bulkheads (tons)
Hood	17,978	4182
Lexington	16,553	3283
BB 49	19,227	4890

Queen Elizabeth and the later Baden are very similar in both the main belt and deck protection but the latter has a thicker upper belt. (The Bismarck of the Second World War was very similar.) In the Royal Sovereign, d'Eyncourt raised the protective deck increasing the protected buoyancy at the expense of a greater chance of the deck being hit by a shell. The bigger Pennsylvania was different; she had a more extensive main belt and a thicker deck and nothing else.

Goodall merely notes the similarity of the two battle-cruisers and the heavy hull of BB 49.[28] The overall similarity conceals some very large individual differences *eg* bulkheads.

Postwar examination of German ships showed that they accepted stresses 10-20 per cent greater than British practice with correspondingly lighter hulls (eg *Baden*'s outer bottom was only ⅝in thick whereas similar British ships would have had 1in). However, this necessitated very elaborate scarphing and rivetting techniques (see Appendix 3) which must have added considerably to the cost of the ships and helped to account for the longer average, pre-war, building time of 37 months compared with an average 28.5 months for a British battleship.

Machinery

Differences in machinery were much more marked; British battleships and all but the last battlecruisers had direct-drive turbines, while both the USN and the German navy built a number of Dreadnoughts with triple-expansion engines. The USN had problems with gearing production and went for steam turbines driving through an electric plant. This had many disadvantages with only a few benefits.

The geared turbine plant of the *Hood* developed 2½ times the shp/ton of the turbo-electric plant of the *Tennessee* or *New Mexico* and 3 times the shp/square foot of floor area. The British plant was very considerably more economical at all speeds; in terms of pounds of steam per shp per hour the differences were 0.5lb at full power, 0.2lb at one-fifth power and 0.2lb at one-tenth power. However, the electric plant permitted much closer subdivision, discussed in the next section.

The *Baden* had three sets of Parsons turbines driving directly. There were fourteen small tube Thornycroft-Schultz boilers of which the forward three burnt oil only and the others coal or oil (normally coal). Goodall says 'The machinery spaces would be described by a naval architect as "compactly arranged" and by a marine engineer as "very congested".'

Subdivision

The US machinery gave exceptional opportunities for close subdivision of the machinery. *Tennessee* had eight large boilers with superheat, each of which was in a separate room, four on either side of the two big turbo-generator rooms. There were three motor rooms, the centre space having two motors. This excellent scheme was degraded by a number of faults; there was a single switchboard room controlling all power with large ventilation trunks reducing its protection.[29] There were glass windows low down in the generator room bulkheads and numerous large ventilation trunks penetrating bulkheads.

The US ships seem to have had by far the best torpedo protection of the day. There were five rows of compartments, each about 3ft wide, the inner and outer being air-filled, the others containing oil.[30] Once again, Goodall was worried by the number of pipes etc, penetrating the bulkheads. He wrote that incidents such as the sinking of the *Audacious* showed that the RN had given insufficient attention to the spread of flooding but the USN was worse.

Baden had a continuous longitudinal bulkhead, 2in thick, with coal bunkers about 6ft wide and, outside that, an air space 7ft wide, less at the ends. Subdivision was generally close but there were exceptions. The fore and aft torpedo rooms were very large[31] and adjacent to the 15in shell rooms, themselves also large. The bunkers had doors in both longitudinal and transverse bulkheads. The ship was divided into five main zones with

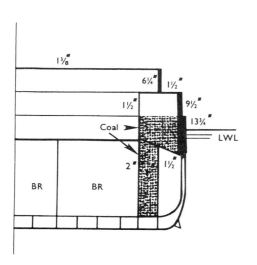

BADEN 31690 Tons

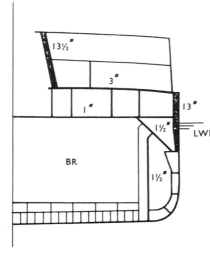

PENNSYLVANIA 32567 Tons

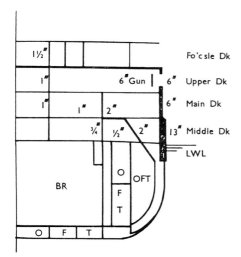

**ROYAL SOVEREIGN (129 Frame)
31000 Tons**

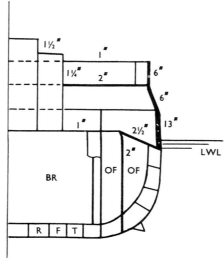

**QUEEN ELIZABETH (129 Frame)
31500 Tons**

two pumps each of at least 900 tons/hour capacity in each zone. The elaborate pumping system required many pipes penetrating bulkheads and there was also a large number of penetrations for voice pipes.

Armament

Baden, like the latest British ships, mounted eight 15in guns in twin turrets. The revolving weight was 1020 tons, very much heavier than the 770 tons of the British Mark I. Goodall notes that there was no handling room for the charges which were exposed to flash when the doors in the trunk were open.

The US triple 14in turret weighed 980 tons. It was very compact but the guns were so close together that there seem to have been interference between adjacent shells in flight, whilst there was also a risk of all guns being disabled by a single hit. The loading arrangements were such that the three guns were unlikely to fire faster than the two in a British mount. Unlike British and German barbettes, those in the US had no framing behind their armour, relying on good joints between plates.

Masts

Goodall went up *New Mexico*'s lattice mast during gunnery trials and noted that there was only slight vibration in the top which died away quickly and would not affect gunnery. Though the lattice mast was lighter, Goodall felt that it would be difficult to adapt to the increasing number of platforms needed for gunnery control.

Accommodation

Goodall wrote: 'Before I had any personal experience of American ships I held the view that in matters affecting comfort our ships came second. I no longer hold this view.' There were some good points; the mess decks were free of clutter and they were well provided with 'luxuries' such as barber's shop, dentist, reading room etc. The 'Heads' called for particular complaint, being smelly with the WCs and urinals in the same space as the washing arrangements. 'The WCs are quite public and the seats consist of two portable boards which are placed over a trough containing running water.' Ventilation was generally adequate but not up to RN standards. There was a lack of isolating valves which would permit the spread of flooding or gas.

E L Atwood visited the *New York* soon after she arrived in the UK and made much the same points on this older ship. He was full of praise for the oil-fired galley and the electric bakery, but thought that the bridge was inadequate and draughty and did not think the lattice mast was a satisfactory support for fire control. Officers' cabins were large and luxuriously equipped. He was very worried by the number of watertight doors and found he could walk from the steering gear to the engine-room at platform deck level. He visited *New Mexico* in 1919 and made similar comments, praising the electrical auxiliary machinery but was most concerned

over the common air intake for all boiler rooms. Like his former (and future) assistant, Goodall, he criticised the toilets.

An American view

The American constructor in London was L B McBride who had interesting and somewhat different views.[32] [Author's response in brackets.] He noted that British ships had heavier hulls than corresponding US ships [it is not certain that this was true in light of Goodall's detailed comparison] and blamed this on the subservience of British constructors to the Navy saying that they were prone to thicken up in way of any failure without thinking it through. [Possibly true when he was writing but not subservience, just lack of time for the staff to think during the war]. He also thought that the British went for cheapness rather than lightness. [Correct, see comparison with *Baden*].

McBride thought that British draughtsmen were less well qualified than those in the US office and hence calculations were all carried out by a few, overworked assistant constructors. In consequence, design calculations were worked out in far less detail than in the US. [Many, perhaps most, draughtsmen had completed 4 years Dockyard school, recognised as the equivalent of a pass degree. They were used extensively on calculation work. However, there was a class distinction and important work was done by ACs. The ability of draughtsmen was undervalued.] He thought that British ships completed overweight because of inadequate calculation but admitted he could not find evidence. [It is quite difficult to check as it is often not clear what was the final legend or what approved changes were made. The table below may not be entirely accurate but it seems to show that ships completed close to the design figure and quite often below.]

Class	Design (tons)	Completed (Load) (tons)
Dreadnought	17,850	18,120
Inflexible	17,250	17,290
Indomitable	17,250	17,410
Invincible	17,250	17,420
Bellerophon	19,018	18,596
Neptune	19,906	19,680
Orion	22,250	21,922
K George V	22,960	25,420 (in 1918)
Tiger	28,120	27,550

Figures for the *Queen Elizabeths* and *Royal Sovereigns* are unclear. There are indications that they completed well above the design figure due to changes – including that from coal to oil in the latter class. [It is likely that McBride was referring to these later classes.] It is sur-

28. The battlecruisers were nearly 200ft longer than the battleship and one might have expected them to be heavier. Much of the difference is due to the battleship's heavy protective deck.

29. In 1942, *Saratoga*, with a similar machinery plant, was immobilised by a single torpedo flooding the control room.

30. Goodall's paper in *Engineering* contains a very detailed drawing of the protection which I would have thought was 'classified' at that date.

31. When *Baden* was mined the forward torpedo room was not restored but more closely divided. The torpedo rooms contributed to the loss of *Lutzow* and the near loss of *Seydlitz*.

32. N Friedman, *US Battleships*, p140.

Life on the mess deck of a battleship in this period was rough. The hammocks and wooden benches and tables were little changed from Nelson's day and few ships had heating or insulation. (Imperial War Museum: Q18676 & Q18666)

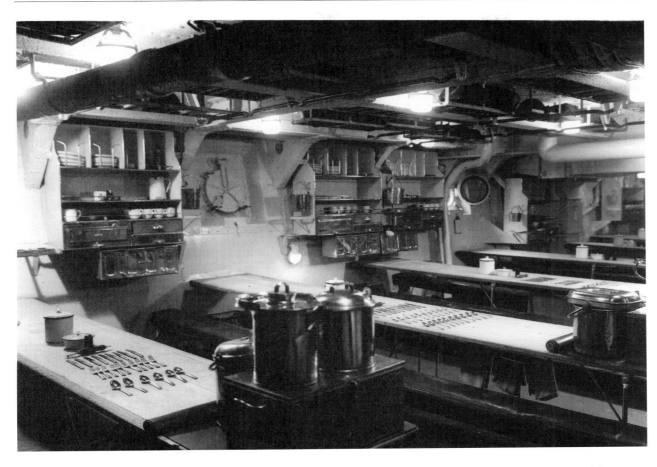

Cooking was likewise basic; the galley did little more than boil simple meals such as stews and duffs prepared on the mess deck. (Imperial War Museum: A20530)

prisingly difficult to measure the displacement of a completed ship; the calculation of hull volume at a given draught is not perfect even if the ship was built exactly to the designed lines. For ships of this size an uncertainty of 200 tons would not be unreasonable – note the three *Invincible*s.

Hindsight

All three navies had very capable designers and their navies got what they wanted. With hindsight, the big weakness lay in underwater protection. The USN had by far the best approach but there were too many detail failings for it to have achieved its potential. The other navies had similar weaknesses, whose problems were revealed in the loss of *Audacious*. German experience (*Lutzow, Seydlitz*) suggests that they may have had even more leak paths.

The 1914 battleship designs

The 1914-15 building programme included four battleships, *Agincourt* of the *Queen Elizabeth* class, to be built at Portsmouth, and three *Royal Sovereign*s, *Resistance* (Devonport), *Repulse* (Palmers) and *Renown* (Fairfields). It has been assumed that these ships were to be similar to the earlier ships of the class but there is strong evidence that they might have been considerably different. A few years ago a notebook came to light which

appears to have been kept as Sir Eustace Tennyson d'Eyncourt's private record of design studies and which contains early designs for the 1914-15 ships.[33]

Design X1 is described as generally on the lines of the *Queen Elizabeth* with the following differences. The 13in side armour was of uniform thickness avoiding the expensive tapered armour of the previous ship. There was a sloped 2in deck arranged as in *Royal Sovereign* and the beam was increased to 94ft to meet the increased displacement. The most important feature was the deck armour which was the style adopted by d'Eyncourt when he took over from Phillip Watts.

X2 was a more radical redesign of the class. The power was reduced to 60,000hp but the speed was kept the same by increasing the length by 20ft. The weight saved was used 'to increase the weight of armour' – as the notebook says, though the figures in the table following show a reduction. The belt came down to 12in though the deck slopes went up to 2½in and the barbette protection went up by 1in on the thickest and 2in on the thinnest portion. The 6in guns were re-arranged with twelve in a two-storey battery amidships. The beam of these ships meant that they could only dock at Rosyth (not yet complete), the locks at Portsmouth and in the large floating dock.

The notebook concludes that X2 was much preferred because of its more economical steaming and general upkeep, fuel consumption being about 20 per cent less

33. Presented to the National Maritime Museum by John Cameron RCNC and held as MS93/011

1914-15 Designs

	Queen Elizabeth	X1	X2	W1	W2	Royal Sovereign
Length (ft)	600	600	620	590	580	580
Beam (ft-in)	90-6	94	94	90-6	88-9	88-6
Draught, load (ft-in)	28-9	28-9	28-9	28-6	28-6	28-9
Load Dspt (tons)	27,500	28,500	27,900	26,700	25,750	25,500
Horse power	75,000	75,000	60,000	31,000	31,000	31,000
Speed (kts)	25	25	25	21	21	21
Oil, max (tons)	3500	3500	3000	3000	3000	3000
Coal (tons)				1500	1500	1500
Armament						
15in (no/rpg)	8/100	8/80	8/80	8/80	8/80	8/80
6in (no/rpg)	16/130	16/150	16/150	16/150	16/150	16/150
3in AA (no/rpg)	2/	4/200	4/200	4/200	4/200	4/200
21in TT (no/torp)	4/	4/20	4/20	4/20	4/20	4/20
Armour (in)						
Side, amid	13	13	12	12	13	13
ford	6	6	6	6	6	6
aft	4	4	4	4	4	4
Bulkheads	6,4	6,4	6,4	6,4	6,4	6,4
Deck						
Focsle	1	1	1	1	1	1
Upper	2	1¼-1½	1¼-1	1¼-1½	1¼-1½	1¼-1½
Main	1¼ end	1-2	1-2	1-2	1-2	1-2
Slope		2½	2½	2½	2	2
Lower	3 ends	2½-1	2½-1	2½-1	2½-1	2½-4
Barbettes	10-7	10-6	11-6	11-6	10-4	10-4
6in Battery	6	6	6	6	6	6
Cost (£million)	c2.5	2.22	2.17	2.035	-	c2.5

Group weights (tons)

	Queen Elizabeth	X1	X2	W1	W2	Royal Sovereign
Equipment	750	710	710	710	700	750
Armament	4550	4600	4600	4600	4550	4550
Machinery	3950	4100	3515	2500	2250	2500
Fuel	650	650	650	900 coal	900 coal	900 coal
Armour*	8600	9450	9150	9150	8600	8100
Hull	8900	9000	9135	8660	8400	8600
Board Margin	100	140	140	130	50	100
Load Dspt	27,500	28,500	27,900	26,700	25,750	25,500

* includes backing

than in X1. These two designs were submitted on 30 May 1914 and rejected. *Agincourt* was cancelled at the outbreak of war and there is no record of a further design study – perhaps it was decided to build a repeat *Queen Elizabeth*.

The two designs for the 1914 *Royal Sovereign*s differ between the Dockyard (W1) and contract-built ships (W2). They are said to be derived from T1, which was the original *Royal Sovereign* design (though the sketch of T1 has two thin funnels very close together). The changes for W1 were a reduction of 1in in the main belt, offset by an extra half-inch on the slopes of the deck. The maximum thickness of the barbette was increased by 1in and the extent of the maximum increased. The stowage for the forward turrets was increased to 100rpg (though 80 taken for the Legend). The 6in guns were rearranged with a double-storey battery amidships, which led to an increase of 140 tons of side and internal armour and a further 140 tons of deck armour. The torpedo bulkheads were increased to 1½in to the middle deck.

Some other changes were noted under W2 though the sketch seems to show them in W1 as well. There was an enlarged torpedo control tower and the conning tower was enlarged and access improved. A protected spotting position was arranged in the stem. The vertical keel was constructed 'in two parts' and the width of the flat keel increased to provide a more rigid structure under docking loads.

The series continued with U1 and 2, described as Canadian battleships. They were based on the *Queen Elizabeth* with a nominal speed of 25kts and the same armament (no drawing). U3 seems to have been fairly similar and had one big funnel. U4 was very different with all four turrets on the same level[34] and the conning tower between A & B (see sketch). U5 had A and B *en echelon* to give bow fire. U4 and 5 had a double-deck 6in battery. The main belt was reduced to 12in in these three designs with increases in decks and elsewhere. The Us and W introduced a spotting station in the stemhead following the *Empress of India* trial.

There was also a 'high speed battleship' for the 1914-15 programme, submitted 8 July 1914 which was not accepted because of poor torpedo protection. It had eight 15in and sixteen 6in guns and a speed of 30kts at an overload power of 108,000hp (normal 85,000hp). Belt armour was 11in with deck 1½in. Slopes were omitted in view of the width of the boiler rooms. There was no room for a second protective bulkhead and it was proposed to fit a coffer dam. An alternative arrangement had X and Y turrets raised 5ft and 55ft added to length to include an upper deck 6in battery aft (weight increased by 385 tons, cost by £50,000). All oil fuel would save 300 tons and £25,000.

34. There were problems with the early director systems in handling turrets at different heights and U4 may have been intended to overcome these. It is more likely that it was to lower the centre of gravity; if the superfiring guns could not fire over the lower turret, what was the point of raising them?

Cruisers | *Four*

Battlecruisers

THE INTRODUCTION of the battlecruiser has been described in an earlier book and more recently by Roberts[1] but for completeness will be outlined briefly in this volume. The battlecruiser was very much the brainchild of Admiral Fisher and, as with many of his dreams, the concept, both of the role and of the technical solution, changed radically as time progressed. It should be noted that the term 'Battlecruiser' was only introduced in November 1911; prior to that, these ships were usually referred to as armoured cruisers.

Like contemporary battleships, the big armoured cruiser of the turn of the century had a mixed armament, which included 9.2in, 7.5in and 6in guns. Such ships were thought capable of playing a supporting role in the line of battle and, after losing one third of their battleships to mines, the Japanese did use their cruisers in this way during the war with Russia. Their main belt was usually 6in Krupp KC, as much as the more lightly-protected battleships, which would keep out all 6in shells, most 9.2in and all high capacity HE at 'battle range' (probably 3000yds).

Fisher's first thoughts in 1902 were not very different from traditional ideas. He envisaged a ship with four 9.2in and twelve 7.5in guns and a 6in belt. By the time he wrote the first volume of 'Naval Necessities' in October 1904, he was thinking of an 'all-big-gun' armoured cruiser with sixteen 9.2in,[2] still with a 6in belt. Shortly afterwards he was persuaded that the arguments which led to an all-12in armament in the *Dreadnought* also applied to the armoured cruiser and the design of *Invincible* was changed to eight 12in guns, but retaining the 6in belt. The reasons for this decision are not recorded but Bacon wrote:

. . . that ships of the size and tonnage necessary . . . should have an additional use in being able to form a fast light squadron to supplement the battleships in action, and to worry the ships in van or rear of the enemy's line. They were never intended to *engage battle ships single handed* [Bacon's italics]; but they were designed to assist in a general action by engaging some of the enemy's ships which were already fighting our battleships.[3]

He also wrote that they should be fast enough to hunt down and destroy any armed merchant ship.[4]

Even in October 1904 Fisher was floating the idea that the battlecruiser could replace the battleship but the First Lord, Lord Selbourne, was not willing to accept

1. D K Brown, *Warrior to Dreadnought*, and J Roberts, *Battlecruisers* (London 1997).

2. He seemed to have preferred a 10in gun but accepted that, logistically, it was expensive to introduce a new calibre so close to the 9.2in.

3. No one seems to have thought of the cost of providing a sufficient number of battlecruisers to hunt down raiders!

4. Admiral Sir R H Bacon, *The Life of Lord Fisher of Kilverstone* (London 1929), Vol I, p256. Note that Bacon's memory is not always reliable.

Inflexible. The section at Frame 121 is of particular interest. *Invincible*, a sister ship was sunk at Jutland as a result of a hit on the roof of Q turret and the flash reached the magazine below. The flash (and possibly hot splinters) travelled inside the ship causing low-order explosions in A and Y turret magazines (see Chapter 11).

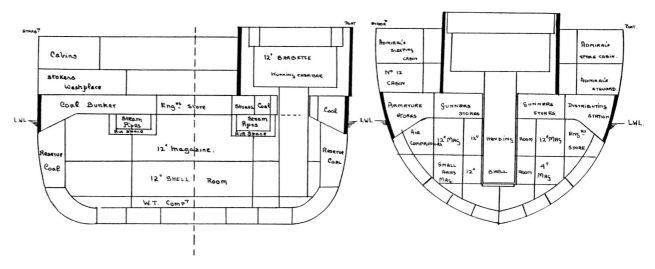

Indefatigable in 1910. The increased spacing of the midships turrets did not permit cross-deck firing without damage to the deck. (WSS)

such a radical proposal. In December 1905 Fisher set up what was effectively a new Committee on Designs to consider the merging of the battleship and armoured cruiser into a 'fusion design' with ten 12in guns and a speed of 25kts, displacing 22,500 tons.[5] However, for once, the committee which he had selected did not support his views.[6] They thought that the *Entente Cordiale* with France and the destruction of the Russian fleet had diminished the need for fast and powerful cruisers whilst the growing threat from Germany should be countered by battleships of the *Dreadnought* type which would be cheaper than the fusion design.[7] There was also growing financial pressure to reduce naval spending and it was the wrong time to propose a more expensive ship.

Indefatigable

The first battlecruiser *Invincible* went to sea in June

1908[8] and began formal trials in October. Studies for the next class, which led to the *Indefatigable*, began in December 1906 and she was finally started in February 1909 under the 1908-09 Programme so that there can have been little or no feedback from the earlier ship to the new design (see later in this chapter for alternative, cheaper ships with 9.2in guns). Design E had eight 12in 50cal and a 9in belt, whilst F had ten 12in guns and a 10in belt. F had triple 12in turrets in A and X positions. These designs were followed by J1–5 which were variants on F, and by J6 with three triple turrets and J7 with four.[9] It was hoped that the triple turret would have a revolving weight of about 500 tons, and first estimates were 610 tons (Vickers) and 655 tons (Elswick); later figures were over 700 tons. This series then died out.

Although while she was building *Indefatigable* was hailed as a great advance on *Invincible*, the actual improvements were small. She was to expose the great weakness of Fisher's original concept for the battle-cruiser. They were to overwhelm the enemy's scouting line with their superior gun power, locate and even engage the enemy battle line, but no thought seems to have been given to the possession of similar ships by the enemy. In fact, the first German battlecruiser *Von der Tann* (which was to sink *Indefatigable* at Jutland) had been laid down in March 1908 and, though details of her design were not known, it was certain that she was a response to the *Invincible* and that something much better was needed.

Indefatigable's main armament was the same as *Invincible* with eight 12in 45 calibre Mk X. The extra 23ft of length gave the wing turrets somewhat better arcs of fire on the opposite beam (70°) though cross-deck firing was still likely to cause damage. P turret was very close to the bridge and could not fire anywhere near the bow because of blast effects on control personnel. Even though the after control top was a little further from the third funnel, it was still unusable and later removed. The anti-destroyer guns were sixteen 4in Mk VII firing a 31lb shell in place of the 25lb of the *Invincible*.

The armour was less than in the earlier ships: the 6in belt extended for only 298ft amidships and the total weight of 6in armour was 721 tons compared with *Invincible*'s 815 tons. In way of the end turrets the belt was only 4in and the end bulkheads were 4in in place of the 6in of the *Invincible*. The high, unarmoured freeboard (c27ft) is often criticised but was necessary in a fast ship.[10] Protection was altered in the two follow-on ships, *Australia* and *New Zealand*. The 2½in protection at the ends was omitted and the belt increased to 5in. Turret armour was the same as *Invincible* but the supporting beams to the roof were strengthened, a change confirmed by the 1907 trials described in Chapter 2.

D'Eyncourt (DNC) was to tell the INA in 1921 that 'In reviewing the whole history of battlecruiser design, I

cannot help thinking it was unfortunate that it was decided virtually to repeat the *Invincibles*–a design already becoming obsolescent–when the *Indefatigable* class was ordered, instead of developing an improved design with protection which should have been at least equal to that of *Moltke* and *Goeben* of about the same

Wing turret of *Indomitable*. The sighting hoods at the front of the turret are conspicuous in this view. Note the 4in guns on the turret roof. (Author's collection)

5. N A Lambert, 'Sir John Fisher and the Concept of Flotilla Defence 1904-1909', *Journal of Military History* (October 1995).

6. It was most unusual for a committee appointed by Fisher to override his views. This topic is discussed in Sumida, *In Defence of Naval Supremacy*.

7. The idea lingered on and may be recognised in Rear-Admiral R H S Bacon, 'The Battleship of the Future', *Trans INA* (1910).

8. She did not officially complete until October 1908; the June voyage was a special trip to Canada for the Quebec Tercentenary.

9. Ship's cover 230.

10. This freeboard corresponds almost exactly with the rule of thumb of 1.1√L.

Lion after her mast had been moved forward of the funnel in 1912. (Author's collection)

date.'[11] In response, Sir Phillip Watts made the valid point that it was the Board of Admiralty and not the DNC who decided on the characteristics of the ships. He suggests that there was a desire to have a homogeneous squadron of six ships but denied that the *Invincible* was obsolete except in the way in which every ship is obsolete on completion. However, it is even harder to justify the later *Australia* and *New Zealand*.

Lion and the 1909-10 Programme

After public pressure (as outlined in the introduction) the next year's programme was to consist of eight capital ships. Fisher wanted them to be all battlecruisers[12] but was opposed by the new Second Sea Lord, Sir Francis Bridgeman, who insisted on the need for battleships to counter the growing strength of Germany. Fisher had a different strategic philosophy, often referred to as 'Flotilla Defence'.[13] He thought that the torpedo launched from destroyers had made both an RN close blockade of Germany and a German invasion of this country impossible. In consequence, home defence would become the role of flotillas of destroyers and submarines. Cruiser warfare in distant waters was still a threat to trade and isolated colonies and Fisher seems to have envisaged battlecruiser squadrons as an overwhelming force to deal with such a threat.[14] This concept does not seem to have been reflected in the endurance of the new battlecruisers which did not differ significantly from that of earlier battleships and battlecruisers. The agreed programme was for three battleships and one battlecruiser (*Lion*) together with a similar four in a 'contingency' programme, *Princess Royal* being the battlecruiser.

Endurance of *Lion*

Speed (kts)	Endurance (nm)
24.6	2420
20.45	3345
10	5610

The early German battlecruisers had much less endurance, *eg Von der Tann* 2500nm at 22½kts and 4400nm at 14kts. *Moltke* was similar.

The *Lion* was 7600 tons larger than her predecessor, allowing a much more powerful armament of eight 13.5in 45 cal MkV guns and a speed of 27kts but only slightly better protection. The main belt was 9in[15] but in way of B barbette it was only 5-6in and by A and X only 5in with a short 4in extension, fore and aft, sealed with 4in bulkheads. There was a 6in upper belt between the main and upper decks. The lower deck was 2in maximum at the ends, mainly 1in.

Damage is discussed in Chapter 11 and need only be summarised here. At Dogger Bank (24 January 1915), *Lion* was hit by seventeen large shells and was disabled. The 9in belt seemed marginally capable of resisting 11in shell but the supports failed under the impact of a 12in from *Derfflinger*. Repairs took about two months. Seventeen large shells form a severe punishment for a lightly-protected ship and it may be thought that she did quite well. At Jutland she was hit by thirteen base-fused HE shells from *Lutzow*. One shell hitting Q turret nearly caused her loss from a magazine explosion but the others did little damage. Her sister-ship *Princess Royal* was unable to keep up at Dogger Bank, while at Jutland she was hit by eight 12in and one 11in without major damage.

Lion completed with a tripod mast supporting a control top abaft the forward funnel (see p39). The top was just 39ft 6in from the mouth of the funnel where gases from the forward ten boilers were vented at a temperature of 550°C. Conditions were intolerable and this mast was replaced by a pole mast forward of the funnel. Later, this was strengthened by struts which did not reach to the control top. *Lion* originally had short second and third funnels which were raised when the mast was altered. *Princess Royal* was similarly modified during completion. These changes cost £68,000 per ship.

Queen Mary

Queen Mary (completed August 1913) was very similar to *Lion* but was the battlecruiser equivalent of *King George V* as *Lion* was of *Orion*, her 13.5in guns firing the heavier 1400lb shell, which made them more accurate. Her secondary battery was better disposed and protected by 3in plate. There were only minor changes to the protection leaving the fore and aft magazines with only 5in side armour.

Queen Mary reverted to the traditional arrangement of officers' accommodation aft which was much preferred. Thanks to the initiative of her first captain, Reginald Hall, she had a considerable number of improvements to ratings' living conditions, including a chapel, bookstall, cinematograph, washing machines and much improved washplaces. Attwood, writing in 1913,[16] drew attention to 'recent' improvements in comfort for the crew, mentioning that washplaces were now provided for seamen instead of only for stokers![17] Hall also introduced some organisational changes which made life a little more pleasant for ratings.

There seems to have been some general interest in living conditions at this time. The table below is simplified from one in the d'Eyncourt papers[18] showing how cramped life was on the lower deck. Imagine living, eating and sleeping in 12½ft²!

Space per man

Ship	No. Officers	No. Men	Space/Officer (ft²)	Space/Man (ft²)
Majestic	50	707	142	21.4
King Edward VII	34	768	306	27.9
Bellerophon	50	679	260	22.7
Orion	46	691	350	32.7
King George V	69	870	219	24
Lion	57	943	305	16.8
Monmouth	38	660	204	21.8
Defence	43	784	342	28.7
Challenger	23	423	305	20.4
Bristol	20	359	138	12.5
Birmingham	21	374	217	22.8

Notes 'Domestics included. Sick bay excluded'.

Tiger

The 1911-12 programme called for one battlecruiser, *Tiger*, whose origins are well described by Roberts.[19] She was the equivalent of the *Iron Dukes*, featuring the same unnecessary 6in secondary battery. Design A of August 1911 had superfiring guns forward and aft but in later studies, X turret was moved well forward. It is probable that the separation of the after two turrets enabled X to fire aft which it could not have done in the more conventional superfiring arrangement due to the blast effects on the lower turret. The provision of an after torpedo flat was another reason for moving the after boiler room to a more forward position.

The secondary battery had 5in armour, adding somewhat to the overall protection of the ship – though at the expense of the exposed 6in ammunition supply. There was also a strip of 3in plate, 2ft 6in deep, below the main belt. This was said to be based on a lesson learnt by the Japanese in the war with Russia[20] and is the only indication that *Tiger* was influenced by *Kongo*.[21] The main

11. Sir Eustace Tennyson d'Eyncourt, 'Notes on some features of German Warship Construction', *Trans INA* (1921) – and discussion.

12. Fisher wrote to Lord Esher 'I've got Sir Phillip Watts into a new *Indomitable* that will make your mouth water when you see it, and the Germans gnash their teeth.'

13. Lambert, 'Sir John Fisher and the Concept of Flotilla Defence 1904-1909'.

14. He still does not seem to have recognised that they might have to fight similar ships.

15. This was only 1in less than that of the later 12in-gun battleships.

16. E L Attwood, *The Modern Warship* (Cambridge 1913).

17. Sailors had previously had to wash – if at all – in buckets wherever they could manage.

18. d'Eyncourt papers, DEY14. National Maritime Museum.

19. J Roberts, 'The Design and Construction of the Battlecruiser *Tiger*', *Warship* 5 and 6 (1978) and *Battlecruisers*, pp36-39.

20. Ships cover. National Maritime Museum.

21. Mr Lars Ahlberg (Private communication) has investigated the origin of *Kongo* using papers by Yasuo Abe and Nakagawa Tsutomu. It does not seem that there was a direct link between that ship and *Tiger* but the Japanese were allowed access to much British thinking as, of course, were Vickers and it is probably best to see *Tiger* and *Kongo* as the independent end-products of similar lines of thought.

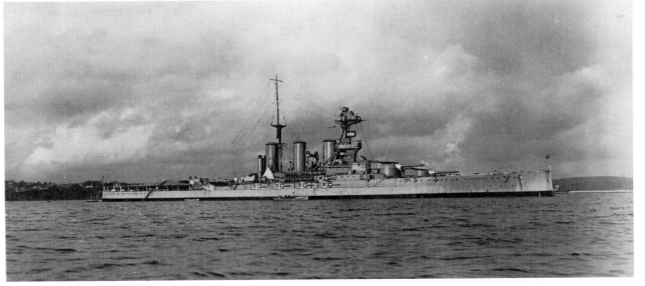

Tiger at the end of the war. The fore-topmast was moved to the derrick post in 1918 but she retains the aircraft platform on B turret. (WSS)

A design study for a big all-
9.2in armoured cruiser c1907.
The study was prepared by S
Payne and the drawing was
given to the author by his son.
The lattice mast aft is
remarkable – and unexplained.

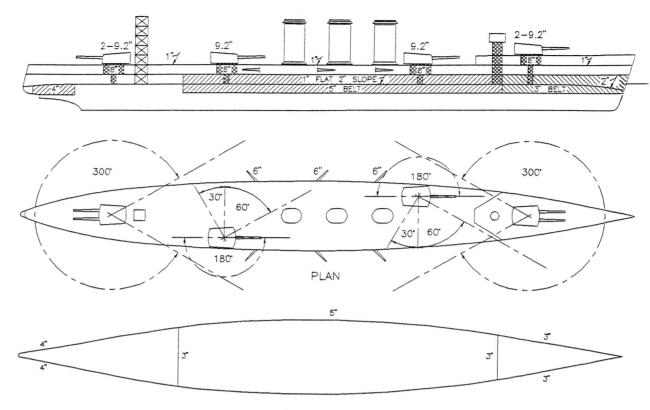

22. At that date thick armour (such
as 9in) cost £92/ton; 2in was
£74/ton.

23. Ships cover 279. Some twenty-
five examples of flooding were
considered but most were trivial.
15° is a very severe list and even
walking, let alone working, would
be very difficult.

24. Sumida, *In Defence of Naval
Supremacy*, p114 (quoting ADM
167/40).

25. Sumida, as above.

26. National Maritime Museum
MS93/011.

27. A similar table appeared in
Warrior to Dreadnought but is
reproduced here as part of the
general discussion of the
battlecruiser concept. Note that the
cruiser described in that book was
E3 not E2 as given.

28. Actual cost £1,677,515.

29. Brown, *Warrior to
Dreadnought*, p147.

30. Brown, *Warrior to
Dreadnought*, p163.

31. *Boadicea* under 1907
programme, *Bellona* in 1908,
Blanche and *Blonde* in 1909, *Active*
and *Amphion* in 1910 and *Fearless* in
1911.

32. Sir A Hezlet, *Electron and Sea
Power* (London 1975).

belt remained at 9in and stopped short of the end turrets.[22] The magazines were protected against torpedo
attack by 1-2½in plate. There were no watertight doors
in transverse bulkheads below the main deck, in the
engine and condenser room longitudinal bulkheads or
in the bunkers between lower and upper decks. It was
calculated that flooding one engine room and the
adjoining condenser room would cause a 15° heel.[23]

Tiger – righting moments (GZ)

Condition	Max GZ	at degrees
Deep	3.71	44
Legend	2.81	42
Light	2.55	41

Battlecruisers were highly stressed ships (tons/in²).

Ship	Hogging		Sagging	
	Deck	Keel	Deck	Keel
Tiger	7.05	5.06	5.48	5.87
Q Mary	7.02	5.12		
Lion	7.02	5.14		

The sagging case was not calculated for the two latter
ships.

There were eleven docks in Home Dockyards plus six
commercial docks in the UK which could accept *Tiger*.

Overseas there were five docks and four more proposed
which could take these ships. *Tiger* was nearly the end
of the type since there were no battlecruisers proposed
in the 1912-13, 1913-14 or the 1914-15 Estimates.

Smaller armoured cruisers

There seems to have been no support within the
Admiralty for smaller battleships but there are indications that there was strong support for smaller – and
cheaper – armoured cruisers. In early 1907 an improved
Invincible for the 1907-08 programme was cancelled.[24]
In June 1907 Jellicoe (DNO) urged that the armoured
cruisers for the 1908-09 programme should be armed
with 9.2in rather than 12in guns to save money. His
views were endorsed by the full Board in June 1907.[25]
An outline of such a ship prepared by S Payne RCNC
probably dates from this period. A legend for the slightly different design E dated November 1911 also refers
(see following table). The first design, with four twin
turrets was estimated to cost £1,454,000. Consideration
was also given to a smaller ship with three twin 9.2in
costing £1,100,000 (the comparative four-turret ship
was now estimated at £1,280,000), but German plans for
big gun (11in) battlecruisers in their 1907-08 and 1908-
09 Programmes led to the cancellation of these 9.2in
ships and hence to the *Indefatigable*.

There was another attempt at a 9.2in cruiser in
October 1913. D'Eyncourt's notebook[26] describes two
variants, E2 and E3 whose particulars are compared

with *Invincible* and the older, armoured cruiser *Warrior*, opposite.[27]

The most important difference between E2 and E3 was that the latter had an upper 4in belt protecting the side under the 6in battery. In a ship to ship duel the odds would clearly favour *Invincible* and the cost saving of the 1913 designs is not enough to have much effect on the numbers which could be built.

Technical considerations

It is clear that cost was a major constraint on the design of the battlecruiser. It was accepted that the cost should not be significantly greater than that of a contemporary battleship, a guideline dating back to the old First Class cruisers.

Direct comparisons with wartime battleships are not possible as there were no corresponding ships, and the changing value of wartime would make such comparison difficult. For the record, the quoted costs of wartime battlecruisers were: *Renown* £3,117,204, *Courageous* £2,038,225, and *Hood* £6,025,000. It is interesting to compare the cost per ton for battlecruisers and, in particular, the effect of wartime inflation. In the table following, cost/ton has been deflated by the retail price index (RPI) at the date of launch. (This is not entirely appropriate but is the best indicator available.)

Class	Cost/ton(£)	RPI	Cost/ton(£), deflated
Invincible	94	106	89
Indefatigable	77	104	74
Lion	75	109	69
Queen Mary	77	115	67
Tiger	74	116	64
Renown	113	186	61
Courageous	95	186	51
Hood	142	267	53

On this basis, cost per ton is remarkably constant. (The high cost of *Invincible* cannot be explained; perhaps a high tender on the grounds of novelty.) Since cost per ton did not vary much, the perceived limit on cost read directly as a limit on displacement, a limit supported by the size of docks available. During the White era considerable efforts had been made to reduce weight in the hull group.[29] It is unlikely that there was much chance of further savings, but the machinery was large and heavy and considerable savings should have been possible (see Chapter 1).

Light cruisers

At the time of the *Dreadnought* committee, Fisher saw no place for ships between the battlecruiser and the destroyer except, possibly, for a very few Scouts as destroyer leaders. Of the earlier Scouts,[30] the Armstrong design was preferred and between 1907 and

Armoured cruisers

	Warrior	Invincible	E	E2	E3
Date, Estimates	1903	1905	1908?	1913	1913
Displacement (tons)	13,350	17,300	15,750	15,500	17,850
Cost (£million)	1.2	1.75	?	1.35	1.5
Armament	6-9.2in,	8-12in,	8-9.2in,	8-9.2in,	8-9.2in
	4-7.5in	16-4in	16-4in	8-6in,	8-6in
Speed (kts)	23	25	25	28	28
Belt thickness, max (ins)	6	6	6	6	6
Weight (tons)					
Hull	5190	6120	5890	5500	6000
Armament	1585	2500	1690	1900	1900
Armour	2845	3370	2985	3560	5070
Machinery	2270	3140	3400	2700	3000

Costs of battleships and battlecruisers

	Battlecruisers			Battleships	
Class (£)	Cost, ship (£)	Cost, guns (£)	Class	Cost, ship (£)	Cost, Guns
Invincible	1,621,015[28]	90,000	*Dreadnought*	1,672,483	113,200
Indefatigable	1,430,091	98,500	*Colossus*	1,540,403	131,700
Lion	1,965,699	118,300	*Orion*	1,711,617	144,300
Q Mary	2,078,491		*K George V*	1,961,096	
Tiger	2,100,000		*Iron Duke*	1,945,824	

1910[31] seven generally similar ships from *Boadicea* onwards were built, all in Pembroke Dockyard. The first pair mounted six 4in BL Mk VIII, increased to ten in 1916. The rest were built with ten 4in. There was a thin protective deck, augmented by coal bunkers. They had four-shaft Parsons direct drive turbines for a speed of 25kts, but it was fairly soon realised that the speed was inadequate and, more slowly, that a 4in shell was too small to be certain of disabling a destroyer with one hit.

Roles envisaged for cruisers included:

(a) Scouting for, and shadowing the enemy battle fleet.
(b) Trade war, protection and raiding.
(c) Colonial police work.
(d) Destroyer leader.
(e) Counter destroyer

A role which was not often stated explicitly was that of 'ship of force' in areas remote from the battle fleet.

Fisher saw the battlecruiser as fulfilling roles (a) and (b) even though their cost meant that there would never be enough, at least for trade route protection. The tasks of scouting, shadowing and trade protection had been made easier by the introduction of wireless[32] but large numbers of ships were still needed.

A general view of light cruisers with at least four 'Town' class in the foreground. British light cruisers from the *Bristol* onwards proved effective and able to withstand a lot of damage. (Author's collection)

Bristol was much bigger, better armed and much better protected than the earlier Scouts. (WSS)

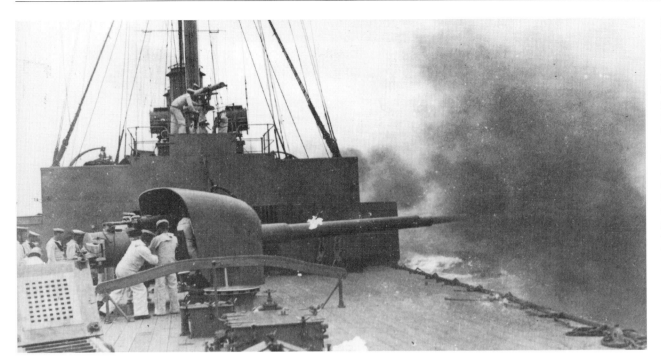

Left: Sydney's after 6in gun firing. The gun is a Mk XII, 45 calibre, 2 tons lighter than the Mk IX fitted in earlier cruisers, making it easier to work in a seaway. Note the depression rail abaft the mounting to prevent it firing into its own ship. (Courtesy Ross Gillett)

Below: Melbourne, one of the Australian *Chatham* class cruisers. This view from above shows the arrangement of guns. In these lightly protected ships it was desirable to space the guns as widely as possible to avoid having more than one disabled by a single hit. Two guns on the beam do not usually have double the effect on displacement as a single centreline gun which may need an increase in ship length. (Courtesy Ross Gillett)

The 'Town' classes

Germany had been building a number of light cruisers generally similar to the Scouts[33] and in 1909 it was decided that the five new cruisers, originally described as 'Improved *Boadiceas*' should mount two single 6in 50 cal Mk IX as well as ten 4in. Speed remained at 25kts and the deck was increased to 2in (plus coal) over magazines and machinery spaces. The *Bristol* class, as they had become, burnt a mixture of coal and oil and had a nominal endurance of 5070 miles at 16kts. *Bristol* had Brown-Curtis turbines and two shafts, the rest had four-shaft Parsons turbines. They were very cramped ships and Fisher's decision to place the officers' accommodation forward, though logical, was not popular. Lack of space meant that they were altered little during the war. Ships with a protective deck at the waterline needed a large metacentric height (GM) to preserve stability with flooding above the deck. This high GM led to severe rolling accelerations making them poor gun platforms.

The next batch of four ships (the *Weymouth* class of 1910) was laid down before the *Bristol*s went to sea, but some of the problems with the earlier class had been recognised and corrected. Instead of a mixed armament, they mounted eight 6in guns. Upper deck guns mounted in the waist were liable to become immersed in a seaway, making them difficult and even dangerous to work, and therefore the forward two beam guns were lifted onto an extended forecastle and the remainder were mounted behind a high bulwark. Since the crews were protected only by a light shield, the guns had to be dis-

33. Armed with ten-twelve 4.1in, which could comfortably outrange the RN's 4in gun.

Adelaide, the last of the Australian *Birmingham* class whose completion was held up by delay in components from the UK. She was to serve in the Second World War. (Courtesy Ross Gillett)

Birkenhead, shown here, and her sister, *Chester*, mounted the lighter 5.5in gun firing an 85lb shell which was easier to handle in a seaway. (WSS)

persed widely to avoid several being disabled by a single hit while separation was also desirable to limit the effects of blast.

Further improvements came in the *Chatham* class (three ships for the RN, three more for Australia laid down 1911-13[34]), again before the previous class had gone to sea. The forecastle now extended for over two-thirds of the length giving fair shelter to the two remaining beam guns on the upper deck at the break of forecastle. Beam was increased by only 6in reducing the metacentric height and making them steadier gun plat-

forms. The eight 6in were the shorter (45 calibre) Mk XII which was 2 tons lighter with virtually the same range of 14,500yds. The reduced inertia of the shorter barrel made elevation and training much easier in a seaway (see Chapter 7).

As a result of the *Edinburgh* trials (Chapter 2), which showed that protective decks were of limited value, the deck was much reduced in thickness, to ¾in over machinery, ⅜in else where. The main protection was a waterline belt of 2in nickel steel over 1in shell plating. Nickel steel could not be given double curvature and hence the hull was parallel sided over the length of the belt. *Southampton* had twin-shaft Brown-Curtis turbines, the rest four-shaft Parsons. These ships were followed by the three very similar ships of the *Birmingham* class (plus one for Australia) which had two 6in on the forecastle, side by side. British cruiser design now took a different turning which will be followed next but the *Birmingham* was to father an 'Improved *Birmingham*' or *Hawkins* class via the abortive 'Atlantic cruisers', discussed later. There were also two very similar ships building for Greece which were taken over early in 1915, and renamed *Chester* and *Birkenhead*. These mounted ten of the excellent Coventry Ordnance Works' 5.5in gun which was about 13 cwt lighter than the 6in. Its projectile weighed 85lbs compared with 100lbs for a 6in and was much easier to handle on a small ship in a seaway. *Birkenhead* had mixed firing giving 25,000shp for 25kts whilst *Chester* was modified for oil only and made 26.5kts with 31,000shp.

Arethusa class

The *Arethusa*s are important in their own right but will be considered in more than usual detail since a first-hand account of their design still exists, written by the constructor in charge, Stanley V Goodall.[35] The initial concept was simple: a speed of 30kts to accompany modern destroyers, six 4in guns and 3in side protection as in the later 'Towns'. Goodall was put in charge of the design even though he was very junior – just five years out of college – supervised by W H Whiting and W Berry. The first sketch design took only two days and this led to further discussions by the Board who asked for a 6in gun to be added at each end. This was of concern to Goodall since experience had shown that a 100lb shell was difficult to handle on a small ship in a seaway. He reduced the GM to 2-2½ft, gave the form a fairly square bilge[36] and fitted deep bilge keels. The change to oil fuel had altered the stability characteristics with a lower centre of gravity in the deep condition. An inclining experiment on *Aurora* gave a GM of 2.21 legend, 2.69 deep, with a range of stability of 83° and 86° respectively.

The first big problem lay in the type of machinery. Conventional cruiser machinery would weigh 1050 tons for 30,000shp whilst the design needed 40,000shp weighing not more than 850 tons. Oil fuel helped considerably but it was necessary to go to destroyer-type machinery as well which led to two further problems.

The lightweight machinery implied the use of high rotational speed (rpm) which meant smaller propellers of lower efficiency. Goodall gives a hilarious account of his discussion with Whiting[37] and Watts. Eventually they drafted a memo to the First Lord (Churchill) pointing out that the speed would be difficult to achieve and that prolonged trials would be needed with several sets of propellers. Trials a few days after the war began were curtailed and *Arethusa* made 27kts at design power (30,000shp) and 29kts at overload power (40,000 shp). Time was short and the design was frozen before model tests were available which showed the form was no more than satisfactory. The E-in-C agreed to smaller, highly-stressed outer shafts and the shaft brackets were forged rather than cast so that they could be smaller and cause less drag.[38]

The new boilers were large and very tall, making it impossible to run a main deck through the boiler rooms. This weakening of the hull structure was particularly unwelcome as these ships had an exceptionally high length/depth ratio and, to make matters even worse, the oil was stowed near the ends giving a very high hogging/bending moment and hence high tensile stresses in the deck.

The protection consisted of 1in HT shell plating with a 2in HT outer layer which could be given double curvature. The plates were very large for the day, the upper strake being 5ft wide and the lower 8ft, both 36ft long. The upper strake was rivetted through the inner plating as well as a 50lb strap – a total thickness of 4½in using 1⅛in rivets, regarded as the largest rivets which could be knocked up satisfactorily. The lower 2in strake was not strapped and was not used in the strength calculation but the designers were aware that it would provide a lit-

34. Much of the equipment was supplied from the UK and slow delivery during the war accounted for much of the lengthy building time of the Australian ships.

35. Goodall gave a lecture to the students of the US Corps of Constructors at MIT, Boston in 1918. His lecture notes came to light in 1982 and were worked into an article by the present author for *Warship International* 1/83 – 'The Design of HMS *Arethusa* 1912'. The passage in this book is much abbreviated from the original.

36. In itself, a square bilge in itself does not help a great deal as it was then thought but it does lead to higher water flow across the keels which is very beneficial.

37. Whiting had the reputation of being an outstanding designer but 'difficult'.

38. Shafts and shaft brackets would account for about 6 per cent of the total drag of a cruiser.

Phaeton of the *Arethusa* class, a new style of light cruiser. It was Stanley Goodall's first design. (WSS)

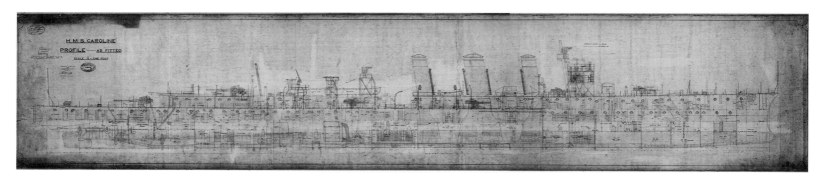

Caroline, one of the first batch of the 'C' class of Improved *Arethusas*. She remains in service (1999) as a reserve training ship at Belfast, the last ship afloat which fought at Jutland. Much of her four-shaft ungeared machinery survives (see Chapter 1). Note the two 6in guns aft and 4in forward. (National Maritime Museum, London: 261228)

tle extra stiffness. The nominal design stresses were 6½ tons/in² in tension and 5½ tons/in² in compression. There was a heavy conning tower of 4 and 6in cast armour plate. This was rarely used in action and removed in late 1917 as weight compensation, being replaced by ¾in splinter protection. The original, thick communication tube remained in place.

Arethusa was in action seventeen days after completion, receiving some thirty hits from 4.1in shells, none of which penetrated the side protection. The design was seen as on the right lines but a little too small and cramped. Their freeboard was only 17.3ft (0.84 √L) and hence they were very wet. They formed the basis for the excellent 'C' class which followed.

The first 'C' class

The eight cruisers of the 1913 programme began as slightly modified *Arethusas*. Two were soon changed to serve as trials vehicles for geared turbine machinery (see Chapter 1). It was intended that one ship should have had the German Föttinger hydraulic transmission and S V Goodall visited the cross channel steamer, *Königen Louise*, to inspect her Föttinger transmission. The other six, the *Caroline* class, had two 4in guns on the forecas-

tle with the second 6in in the superfiring position aft as did the geared ships.[39] The idea was that the semi-automatic 4in was better for chasing destroyers whilst the 6in guns aft were appropriate to running from a more powerful ship. Wartime experience soon led to the forecastle guns being replaced by a single 6in. This class were bigger than the *Arethusas*; 10ft more on length and 18in on beam which made them less cramped[40] and gave them a sufficient stability margin for changes to be made in service. The wartime developments of these ships will be discussed later.

Atlantic cruisers

In 1912, (false) reports reached the Admiralty that the Germans were planning larger cruisers with 170mm (6.8in) guns for raiding on the trade routes and the First Lord, Churchill, asked for design studies for a counter to be prepared 'in case' the reports were true.[41] The head of cruiser design, William Berry, responded with designs A, B1 and B2 (see table). Papers on these ships are incomplete but it may be assumed that A was rejected for inadequate armament and the Bs as being too expensive, although a combination of heavy armament, extensive protection and high speed is bound to be

39. There was considerable debate over the armament in the early stages, all 6in, all 4in and mixed armament all had their advocates. (See Records of Warship Construction during the War, DNC Dept. Originally Confidential.)

40. Though there were twenty extra men to be accommodated.

41. This account is largely based on a summary of design studies kept by d'Eyncourt and now held in the Maritime Museum as MS93/011. I am also grateful for help from K McBride. Also material in Ships cover 319

42. *Hawkins* is said to have fired 5 rounds a minute off Normandy in 1944 for a short time.

43. D K Brown, 'Atlantic Cruisers'. To be published in *WARSHIPS* (World Ship Society).

44. Conceived at a Sea Lords meeting on 9 June 1915.

45. After *Raleigh* was wrecked in 1922, the class was known by a variety of names, most often *Hawkins*.

Caroline in original configuration. (Author's collection)

expensive. In July 1913, d'Eyncourt submitted B3 with a heavier armament of eight 7.5in guns and a little cheaper as a consequence of reduced speed.

They were intended to serve in distant waters so most studies had mixed coal and oil firing. It is interesting to see the cost of this in comparing B4 with the oil-only B3. They were quite well protected though the 6in belt of B1 and B2 was rather shallow. They had adequate freeboard and draught and should have been able to maintain speed in a seaway without difficulty.

The 7.5in gun was presumably introduced as a response to the rumoured bigger gun on German ships. This was hand-loaded by two men carrying the 200lb shell in a grab between them and the sustained rate of fire was probably about 3 rounds a minute.[42] A 6in gun could fire twelve rounds a minute in the gunlayers' test and a more realistic four rounds in the battle practice. Fire control was almost non-existent for cruisers in 1913 and neither gun would be likely to hit over 6000yds. It is likely that the more numerous armament of 6in would have been more effective. Note that this is the opposite of the argument put forward for all-big-gun battleships and is justified because of the lesser protection given to smaller ships and the reduced chance of hitting at long range due to the motion of a smaller ship and their lack of fire control. The Atlantic cruiser died soon after, presumably as it was realised that the reports of big German cruisers were wrong. Since these ships are little known,[43] a table of particulars follows.

At the same time there were a number of studies for Third Class colonial cruisers, usually with two 6in and four 4in. These drew the wrath of Churchill who said that you should not build obsolete ships – the eternal problem of quality versus quantity.

The Raleigh class

In 1915 a new class of cruiser was designed to hunt German cruisers on the trade routes[44] – the *Raleigh* class,[45] also known as 'Improved *Birmingham*s'. They were to be fast, carry a heavy armament and would therefore be big ships. Alternative designs were prepared with eight, twelve and fourteen 6in guns and also one with two 9.2in and eight 6in. However, the final armament was seven 7.5in together with ten 12pdrs (four on AA mountings), on a displacement of 9750 tons legend and a speed of 30-31kts. They retained the mixed firing of the 'Atlantics' and their line of descent from *Birmingham*, which puzzled historians so long, is now clear with the 'Atlantics' forming the missing link. The design power was 60,000shp on four shafts giving a speed of 30kts (legend). All but the first two were changed to all-oil fuel during building giving an extra 10,000shp.

The sides sloped inward from deck to bottom adding to the effectiveness of the 3in (2+1) (max) belt. Underwater, there was a shallow bulge with a single space. As designed, a coal bunker inboard of the bulge

might have given further protection. They were costly ships at £750,000, excluding guns and mountings and hence only five ships could be ordered and one, *Cavendish*, was converted into the carrier *Vindictive* during construction.

A selection of studies for the 'Atlantic Cruiser' (See table below for details). Taken from d'Eyncourt's note book and redrawn by Rear-Admiral Roger Morris.

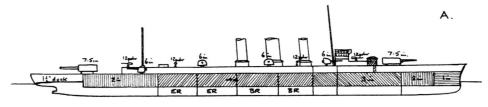

A.

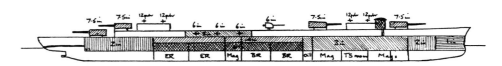

B1

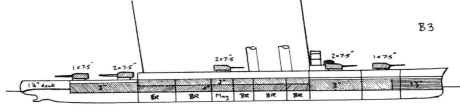

B2

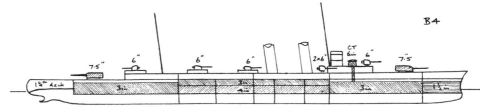

B3

B4

Atlantic Cruisers – particulars

Design	A	B1	B2	B3	B4 oil	B4 mix
Length (ft)	500	540	540	540	510	510
shp x 1000	40	40	40	30	30	28
Speed (kts)	28	28	28	26	27.5	26.5
Guns – 7.5in	2	4	4	8	2	2
6in BL 50 cal	8	8	8	–	6	6
Main belt, max (ins)	4	6	6	4	4	4
Dispt, load (tons)	6150	8150	8000	7400	6500	7000
Cost (£ x 1000)	550	750	740	700	548	588

Five | Destroyers and Early Naval Aviation

Grasshopper (foreground), a coal-burning destroyer of the *Beagle* class, seen at Malta. (WSS)

Destroyers

THE DEVELOPMENT of destroyers in the years leading up to war was continuous with several major technical advances, which have been described in some detail. At the beginning of the war the 'M' class was building and, during the war, large numbers were built to this design and to that of the 'R' and 'S' classes developed from the 'Ms'. Just before the war a few larger ships were built as flotilla leaders and these would lead to the 'V' class, one of the great designs of all time, in which leaders began to merge with the standard destroyer.

The 'River' class had shown the value of a high forecastle, confirmed by unhappy experience with the 'Tribal' class which had low, turtledeck forecastles. Comparison of these two classes at sea showed that high trial speeds were very expensive and of little value in service. Finally, the Russo-Japanese War showed the need for heavier gun armament.

The 'River' ('E') and 'Tribal' classes ('F') have been discussed in an earlier book.[1] The design of the *Beagles* of the 1908-09 programme began with a lengthy discussion of the role of the destroyer, summarised in March.[2] The consensus view was that they were primarily 'destroyers', protecting British battleships from torpedo attack with a secondary role of attacking the enemy battle line. To this end, the early design studies showed six 12pdrs of which the two on the forecastle were replaced by a single 4in Mk VIII as the design developed. It is surprising that the relatively ineffective 12pdr was used at this date. At 28kts, they were a little faster than the 'Rivers'.

Though the earliest study showed oil fuel, this was changed to coal by the Controller, presumably because of doubts over the availability of oil in wartime.[3] For the same radius of action, the ship carried 185 tons of coal

Particulars of pre-war destroyers

Class	Beagle	Acorn	Acheron	Acasta	Laforey	'M'
Programme	1908-09	09-10	10-11	11-12	12-13	13-14
Displacement (tons)	945	772	778	1072	965	900
Cost (£x1000)	110	94	88	100	98	110
Cost/ton	116	121	113	93	98	122
Fuel	Coal	Oil	-	-	-	-
Speed (kts)	27	27	27	29	29	34
No. in class	16	20	14	12	22	6
No. of 'Specials'			15	8		7
Armt 4in	1	2	2	3	3	3
12pdr	3	2	-	-	-	-
21in TT*	2	2	2	2	4	4
Freeboard F (ft)**	13.9	13.4	15.5	[18]	17	15.8
F/√L	0.84	0.85	0.99	[1.1]	1.03	0.96
Bridge abaft/L	0.24	0.23	0.27	0.22	0.25	0.21

* Two reloads in the classes with 2 tubes.
** Figures approximate, from photos, those in [ ] doubtful.

Redpole of the *Acorn* class seen in 1917. They were oil burners which made them smaller and cheaper than the *Beagles*. (Imperial War Museum: SP320)

1. D K Brown, *Warrior to Dreadnought*, p194.

2. E J March *British Destroyers* (London 1966), p102.

3. In fact, they served in the Mediterranean during the war where oil was scarce. There was even a proposal to build further, similar ships.

4. 18in and 21in torpedoes were numbered in different sequences. The 18in RGF Mk VII was the first 18in heater but March is incorrect in saying it was carried in the *Beagle* class.

instead of 140 tons of oil which, in turn, led to a bigger and more expensive ship. Direct-drive turbines drove three shafts at a maximum of 720-740rpm. As a cost-saving measure, one of the 12pdrs was omitted and the speed was reduced to 27kts, but they were still expensive at an average cost of £110,000.

The *Beagle* class was the last in which the ships were designed by their builder working from a loose DNC specification. Differences between ships of this class were less than in previous classes suggesting that the specification was more detailed than before. DNC complained that the work involved in checking a number of individual designs was greater than completing the design in house – it still is.

The 'heater' torpedo developed by Engineer Lieutenant Hardcastle had proved successful on trial and was introduced in this class as the 21in Mk I with a 200lb guncotton charge.[4] It was a short torpedo and during the war was replaced in this class by the Mk II which was longer than the tube and stuck out. It could reach 5500yds at 30kts and 3000yds at 45kts. It was inclined to run erratically at the higher speed and this was reduced to 35kts during the war. The long range of the heater torpedo combined with the increased accuracy imparted by the gyro was a major factor influencing the move to long range gunnery (see Chapter 1). However, the lessons of the Russo-Japanese War had not been fully appreciated and the chance of a hit with only two single tubes was remote.

The *Beagle*s were the first class to carry the new stockless anchor in a hawsepipe and there were fears that it might cause more spray, but early reports from sea were encouraging. Trials of mess-deck heating were

in hand in six of the 'Tribals' but the *Beagle*s remained unheated and unlined.

Acorn to Laforey classes

The twenty ships of the *Acorn* class ('H' class – 1909-10 Estimates) were oil burners and hence smaller and cheaper at about £94,000. Their cost per ton was slightly greater at £121, presumably because of the still novel oil-burning boilers. The armament was a little heavier with two 4in and two 12pdrs. The torpedoes were the longer Mk II with a charge of 280lbs of guncotton. They were followed by the generally similar *Acheron*s ('I' class, 1910-11) of which there were fourteen built to the standard Admiralty design, six slightly modified Australian vessels and nine 'Specials' designed by three different builders. Specials are discussed in Appendix 2

Ruby of the *Acorn* class getting wet. Sea States are difficult to estimate from photos but this is probably Sea State 6 with waves typically 17ft high. Though reasonable sea boats for their size, they were still very small ships. (Courtesy John Roberts)

Lennox of the *Laforey* class. The standard British destroyer of the war in near definitive form. (WSS)

but their main difference was in increased speed, usually at greatly increased cost. The Admiralty boats showed the benefit of the learning curve and their cost per ton came down from £121 to £113.

The *Acastas* ('K' class, 1911-12) were faster at 29kts and had a more powerful armament of three 4in and two twin torpedo tubes, which was to be the standard for most of the war. Despite this, the cost per ton fell again to £93 though increased size brought the total to about £100,000. There were twelve Admiralty design and eight Specials built. Two of the Specials had interesting design features, discussed later; *Ardent* had a longitudinally-framed hull while *Hardy* was intended to have a diesel cruising engine.

The twenty-two *Laforeys* ('L' class, 1912-13) were generally similar. *Leonidas* and *Lucifer* had experimental, single reduction-geared turbine driving the shaft at 360-370rpm instead of over 600rpm in the direct-drive ships with a most marked reduction in fuel consumption (see Chapter 1). There was a further reduction in cost to £98,000 (£98/ton)

Ardent and longitudinal framing

During the tendering process for the *Acasta* class of 1911-12, builders were encouraged to submit alternative proposals, and Denny wrote saying that a destroyer was a 'peculiarly suitable type of vessel in which to propose a longitudinal system of framing'.[5] The closely-spaced

Laverock aground. This unfortunate event shows off her underwater form. (Author's collection)

transverse bulkheads would maintain form and reduce the need for many 'webs' – transverse frames. It was suggested that these webs should be about 8ft 9in apart though it was pointed out that there was much greater flexibility to vary spacing and hence compartment length than in the conventional system of transverse framing.

The distinction between the systems of transverse and longitudinal framing is not entirely clear cut. The traditional transversely-framed ship would have a few longitudinals to hold things together whilst the longitudinally-framed ship would have a number of deep transverse frames. The main distinction came at the intersections; in the traditional system the transverse frame was continuous whilst the longitudinal was continuous in the later system.

The closely-spaced longitudinals would strengthen the deck and bottom against buckling and, on the deck, would be integrated with the machinery space coamings.[6] As the girth of the hull reduced towards the end, the longitudinal frames would come closer together, providing the increased strength in that area which experience had shown to be necessary. Denny sent a quarter-scale model of the proposed design.

Denny's submission was complicated with three different machinery options and alternative transverse or longitudinal framing for each. Figures for one option were:

	Transverse Framing	*Longitudinal Framing*
Displacement (tons)	1098	1077
Hull weight (tons)	393	372
CG above keel (ft)	12	12.15

For the longitudinally framed ship the stresses were:

	Stress (tons/in2)	
Sagging	keel 5.0	deck 5.2
Hogging	5.3	7.1

The Admiralty's reaction was enthusiastic: 'vessel appears to be very well designed'. The design was checked by Hannaford[7] and Smith, reporting to Pethick, then head of destroyer design. Denny was asked to stiffen the deck and bottom,[8] to justify the wide spacing of the transverse frames and to investigate the strength of the large plate panels under lateral load from water pressure. It was also suggested that the brackets at the deck edge be re-examined. The deep displacement of the agreed version was 1091 tons with 9½in trim by the bow. The bow freeboard was 15ft 4in. A revised strength calculation gave the following figures:

	Hogging	*Sagging*
Displacement (tons)	1019	861
Moment of Inertia Ins²Ft²	16,866	17,200
Bending moment (tons ft)	11,880	10,860
Stress deck (tons/in²)	6.96 (7.22)T	5.4 (5.79)C
Stress keel (tons/in²)	5.1 (5.67)C	5.4 (6.25)T

Notes; T means tensile stress, C compressive. Figures in brackets are for standard ships of the class. The displacement differs as variable load, mainly fuel, was adjusted to give a 'worst case' for each condition.

Buckling of the deck was investigated using the 'Gordon formula'.[9] It was not possible to calculate the overall buckling strength of a large panel of plating with stiffeners until long after the Second World War when computers became available. A single stiffener with 'equivalent' breadth of plating was considered as a strut. A little later, it was conventional to take the equivalent breadth as 25 times the thickness each side; for *Ardent* it was taken as 9in either side which sounds about the same. It was estimated that in the most severe loading considered there would be a factor of safety of 2.05. A note in the Ship's Cover says that the standard design was considerably stronger and changes were made.[10] Denny went on to investigate transverse strength using the Bruhn method.[11] There was then a very friendly exchange of letters in which Denny and the Admiralty each thanked the other for their help.

There are no records of the actual building. With rivetted construction it is easier to build a transversely-framed ship. The transverse ribs can be put in place and held together with temporary wood ribbands, bolted through the rivet holes, until the plates are put on to hold it all together. Longitudinal framing would probably require more temporary support and would only really come into its own with welded construction. The design seems to have been a success. Denny was paid £100 to weigh everything built into the ship which seems to have completed to the design figure. The first table showed a weight saving of about 20 tons which would have corresponded to an increase of 0.4 knots in speed. The trials officer (Dippy) reported that she made 29.54kts for 6 hours at 582rpm. It was reported that she was notably free of vibration. The agreed cost was £102,490 (hull only £41,264) exactly as estimated but among the most expensive of the class.

There is no record of her service nor why longitudinal framing was not repeated until the *Javelin* class of 1936. I suspect that the war came before she had been fully evaluated and the delay in changing to a novel construction was unacceptable under wartime conditions.

Diesels

In 1905 the torpedo-boat *TB 047* was due for re-boilering and it was proposed that she be converted to diesel engines. There was difficulty in finding a suitable

5. Ships cover 277, National Maritime Museum.

6. While this statement is true, it is not clear that buckling had been a problem with existing ships.

7. Later to be in charge of destroyer design himself and responsible for the 'V' and 'W' classes.

8. Bottom longitudinals 1-7; 6in x 3in-9lbs, deck 5in x 2in-6lbs

9. A complicated semi-empirical formula which remained in use until after the Second World War which related load to cause failure to the size, shape and material of the strut.

10. I find this hard to believe as the paper goes on to say that the whole of the deck plating was effective in compression whereas only half was effective in the Admiralty design. It may even have been a typing error.

11. I don't recognise this method. Denny admitted they were not sure if they understood it!

Murray of the first batch of the 'M' class. (WSS)

design until 1908 and even then the only tender submitted was found unconvincing. Vickers had proposed a Vogt engine which never worked! Oram, the Engineer-in-Chief, suggested a 600bhp plant for another torpedo boat with 150hp per cylinder but there were no tenders.

Yarrows were proposing an all-diesel ship for the *Acasta* class and Thornycroft suggested a steam plant for full power with a diesel cruising engine. The Admiralty were clearly enthusiastic but doubted the ability of engine builders to deliver.[12] Eventually *Hardy* was ordered from Thornycroft with an 1800bhp Sulzer diesel on the centre shaft, but it was never installed. It would have cost £19,600 (total ship cost £113,650).

Taurus of the Thornycroft 'R' class. The 'R' class had geared turbines which were much more economical on fuel than earlier ships with ungeared turbines and fast turning propellers. (WSS)

The 'M' classes and similar

The six Admiralty 'M 'class destroyers of 1913-14 had their speed greatly increased to 34kts with the seven Specials even faster at 35kts. This increase in speed was of course expensive, the Admiralty Ms costing about £110,000 (£122/ton) while the Specials cost some £127,000.

When the war broke out, four destroyers building for Greece and generally similar to the Admiralty 'Ms' were purchased as the *Medea* class, and four slightly larger ships building by Hawthorn Leslie and with four 4in guns were purchased as the *Talisman* class.[13]

A very large number of additional Ms were ordered in the early part of the war.

'M' class destroyer orders

	Admiralty	Specials
1913-14 Estimates	6	7 (3 not ordered)
Medea		4
Talisman		4
1st Order, Sep 14	12	8
2nd, Nov 14	7	3
3rd, late Nov 14	22	-
4th, Feb 15	16	2
5th, May 15	16	4
TOTAL	79	32

Later Admiralty vessels had a slightly raked stem and more flare to keep them dry.[14] All the later ships had the second gun on a bandstand. They were a very successful design but, as most were built of ungalvanised plate, they had a short life. Since there were more than enough better destroyers at the end of the war the 'Ms' were soon disposed of.

By July 1915 the Admiralty had decided that all future destroyers should have two-shaft geared turbines (Brown-Curtis preferred). This led to the 'R' class which was similar to the 'Ms' but with the after gun on a bandstand, 1ft more freeboard, more flare and a more robust bridge. Comparative trials of *Romola* with the ungeared *Norman* showed a 15 per cent fuel saving at 18kts and 28 per cent at 25kts. There were also eleven 'Modified Rs' in which the forward two funnels were combined so that the bridge could be moved aft. They also mounted the 4in Mk V gun with a range of 12,000yds and a rate of fire of 19-20 rounds per minute.

This design was further developed into the 'S' class, designed in February 1915, when it was realised that the Germans were only building small numbers of big destroyers and hence the British did not need all their ships to be as big as the 'Vs' and 'Ws'. The 'S' class had a more heavily raked stem, and considerable sheer to the forecastle which had a vestigial turtle deck. Some of the earlier ships had a fixed athwartships torpedo tube either side abaft the break of forecastle. The Thornycroft Specials had a higher freeboard and, even so, mounted A gun on a raised platform.

12. Ships cover 370.

13. The origin of these ships is obscure. See R Gardiner (ed), *Conway's All the World's Fighting Ships, 1906-1921* (London 1985), p78. Also K McBride. 'British M Class destroyers of 1913-14', *Warship 1991.* A destroyer building in Portugal was also briefly in British hands as the *Arno* before ending in Italy. See *Warship International* 1/97, p84 for an incomplete story.

14. Rake of stem is helpful in keeping ships dry but the effect of the small rake in these ships would have been negligible.

Stonehenge of the second batch of Admiralty 'S' class. By trunking the forward funnels it was possible to move the bridge aft making it drier and reducing the perceived motions. (WSS)

The pre-dreadnought battleship *Hibernia* rigged for the experimental launch of an aircraft in 1912. (WSS)

Aircraft carriers

The early history of naval aviation has been well described by Layman[15] and others and will only be outlined briefly in this chapter which deals with the ships from which the aircraft operated. The Royal Navy gets the first mention for Cochrane's use of kites from *Pallas* to distribute propaganda leaflets in 1806. Many navies experimented with balloons during the nineteenth century but the RN did not. While there may have been a reactionary element in this disinterest, it seems that there was a well-justified conviction that spherical balloons had little to offer at sea, due to control problems, and there was a trial in 1903-4 involving an army balloon unit which confirmed this view. There was greater interest in kites, probably because of the charisma of S F Cody, an American pioneer resident in the United Kingdom. There were several trials between 1903 and 1908[16] when the Admiralty decided that kites as then known had little to offer.[17]

The aeroplane

The USN was the first to launch and recover an aeroplane from a ship. After an unsuccessful trial in 1910 from the torpedo-boat *Bagley*, on 4 November 1910 Eugene P Ely took off in a Curtis pusher plane from a platform built over the forecastle of the cruiser *Birming-*

ham. On 18 January 1911 he landed a similar plane on a platform at the stern of the *Pennsylvania*. In both these trials the ship was at anchor in calm water. The RN began to show an interest in aviation in 1909 with the decision to build the rigid airship *Mayfly*, and in 1912 there were a series of trials similar to Ely's earlier flights with Lieutenant C R Samson as pilot. These trials have often been confused and are outlined in tabular form below.

Early RN Flights

Date	Ship	Comments
10 Jan 1912	*Africa*	Take off at rest. Short pusher landplane[18]
2 May 1912	*Hibernia*	Take off while steaming at 10½kts. Short pusher.
4 Jul 1912	*London*	10-15kts, 25ft run

The take-off ramp on *Africa* sloped down quite steeply to the bow whilst *Hibernia*'s was nearly flat. Neither Ely's nor Samson's flights contributed much to the solution of operating aircraft from warships since the platforms obstructed much of the main armament. Between these flights the Royal Flying Corps was set up with a Military Wing, a Naval Wing and a Central Flying School.

15. R D Layman, *To Ascend from a Floating Base* (Cranbury N J 1979).

16. R D Layman, 'Naval Kite Trials', *Warship 1994*.

17. It is interesting that the problem of the disturbed air behind funnels and superstructure was already apparent – it still is.

18. The cylinders under the wings were buoyancy bags, not seaplane floats.

19. I Johnston, *Beardmore Built* (Clydebank Libraries 1993).

20. Sir A W Johns.,'Aircraft Carriers', *Trans INA* (1934).

21. These proposals from senior admirals help to demolish the myth that the RN was opposed to aircraft.

Beardmore's avaiation ship design

On 23 October 1912 Beardmore's submitted a design to the Admiralty for 'a parent ship for naval aeroplanes' based on a concept by the Marquis of Graham, a pioneer flyer.[19] The proposal was well received but after discussion with two naval enthusiasts, Rear Admiral Moore and Captain Murray Sueter, a second, smaller design was drawn up.

The illustration shows her with two superstructures, each holding three hangars, and funnels with a 'bridge' between. The Admiralty finally rejected the proposal as without further experience it was not certain what was required.[20] This Beardmore design was the starting-point for most wartime carrier designs and reflects great credit on this fledgling company. However, some years later, wind tunnel tests, discussed in Chapter 8, would show that the proposed layout was quite impractical.

Hermes and operations up to the war

There were two proposals for aviation ships in 1913, Admiral Mark Kerr suggesting a purpose-built 'true'

carrier while the First Sea Lord, Admiral of the Fleet Sir Arthur Wilson, had a less ambitious scheme.[21] He wanted to convert an *Eclipse* class cruiser, removing the main mast and building a landing platform aft with a take-off platform forward. Special cranes would lift planes from one deck to the other. In the event, an even more limited scheme was adopted.

The thirteen-year-old cruiser *Hermes* was commissioned for the manoeuvres in May 1913. She was given a

Beardmore's aviation ships

	1st version	2nd version
Length x Beam x Draught (ft)	450 x 110 x 20	430 x 110 x?
Displacement (tons)*	11,500	15,000
shp	22,000	?
Speed (kts)	21	15
Armament	12-6in, 4-47mm AA	8-4in
Aircraft	6 + spares	6 in hangars, 4 in hold

* These figures seem suspect but were quoted at the time.

This close-up of *Hibernia's* arrangements shows that they were not operationally practical as half the ship's main armament is out of action. The plane is a Short pusher landplane – the cylinders under the wing are not floats as often described but could provide buoyancy in a forced landing. (Author's collection)

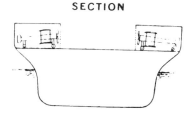

SECTION

launching platform forward and canvas hangars fore and aft, each served by a very long derrick. She was fitted to carry 2000 gallons of petrol. Some nine flights were made in early July and on 17 July two seaplanes joined for the manoeuvres. There were about twenty flights during and after the manoeuvres including two in which a Caudron seaplane took off from the ramp. The other plane was a Short S64 with twin floats and was the first plane with folding wings, hence it became known as the Short 'Folder'. *Hermes* contributed nothing to the result of the manoeuvres but she had demonstrated that it was possible to carry out sustained air operations

from a ship. It was also shown that it was essential for naval aircraft to have a radio. *Hermes* was recommissioned in much the same condition on the outbreak of war but was torpedoed and sunk on 31 October 1914, the first carrier to be sunk.

In 1913 the first plane designed to carry a torpedo, the Short Type C, took to the air. The first drop of the 14in, 810lb weapon took place in March 1914. On 1 July the Naval Wing seceded from the RFC and became the Royal Naval Air Service (RNAS). The air department of the Admiralty was established under Captain Murray Sueter. The RNAS was well represented at the Naval Review at Spithead with three airships and seventeen seaplanes. A Sopwith 'Batboat' flew round the fleet after dark with lights blazing. The total strength of the RNAS at the outbreak of war was seven airships, fifty-two seaplanes and thirty-nine landplanes (not all serviceable). Sixteen of the seaplanes had lightweight (70lb) radios with a range of up to 120 miles. This was by far the largest naval air force in the world.

Ark Royal (1913)

Someone had noted the potential of *Hermes*' manoeuvres and £81,000 was allocated for an aircraft-carrying ship in the 1914-15 Estimates.[22] In May 1914 a merchant ship which had just commenced building at Blyth was purchased, to be named *Ark Royal*. This ship was completely re-designed, the engine being moved from amidships to aft. The design was led by J H Narbeth,[23] assisted by C J W Hopkins. The requirements were set out by Murray Sueter assisted by Commander L'Estrange Malone, and between them this team produced a magnificent first shot at a carrier.[24]

Moving the engines aft left a clear hold – hangar – 150ft long, 45ft wide and 15ft high forward which could accommodate ten seaplanes. A sliding hatch 40ft x 30ft allowed the two steam cranes to lift the planes to the upper deck. This was one of her few failings as the cranes could only be used when the ship was not rolling. To get her to a reasonable draught, a considerable amount of water ballast was necessary and much of this was arranged high in the ship, reducing her excessive metacentric height and helping to make rolling less severe. The cranes were also used to lift planes onto and out of the water.

She was well equipped with workshops and all the multifarious stores needed even by early warplanes. Petrol was stowed in cans in a special compartment surrounded by a water jacket for fire protection. There was a space under the bridge, open at both ends, in which the engine of a plane could be run up under cover for testing. The forecastle was clear of all obstructions so that seaplanes on a wheeled trolley could take off.[25] There were ballast tanks well forward so that she be trimmed by the bow for take off. The anchor and cable gear were on the deck below. Her truly unique feature was the steadying sail on the mizzen to help keep her head to

Hermes was used as a seaplane carrier at the outbreak of war but was sunk by *U 27* on 14 October 1914. The remains of the after seaplane can be made out and the imposing row of broadside 6in guns are clearly seen. (Author's collection)

wind; she remains the only aircraft carrier to have been fitted with a sail.

It seems clear that she was envisaged as a 'depot ship' and, as such, her speed of 11kts was adequate but it was too low for operational work. *Ark Royal* gave good service in the Dardanelles campaign and between the wars she was used for catapult development trials, being renamed *Pegasus* in December 1935 to free her name for the new *Ark Royal*. As *Pegasus* she was to operate Fulmar monoplane fighters in the Second World War but her true value was in proving most of the features of a modern carrier.

22. There are indications that it was the First Lord, Winston Churchill, presumably briefed by Murray Sueter. It is certain that her name was selected by Churchill.

23. J H Narbeth, 'Fifty years of Naval Progress', *The Shipbuilder* (December 1927). His rank at the time is uncertain (probably constructor). Narbeth was an aviation enthusiast who had read works on aerodynamics.

24. J H Narbeth. 'A Naval Architect's Practical Experiences in the Behaviour of Ships', *Trans INA* (1941).

25. C J W Hopkins, 'The Development of the Aircraft Carrier', *RCNC Journal*, Vol II (copies held in National Maritime Museum). Writing many years later, he says that one plane did attempt, unsuccessfully, to take off from her deck but no confirmation has been found.

The *Ark Royal* of 1914 had many features of the aircraft carrier with careful thought to workshops, petrol stowage etc and she was the only carrier to have a sail – on the mizzen to help keep her head to wind. Her only faults were that she was too slow and it was difficult to lift the planes from the hangar by crane. She was renamed when the 1934 carrier took the name of *Ark Royal* and, as *Pegasus*, operated fighters in the Second World War. (Author's collection)

Six | Submarines

THE EARLY HISTORY of submarines is well known[1] and needs only to be outlined here, concentrating on Royal Navy involvement. Other than Cornelius Drebbel's legendary rowing submarine, one may see Fulton's demonstration of 1804 as marking the start of submarines in Britain. Fulton had built a submarine in France, the *Nautilus*, but became disillusioned with his treatment and crossed the Channel. In a demonstration backed by the Prime Minister, Pitt, he sank the brig *Dorothea* off Walmer. This drew Lord St Vincent to remark: 'Pitt was the greatest fool that ever existed to encourage a mode of warfare which those that command the sea did not want, and which, if successful, would deprive them of it.'

St Vincent was surely right and his approach was to guide the Royal Navy for the next century, but this did not mean that the Navy turned a blind eye to all developments. During the Crimean War the German Wilhelm Bauer began building a submarine in Scott Russell's yard on the Thames, but he thought Scott Russell was stealing his ideas and moved to St Petersburg where he completed a submarine after the war. Scott Russell was building a submarine device; details are scanty but it seems that it was a diving bell, walked along the bottom to attack enemy ships at anchor.[2] Though completed and tried, it does not seem to have been successful.

Due note was taken of the numerous attempts at submarine warfare during the American Civil War, almost all were of which failures, many suicidal, but they showed potential for the future. In 1878 the Reverend G W Garrett completed a 4½-ton submarine, *Resurgam I*. Results were encouraging and in 1879 he decided to build a 30-ton steam-propelled vessel, *Resurgam II*. Steam was stored at 150lbs/in² and it was claimed to be able to drive her for 12 miles at 3kts. In February 1880 *Resurgam* set off from Liverpool for Portsmouth to demonstrate to Nordenfelt and the Admiralty but sank in tow off Rhyl on the way, where her remains have recently been found. Garrett joined Nordenfelt for whom he designed several craft, two of which were built at Barrow-in-Furness, opening that yard's continuing involvement in submarine building. These Nordenfelt submarines were generally unsuccessful, mainly because their trim could not be controlled when submerged.

The new navy in the shape of submarine *A 13* passes the old navy, HMS *Victory* in Portsmouth Harbour. She was the first diesel-engined submarine. (Author's collection)

In December 1886 William White[3] and Lord Charles Beresford were given a trial dive in a French-built submarine, *Nautilus*. She stuck on the bottom and was only freed from the mud by violent rocking. Later White was to advise Captain Bacon when he commanded the first RN submarines that he should not dive in one!

Up to the end of the nineteenth century there were no practical submarines but at about that date a number of reasonably successful designs appeared in France and the USA and it became apparent that the RN should learn more of the capability of these boats.

Submarines of the RN – Holland and his boats

J P Holland was born in Ireland and emigrated to the USA in 1872. He soon became interested in submarines and completed a number of increasingly successful designs, leading to the purchase of his No. VI by the USN in 1900. The RN did not wish to purchase boats from France, a potential enemy, and were offered an attractive deal by Mr Isaac Rice of the Electric Boat Company which now owned the rights to Holland designs. Five submarines of Holland design would be built by Vickers at Barrow costing £35,000 each.[4] The American company would supply technical assistance. The drawings were based on Holland's No. VII design but as forwarded to the UK, they seem to have incorporated a considerable number of unwanted extras, which were eventually eliminated by Vickers.

The contract called for the following performance attributes.

Speed surfaced: 8kts, 7kts in 'ordinary' weather.
Endurance: 250 miles at 7kts
Speed submerged: 7kts, endurance 25 miles.[5]
Crew endurance submerged: 15 miles.
Depth-keeping: normally ± 2ft, max 4ft.
Time to dive: 2 – 10 mins, depending on crew experience.
Diving depth: normal 50ft, maximum safe 100ft.

Submarine *No.1* was launched in great secrecy on 2 October 1901 and began trials in the following January. By and large, the requirements were met.[6] Surface speed was about 7.5kts with a full-power endurance of 236 miles. Submerged, the boats were uncontrollable at speeds of less than 5-6kts at which speed they had an endurance of 3¾ hours.[7] Normally, they did not dive below 50ft though one is said to have reached 78ft.

Strength calculations then and until after the Second World War were approximate. There was a simple formula which was fairly accurate for the stress in the plating but it assumed that the frames were strong enough and that the hull was built and remained circular.[8] When Holland *No. 1* was salvaged, her strength was examined using modern methods which predicted collapse at 80ft! The critical elements of submarine design were – and are – strength and control, both usually neglected.

Though the Holland boats carried a single 18in torpedo tube with three torpedoes, they had very limited operational capability. They were intended as developmental and ASW training craft and as such did very well.[9] The fitting of a crude periscope was a major improvement over the basic Holland design.

Holland Number 4. Note the low freeboard and lack of a conning tower making them liable to flooding. The tallest tube is a periscope. (WSS)

1. See R Compton-Hall, *Submarine Boats* (London 1983), and M Wilson, 'Early Submarines' in Dr A Lambert (ed), *Steam, Steel and Shellfire* (London 1992).

2. 'J Scott Russell', entry to be published in *New Dictionary of National Biography* by D K Brown.

3. F Manning, *Life of Sir William White* (London 1923).

4. The contract was placed by the Controller, A K Wilson, who is better known for saying that submarine captains were pirates and should be hanged if captured in war. This seems to be another example of the conflict between words and deeds. Making a responsible decision at his desk, Wilson acted rationally, regardless of his words outside.

5. It appears that Vickers claimed 25 miles at 7kts which was wrong.

6. There is doubt over all the performance figures for early submarines; see A N Harrison (ed J Maber). *The Development of HM Submarines* (BR 3043) (HMSO, London 1979).

7. Good control at low speed requires bow hydroplanes.

8. D K Brown, 'Submarine Pressure Hull Strength', *Warship International* 3 (1987).

9. They were prepared to attack the Russian fleet following the Dogger Bank incident in 1904.

Above: A 3 has a small conning tower but the class were still liable to flooding. There appears to be a magnetic compass just abaft the conning tower. (WSS)

Below: The 'A' class were designed by Vickers but there was some Admiralty involvement. This illustration shows arrangements for testing a submerged model in the ship model tank at Haslar, the first time such a test had been made. (Admiralty Experiment Works)

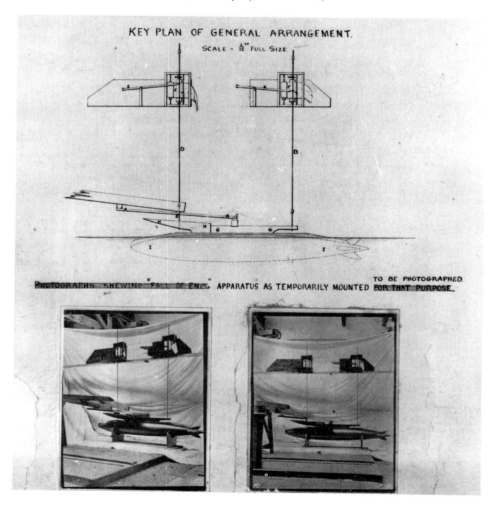

'A', 'B' and 'C' classes

These successors to the Holland boats were designed by Vickers[10] and though they may be regarded as improvements on the Hollands, there was no American (Electric Boat Co) contribution. There was, however, some Admiralty involvement in the design as Edmund Froude tested a model of the 'A' class in the tank at Haslar. In service, the 'As' were seen as only a slight improvement on the Hollands but the 'Bs' and even more so the 'Cs' were thought to be fully-capable warships and more than the equal of any foreign design. Their more extensive casings and taller conning towers made them better seaboats on the surface.

Particulars of early submarines

Class	Holland	A 1*	B	C
Number built	5	13	11	38
Dispt. sub (tons)	122	205	316	320
Length (ft-in)	63-10	103-6	142-2½	142-2½
Speed (surface/subm, kts)	7½/6	9½/6	12/6	13/7
18in TT	1	1	2	2
Torpedoes	3	3	4	4
Complement	8	11	15	16
Reserve buoyancy (%)	8.2	9.2	10.1	10.1
Cost (£x1000)	35	41	47	47-49

*A 2 onwards had two tubes and differed in other ways. There were differences within classes and there is some confusion over the exact figures. (See Harrison)

They were all built by Vickers at Barrow with the exception of six 'C' class at Chatham Dockyard. The number built is impressive, showing Admiralty confidence in their new arm. The Hollands were included in the 1901-02 Estimates and the last of the 'Cs' under the

1908-09 Estimates. These classes were short-ranged but, within their limits, had a useful operational role. It is often suggested that the coast defence role, linked to their small size, was a deliberate policy, possibly due to Fisher. However, it is likely that the designers felt that the technology was as yet insufficiently developed for larger boats. Costs rose slowly up to £50,350 in the last 'Cs'.

These early boats all had Wolsley petrol engines built by Vickers except for *A 13* which had an experimental six-cylinder Hornsby-Acroyd heavy oil engine[11]. It was 3 tons heavier than the petrol engine but the fuel consumption was 0.42lbs/bhp/hr instead of 0.9lbs/bhp/hr for petrol engines. Petrol fumes were both toxic and explosive but there was no alternative at that date. The figures for reserve of buoyancy are as completed and would soon be eroded in service. If weights were added

high in the boat it would be necessary to add ballast as well to restore stability, a double encroachment on the reserve. None of these boats had any internal bulkheads which might affect their safe diving depth, probably not then appreciated. *C 21* had the first ballast keel, which was 49½ft long and weighed 9 tons

The combination of a small reserve of buoyancy and the lack of bulkheads was a contributory factor in the numerous accidents to early submarines. Of the 'A' class, three were lost in collisions and two foundered, while one 'B' and three 'Cs' were lost in collision. The sheer difficulty of seeing these small, low-lying craft must have been a factor in the collisions. Their form generated a high bow wave which, rising above the hull forward, could lead to an unintentional dive. This was cured, at least partially, by adding buoyancy spaces high up, forward. The problem, and cure, were to recur.

B 8 in dock in 1908. This clearly shows the spindle-shaped, single hull construction. (Author's collection)

10. Vickers' house magazine (Link Supplement, 1981) names Captain Bacon, Inspecting officer of submarines, as co-designer.

11. 'Firsts' are always difficult but in my opinion *A 13* was the world's first diesel-engined submarine.

C 6 showing the steady increase in size of the conning tower. The 'C' class may be regarded as the first really operationally-capable boats though they were still very much a coastal design. (WSS)

The 'D' class were the first overseas submarine and were diesel engined. *D 4* had an experimental 12pdr gun on a disappearing mounting (seen here), but it proved unsuccessful. (WSS)

The 'D' class

D 1 was ordered as a prototype under the 1906-07 Estimates, *D 2* two years later, and *D 3-8* under the 1909-10 Estimates. This class was the first Admiralty design.[12] They were nearly twice the displacement of the 'C' class and, of course, much more expensive – *D 1* cost £79,910, and later boats up to £89,000 (about the same as a destroyer). They had diesel engines on twin shafts, much improved ballasting systems which gave them double the reserve of buoyancy, and greater internal volume. They also had two way radio. All these features combined made them the first class capable of overseas patrol. The main technical advances will be explored in detail.

Ballast tanks

Submarines, both on the surface and below, must satisfy Archimedes' Principle – weight = buoyancy – and both weight and buoyancy can vary during a patrol. A moderate reserve of buoyancy on the surface is provided by the empty main ballast tanks, which, when completely filled with water should leave the submarine submerged with neutral buoyancy.[13] Buoyancy is the product of volume and density, both of which may change. The specific gravity of sea water varies from 1.005 to 1.03 while the volume of the hull may change as it is compressed at depth. Rivetted boats were particularly liable to this problem; Oram describes how 'V' class boats would compress suddenly at 25ft going down and spring back at 19ft on the way up, making depth-keeping very difficult.[14] The weight of the boat changes as fuel and stores are consumed and, most important, as torpedoes are fired. Compensating tanks are needed into which water can be admitted to offset these changes and these tanks must be arranged so that there is little change in the position of the centre of gravity of the boat. Compensation for torpedo firing was usually automatic. In addition, there was usually a 'quick diving tank' (Q) which would be full on the surface so that,

when the main ballast tanks were filled, the boat would be heavy and dive quickly. Q tank would be blown as soon as the boat was submerged. For stability when submerged, the centre of gravity (G) must lie below the centre of buoyancy (B) and a value of BG of about 10in was usually selected.

The three main arrangements of ballast tanks are shown in the sketch on page 86 though the distinction between saddle tank and double hull could be blurred. If internal ballast tanks are used, as in classes prior to the 'Ds',[15] their structure must be able to withstand sea pressure at depth or valves have to be fitted to close the tank off from the sea as it dives.[16] British practice was to design the structure to take full diving pressure but to close the valves as well.[17] During the act of surfacing weight and buoyancy and the position of their centres are all changing rapidly and a number of classes had a transient condition while surfacing in which stability was poor and, in bad weather, even hazardous. The double-hull design had ballast a little higher up which made it more difficult to ensure adequate stability when surfacing. It should be appreciated that calculations on transient characteristics are almost impossible without a computer and, though designers in all countries were aware of the problem, their intuitive solutions were not always sufficient.

The 'Ds' had saddle tanks which proved successful in use. They enabled a reserve of buoyancy of about 20 per cent to be achieved and, at the same time, made more internal space available. The external tanks had valves top and bottom but, during the war, boats in enemy waters ran on the surface with the lower valves open for quicker diving[18] and these valves were eventually omitted.

Though earlier submarines had a small radio receiving set, they could not transmit. The 'Ds' had a much more powerful set which could transmit as well, though a mast had to be raised to use it. This much increased their operational capability in more distant waters. *D 4* had an experimental gun mounting, a 12pdr which could be

12. It appears that the weight and stability calculations were carried out by Vickers and that the company accepted responsibility for performance. The Admiralty team was led by H G Williams RCNC who later moved to Armstrongs to set up their submarine programme.

13. The reserve was about 10 per cent in the early classes, increasing to 20 per cent in the 'Ds'.

14. H K Oram, *Ready for Sea* (London 1974), Ch 15.

15. Tanks were tested to 50lbs/in² in these classes, roughly 100ft diving depth.

16. Structure strong enough to take diving pressure on flat panels would be very heavy.

17. It is believed that the French *Lutin* was lost when a stone prevented the valves from closing properly.

18. It was common practice to run with two main ballast tanks flooded in the interest of quicker diving.

19. Also *AE 1* and *AE 2* for Australia.

20. The battery was not moved, other changes were incorporated.

21. The arrangement of valves would vary from one builder to another increasing the hazard. This system was used until the 'A' class at the end of the Second World War.

folded down into the casing. The mount was not a success and the gun was eventually left exposed.

The brave decision was made to replace the hazardous petrol engine with diesels in the 'Ds', even though the experimental unit in *A 13* had yet to go to sea. The diesel was heavier – approximately 70lbs/bhp compared with 60lbs/bhp for the petrol engine of the 'Cs'. It was also longer and higher but these increases were partially offset by much reduced fuel consumption. The twin-shaft arrangement permitted a stern torpedo tube to be fitted. At the time, there was some criticism of the 'Ds' as too big but, as usual, the next class were bigger.

The 'E' class

Though the 'Ds' were generally liked, technology was advancing so rapidly that an even better design was both possible and necessary. The result was the 'E' class, possibly the best British submarine design of all time and among the best in the world at the outbreak of war (see table). The design began as a slightly improved 'D' but as usual the number of changes grew. It was feared that the 'Ds' were already too long to manoeuvre for a bow shot and as a result the 'Es' were given a pair of beam tubes. There was a single bow tube in the first eight boats after which a second was fitted and they had a single stern tube, all tubes being 18in. More powerful engines and motors were fitted increasing speed both on the surface and submerged at the expense of further increases in size and cost, which rose to up to £101,900 in the first six.

The 'C' and 'D' class boats had a collision bulkhead, well forward, but the rest of the boat was open. One reason for this was that controls and valves were usually operated locally and in a small, undivided boat the captain could control the operators and see what they were doing. The 'E' class had two bulkheads dividing the boat into three. This was a slightly strange decision since the boat would sink if either of the two biggest spaces was fully flooded. Apparently it was hoped that sufficient air would be trapped in the crown of the damaged space to keep the boat afloat.

E 1-6 were ordered from Vickers under the 1910-11 Programme[19] and the fifty-sixth and last of the class was ordered in November 1914. *E 7* and *8* of the following year's Programme were built at Chatham to the same design. The Vickers boats *E 9-11* and *E 14-16* were considerably modified with two bow 18in TT, three bulkheads, the engines moved forward and a quarter of the batteries moved aft, while the conning tower was enlarged to make a steering position. The cost had risen to £105,700 (excluding broadside tubes). Chatham produced a simplified version of the design for *E 12* and *E 13*[20] and this was the basis for all wartime boats including the Vickers boats. A meeting was held on 11 November 1914 as a result of which orders were placed for *E 19-56* with Vickers and twelve other builders.

Though they were a very successful design, wartime experience led to many changes. Perhaps the most important addition was a toilet which could be used submerged. This involved operating a complicated sequence of valves and levers with the penalty of 'getting your own back' for a mistake in operating the high-pressure air.[21] A much larger radio was fitted which needed two large folding masts, and a 12pdr gun was mounted on the casing. Other additions were Fessenden underwater signalling gear, sounding machines, sky-

E 4 was used in trials of steering with and without a top rudder (just visible in this photo). It was found to be useless and was removed from boats which had already been fitted. (WSS)

The 'F' class were an Admiralty design, double hull coastal boat. Though quite satisfactory, there was no real role for such craft and only three were built. (Imperial War Museum: SP1238)

Nautilus was intended to be a large and fast overseas submarine. However, her building was given low priority and she was out of date before completion and never entered operational service. (Imperial War Museum: Q22765)

guard periscopes, hydroplane guards and slopchutes. From *E 19* on a flared bow was incorporated. There were other minor variations between different orders.

An upper rudder, above the pressure hull, had been introduced in the 'D' class but trials of *E 4* with and without this rudder showed that it was of no value and it was removed from completed boats and omitted in new construction. Six boats were fitted as minelayers with twenty mines carried in the ballast tanks in lieu of the beam torpedo tubes.

The Vickers contract

Vickers' original contract with the Electric Boat Company specified that Holland patents could only be used on boats built at Barrow or, for a royalty of £2500,

in the Dockyards. Vickers asked for a royalty of £10,000 should any boats be built in another commercial yard, but this was not agreed and left open as it was not then intended to use other yards. No Holland patents were involved in the 'A' or later classes but it would seem that a somewhat similar contract was negotiated with Vickers covering the use of their designs. This was seen as preventing the building of submarines other than at Barrow or the Dockyards and it was claimed that this was in the public interest as preserving Vickers' expertise. Two years' notice of cancellation was required and this notice was given on 31 March 1911.

Innovation or aberration?

In 1910 Captain Roger Keyes was appointed as Inspecting Captain of Submarines. He inherited the 'A' to 'C' classes, *D 1* with eight more of the class completing and the first 'Es' about to be ordered. His advisory committee persuaded him that the Admiralty/Vickers designs were inferior to those of Italian and French companies and that Vickers could not build sufficient numbers of submarines.

Later that year, one of Keyes' staff together with representatives of DNC and E-in-C visited Italian and French yards. As a result Scotts were licensed to build FIAT designs under licence which became *S 1-3* at a cost of £70,000 each. Against the recommendations of the inspecting team, Armstrong's were licensed by the French company Schneider to build *W 1-4* to a Laubeuf design. All seven of these vessels were handed over to the Italian Navy soon after completion as they were not thought worth the waste of scarce submarine crew.

A committee of submarine officers in 1912 recom-

mended the building of two types of submarine, coastal and overseas. Two designs of coastal submarine were prepared, the 'V' class by Vickers costing £75,799, and the Admiralty 'F' class. Both classes were about 450-500 tons submerged displacement and were satisfactory in meeting requirements but the war showed there was little use for such small boats and only three 'Fs' and four 'Vs' were built.

It was hoped that the overseas requirement could be met with a boat of 1000 tons (surface) with a maximum surface speed of 20kts. The Vickers design, *Nautilus*, completed late in 1917 at 1441 tons with a speed of 17kts but never entered operational service. Her completion was delayed by more urgent work and by the time she did complete she was outdated by wartime developments. Her engines were a new design by Vickers and were never developed into reliability. She cost at least £203,850.

Scotts offered a modified Laurenti (FIAT) design with steam propulsion for an estimated £125,000 (probably exceeded), the *Swordfish*. She displaced 932 tons on the surface and reached 18kts. It took only 1½ minutes to close her funnel for diving but *Swordfish* was thought unsatisfactory and, after trials, was converted into a surface patrol boat. Part of the problem was that the high reserve of buoyancy came from spaces high in the double hull which were slow in draining when surfacing leading to stability problems. In many ways she was a very advanced design and many of her novel features were copied in later British submarines. She had a central hydraulic system – telemotor – operating all the main flooding valves from the control room. The high-pressure air system was likewise operated from the control room. She was very well subdivided with eight main bulkheads which were dished so that they needed no stiffeners. Doors in the bulkheads were double so that flooding would always force one shut. There were rescue buoys and arrangements to supply liquids to a boat trapped on the bottom.

Double hulls: the 'G' class

Naval submariners of the day were much attracted by the advantages of the double hull design, which permitted a much larger reserve of buoyancy on the surface; 45-50 per cent instead of 20 per cent in saddle tank designs. The shape of the outer hull could also be optimised for good performance on the surface, then important since submarines were on the surface for much of a patrol. The nature of design is that improvements in one aspect lead to penalties elsewhere: in this case the greater reserve of buoyancy meant bigger ballast tanks which were slower to fill (particularly the uppermost ones) giving longer diving times. They were also slow to drain, leading to stability problems on surfacing.

A less obvious advantage of the double hull was that it was possible to arrange the frames outside the pressure hull, within the ballast spaces. This increased the usable space within the hull. Most submarine designers feel happier with internal frames since water pressure forces the plating onto the frames rather than away as in external framing. Rivets can be weak in tension, particularly under explosive loading such as depth-charge attack but there is no direct evidence of failures associated with external frames. The distinction between the

The steam-driven *Swordfish* was designed and built by Scotts to the same requirement as *Nautilus* using Laurenti patents. She did not enter service as a submarine and was converted into a surface patrol boat. However, her many advanced features such as the hydraulic and HP air system were developed in later classes. (Imperial War Museum: SP25)

Swordfish. Note the large number of domed bulkheads to limit flooding in the event of an accident. The sections show the double hull construction. (National Maritime Museum, London: 327103)

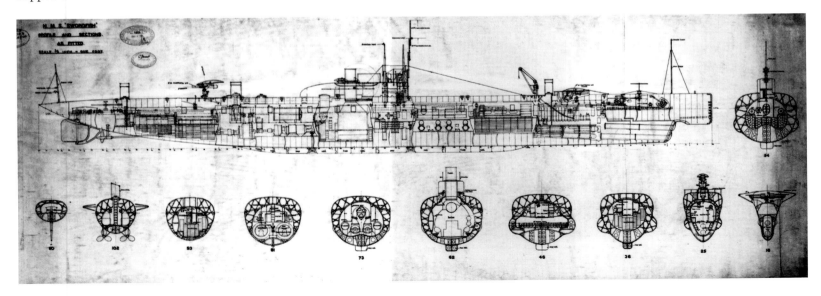

From top to bottom these sketches show single hull (internal ballast), saddle tank and double hull arrangements. The ballast tank is indicated by the letter **B**. Note the flat panels in the single hull which could be exposed to full diving pressure. If the upper part of the double hull is made free flooding, as it often was, it becomes almost indistinguishable from the saddle tank.

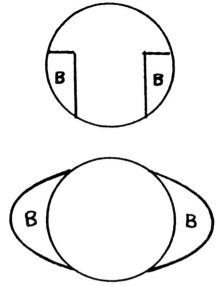

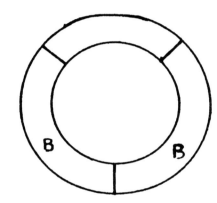

G 14. The 'G' class were a double hull design, equivalent to the saddle tank 'E' class. Though they were quite successful, the 'E' class were preferred. It had been intended to try a number of alternative engine designs in the 'G' class but the outbreak of war prevented this. (Imperial War Museum: SP2511)

double hull and saddle tank designs tended to blur during the war. Most 'double hull' designs faired off the outer hull towards the ends while the upper portion was often free-flooding rather than ballast tank.

As a result of this enthusiasm for double hulls, DNC prepared a design similar in capability to the 'Es'. Initially, the new class ('G') was intended to have a single 21in torpedo tube fore and aft and an 18in on either beam but the single forward tube was replaced by two 18in. Fourteen boats were completed (one cancelled) and were found satisfactory, although the saddle tank 'E' and, later, the 'L' classes were preferred. The Gs had a telemotor system similar to *Swordfish*.

It was originally intended to try a number of different designs of diesel engine in the 'G' class. Armstrongs were to fit MAN engines in *G 6* and Sulzers in *G 7*, Scotts were to use FIAT in *G 14* while Whites would put their own modified type of MAN in *G 5* (which was cancelled in 1915). The war put an end to these plans and they all completed with Vickers engines (some built at Chatham). The major failing of wartime British submarines lay in their obsolescent engines. It is clear that this was already recognised in 1914 and measures taken which should have led to an improvement.

British submarines at the outbreak of war

At the outbreak of war, the RN had more submarines than any other navy.

Navy	No. of submarines
Britain	77
France	45
USA	35
Germany	29
Russia	28
Italy	18
Japan	13

These figures do not tell the whole truth since many boats of every navy were old or experimental.[22] However, the enormous numerical superiority of the RN goes far to destroy the myth that the Board of Admiralty were opposed to submarines. The next table compares some of the latest submarines at the outbreak of war.

One of the most important aspects of a submarine, diving depth, is not given in the table. Diving depth was rarely quoted, mainly because no one really knew what was safe; some figures are given in Chapter 9. Diving depth only became important when sonar and depth charges became effective; the early boats were content to be out of sight and rarely went deeper except by accident.

Particulars of submarines, 1914

Country	GB	GB	USA	Germany	France
Design	D 1	E 1	M 1	U 23	Amphitrite
Surface dspt (tons)	483	667	488	669	414
Length (ft)	163	178	196	212	177
Torpedo tubes – no.	3	4	4	4	8
– diameter (in)	18	18	18	19.7	17.7
Speed (kts) surfaced	14	15	14	16.7	13
submerged	9	9	10.5	10.3	9.5
Crew	25	30	28	35	29

22. Germany was late in starting and, in consequence, had a higher proportion of modern boats.

PART III:
Wartime Experience and Design

Seven | Major Vessels

Sir Eustace Tennyson d'Eyncourt, Director of Naval Construction 1912-23. He was very well liked and attended RCNC social events until his death. (RCNC)

THE BUILDING TIME for battleships and battlecruisers was too long for any ship to be completed incorporating wartime lessons during the war, particularly since the perceived need for additional capital ships was reduced in later years when the ten battleships with 15in guns had joined. The battlecruisers which were eventually built introduced small tube boilers with consequent savings in weight and space. Light cruisers and destroyers were built in large numbers, mainly based on pre-war designs. Continuing improvements were made, mainly to armament and seakeeping. Naval aviation grew enormously and by the end of the war the first true aircraft carrier was in service. Submarines developed into the very successful 'L' class, whilst there were technically interesting, if sometimes freakish, variants. In both cruisers and destroyers the 4in gun was replaced by larger-calibre weapons since the 31lb shell was found insufficient to disable a destroyer, let alone a cruiser, with certainty.

The DNC at the outbreak of war in 1914 was Sir Eustace Tennyson d'Eyncourt.[1] His two predeccessors in the post had been Admiralty-trained men who had worked at Armstrongs, but he inverted this procedure, being an Armstrong apprentice who moved to the Admiralty. He was born in 1868 and brought up in a prosperous home near Barnet Green. On leaving school he was persuaded by Edward Reed's daughter, herself an

engineer, to become a naval architect. He was apprenticed to Armstrongs eventually working under their chief designer, J R Perrett, a former constructor. He then attended the Greenwich constructors' course under Professor Whiting.

On his return to Elswick he was much involved with speed trials, even surveying a new mile at St Abbs Head. He moved to Fairfield in 1899. When Phillip Watts rejoined the Admiralty in 1902 Perrett was promoted and d'Eyncourt returned to Armstrong in his place. He was involved in many visits abroad to discuss the requirements of potential customers. He was on one such visit to Brazil in 1912 when he received a telegram from Perrett saying that Watts was leaving the Admiralty and suggesting he applied.[2] W E Smith had been selected but there was a change in government and the new First Lord, Churchill, chose d'Eyncourt instead. D'Eyncourt was the only DNC who was not a member of the Royal Corps but his background was similar and his natural charm soon ensured his popularity. He attended Corps sporting and social events until his death.

Seakeeping, wetness and motions

Continuous high-speed steaming in any weather revealed problems in seakeeping. Many, perhaps most,

HMS *Valiant* at sea late in the war. Even battleships could suffer in bad weather. This looks like Sea State 5-6, waves about 13-15ft high. (Courtesy John Roberts)

warships of 1914 were wet, with spray and green seas sweeping decks, guns and even bridges. Severe motions also made it difficult to load and train the guns as well as reducing crew efficiency due to seasickness and exhaustion. The reason was that freeboard was inadequate in most ships and the bridge was too far forward. It can never be said too often that all design is a compromise, and the problem of freeboard was recognised before the war, but the desire to cut down on unprotected sides in the larger ships and to minimise the visual silhouette in smaller ones led to a choice of freeboard which was too low. This had not been appreciated because peacetime exercises were usually held in the summer when bad weather was less likely and, if a storm blew up, the ship's course would be altered and speed reduced to prevent damage. New designs of light cruisers and destroyers were given higher freeboard and other features to reduce wetness, whilst bridges and guns were moved further aft where motions were less. These aspects will be examined in the context of contemporary ships.

The Grand Fleet, based in Scapa Flow, had to traverse the Pentland Firth, one of the most stormy seas in the world. Major damage to ships was not uncommon: for example on 15 December 1914 the light cruiser *Boadicea* lost her bridge and several men were drowned whilst the *Blanche* received lesser damage. Worse was to come; on the night of 6-7 November 1915 the battleship *Albemarle* had her complete forebridge washed away – 135ft abaft the bow and 40ft up – and even the armoured conning tower was damaged. Her captain found himself on the upper deck amongst the wreckage of his bridge and two men were drowned. Hundreds of tons of water poured below. *Zealandia* was slightly damaged and *Albemarle* was escorted to Scapa by the *Hibernia*.[3]

There are many different aspects to the behaviour of

The battlecruiser *Princess Royal* in heavy weather; probably Sea State 5-6, waves 13-15ft high. (Author's collection)

ships in rough seas, particularly small ships like First World War destroyers, and the more important will be considered in turn. A modern designer would use a detailed computer analysis, backed up by model tests but, for historical analysis, cost and time enforce the use of approximate formulae and trend curves. These formulae were not available until after the Second World War (though it will be suggested that they could have been).

Wetness

The chance of taking a green sea over the bow depends very much on the ratio of freeboard to length. A rule of thumb introduced at the end of the Second World War suggests that freeboard should be at least 1.1 times the square root of the length[4] (but post-war designs tended to 1.3 times). From the 'River' class onward, most destroyers had a freeboard in the average load condition, as designed, which was close to that figure.

1. Sir Eustace Tennyson d'Eyncourt, *A Shipbuilder's Yarn* (London 1948) and D K Brown, *A Century of Naval Construction*.

2. This led to the strange battleship which eventually became HMS *Agincourt*.

3. John Jellicoe, *The Grand Fleet 1914-16* (London 1919), p256.

4. This guideline was based on the number of complaints. Ships with freeboards less than the guideline complained often. The higher guideline for later ships reflects the need to maintain high speed in any weather during anti-submarine operations.

A battleship, probably *Orion*, pitching into a very moderate sea, probably Sea State 4, waves some 6ft high. (Author's collection)

Fig 1: Pitch in head seas

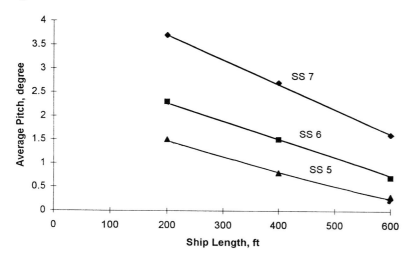

Fig 2: Heave in head seas

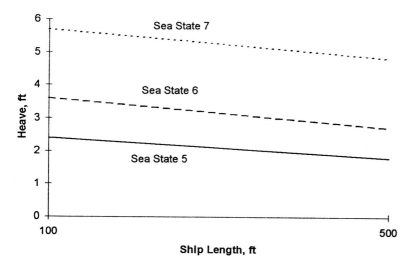

Fig 3: Incidence of seasickness

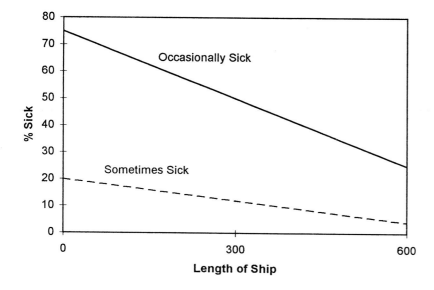

However, addition of weight, particularly during the war, reduced the freeboard considerably, adding to wetness. Most of these destroyers had less flare than would be adopted today, also contributing slightly to their wetness. All would have benefited from a sharply raked stem.

Most battleships were wet in a seaway and this was usually blamed on their weight, making them plough through heavy seas, but it is much more likely that the problem was simply inadequate freeboard exacerbated by projections which generated heavy spray. An interesting example of this is in Admiral Charles Madden's letter to d'Eyncourt describing the relative performance of some battleships in April 1916.[5] He says (adapted slightly):

> The classes in order of wetness were *Revenge, Canada, Iron Duke, Erin, St Vincent, Orion, Hercules* and *Neptune*. *Revenge* was a continual cloud of spray forward, free running with numerous cascades and a long feather of spray blown off the water as it left the deck going over the turrets. *Canada* – nearly as bad. *Iron Duke* less, no cascades, water running off forecastle by breakwater and scuppers only. *Erin* was fairly dry. The remainder practically dry except for occasional waves striking anchors and throwing spray inboard. Observation shows that the spray was entirely due to the seas striking the flat crowns of the anchors, that the low freeboard ships with low stowed anchors took each sea and as the anchors are higher fewer seas reached the anchors. Of cruisers, *Calliope* was about equal to the *Orion* and *Bellona* to the *Erin*.

In the table below the actual freeboards[6] of the ships mentioned by Madden are divided by 1.1 x square root of the length (ft) giving a ranking which places them in very much the same order of merit as given by Madden.

Wetness and freeboard

Ship	Length (ft)	Freeboard (ft)	F/1.1(L)[0.5]	Rank	Observed
St Vincent	536	26	1.02	1	2
Orion	581	26	0.98	2	1
Iron Duke	622.9	20	0.73	5	4
Revenge	620.5	22.5	0.82	4	6
Erin	559.5	23.2	0.89	3	3
Canada	661	20	0.70	6	5
Calliope	446	17.5	0.75		
Bellona	405	[20.0]	[.90]		

Bellona's freeboard is suspect – high – but ranking with *Erin* seems reasonable. *Calliope* seems accurate but one would not expect her to rank with *Orion*. Later light cruisers of the 'C' and 'D' classes had their forecastles raised to reduce wetness (see below).

Size and motions

A good big ship will always be better than a good small ship in this respect. Fig 1 shows the angle of pitch[7] for ships of different length in various sea states,[8] whilst Fig 2 shows values of heave in head seas.[9] Note that the effect of increasing length is much greater on small ships than on longer vessels. It was the study of curves like these which led the author to decide that the length of the current 'Castle' class OPVs should be of the same order as that of the Admiralty 'S' class, though this was refined later as a result of computer analysis. Not surprisingly the reduction of motion with increase in length leads to a reduction in the occurrence of seasickness in the crew, shown for recent ships in Fig 3. The overall effect of size on the maximum speed in head seas is shown in Fig 4; the lines are for 'well designed' modern ships, assuming that proportions and form are appropriate.

When the bow pitches out of the water and re-enters with a sudden impact – sometimes called 'hitting a milestone' – it is said to be slamming. Less often, slamming occurs at the stern or under the flare if that is excessive (*eg* under the fore end of the flight deck in some Second World War aircraft carriers). Of all motion-related characteristics, slamming is the most likely to cause a captain to slow down and this is a wise decision because slamming can cause local damage, tearing plates at the point of impact or, sometimes, causing cracking at highly-stressed areas near amidships.[10] Slamming is a very complex phenomenon depending on many factors, in particular, section shape forward. However, for ships of generally similar shape, as were these destroyers, the incidence of slamming depends mainly on draught. Fig 5 shows how the speed at which slamming occurs varies with both draft and wave height for typical ships. The scatter of recorded data about these mean lines is considerable (indicated by the vertical lines on the graph) but, at the very least, they indicate the difference between classes.

Speed for slamming in sea state 6, wave height *c*18ft[11]

Draught (ft)	Slamming starts at (kts)
8	10
9	12
10	14
12	18

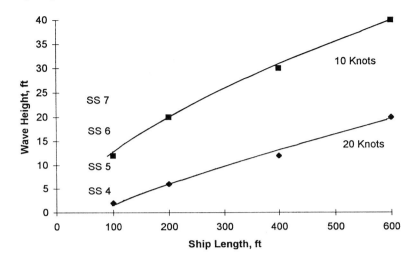

Fig 4: Speed in head seas

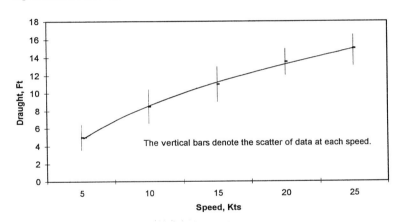

Fig 5: Slam limited speeds

The vertical bars denote the scatter of data at each speed.

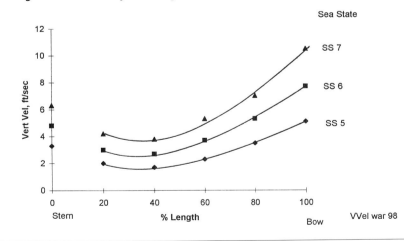

Fig 6: Vertical velocity over length

VVel war 98

---

5. K McBride, 'Seakeeping, Easter, 1916 Style', *Warship International* No 1 (1990), p50. See also discussion by D K Brown in the same issue.

6. The freeboards are measured off photographs in as near 1916 condition as possible. Drawings normally show the design waterline.

7. Pitch is a measure of the see-saw, angular motion in degrees.

8. Both wave height and the magnitude of the motions are expressed as 'significant'. This is the average of the one-third highest and corresponds well with the subjective value assigned by an experienced observer. See note at the end of this section for figure defining sea state. (Beaufort number is often confused with sea state which is incorrect as Beaufort number relates to wind speed and Sea State to wave height with only a loose connection.)

9. Heave is the bodily up and down motion of the ship in feet (or metres).

10. Cracking is most likely to occur as the result of repeated slams leading to fatigue failure.

11. Wave heights are 'significant' ie the average of the one third highest which is roughly what an experienced seaman will give as a subjective estimate.

The destroyer *Versatile* making heavy weather of Sea State 5, 10-12ft waves. (Courtesy John Roberts)

Perceived motions – nausea, etc

Human beings are most sensitive to vertical acceleration, the combination of pitch and heave motions. Seasickness is most common in the frequency band 0.18-0.3 Hz (cycles/second) and many people will be ill at an acceleration of about 2½ft/sec² (0.8m/sec²). The vertical acceleration varies considerably along the length being highest at the ends where pitching makes the most contribution. Though this variation was always known, it does not seem that its magnitude was appreciated. Most reports on a ship are written by the captain and he will describe what it seems like to him on the bridge. Hence, motion at the bridge is an important parameter, linked to the distance of the bridge from the bow. Fig 6 shows how the vertical velocity varies along the length. The motion at the A gun position would be considerably worse and much worse still in the forward mess decks. It is virtually certain that decision-making is affected by vertical acceleration even amongst people not actually sick.

Class	Bridge abaft bow as %L	Freeboard[12] F (ft)	F/√L
'River' E	26	16	1.06
Beagle G	22	13.2	0.81
Acorn H	24		
Acheron – I	26	18	1.15
Oak – I special	23	19	1.2
Mastiff M	23	17	1.04
Lightfoot	21	17	0.96
Faulknor	23	19.9	1.11
Admiralty 'R'	21	17	1.03
Admiralty 'S'	31	17	0.84
V & W	27	19.4	1.10
Scott	25	18.6	1.02
Some foreign ships			
Decatur (US)	24		
B98 (Germany)	26		

During the war there were numerous complaints from the fleet that the bridges were too far forward, though many complaints related to spray on the bridge rather than motions. One such complaint is in a letter from Jellicoe to d'Eyncourt dated 6 April 1916.[13]

> Do put the bridges of TBDs in the early stages of construction further aft. We are immensely handicapped in this respect compared to the Germans. We can't look at a head sea at any speed at all and it will force us into fighting from *windward* in anything but a calm. It is a most serious defect in our vessels.

Jellicoe was correct in his criticism of British designs but very wrong in suggesting that the Germans were better.

A destroyer was very congested and there were strong pressures to keep them as small as possible. The bridge and mast were hard against the forward funnel and it was a surprisingly long time before this was trunked with the second funnel permitting the bridge to move aft. However, there is considerable evidence that moving the bridge aft will lead to captains driving their ships harder until the perceived acceleration is what they are used to accepting, so causing slamming damage.

The position of the bridge is important but only part of the story. The bridges on German ships were low and the forecastle short, ending well forward of the bridge. In 1919 Commander England in the destroyer *Vivien* escorted *B 98* of about the same length across the North Sea at 15kts in Beaufort wind force 6-7 and a 'rough sea'.[14]

> I considered her [*B 98*] incapable of fighting at this speed, though my own ship could have been fought comfortably with the exception of No 1 gun. On the upper bridge *Vivien* was dry and I did not find it necessary to wear an oil skin.[15]

The USN destroyers of the day – fifty of which were to serve in the RN during the Second World War – were longer and should have had lower motions but they suffered from flimsy superstructures and had to ease off to avoid damage.

Roll

The rolling behaviour of First World War ships is not well documented and there are no simple rules to predict behaviour. Subjective accounts make it clear that all the ships described in this chapter rolled heavily and this could have been reduced by fitting bigger (deeper) bilge keels.[16] There was concern in the summer of 1911 over reports of heavy rolling in the cruiser *Liverpool*. DNC was reluctant to believe these reports as her form and stability were similar to earlier cruisers about which there had been no complaint, and it was thought that she might have met a resonant sea.[17] A comparison of bilge keel sizes was made and as these are rarely recorded it is reproduced here.

Bilge keel size and stability

Ship	Keel area (ft²)	Length x Depth (ft)	GM (ft)	Period full (sec)
Liverpool	486	162 x 1.5	3.15	9.0
Boadicea	442	144 x 1.5	2.8	10.16
Amethyst	417	139 x 1.5	3.5	8.2
Adventure	420	140 x 1.5	2.34	9.68
Pioneer	360	120 x 1.5	2.2	10.72
Bellerophon	1516		5.5	13.8

There is no simple way of relating bilge keel size and roll behaviour even today (1998). For one specific case the roll amplitudes for different sized keels were:

Average roll angle, degrees, in Sea State 6

Base line depth of keel	10.4
Half Base line depth of keel	15.4
1.5 x Base line depth of keel	7.7

Consideration was given to converting *Liverpool*'s 18in single plate bilge keel[18] to a V with a 6in plate extension but it is not clear if this was done. A study was made of an anti-rolling tank which would need 68 tons of water and reduce the GM from 3.13ft to 2.55ft. (There is a reference to a merchant ship in which the tanks were said to sound like 'Scylla swearing at Charybdis'.)

Roll accelerations acting on people or weights cause large lateral forces. Such forces particularly affect manual tasks such as loading a gun, and this was probably the main reason for the failure of the 6in Mk VII BL in *Swift* and *Viking* and for the similar failure of 5.9in guns in German ships. The inertia forces on a long barrel subject to lateral accelerations are high and manual training and elevation would be difficult in a heavy sea. (Note the introduction of a shorter 6in in light cruisers and see also discussion of the *Royal Sovereigns* in Chapter 3) After the war an experimental gyroscope stabiliser was fitted in the destroyer *Vivien*, but it does not appear to have been successful.

Hindsight

The TBD Committee of 1901 carried out an excellent survey of seakeeping of the earliest destroyers. It would have been possible to extend this into later classes and with the instruments of the day to quantify the results, generating trend curves similar to those reproduced in this section. Model tests could be incorporated where appropriate. It is not clear why this was not done as designers were quite keen to produce graphs and formulae for other design aspects. Since the destroyers' main opponents were the generally similar destroyers of other navies, there probably seemed little tactical advantage in improving seakeeping. Their officers and men did not realise that improvement was possible and suf-fered in comparative silence. They certainly earned the 'hard-lying money' paid as compensation for discomfort.

The problems of severe motions and wetness near the bow were understood in principle but lack of experience in bad weather caused such problems to be underestimated. Pressure to keep down the size and hence cost contributed to a short upper deck which forced the bridge and A gun towards the bow. Palliative measures on later ships included an increase in freeboard whilst funnels were trunked so that the bridge could be moved aft.

Sea state and wind speed

The connection between wind speed and wave height is not very consistent but the values given are typical for a steady wind which has been blowing for some time in the open ocean. The probability is the percentage of the year for which these conditions apply in the North Atlantic. There are strong indications that average waves have increased in height in recent years but the figures above are suitable for the two World Wars.

Sea State	Wave height (ft)	Wind speed*	Probability
0-4	0-8	0-21	59
5	8-13	22-27	21
6	13-20	28-47	13
7	20-30	48-55	6
Over	30+	55+	1

Machinery: availability, reliability, and maintainability

The machinery of British warships was generally reliable in the sense that breakdowns were rare but this was achieved only by a great deal of hard maintenance work from the engineering staff. This need for frequent maintenance reduced the number of ships available for operations; Jellicoe suggests that, typically, two battleships (10 per cent), a similar percentage of light cruisers and up to 25 per cent of destroyers might be under some form of refit at any one time. There are indications that the German fleet had even more problems.

One serious problem, later known as 'condenseritis', appeared as early as 17 August 1914 when the battleship *Orion* reported serious leakage in her condenser tubes. This would contaminate the feed water with salt which would damage the boilers; it might even lead to 'priming' – water droplets in the steam – which would damage steam joints and could cause an explosion in the valves.[19] Dockyard mechanics were brought in to help with re-tubing and every ship turned over spare tubes. By October *Iron Duke* developed similar problems but this time the work was largely carried out by ship's staff, working as opportunity offered, between trips to sea.

12. Freeboard for ships in service has been scaled from photographs. This depends on the photo being truly broadside and having a clear waterline and it is easy to make a mistake. However, when several photos for the class come up with similar figures, it may be believed.

13. D'Eyncourt papers, DEY 37. National Maritime Museum.

14. Probably 9-12ft significant wave height.

15. A Preston, *V and W Class Destroyers* (London 1971), p20.

16. Other navies may have been worse. *Baden* had bilge keels of 2500sq ft area; *Royal Sovereign* 5370sq ft. It may be of interest that they added 2.9 per cent and 7.6 per cent respectively to the power required.

17. This is a perfectly reasonable line to take as roll is so dependent on the frequency with which waves encounter the ship. Sailors rarely complained of roll in those days.

18. This is a good deal shallower than I would use on a modern ship of that size.

19. Vice Admiral Sir L le Bailly, *From Fisher to the Falklands* (London 1991), p23.

Jellicoe wrote that this '. . . demonstrated the extreme efficiency and the very fine spirit of the engine-room departments of the ships of the Grand Fleet.'[20]

It should be recognised that a single condenser might have 4000 tubes, each up to 12ft in length. The tube were brass (either 30 per cent copper, 69 per cent zinc and 1 per cent tin or, later, 40/60) and the main problem was impingement attack which is critically dependent on water velocity, which had been increased in turbine ships but the problem had not occurred in the relatively slow steaming of peacetime. The were also problems with the gland packing where the tubes met the end plates of the condenser. All the navies of the First World War had similar problems which persisted until about 1930 when a partial cure was found by adding 1 per cent aluminium to the brass of the tubes. At Jutland the German battleships *Kaiserin* and *Grosser Kurfurst* both lost the use of one engine due to condenser problems and the battlecruiser *Von der Tann* lost speed from dirty coal.

There were also problems with the Yarrow small tube boilers in cruisers, beginning with *Liverpool* in December 1914. The Boiler Committee of 1904[21] had insisted that the tubes should be straight which meant that the lower drums were D-shaped, leading to failures at the joint – known as 'wrapperitis'. Engineer Rear-Admiral Gaudin was called before the First Lord, A J Balfour, and was asked who was responsible for these boiler problems. He replied:

> You are, sir . . . When you were Prime Minister, sir, you appointed a committee of people who knew nothing about naval boilers, to investigate. Amongst their recommendations they said 'All boiler tubes must be straight'. Hence the D shaped drums at the junction of the tube plate and wrapper.[22]

Though these troubles were fairly minor compared with the many hours of reliable steaming, they did give Jellicoe cause for concern that the Germans could choose their moment when all their ships were available and attack a weakened Grand Fleet. He quotes May 1916 (the month of Jutland) when the strength of the fleet was reduced by repair, refit and detachment by two battleships, three battlecruisers, three armoured cruisers, three light cruisers and twelve destroyers.

Sloping armour

In the development of the designs for the 1914-15 battleships, it was realised that 13.5in shells were available which could penetrate 13in armour at fighting range.[23] Someone, possibly E L Attwood RCNC, suggested the use of sloping armour with the top outboard of the bottom. Shells would strike at an angle and be less likely to penetrate, so that armour sloped at 20° would be equivalent to vertical armour 25 per cent thicker.

The most comprehensive discussion of the value of sloped armour is found in discussions with the British constructor in Washington, Stanley Goodall, concerning the protection of BB 49 (*South Dakota*) who also made comparisons of British and US tests of armour. In March 1918 he sent a memo to the Bureau of Construction and Repair (Admiral David Taylor) on the value of inclined armour.[24] The British tests had been carried out against face-hardened side armour at both normal impact and at 20° to the normal and against high tensile steel plates (uncemented) as used for turret roofs and decks at angles between 55° and 75° to the normal. It was thought that these angles corresponded to 'modern fighting ranges, 12–16,000 yards'.

There were considerable differences between the results of the British tests and similar USN tests, which Goodall thought were due to the earlier date of US testing and their use of smaller shells but both sets of tests showed there was a considerable advantage in inclining the armour so that impact would be at 20° or more to the normal (at 12-16,000yds). Under these conditions British tests showed the thickness of armour needed to defeat a German 15in shell was reduced by 25 per cent while US tests gave a 15-20 per cent reduction from that of vertical armour.[25] This meant the thickness needed to keep out a German 15in APC at 12,000yds was 15in of US armour (based on the US tests), or 12in of British armour (British tests).

There is a brief note in November 1918 which mentions tests against 12in plates from both British and US sources by shells from both countries. Goodall suggests that British armour did not do very well but the few figures quoted suggest that the quality of the plates were similar and that US shells were better. Goodall had been on the post-Jutland committee investigating shells and pointed out in his 1918 memo that the action of a capped shell at 20° impact is very different from that at normal incidence, because:

(a) The cap, designed for normal impact, did not assist the point to function correctly.
(b) The shell was so highly stressed at the shoulder, alongside the head of the cavity, that it broke up and the plate was not defeated even at high striking velocities.

The results of the British tests are summarised below.

In tests of roof armour there were again differences between British and US results but not to the same extent. At 12-16,000yds the angle of descent of a German 15in shell would be between 9° and 15° and under these conditions the benefit of a horizontal roof compared with the conventional roof with a 5° slope was equivalent to about 15 per cent in thickness. The table below shows the thickness of horizontal plate needed to resist a German 15in shell when the ship was rolling through 8° giving impact at 60° to the normal.

20. J Jellicoe, *The Grand Fleet 1914-16*, p153.

21. D K Brown, *Warrior to Dreadnought*, pp165-166.

22. Engineer Rear-Admiral Scott Hill, 'The Battle of the Boilers', *Journal of Naval Engineering* (July 1985).

23. D'Eyncourt papers, DEY 37. National Maritime Museum.

24. There are indications that inclined armour was proposed by Attwood during the designs whilst Goodall was his assistant. Goodall's letters are now in the PRO.

25. Partially offset by a 6 per cent increase in the area covered.

26. It was assumed that the angle of descent was 30° and that the shell would burst 18ft from impact.

27. Inclined armour was abandoned after the war by the renewed design team of Attwood and Goodall because it was incompatible with the new-style torpedo protection.

28. He does not seem to have considered a bomb hitting at normal impact. There were bombs in 1918 which could penetrate 3½in at normal impact if dropped from a great height – if it hit!

29. Though this strengthens the belt it also allows shock to be passed from one plate to the next and may increase damage. It is also very difficult to remove keyed plates for repair.

30. Letter of 14 July 1916. Held in ADM 1/8463/176.

	At 20,000yds	*At 12-18,000yds*
US tests	6in STS (US plate)	4¾in
UK tests	5½in	3½in

It was suggested that further tests were needed since impact could be at angles up to 30°.

The following month, April 1918, Goodall wrote another memo to the Bureau comparing two schemes of protection for BB 49. The first of these was proposed by the Bureau with a near vertical 13in belt to the 3½in second deck. The alternative, which Goodall preferred, had a 12in belt sloped at 80° (a restriction on beam prevented a greater slope) to be carried up to the main deck. The second deck was to be thin but the third was 2in thick and sloped at the sides to meet the bottom of the belt.[26] The second scheme was slightly lighter (and very similar to *Hood*).

Goodall maintained that the sloped 12in armour was equivalent to 15in vertical and would resist 15in shell at fighting ranges. Since the belt was high, few shells would hit the deck and these would burst well above the third deck which he thought was quite thick enough to stop all splinters. The height of the belt would also help to protect stability after damage. The first scheme would allow the direct impact of unburst shells on the 3½in second deck (see the debate between d'Eyncourt and Watts on deck height in the *Royal Sovereign* in Chapter 3) which would penetrate and allow shells to burst in the magazines or machinery spaces. The second scheme had a higher centre of gravity which meant increasing the beam (and hence the weight of deck armour) and complicated the torpedo protection.[27] Goodall returned in later papers to the folly of putting so much weight into the 3½in deck which was still insufficient to resist the impact of intact shells.

The Bureau thought that Goodall's proposal was too radical and preferred their own. Some estimates were made of the weight involved in increasing deck protec-

tion but it was too great. Goodall argued that the deck protection which would keep out a 2000lb plunging shell would resist all known bombs.[28] The first application of sloped armour was in the battlecruiser *Hood*, discussed later in this chapter. Her 12in belt was sloped at about 12° and was probably equivalent to 14in of vertical armour.

Goodall was interested in the differences between US and British practice for framing behind armour in both turrets and barbettes. In the battleship *Mississippi*,

> while heavy girders were fitted behind turret shield armour and under turret roof plates, contrary to British practice, no framing was fitted behind barbette armour, also contrary to British practice. The barbette armour relied for strength on keys and heavy butt straps and the impression given was that a turret would be put out of action by a heavy direct hit on the barbette armour.

The frames behind side armour were much lighter in USN ships '. . . but as the main armour belt plates are keyed at the butts[29] it is a matter of argument whether the American system is not as effective as the British, with the added advantage that considerable gain in weight is effected' – but it will be argued in Chapter 8 that even the heavier British framing was insufficient. The heavy armour round the uptakes was interesting, though RN war experience suggested that it was unnecessary. In 1916 Beatty objected to the sloping face and roof of British turrets as this would make impact closer to normal at longer range.[30]

Wartime changes

Director control was being fitted for the main armament of battleships before the war and, by the time of Jutland, all, with the exception of the purchased ships *Erin* and *Agincourt*, had been so equipped. Directors

Iron Duke late in the war. Comparison with the photograph in Chapter 3 shows the extent of alterations during the war, including aircraft on B and Q turrets, training marks on B turret, remote control searchlights etc. (WSS)

were then fitted to control the secondary armament[31] and to cruisers during 1917-18. Henderson gyro equipment was fitted in 1917 to ensure that guns only fired as the ship rolled through the upright.[32] Improved Dreyer tables for longer range firing were fitted. A very few ships had bulge protection. There was some increase in the number of anti-aircraft guns but most retained the 3in gun. Lacking any control system, the chance of hitting an aircraft was remote.[33] The number and size of searchlights were increased and most were remote-operated to reduce the effects of dazzle on the operator. Paravanes and longer rangefinders were added.[34] During 1917-18 range clocks and turret training scales became the visible sign of attempts to coordinate the fire of several ships on the same target. The most conspicuous addition was of aircraft platforms, covered under aviation in the next chapter. It is significant that all these changes may be seen as normal development, speeded up by war, and not as weakness in pre-war thinking.

New shells for old

After Jutland, two committees were set up, the Projectile Committee[35] and, later, the Shell Committee.[36] During their hearings there were two powerful letters from Admiral Beatty mainly on the subject of shells. The Projectile Committee was tasked with identifying faults in current shells, recommending stop gap actions and pointing the way ahead. They reported in 1917.[37]

One of the first actions was to withdraw HE Lyddite-filled shells except from ships likely to take part in shore bombardment as these shells were ineffective against ships and a potential hazard since their Mk 13 fuse could detonate if given a severe knock.[38] Those ships which retained HE were warned not to stow them in the turret or working chamber.

There was then a prolonged discussion of the advantages and disadvantages of CPC (powder-filled, Mk 15 fuse with no delay though normal functioning would lead to an explosion about 20-25 ft from impact) and APC (Lyddite-filled, Mk 16 fuse). New tests showed that APC was even worse under oblique impact than had been shown by the *Edinburgh* trials – at 20° an inert-filled shell would be broken by a ⅔ calibre plate. Overall, there was little to choose between the two types of shell in terms of the damage caused: APC was slightly better against thick armour at short range (6000yds), beam to beam (*ie* normal impact), while CPC was better in attacking decks – at 16,000yds, 35-44 per cent of the target presented was deck with angles of descent of 14½° for 15in, and 16° for 12in Mk X. In order to increase the obliquity of impact ships could change course by 1½-2 points.[39] Beatty pointed out that at Dogger Bank *Lion* had been firing 55° before the beam and this angle had to be added to the 20-24° angle of descent. Even so, an 11in shell penetrated the 5in armour and a 12in shell went through 6in plate.

Some underwater hits had caused serious damage at Jutland and shells were exploded against a mock-up of the hull of *Lion* below the belt, APC causing slightly more damage. Powder-filled shells caused much more incendiary effect (as had been seen at Tsushima). The performance of German APC shells was not thought to be outstanding. The delay was very variable; usually 6-20ft, sometimes as much as 40-50ft – and 12 per cent failed to explode. Descending at 20-25° the fuse would be actuated by the top deck and the shell would burst on or just above the next deck. There was no case of a shell exploding below the second deck. Few detonated completely. Having established the need for stronger shells, less sensitive filling and better fuses the Projectile Committee was wound up and a new committee formed.

In their final report the new Shell Committee said that by May 1919 29,900 new shells had passed proof with only 7 failures.[40] Even as early as February 1918 some 70 per cent of the shells in the Grand Fleet were of the new type, filled with 'Shellite', a mixture of Lyddite and dinitro phenol, a less sensitive and less powerful explosive (Shellite 60/40 would be 60 per cent Lyddite). It was hoped for a delay of 40-60ft but the average was more like 35 feet. The post-war trials against *Baden* and others (Chapter 11) showed that these new shells were very effective. Tests were carried out to ensure that the detonation of one shell would not set off adjacent shells in a magazine.

New capital ship designs 1914-1918

No battleships were designed and built during the war. Some preliminary designs were started in 1914 but, as will be described, they changed radically, emerging as the battlecruiser *Hood*.

Renown and Repulse

These two battlecruisers were very much the personal creation of Admiral Fisher, who had been reappointed as First Sea Lord in 1914. Work on the battleships of the 1914 Programme had stopped on the outbreak of war to free effort for ships which could be completed during the war, then expected to last no more than 6 months. After the Falklands battle, Fisher obtained approval for two battlecruisers to be designed and built very quickly. Design work began on the morning of 19 December for a ship mounting two twin 15in turrets, which were already in hand for the stopped battleships. By the afternoon of that day, Fisher had changed the armament to three twin 15in. The design was approved on 28 December, the first keel laid on 25 January 1915 and *Repulse* completed a full-power trial on 15 August 1916.[41] It was a magnificent achievement on the part of DNC department and the builders, but Jutland had been fought before they entered service and their light protection immediately came in for criticism.

They had a 6in belt from the centre of A turret to the

31. A few ships received temporary arrangements in 1916 and, by the end of the war, all ships with 6in guns were so fitted.

32. Unfortunately, this position corresponds to the maximum angular velocity and may not have been a wise choice.

33. A Raven and J Roberts, *British Battleships of World War II* (London 1976), p90.

34. Eventually, a 30ft rangefinder was selected but fitting only began in 1919.

35. Membership – V Ad R B Farquarson, Cdr L J L Hayward, S V Goodall RCNC.

36. Membership (Final) – Capt H R Crooke, Lt Col K E Haynes RA, Lt Col H A Lewis, Cdr W B C Ross (from DNO).

37. Final report; ADM 186/166.

38. A considerable number of 12in and 13.5in (not 15in) HE shells were carried and used at Jutland. It is not inconceivable that they played a part in the magazine explosions though there is no direct evidence.

39. A 'point' is 11° 15'.

40. ADM 186/189 dated 1 May 1919.

41. D K Brown, *A Century of Naval Construction*, p112. (This passage was based on the d'Eyncourt papers, National Maritime Museum.)

The battlecruiser *Renown* was designed and built very quickly. The double row of side scuttles indicate the very limited armour. Note the triple 4in mounts aft which were not successful. (Author's collection)

centre of Y turret but it was only 9ft deep. There was a short continuation, 4in forward and 3in aft. End bulkheads were 4in forward and 3in aft. The deck was 1in on the flat, 2in slopes (increased to 2in on the flat over the magazines after Jutland). There was a very shallow bulge which would have provided little protection against contemporary torpedoes. To speed production, they had the same machinery as *Tiger*. They were fast ships and would have been valuable in a pursuit. Though much criticised, both ships gave valuable service in the Second World War, due to their speed. Though their protection had been improved it was not tested except in the sinking of *Repulse* by Japanese torpedo bombers on 10 December 1941.

The 'large light cruisers'

Fisher could not get approval for more battlecruisers so in 1915 he proposed three 'large light cruisers', which became the *Courageous*, *Glorious* and *Furious*. Twelve 15in turrets were in hand for the first of the 1914 battleships of which *Repulse* and *Renown* had six while two more had been allocated to monitors. This left two each for *Courageous* and *Glorious*. It is not at all clear how it was proposed to fire two twin turrets, one mounted forward, the other aft; salvo firing needed about four shots for reliable spotting but firing broadsides would mean a long interval (and probably strain the hull). The only time they went into action, on 17 November 1917, they

Courageous was one of three 'large light cruisers' conceived by Fisher to evade a government decision that no new capital ships were to be built. (WSS)

were chasing and much of the firing was from A turret alone.[42]

The protection was the only feature which was really light cruiser style; 2in over 1in hull plating. Fisher was insistent on shallow draught, of 21-22ft, since their construction was to be justified by his plan.[43] They were intended to scout at high speed even in rough weather but the hull was initially not strong enough. The problem appears to have been the discontinuity where the relatively flexible bow joined to the rigid A barbette, supported by the side armour. Like *Repulse*, the anti-destroyer armament of *Courageous* and *Glorious* was the 4in gun, firing the 31lb shell. Unfortunately, most of the guns in both classes were in a new triple mount, which was not a success, as its crew of 26 men got in each other's way.

The third ship, *Furious*, carried the concept to extremes and was intended to mount two single 18in guns. The forward turret was removed before the ship was completed to make way for a flying deck (see Chapter 8). She mounted single 5.5in in place of 4in against destroyers. These ships were ridiculed and were not repeated. However, the USN had some very similar schemes and the Germans were impressed and designed an equivalent vessel.[44]

Hood

The starting point for *Hood* was a note from Controller (Admiral Sir F C Tudor) late in 1915 to DNC proposing an 'experimental' battleship with the armament, armour and engine power of the *Queen Elizabeth* but drawing as little water as possible (50 per cent reduction if possible) and incorporating the latest thoughts on underwater protection. The idea of shallow draught, combined with greater freeboard, was to reduce the hydrostatic pressure on bulkheads after damage and to ensure a greater reserve of buoyancy. It was also intended to mount the secondary armament (twelve 5in guns of a new design) much higher so that the gun ports would not flood.

D'Eyncourt responded on 29 November with a ship 760ft long (oa), with a beam of 104ft and a draught of

23ft 6in (a 22 per cent reduction on the *Queen Elizabeth* class). Protection was said to be the equal of *Queen Elizabeth* despite being thinner (10in) due to the use of sloped armour. However, there were only three graving docks in the Royal Dockyards which could accept such a ship and few building slips. Variants[45] were examined with reduced length and beam but, not surprisingly, their underwater protection was inferior.[46] Tests on the Chatham Float[47] had shown that effective bulge protection was possible but the overall beam required was considerable. These studies were forwarded to Jellicoe for comment. He thought that there was little need for battleships in the light of the Grand Fleet's superiority but he believed that the Germans were building at least three heavily-armed battlecruisers with a speed approaching 30kts and armed with 15.2in guns and suggested a new, fast British battlecruiser with guns larger than 15in if possible to counter them.

Two design studies were submitted on 1 February and four more on the 17th; three carried eight 15in guns, the others four, six or eight 18in. All but the first had small tube boilers saving some 3500 tons. Even so, they were all very large ships – 32,500 to 39,500 tons. Most had an 8in main belt. Study '3' was selected for development with eight 15in guns, since the 18in weapon was not ready, and a speed of 32kts. It had a 10in belt as initially designed instead of the 8in of the others but this was reduced to 8in in the final version. Two slightly modified versions of the design were forwarded on 27 March 1916 and Design B was accepted. Since this represented the considered views of the Board and the C-in-C on the best achievable battlecruiser just before Jutland, its particulars are given below.

Hood, prior to Jutland

Displacement: 36,300 tons
Length x beam x draught (ft): 860(oa) x 104 x 25.5
Armament: 8-15in, 16-5.5in, 2-21in submerged TT
Armour: belt 8in, 5in upper, 4-5in forward, 3-4in aft.
Machinery: 144,000shp = 32 knots
Oil (tons): 1200 at load, 4000 max

42. The turrets were later modernised and fitted in *Vanguard*, the last British battleship (completed 1946).

43. Note, however, the alternative justification for shallow draught in the early studies for *Hood*.

44. K McBride. 'The Weird Sisters', *WARSHIP 1990* (1990).

45. A Raven and J Roberts, *British Battleships of World War Two*, Ch 4. The authors describe the design studies for both battleships and battlecruisers in fascinating detail.

46. J Roberts, *Battlecruisers* (London 1997), pp55-56.

47. D K Brown, 'Attack and Defence', *WARSHIP 24* (October 1982).

48. In the immediate aftermath of Jutland there was understandable confusion; some accounts say June.

49. A Raven and J Roberts, *British Battleships of World War Two*, p64.

50. R A Burt, *British Battleships 1919-1939* (London 1993), p30. (Also Roberts and Jurens below.)

Hood as completed. Note that the shell rooms are below the magazines; her sisters would have had them the other way round.

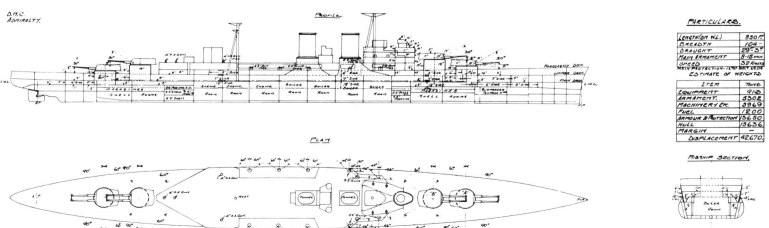

The final design was approved on 7 April 1916 and three ships were ordered that day; a fourth was ordered in July.[48] *Hood* was laid down on 31 May 1916, the day that Jutland was fought and work was therefore suspended. As a result of studies within the Grand Fleet, Jellicoe pressed for better flash precautions and for thicker deck protection over the magazines. He and Beatty put these views forward at a meeting on 25 June 1916 where the need for thicker deck protection was opposed by the DNC, presumably on the basis of the Payne-Goodall report (see Chapter 11). A revised legend of 12 July showed fairly minor changes in protection. The 8in belt was increased in depth by 1ft 8in with the 5in upper belt reduced to 3in and there were slight increases in the thickness of decks. The protection of the turrets was considerably increased and other minor changes made. The number of dynamos was doubled to eight. These changes brought the legend displacement to 37,500 tons and would have resulted in a ¼kt loss of speed.

However, on the same date in July DNC proposed some major increases in vertical protection which would increase draught by 2ft with a 1kt loss of speed. The belt was to be increased to 12in, the upper belt to 6in and the barbettes to 15in. Such a ship would have the same armament as *Queen Elizabeth* and be some 7kts faster with protection at least as good. She was re-started to this design on 1 September. Alternative designs were considered later in July with triple 15in mounts, but rejected.[49] Further changes were made in September including an increase in the deck over magazines to 3in.

The final design was only approved in August 1917 by which time the displacement had risen a further 600 tons. Further changes would have been made to the three later ships, mainly increased turret armour.

Armour weights – percentage of load or standard displacement

Ship	%
Invincible	20
Hood	33
Nelson	29
King George V (1936)	36
Hindenburg	34
Lexington	28.5 (1919 design)

Hood's 12in side armour was angled at 12° making it the equivalent of about 14-15in of vertical armour. In criticising *Hood*'s 'weak' protection it is well to remember that her main belt was more effective than any ship of the First World War and better than many later ships, but deck protection was a different story. In the autumn of 1919 tests were carried out using the new 15in APC shell against replica targets of *Hood*.[50] In the first series the impact was on the thin upper belt, which allowed the shell to reach the magazine crown. The results seem to have been marginal and it was decided to increase the deck over the after magazines to 6in and to 5in forward but this work was not carried out. Later trials suggested a vulnerability to plunging shells below the belt. *Hood*'s

Hood was the end product of a number of design studies prior to Jutland. She was then redesigned after the battle with a great deal of extra armour making a not very satisfactory compromise. However, between the wars she was the largest and fastest capital ship in the world. She is seen here on trials when she made 31.9kts with 150,220shp at 44,600 tons deep displacement. (Imperial War Museum: Q17879)

Hood in 1932. She had an improved turret design without sighting hoods and the upper turrets were capable of axial fire. (Author's collection)

armour weight amounted to 33.5 per cent of her total displacement, making her a fast battleship rather than a lightly armoured battlecruiser. The numerous changes made led to a poor use of this weight and, ultimately, to her loss.[51] She had an anti-torpedo bulge, 562ft long and 10ft deep with a 1½in inner bulkhead. The inner space was packed with sealed, hollow steel tubes which tests on the Chatham Float had shown were effective in absorbing explosions.[52]

The 15in mounts were the Mark II giving 30° elevation – though they could not be loaded over 20° – and, at last, the spotting hood on the roof was eliminated in favour of a position in the front plate enabling the superfiring turrets to fire over the lower ones. The turret roof was flatter than in earlier ships and was to be 5in thick in the follow-on ships. The magazines were above the shell rooms, though the positions would have been reversed in the three follow-on ships. The conning tower weighed 600 tons, the heaviest fitted to a British ship – a waste of weight.

There do not seem to have been any later British battlecruiser designs during the war but design work began soon afterwards, leading to the 'G 3s' as described later. German design work continued until the Armistice and the USN was designing its first battlecruiser, *Lexington*.

Hood's machinery was representative of the best available in the war and, as such, is worth describing in detail.[53] There were twenty-four oil-fired Yarrow small tube boilers generating steam at 230lbs/in² without superheat. Each of these was 13ft 3in long, 16ft 10in

wide and 16ft 7in high. There were four sets of Brown-Curtis turbines with the two sets driving the wing shafts in the forward engine room. The middle room had the inner port unit and the inner starboard was in the after room. Each set had a cruising turbine which could be coupled to the high pressure (HP) turbine driving through one pinion (55 teeth) whilst the low pressure turbine (LP) with a built-in astern turbine drove the other pinion (75 teeth). The main gear wheel had 392 teeth and was 12ft in diameter.

	Horsepower	rpm
HP Turbine	17,500	1497
LP Turbine	18,500	1098
Propeller	36,000	210

The cruising turbines could produce about 15 per cent of full power, giving half full speed, and had four wheels. The main HP turbines had two double Curtis wheels followed by eight single-impulse wheels. The blades were phosphor bronze with forged steel disks and shafts. The LP turbines had eight ahead wheels and two triple Curtis wheels for going astern. The design was said to be 'conservative' with HP blade tip speed of 426ft/sec. and 492ft/sec for the LP. The condensers were under the LP turbines.

The four three-bladed propellers were 15ft diameter, 19ft 3in pitch with a developed area of 125sq ft. Progress in machinery design is illustrated in the table opposite.

British battlecruisers with the blessing of hindsight

At the time *Invincible* was conceived it was customary to protect a battleship or First Class cruiser against guns similar to those which she herself mounted. This was not a universal rule, *eg* the pre-dreadnought *Duncan* which had a thin belt for increased speed. The 6in belt of the *Invincible* would keep out all sizes of high-capacity HE shells, whose threat was then taken very seriously, and all types of shell of 6in calibre and below, and at most ranges and angles it would have a good chance of resisting the impact of 9.2in shells. The designer should then have ensured that there was little chance of the ship

Machinery weights for *Hood*

Engine room weights	Tons	Boiler room weights	Tons
Main engines circ pumps, shaft in ER	1776	Boilers, main steam pipes	1234
Aux. M/C	506	Feed pumps & water	169
Floor plates, ladders, spares	186	Auxiliary	291
Water	192	Funnels etc	377
Steam pipes outside	38		
Propellers	87		
Shafting abaft M/C	520		
Floors	9		

being disabled or sunk by a small number of hits from 11in or larger AP shells (or underwater explosion). The battlecruiser concept implied disabling the enemy before he could inflict serious damage. They had the guns to do this but it is surprising that, except for *Queen Mary*, they were not given Pollen Argo fire control.

Up till the war, very little thought had been given in any navy to limiting the effect of an explosion; efforts had rather been devoted to keeping the projectile out in the first place. There were traces of damage limitation in the 'protected cruiser system' and elements of this could be seen in the arrangement of bunkers in the coal-fired battlecruisers. Ammunition explosions were recognised as the most serious hazard to lightly-protected ships but, as described in Chapter 2, it was thought that full-scale trials had shown that cordite would only burn and not explode. The risk from detonation of shells was thought to be greater so shell rooms were placed below magazines.

If the magazine did not explode, battlecruisers stood up quite well to shell fire. At the Falklands, *Invincible* was hit by twelve 8.2in, six 5.9in and four unidentified shells with little damage. At Dogger Bank, *Lion* was disabled, receiving seventeen hits from 11in and 12in shells.[54] However, most of the serious damage was caused by one 12in hit from *Derfflinger* which forced in a 9in plate by the port engine room. This caused flooding in the port reserve feed tank so that the port engines had to be stopped. It also stopped the last dynamo so that all light and power failed. The reason was that the framing was insufficiently strong and the edge of the plate had a sharp corner which cut into the frame. This was part of a wider problem. DNC's department was overworked and the enormous building programme before the war overloaded the system so that mistakes were made and not noticed.[55] Sir Phillip Watts had the reputation of being a brilliant conceptual designer but lacking an eye for detail.

Tiger took fifteen hits from heavy shells at Jutland and remained in action with six of her eight guns. *Inflexible*'s mine damage at the Dardanelles in 1915 was the only serious underwater damage suffered by a battlecruiser and the results were not encouraging. If *Lion*'s port engine room had flooded at Dogger Bank, that, with other damage, could have sunk her.

As discussed in an earlier book, the author believes that the basic concept of the battlecruiser was sound. *Invincible*'s glorious career at Heligoland Bight, Falklands and Jutland justifies that statement. The three magazine explosions at Jutland (and the later case of *Hood*) have obscured the real value of such ships. As discussed, it was believed at the time that full-scale trials had shown that cordite was very unlikely to explode and hence protection to magazines was often less than that given to machinery. Even the thickest armour could be penetrated by guns of the calibre mounted in the ship (given decent shells) or by contemporary German ships.

Progress in machinery design 1905-1916

Ship	Year	shp	Wt (lbs/shp)	Space (sq ft/shp)	Fuel (lbs/shp/hr)
Dreadnought	1905	23,000	184	0.45	1.522
Lion	1909	70,000	154	0.25	1.67
Repulse	1914	112,000	113	0.166	1.28
Hood	1916	144,000	84	0.136	1.11

It seems to have been thought that the machinery spaces were sufficiently sub-divided to prevent the ship being disabled by a single shell and probably by a single torpedo. The greatest weakness lay in the centreline bulkhead of the engine room. Flooding of one side and the adjoining boiler room would cause a very large angle of heel and it would probably be necessary to flood the intact engine room to save the ship. There must be some doubt as to the separation of secondary systems such as the lubrication system which would bring all machinery to a stop.

Wartime light cruisers

The *Arethusa*s and the derivative 'C' class were clearly seen as the right type of ship for a war in the North Sea, but the battle of Heligoland Bight on 28 August 1914 showed that a 6in gun on the centreline was worth far more than a pair of 4in.[56] (It is not clear how this conclusion was reached; the RN can have had little knowledge of the damage to German ships. Perhaps it was the inability of German 4.1in to penetrate *Arethusa*'s light belt. The unreliability of the semi-automatic 4in Mk IV may have been a factor.) This section begins with a chronological survey of the principal features of wartime light cruisers after which lesser developments are outlined.

Later 'C' class

The limited stability and cramped arrangement of the *Arethusa*s made modifications difficult but in 1918 five of them had the after pair of 4in guns replaced by a single 6in. The forward pair of 4in in the *Caroline*s and *Calliope*s were replaced by a 6in in 1916-17 and the remainder went in 1918. The four ships of the *Cambrian* class were originally repeats of *Calliope*, though laid down well before that ship went to sea. The last, *Constance*, had the forecastle 4in replaced before completion, the others being altered at the same time as the earlier ships.

There were two other ships of the 1914-15 programme: *Centaur* and *Concord*. To save time they adopted the four-shaft, impulse-reaction turbine plant intended for two Turkish cruisers ordered from Vickers. They were designed for five 6in guns – one on the forecastle, one forward and one aft of the funnels and two superfiring aft. Four (originally six) improved *Concord*s

51. The loss of *Hood* will be discussed in a later volume. The best available account is that by W J Jurens, *Warship International* 2/87. It is probable that a 15in shell from *Bismarck* exploded the 4in magazine which, in turn, caused the after 15in magazine to explode, venting back through the 4in space.

52. The last visible remains of the *Hood* after her sinking were these steel tubes which had floated free.

53. I Jung, *The Marine Turbine* (Greenwich 1982) and the RN College notes. Greenwich ca 1940.

54. A good rule of thumb is that a twentieth-century battleship will be disabled by about 20 hits. This seems to work even with *Bismarck* as though she endured more than 400 hits, she was disabled quite soon after the first hit.

55. D K Brown, *A Century of Naval Construction*, p92.

56. J Goldrick, *The Kings Ships were at Sea* (Annapolis 1984), pp83 et seq.

The cruiser *Castor*. The original two 4in mounts on the forecastle have been replaced by a single 6in. (WSS)

were ordered in December 1915 as the *Caledon* class. They had a raked bow and an extra 9in of beam to give satisfactory stability with wartime additions. The three survivors of this class were to take part in the Second World War.

The five cruisers of the *Ceres* class, ordered in March-April 1916, were redesigned; the bridge was moved aft and the second 6in gun was mounted in a superfiring position forward. For an 8in increase in beam and a small increase in displacement their fighting capability had been greatly increased. 'B' gun had a much wider arc of fire and its raised position made it capable of use in bad weather. The re-positioning of the bridge reduced both motion and wetness on the compass platform. All but one had Brown Curtis turbines on two shafts.

The five *Capetowns* of June-July 1917 were near repeats of the *Ceres*, but by the time they were ordered it had become apparent that all the early ships were very wet due to inadequate freeboard forward. In these ships the forecastle deck was lifted 5ft at the stem and sloped down to the original level at A gun position. The section shapes were retained up to the original line of the forecastle and then run up vertically to the new deck line, forming a knuckle. This change seems to have been very successful and was repeated in later classes. The 'Cs' had fairly thick side plating which lapped onto the stem forging and a plume of spray ran up the groove so formed and landing on the compass platform![57]

The 'D' class

In September 1916 the first three cruisers of the 'D' class (*Danae*, *Dauntless* and *Dragon*) were ordered as a fur-

Concord and her sister were 'C' class cruisers built under the 1914-15 programme but used machinery ordered for two Turkish cruisers. (Author's collection)

Dragon was a 'D' class cruiser with the original low freeboard forward. In this photo she has an aircraft hangar built into the bridge. In 1921 an experimental 6-barrel pom-pom was mounted in B gun position. (WSS)

ther enlargement of the 'C' class design in response to a mythical report of more heavily-armed German cruisers. They were lengthened by about 20ft and given 2ft more beam to accommodate a sixth 6in gun between bridge and funnel. The 670 tons extra displacement allowed them to carry twelve torpedo tubes in four triple mounts. Three more ships were ordered in July 1917 and six, later reduced to two, in March 1918. All but the first three had the raised 'trawler' bow fitted in *Ceres*. They had larger propellers running at lower rpm for greater efficiency. Late in the war there was a proposal to lengthen the 'Ds' by 15ft to carry 50 tons more oil bringing the legend displacement to 5100 tons.

The 'E' class

The *Emerald, Enterprise* and *Euphrates* were designed for very high speed to match exaggerated reports of the speed of the German minelayers *Brummer* and *Bremse*.[58] At the end of the war one was cancelled and the others completing in leisurely fashion in 1926. Two sets of *Shakespeare* class flotilla leader machinery were fitted giving a total of 80,000shp and a speed of 33kts trial, 32kts deep. They were designed with a knuckle following the success of this feature in earlier ships.

The relationship between length, speed and power of the 'C', 'D' and 'E' classes is interesting.

57. The 'County' class guided missile destroyers had a similar problem - but an enclosed bridge.

58. They achieved 28kts on trial.

Despatch showing the raised bow of later C and D class. (WSS)

Frobisher of the *Hawkins* class, often known as 'Improved Birminghams', the ancestry through the Atlantic cruisers now being clear. (Author's collection)

Emerald was a stretched 'D' with double the power, giving 33kts to counter mythical very fast German cruisers. The accidental knuckle formed by the trawler bow in the later 'C' and 'D' classes seemed successful so the 'Es' were designed with a knuckle – as were almost all later RN cruisers. (Author's collection)

Length, speed and power

	Colombo	Dunedin	Emerald
Length (ft)	445	465	560
Displacement (tons)	4270	4530	8160
shp	40,000	40,000	80,000
Power for 29kts	37,125	41,100	41,100
shp/Dspt x V @ 29kts	0.30	0.26	0.17
Circ M*	8.4	8.59	8.51
rpm full speed	340	275	?

*Circ M, a Froude coefficient, is the length divided by the cube root of the displaced volume (35 x Dspt, tons).

The value of increasing length in giving much bigger ships the same speed for the same power is clear though

the 'Ds' undoubtedly benefited from the lower rpm. The additional horsepower in the 'Es,' nearly 40,000, only increased the speed by 3-4kts.

In 1918 there were designs based on the 'E' class with either four or five 7.5 inch in response to yet another incorrect report of fast German cruisers with two 8.2in guns.

General trends

The clear trend in wartime cruiser design was to replace the 4in guns of a mixed armament with an all 6in armament, to improve the arcs of fire and to increase the number of guns. The sudden jump in speed with the 'E' class is, perhaps, best seen as an aberration rather than necessary though high speed was seen as essential in the first post-war cruisers. Experience was to show that

these small ships ('C' and 'D' classes) were very wet and the freeboard was increased.

Cruiser freeboard

	Early 'C'	Later 'C'	Early 'D'	Later 'D'
Freeboard, design, for'd (ft)	24	29	24	30
Length (L)	450	450	471	471
f/(sq rt L)	1.13	1.37	1.10	1.38

The forecastle deck was raised some 5-6ft at the stem head and the sides were brought up vertically from the line of the original deckline. This formed a 'knuckle' at the old deck level and this was thought to throw water clear of the deck. A knuckle featured in almost all later British cruisers.[59]

Other features and changes

MASTS AND FIRE CONTROL. The *Arethusa*s and the earlier 'Cs' up to the four *Cambrian*s completed with a pole mast, which was changed to a tripod carrying a director in 1917-18 following the trial conversion of *Penelope* in 1916. She was inclined in September 1916 and when the results were seen to be successful work began on other ships. The extra weight, high up, amounted to about 18 tons. The *Caledon*s, later 'Cs' and the 'Ds' were completed with tripod masts and directors.

ANTI-AIRCRAFT GUNS. These varied from time to time and between individual ships; the notes which follow are a generalisation. The *Arethusa*s began with a single 3pdr, replaced by a single 3in in 1915. In 1917 this was increased in five ships to two 3in whilst two were given a single 4in. The *Caroline* class completed with a 13pdr AA[60] which was replaced in three ships by two 3in, in one by two 4in and in two by one 4in. Two received two single pom-poms as well.

Calliope ended the war with two 3in AA and *Champion* with one 4in. The *Cambrian*s and *Centaur*s also changed from a 13pdr to two 3in (five ships) or a 4in (one ship). The later 'Cs' and the 'Ds' completed with two 3in and, after *Caledon*, two single pom-poms as well. The 'Es', completing after the war' had five 4in and four pom-poms.

TORPEDO TUBES. The *Arethusa*s and *Caroline*s completed with two twin 21in torpedo tubes and five reloads, which were replaced by two more twin mounts in 1916-17. The *Calliope*, *Cambrian* and *Centaur*s completed with a single, submerged torpedo tube on either beam which proved of little value as they could not be fired at speed. Approval was given to fit two twin above-water tubes in all except *Centaur* and *Concord* where gun blast made it impossible to find a site for them.[61] The *Caledon*s and later 'Cs' completed with four, twin 21in tubes and the 'Ds' and 'Es' with four triple tubes.[62]

Stability and weight growth

The metacentric height of the *Arethusa* design was deliberately low to reduce the severity of rolling and make them better gun platforms.[63] *Aurora* was inclined on completion and *Penelope* after fitting the tripod mast. Figures for these and others follow.

Ship	Condition	GM (ft)	Range, deg
Aurora	Legend	2.21	83
	Deep	2.69	86
Penelope	Legend	2.05	82
	Deep	2.65	86
Cordelia	Legend	2.0	73 As built
	Deep	2.75	84
Cordelia	Legend	1.6	70 With tripod and three 6in
	Deep	2.5	76
Cleopatra	Legend	1.5	69 With tripod, four 6in
	Deep	2.5	79

A detailed list of additional items for the *Arethusa*s is given by Raven and Roberts.[64] By 1916 126 tons had been added and a further 79 tons by 1918, partially offset by the removal of the conning tower (20 tons). The bigger items included AA guns, torpedo tubes and stowage, ready-use lockers, paravanes, tripod and director, minelaying gear, flying-off platform, 36in searchlight and platform, and the change to 6in guns. Other classes would have had similar growth – *Caledon* is said to have grown by 250 tons by 1921. *Cleopatra*'s inclining seems to have been a cause of concern and it was decided not to fit flying platforms to the earlier classes and to remove any already fitted.[65]

Building times

They were fairly small and simple ships and did not take long to build. The wartime Cs usually completed in about 20 months from order. *Caroline* seems the fastest; about 17 months from order, 12 months from laying down. Resistance to damage was very good and is covered in Chapter 11.

Aesthetics

In this writer's view, many of the late wartime ships were beautiful in their day and are seen as such by many modern enthusiasts. Ships like *Hood, Glorious, Raleigh*, the 'C' class cruisers and 'S' class destroyers have an appearance related to function which attracts the eye. To invert the old saying 'If it looks right, it is right' – 'If it is right, it will come to be seen as looking right'. These ships did not all look the same: d'Eyncourt clearly left his section heads some discretion but, equally clearly, he made sure their output was pleasing.

59. The value of a knuckle remains a matter of controversy. The author is a firm believer, demonstrated by the prominent knuckle on the current 'Castle' class for which he was responsible.

60. A short gun originally used by the Royal Horse Artillery.

61. It is unclear how many received the extra tubes; Roberts suggests only *Calliope, Champion* and *Canterbury*.

62. The 'Es' were later changed to four quadruple tubes.

63. A committee chaired by Captain Grant of the *Falmouth* had reported that the 6in gun was too heavy for manual operation and recommended a 5in but this proposal was not adopted. (Cf *Narvik*)

64. A Raven and J Roberts, *British Cruisers of World War Two* (London 1980), p33.

65. The figures quoted are not in themselves sufficient to judge the adequacy of their stability. The maximum righting lever (GZ) and the angle at which it occurs are the critical figures, together with the wind loading on the ship.

Wartime Destroyers and Aviation Vessels

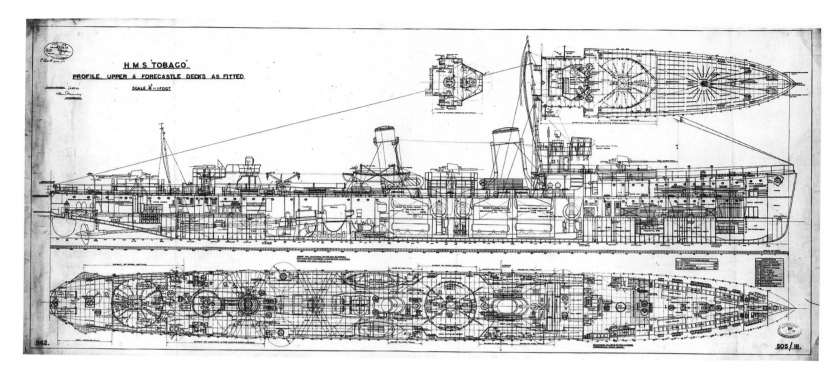

Tobago was a Thornycroft special 'S' class. They had a little more beam than the Admiralty ships which enabled the forward gun to be raised. (National Maritime Museum, London: 31918)

Destroyers

Flotilla leaders

The Captain 'D' commanding a flotilla of up to twenty earlier destroyers would normally be accommodated in a 'Scout' – light cruiser – with a speed of 23-25kts. It was clear that this arrangement would be unsuitable for the much faster 'M' class destroyers and in 1913 a design was begun for a flotilla leader which, after the usual consideration of options, appeared as the *Lightfoot*. Two ships were ordered in December 1913, two more under the 1914-15 Estimates and a further three in November

1914. They provided the space for the Captain, his staff and the communications team. The latter were given a long-range (150 mile!) wireless set. During 1915 a further six ships were ordered to a design which was modified to improve behaviour at sea. The forward two funnels were combined so that the bridge could be moved aft by 13ft making it possible to mount a gun superfiring in B position. It was hoped to increase the freeboard by 1ft but the ships were already under construction and this change was only possible in the last ship. There were also four slightly bigger ships being built by White at Cowes for Chile which were purchased as the *Faulknor* class leaders.[1]

Gabriel, a *Lightfoot* class leader. She is seen here as a minelayer with canvas screens from the after funnel to the stern. (WSS)

The 'V' and 'W' class

The advent of the faster 'R' class meant that even the new leaders were not fast enough and DNC was asked to design a new leader with a speed of 34kts using the same machinery as the 'R' class – 26,000shp geared turbines.[2] Length was saved by adopting superfiring guns forward and aft and only two funnels were fitted; tall and thin forward, short and fat aft. This enabled the bridge to move further aft, reducing the motions per-

ceived there. Initially, five ships were ordered (*Vampire*, *Valentine*, *Valhalla*, *Valorous* and *Valkyrie*), described as divisional or half leaders. They cost about £200,000, some £50,000 less than a *Lightfoot* and only £6000 more than some of the more expensive standard destroyers. This design, by Hannaford, almost accidentally,[3] became one of the greatest warship designs of all time and was the model for two decades of future British and many foreign destroyers.

In 1916 reports suggested that the Germans were

Broke, a *Faulknor* class leader. These ships were building for Chile and were purchased on the outbreak of war. Four of their original six 4in were replaced by two 4.7in late in the war. (Author's collection)

1. It has been suggested that these ships derived from Fisher's super *Swift* which he wanted instead of light cruisers. There is no evidence to support this story but it could be true.

2. What a requirement! – Same speed with a much bigger ship using the same machinery – and the 'Rs' were good.

3. One is reminded of Louis Pasteur's remark – 'Chance favours the trained observer'.

Valentine was an early 'V' leader, seen here post-war but little changed from her original configuration. (Author's collection)

building numerous large destroyers and twenty-five repeats were ordered in June as the 'V' class destroyers. Initially, these ships carried two twin 21in torpedo tubes, but *Vampire* had the prototype triple tubes which were later fitted to most of the class.[4] Twenty-one 'W' class (plus two cancelled) followed in December 1916. A repeat 'W' class of sixteen boats was ordered in January 1918 and thirty-eight more in the spring but only nine of the first batch and seven of the second were completed. In the second batch the longer boiler room was forward of the smaller one so that the forward, tall funnel was the thicker one. The engine room was the longest compartment in the ship and it was desirable to have a short space adjacent to limit the extent of flooding from damage extending over the bulkhead.

Armament

The majority of the ships described mounted the 4in Mk VIII gun firing a 31lb shell with a range of 10,000yds. Extreme range was of little importance as hits over 1000yds were unlikely from a hand-operated gun without director. Trials described in Chapter 2 seemed to show that a single hit with a 31lb shell would disable a destroyer but wartime experience showed that only a hit in the machinery spaces would actually do so. A 6in gun was mounted for trials in two ships but problems with working such a gun in a seaway (discussed in Chapter 7) meant it was unsuccessful.

The repeat 'Ws' had a 4.7in BL[5] (50lb shell) to counter the rumoured heavier armament in German ships. Two classes of even bigger leaders, both with five 4.7in guns, were built; the *Shakespeare* class by Thornycroft and the more conservative Admiralty *Scott* class. Both are discussed later in Appendix 2 under specials.

Endurance

During the war the main complaint about destroyers was their lack of endurance; Jellicoe wrote that three days was their effective time at sea, which limited Grand Fleet sweeps to that time.[6] The table which follows gives the nominal endurance, usually the design intention. In practice, there was considerable variation between ships of the same class, whilst fouling, deterioration of machinery and even maloperation meant that the endurance achieved was much less. Furthermore, no captain would wish to reach harbour with empty tanks and it was thought prudent to refuel, if possible, when half the fuel was used.

Nominal endurance

Class	Oil (tons)	Endurance (miles)	At speed (kts)
Beagle	205-236	2000	15
Acheron	178		
Acorn	170	2250	13
Acasta	258	2750	15
		600	29
'L'	268	2240	15
'M'	278	2530	15
Yarrow 'M'	228	1940	15
Thornycroft 'M'		1510	15
'R'	296	3440	15
		1860	20
Modified 'R'	300		
'V' Leader	367	3500	15
		600	34
Shakespeare	500		
Scott	500	5000	15
'S'	301		
Repeat 'W'	367	3210	15

Acheron carried 148 tons in war tanks with 30 in peace tanks. *Shakespeare* war 398 tons, 102 tons peace. *Beagle* coal only. A few figures follow showing variations between ships of the same class. At full speed the *Acorns* on average burnt 7 tons per hour, ranging from *Chameleon* at 6.4 to *Redpole* at 8.0. In the *Acherons*, full power consumption per hour varied from 50.6 to 61 tons. Some endurance figures for the 'M' class at 15 knots are:

4. Those fitted for minelaying had a triple TT mount forward and a twin aft.

5. This gun seems to have been successful. When the 'Vs' and 'Ws' were being scrapped in the thirties, preference was given to retaining those with 4.7in guns. It was a new gun and not an adapted army gun as is sometimes claimed.

6. Jellicoe, *The Grand Fleet 1914-1916*, p18.

A German destroyer firing a torpedo. At Jutland the performance of the torpedo was disappointing for both sides. (Courtesy Julian Mannering)

Destroyer torpedoes at Jutland

	British		German	
Number of TT	260		326	
	Day	*Night*	*Day*	*Night*
Torpedoes fired	33	38	78	19
Hits scored by destroyers	3	2	1	1

Torpedoes used to sink disabled ships have been omitted.

The first point to note is the small proportion of the torpedoes carried which were actually launched. This was mainly due to the difficulty in reaching a good firing position but, in part, captains tended to fire single shots in the hope of a better opportunity later. Since the chance of a hit from a single shot was very low,[9] this practice contributed to the low score. On the other hand, British destroyers do seem to have been quite effective in spoiling German attacks.

Typically, the speed of a torpedo was about twice that of its target. Since the range is usually quoted in yards, the speeds quoted in the following passage are shown in brackets as yards per minute and the running time in minutes is given behind the range.[10] The latest Mk II**** had a high-speed setting of 45kts (1500yds/min) for a range of 4200yds (3min) and a long-range setting of 19kts (1000yds/min) for 10,750yds (11min). Earlier versions had the same speed settings but about 10 per cent less range. With these long running times, there was every possibility of the target changing course or speed – even if these had been correctly estimated before firing.

German torpedo performance was broadly similar with much the same sized warhead. There is some evidence that depth keeping was unreliable in German torpedoes as several were seen to pass beneath stationary ships. It is interesting that German destroyers had a more numerous torpedo outfit than British, at the expense of guns, but were less successful in scoring hits.

A significant number of hits were only likely from a co-ordinated attack by several ships each firing a number of torpedoes. Such co-ordination was virtually impossible before the introduction of reliable voice radio (and radar for night attacks).

Comparison with other navies

Only three navies built destroyers in large numbers during the war, Britain, Germany and the USA.[11] There were considerable differences in style between these navies but each seems to have been well satisfied with their pre-war designs and continued to build and develop them in considerable numbers. Towards the end of the war a number of bigger and more heavily armed destroyers were built, mainly in reaction to scare stories that the enemy was building such ships. These bigger ships, such as the 'Vs' and 'Ws', formed the basis for post-war designs.

British engineers had adopted oil firing before the

Ship	Endurance (miles)
Minos	3060
Milne	3710
Mastiff	2100

It may be interesting to look at the effects[7] of doubling the endurance of the 'M' class. Fuel and reserve feed water totalled 294 tons as designed but if this is doubled the ship will get bigger – a lot bigger. In fact the displacement goes up from 1103 tons to 1963 tons with large increases in hull and machinery weight and the fuel and reserve feed water to 840 tons (not just twice 294 as the ship is bigger). The bigger ship would be a better seaboat, the armament layout would be improved and even the crew might get a little more space, but it would be a costly change.

Effectiveness of destroyer torpedoes

British destroyers were intended primarily to protect the battle line from torpedo attack and, secondarily, to attack enemy battleships. These two roles were reversed for German destroyers. The only significant example of such attacks was at Jutland;[8] the figures speak for themselves.

war and moved to geared turbines early in the war, much improving endurance and sustainable speed. Even so, the need for even more endurance was recognised and fuel stowage was increased. Freeboard and flare were increased and the bridge moved aft to improve sea keeping. The greater size of the 'Vs' and 'Ws' made them even better sea boats.

At the outbreak of war, most German destroyers had the weak gun armament of three 88mm (22pdr), but in the majority this was changed to three 4.1in (38lb shell) by 1916. Initially, most of their ships were coal-burning but full oil-firing was introduced in wartime ships; there were no geared turbine ships. Jellicoe frequently complained (see Chapter 7) that German destroyers were better sea boats but he quotes no evidence to support this unlikely view. German sources suggest that their boats with a short forecastle and a well deck forward of the bridge were very wet.[12] Later boats were bigger and the forecastle was both longer and higher, but they were still inferior to their British contemporaries (see *Vivien*, Chapter 7)

In general, USN destroyers were bigger, partly to get the endurance needed for the Pacific but, more directly, because they were used as scouts for the battlefleet. Even in peacetime they would normally cruise at 20kts and would use full power frequently. The last pre-war ships of the '1000 ton' class mounted four 4in guns and twelve torpedo tubes. Speed was just under 30kts but their endurance was 2500 miles at 20kts. The hull form had a low resistance (in still water) and a model was made and tested at Haslar. USN reports suggests that their sea keeping was inferior to the earlier '750 ton' boats.[13] The wartime destroyers, the famous 'Flush

Deckers', were larger still, with the same armament and a trial speed of 35kts. Endurance was specified as 3400 miles at 20kts (5000 miles at 15kts) but much exceeded on trial by many ships.[14] USN reports of their ships operating with RN destroyers in the Irish Sea claim that the Americans were the better sea boats, but this comparison is presumably with the small, pre-war British ships. Certainly, no one in the Second World War had any doubts about the superiority of the 'V' & 'W's over the 'Towns'. The USN ships suffered from flimsy upperworks and very large turning circles, exacerbated by unreliable chain-operated steering gear.

Action damage is discussed in Chapter 11; in brief, they were all tough ships, hard to sink but easily disabled by a hit in the machinery spaces. The main steam pipes, just under the upper deck, were particularly vulnerable. The only solution would have been to arrange the machinery on the unit system with alternating boiler room, engine room, boiler room, engine room. This arrangement had not then been tried by any navy and would have meant a considerable increase in size.

Aircraft carriers and aviation

War, the first phase

On 11 August 1914, only one week after the outbreak of war, the RN requisitioned and later purchased three cross-channel steamers – *Riviera, Engadine* and *Empress*, apparently at the behest of Captain Murray Sueter, who had been appointed director of the Admiralty's newly-formed Air Department in November 1912. The first two were converted to simple seaplane carriers at Chatham and were in service at the

7. These changes have been estimated using what naval architects call the 'Weight Equation'. In fact, the change is too great for that method to be truly valid but the figures above are of the right order.

8. D K Brown, 'Torpedoes at Jutland', *Warship World* 5/2 (1995).

9. P Pugh has calculated that had all available torpedoes been fired, there might have been an additional twenty-three hits, thirty-two total. (Private communication)

10. Since gunnery fire-control had difficulty in dealing with times of flight measured in a few seconds, it is not surprising that torpedo running times of many minutes proved difficult.

11. Japan built a number right at the end of the war, generally similar to the 'R' class.

12. E Groner, *German Warships 1815-1945* (London 1990), pp173, 181.

13. N Friedman, *U S Destroyers* (Annapolis 1982), p33.

14. In the Second World War, British sources quote boats up to DD 185 as having 275 tons of oil giving 2000 miles at 10kts. Later boats with 390 tons had an endurance of 2900 miles at 10kts. A Hague, *The Town Class* (Kendal 1988).

Ben-my-Chree as a seaplane carrier. An aircraft of hers carried out the first successful air-launched torpedo attack. (Imperial War Museum: SP9950)

Campania after her second conversion in November 1915. The fore funnel was divided so that a longer and more steeply sloping flight deck could be fitted. (Imperial War Museum: SP114)

beginning of September, *Empress* following a month later. The 'conversion' consisted of building a canvas shelter at each end with handling booms for the aircraft and two or three 2pdr guns. One may assume that Chatham Dockyard were told to 'do it like *Hermes* but without the launching ramp'.

By the end of September one squadron of the RNAS was based on land in France tasked with attacking the German Zeppelin force. One army airship was destroyed in a raid on Dusseldorf on 8 October but the famous raid on the factory at Freidrichshaven caused no damage, although it did show the potential of strategic bombing and also demonstrated the enthusiasm of the Admiralty for its new arm. On Christmas Day 1914 the three converted steamers launched seven seaplanes against the airship sheds at Cuxhaven. Only three returned and there was no damage but it is deservedly

remembered as the first seaborne airstrike against a land target.[15]

The three steamers were further modified at Liverpool in 1915 with the fitting of a large, permanent hangar aft. An Isle of Man steamer, the *Ben-my-Chree*, had been given a similar modification earlier in the year, going to the Dardanelles later that year where one of her aircraft carried out the world's first aerial torpedo attack in August. She was sunk by Turkish artillery whilst at anchor at Castelorizo in January 1917, her stored aviation fuel burning furiously before sinking, a fire which was to influence all later British carrier designs (see under *Argus* below).

Campania[16]

The liner *Campania* was built for the Cunard line in 1883 and had already been sold for scrap when the

Campania sinking on 5 November 1918. She dragged her anchors and impaled herself, first on the bow of *Royal Oak* and then that of *Glorious*. (Author's copllection)

Admiralty purchased her for £32,500 as an armed merchant cruiser in November 1914. However, she completed as a seaplane carrier in April 1915 with a 120ft flying-off deck long on the forecastle. The deck sloped down very gently[17] and take-off was very difficult, so she usually hoisted her seaplanes onto the water for normal take-off at this stage of her career. Her speed of 18kts at best, with her worn-out machinery, just enabled her to operate with the fleet.

Her captain, O Schwann, another aviation enthusiast, reported that, despite her problems, she could still be the most promising aviation ship for the fleet. In November 1915 she was taken in hand for further modification at Cammell Laird. The fore funnel was split, port and starboard, to allow the flight deck to be increased to 200ft in length and it was given greater slope. Hangars for ten planes were provided under the aft end of the deck, the aircraft being hoisted up by derricks, and she could operate a kite balloon aft. She missed the battle of Jutland having failed to receive the sailing signal. By the end of 1916 she was worn out but she remained with the fleet, until in April 1918 she dragged her anchors in a gale and fell across the bows of *Royal Oak* and then *Glorious*, finally sinking. However, she had demonstarted the value of a fast aviation vessel operating with the fleet.

Furious

Furious was the third and most 'curious'[18] of Fisher's 'large light cruisers' and was nearing completion in March 1917 when it was decided to convert her to carry aircraft. The forward 18in turret was removed[19] and a sloped flying-off deck fitted with a hangar for five Sopwith Pups and three Short 184 seaplanes. She joined the fleet on 4 July 1917. Her speed of 31½kts was not far off the stalling speed of a Pup and on 2 August 1917 Squadron Commander E H Dunning flew onto the flying-off deck and was pulled from the sky by a team of handlers. He repeated this feat on 7 August but was killed when trying a third time. By November it was decided that she should be given landing-on deck aft and she was taken in hand by Armstrongs.

She emerged in March 1918 with a flight deck 300ft long in place of the after 18in turret. There was another hangar below this deck, increasing her aircraft complement to sixteen. Both hangars now had lifts and the two flight decks were connected by 11ft wide gangways, port and starboard. Longitudinal wires were supported just above the landing deck to engage with hooks on the Pups' skid undercarriage. Transverse wires attached to sandbags were intended to slow planes down and at the fore end a safety barrier of vertical ropes on a 'goalpost' prevented the planes from hitting the funnel. In fact, a safe landing was virtually impossible; of thirteen attempts, nine ended in a crash. The problem was the turbulent air flow behind the bridge, funnel and heavy tripod mast which was too much for the light, low-powered aircraft. One landing was made by an SSZ airship, but the ship was at rest at the time.

Furious was used operationally for the rest of the war but with no more landings. Her fighters shot down a German seaplane on 19 June and on 17 July she flew off

15. R D Layman, *The Cuxhaven Raid* (London 1985).

16. J M Maber, 'HMS *Campania* 1914-1918', *WARSHIP 26* (April 1983).

17. 15 minutes slope is often quoted, but photographs suggest it was more than this, though still insufficient.

18. It was said of these three ships '. . . they may be large and curious'.

19. It is believed that, though the forward turret was in place, the gun itself was never installed, though it was on the quayside ready. The barbette structure remained.

Furious in her first appearance. The forward 18in turret has been removed and a flight deck installed with a hangar below. (WSS)

In 1917-18 *Furious* was further modified. The after 18in turret was removed to make way for a landing deck. It was not a success; of thirteen attempted landings, nine were crashes. The problem was air turbulence behind the superstructure. However, on 17 July 1918 she flew off seven Camels which destroyed the airship sheds at Tondern together with two Zeppelins. (Author's collection)

a strike of seven Camels which destroyed the airship sheds at Tondern, together with two Zeppelins, the first really successful air strike from the sea.

Vindictive

This ship was laid down in 1917 as the cruiser *Cavendish* of the *Hawkins* class but during construction it was decided to convert her into an aircraft carrier. She was, in most respects, a smaller *Furious* with a flying-off deck forward and a landing deck aft and the original mast, bridge and funnels between. She retained four of her original 7.5in guns and attracted a great deal of attention as a hybrid gun and aviation ship. In fact, she was a failure and only one landing was ever made. She joined the Grand Fleet in October 1918, too late for operations. In 1919 she took twelve aircraft to the Baltic

but they normally operated from land bases. Some consideration was given to converting her to an 'island carrier' with a full flight deck, and a model was tested in the wind tunnel in 1918, but the plan was abandoned. In 1923 she was rebuilt as a cruiser, but retained her hangar with a catapult installed on top, the first catapult in a conventional warship.

The 1917 plan

In December 1916, Murray Sueter proposed an ambitious scheme for an attack on the German fleet at its anchorage using torpedo bombers.[20] This was developed during 1917 and formally submitted by Admiral Beatty, C-in-C Grand Fleet, in September 1917. It envisaged 120 aircraft flying in three waves from eight converted liners, supported by bombing from big flying

Vindictive was converted on similar lines to *Furious*. Only one landing was attempted and though this was successful, it was not repeated. She retained five 7.5in guns and attracted a lot of attention abroad as a 'hybrid' warship. (Author's collection)

Vindex, a later seaplane carrier; she carried five seaplanes and two landplanes. (Imperial War Museum: SP1452)

boats. This won support in the Admiralty but there was no way in which eight big, fast liners could be spared for conversion. As a first step it was decided to build four carriers with speeds of 24-25kts. Two would have full-length flight decks and carry fourteen planes and the smaller ones would only have a flying-off deck and carry eight planes. This scheme was changed at various times but one may see the *Hermes* and *Eagle*, discussed later, as the outcome of the bigger ships while the small ships became more cross-channel steamer conversions.

Small conversions

The last four conversions had a hangar aft for seaplanes and a launching platform forward for landplanes.

Aircraft carried

Ship	Seaplanes	Landplanes
Vindex	5	2
Manxman	4	4
Nairana	4	4
Pegasus	4	5

Pegasus was the last and best of these conversions and remained in service until 1931 though in reserve for much of the time.[21] One must also mention two ex-German prizes which carried seaplanes in the Eastern Mediterranean, two paddle steamers which briefly operated seaplane fighters in the Humber and even two seaplane carriers in the Caspian in 1918-19.[22] None of these were of interest as ships but further demonstrated the RN's enthusiasm for air power.

Argus, the first true aircraft carrier

At the outbreak of war, Beardmores were well advanced with building the liner *Conte Rosso* for the Italian Lloyd Sabaudo line. Various uses were considered for this ship including a scheme in 1915 to complete her as a seaplane carrier.[23] By the time she was purchased in August 1916 there were a number of alternative proposals for her layout. One was for a flush flightdeck ship put forward by Lieutenant R A Holmes, a naval architect for the Cunard line who had served in *Riviera* and was then in the Air Department. Smoke was to be discharged through long horizontal ducts to the stern and there was to be a ramp aft for seaplanes. In 1915 Flight Lieutenant H A Williamson[24] proposed a design with an island superstructure to starboard.[25]

When Narbeth started the real design he looked hard at both schemes, incorporating some features, but most of the style was his. The hangar was the central feature of the ship, 330ft long, 48ft clear width and 20ft clear height. The width was up to 68ft between frames, and the height was great enough for planes to be lifted by a gantry crane to move them along the hangar, above other aircraft parked there. The hangar was isolated from the rest of the ship by air locks and it was subdivided by four fire-resistant roller curtains. There was a steel roller door at the aft end so that seaplanes could be embarked over the quarterdeck by two cranes. These fire precautions were part of the lesson from the sinking of the *Ben-my-Chree* and were to be a feature of all future British carrier designs. Good ventilation was installed to disperse petrol fumes and the hangar deck was given steel non-skid strips rather than planking which might become soaked in oil and petrol. Large sand boxes and numerous Pyrene extinguishers were fitted at gallery level for firefighting.

Care, too, was taken over the safe stowage of petrol; bulk storage was ruled out as it was thought that it would be impossible to ensure that pipe joints did not leak. The 4000 two-gallon cans were stored in a separate hold space forward which was separately ventilated and

20. The design of the Sopwith Cuckoo to carry an 18in torpedo weighing 1000lbs (170lb warhead) had just started at Sueter's instigation.

21. G E Livock, *To the Ends of the Air* (London HMSO, 1973).

22. A forthcoming book by R D Layman describes the Caspian operations in detail.

23. No details of this scheme have been found but it may be assumed that she would have been similar to *Campania*.

24. R D Layman, 'Hugh Williamson and the Creation of the Aircraft Carrier'.

25. See Layman, *Before the Aircraft Carrier*, for discussion of why the island was to be to starboard. It is interesting that the first wind tunnel models with a single island have it to port. DNC records are clear that pilots had already become accustomed to abort a landing, even on a field, by turning to port as with a rotary engine it was much easier to turn that way.

was isolated from the rest of the ships by void spaces. The cans were taken to the flight deck on a two-stage lift with a fire barrier half way up. Even in this first carrier attention to the safety of petrol was taken very seriously. A continuing preoccupation with the subject accounted, on the one hand for the small number of serious fires in British carriers but, on the other, for their rather limited stowage for aircraft fuel.

The original liner sides of *Argus* were carried up to the level of the hangar roof which became the strength deck, another feature perpetuated in most later British designs. The flight deck was supported 14ft 6in above the hangar on a light lattice structure and had expansion joints to ensure that it did not carry longitudinal bending loads. There seem to have been some hope that air could flow through this space, preventing eddies at the aft end but it was quite congested and it is unlikely that much air went that way.

Boiler smoke was carried away in two large ducts between hangar and deck. Each duct was surrounded by an outer annulus through which cool air was blown and there were fans in the exhaust ducts themselves to pre-

vent a backdraught in a following wind. It was not a very successful scheme; even with the cooling air and lagging the ducts got very hot, and the hot gases were discharged just under the spot where aircraft needed undisturbed air for touchdown.

Conte Rosso had been designed for a maximum speed of 19½kts but the Admiralty would have preferred 25kts so her original five double-ended and four single-ended boilers were increased to six of each, oil fired (coal dust had caused wear in the engines of *Campania*'s planes). These delivered 21,376shp on trial for a speed of 20½kts, the most that could be expected. She was given newish boilers, ex-destroyer, in 1936.

The initial design had two small superstructures, port and starboard, but wind tunnel tests from November 1916 showed that there would be serious turbulence in the landing area. These were amongst the earliest wind tunnel tests ever carried out on other than aircraft and when they had been validated by the failure of *Furious'* deck, the design was changed to a flush deck. The photo below shows the starboard superstructure still on the deck but moved inboard while the port structure is on

Argus fitting out. She was intended to have two islands, port and starboard. The starboard one is on the flight deck with lifting beams attached; a very early example of prefabrication by Beardmore. The port island appears to be on the quayside. (Author's collection)

the quayside. It seems that they had been prefabricated and lifted on (and off) in one piece, a very early example of such a technique, reflecting on Beardmore's reputation for new technology. Control positions were provided in galleries either side of the flight deck, forward, but when flying was not taking place, a retractable chart house was raised on a hydraulic ram at the fore end of the deck.

She completed with two lifts, both of which had to be forward of the ducts. The after one was of little use and was soon fixed shut. The remaining lift was 30ft x 36ft so that during the Second World War *Argus* was the only carrier which could take fixed-wing Seafires into her hangar! She commissioned on 14 September 1918 and the first landings were made on 24 September. Within two days twenty-one landings with different aircraft had been completed without incident. Narbeth was still attracted by Williamson's idea of an island superstructure, and a wood and canvas mock-up was fitted to *Argus* and tried in early October. There were no problems; if anything, pilots preferred the island as it helped them to judge their height. With only one island, the wind can be put slightly off the bow so that the turbulence is shed outboard but with two there will always be interference. These trials led to the decision to complete *Eagle* and *Hermes* with islands.

Argus embarked her squadron of Sopwith Cuckoo torpedo bombers on 10 October and began to work up for an attack on the German fleet, but the war ended before they were ready. She remained an operational carrier until 1930 when she went into reserve. She had a big refit in 1936-8 and re-emerged to operate 'Queen Bees', radio-controlled Tiger Moths for anti-aircraft gunnery practice. During the Second World War she served mainly as an aircraft transport, but was pressed into active service when necessary. It cannot be emphasised too strongly that she was the only true carrier to operate during the war – or for some time after – and there are still people who claim the Admiralty of the day was opposed to aircraft.

Argus had a large, high and unobstructed hangar with a big lift. She was the only Second World War carrier able to strike down fighters with non-folding wings – Hurricanes in this photo. (Author's collection)

Very soon after completion *Argus* was given a wood and canvas mock-up funnel and island for trials. Pilots found no difficulty, if anything, the island helped them to judge their height. (R D Layman)

Wind Tunnel Experiments

In November 1916 a series of wind tunnel experiments were carried out on various carrier arrangements. These must have been amongst the first such experiments other than on aircraft showing how progressive was the carrier team, naval and constructor. A further series took place in January 1918 in an attempt to improve conditions on *Furious*. (All photos National Maritime Institute)

The original style for *Argus*. She would have had two islands port and starboard but the experiments showed that the eddies from one of the islands would make landing dangerous. This test also showed that Beardmore's ingenious 1912 design was impractical.

The first thought for *Furious* was a small bridge and a streamlined funnel but it was unsuccessful.

A two-island scheme also failed.

A single island, originally to port, was encouraging. The island was moved to starboard as aircraft with rotary engines could turn more easily to port.

Furious with a large starboard island. Though this scheme was not adopted, it probably formed the basis for *Glorious*.

A proposal for *Vindictive* with a starboard island and retaining five 7.5in guns.

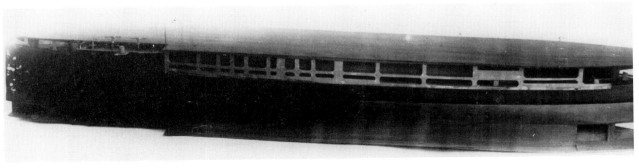

Eagle was tried without an island. Since there is no provision for smoke ducts, this cannot have been a serious project but for comparison with the scheme adopted.

Hermes

Hermes was ordered from Armstrong on 14 July 1917 as a carrier of 10,000 tons.[26] Her intended air weapon load was 12 100lb bombs, 120 65lb bombs, 102 16lb bombs and 8 18in torpedoes, each weighing 1000lb. She was also to carry 200 rockets and 500 explosive darts. It is often forgotten that a carrier has to stow a numerous and varied stock of aircraft weapons. There was even a suggestion that she should be designed so that she could be rebuilt as a cruiser should she not succeed as a carrier.

Work was stopped at the hangar deck in April 1918 as a major redesign of the upper works was in hand. Building restarted in June only to stop again at the armistice pending trials of *Argus* and *Eagle*. Rutland, now a major in the RAF, wrote an influential paper in 1918 pointing out the need for a carrier to have a substantial margin of speed over the battlefleet (then capable of 21kts) and suggested 26-27kts at least. *Hermes* could make 26.2kts and was thought acceptable. She was towed to Devonport in 1920 and completed in 1924.

Hermes' flight deck was the strength deck with the sides taking the shear forces. This meant that openings in the side were restricted in size, number and position. At the bow, this worked to advantage with unbroken sides, flaring continuously to the flight deck which was only 32ft above the design waterline. However, Admiral Beatty was keen on a heavy gun armament which was more difficult to reconcile. Various armaments were considered with up to eleven 6in but she completed with six 5.5in and three 4in AA.[27] She had a very tall island topped by a heavy tripod carrying her gunnery control top which made her hard to control in a strong wind. This problem was exacerbated by the fact that she trimmed by the bow with a full load of fuel. She also heeled 4° to port, presumably because the designers had over-compensated for the weight of the starboard island.[28] Her stability was poor and, like most early carriers, the boiler room intakes were rather low, much reducing her effective range of stability. Seaplanes could be embarked over the quarter deck and taken into the hangar through a shuttered door or up to flight deck on the after lift which worked outside the hangar. She was always too small to be an effective carrier.

Eagle

She was commenced by Armstrong as the Chilean battleship *Almirante Cochrane* but work was stopped when war came. She was requisitioned in 1918 for conversion to an aircraft carrier, suffering the usual frequent design changes as experience was gained both at sea and in the wind tunnel. The details of her structural design are uncertain but the most likely is that the flight deck (hangar roof) was the strength deck, with the hangar sides carrying the shear forces.

There was still doubt over the viability of the island style so she was sent to sea for preliminary trials in 1920 while incomplete. She had only one funnel, was limited to 15kts and the masts were not fitted. One hundred and forty-three landings were made with only a few minor incidents even though some were deliberately carried out in bad weather. Many of the trials were devoted to developing an effective arrester gear.

Further wind tunnel tests were carried out in parallel, in an attempt to improve the air flow round the island. Both tests and ship trials showed that it was important to keep the wind directly ahead since even a few degrees off would cause eddies from the edges of the deck. As with *Hermes*, the island was dominated by a heavy tripod mast carrying the controls for her nine 6in guns, then thought essential. She was intended to have twelve torpedo tubes for self defence but these were deleted from the design at a late stage (see next section).

The original intention was to stow petrol in cans, but she completed with a bulk stowage for 5100 gallons (later increased to 14,000 gallons) in special tanks separated from the main structure and surrounded by a coffer dam. She completed with four steel shutter fire curtains in the hangar and, in 1929, she had a salt water spray fitted to the hangar. In 1932 a foam firefighting system was fitted to the weather deck. Weapon stowage was still a problem and by 1939 her 23 aircraft needed 27 18in Mk XII torpedoes, 48 500lb SAP, 342 250lb bombs (SAP and 'B'), 130 100lb AS, and 360 20lb bombs anti-personnel with 54 depth charges and 24 mines.

Balloons at sea

Early attempts to use balloons at sea had been with spherical balloons which could not be towed and were difficult to use in winds. By 1915 kite balloons were available and the merchant ship *Manica* was hurriedly adapted to support a kite balloon for spotting in the Dardanelles. She was given a hydrogen generator and a compressor to fill bottles at 1800 lbs/in². She had stores and workshops and the fore deck was cleared to operate a kite balloon. She arrived in April 1915, prior to the landings, and proved very useful for gunnery spotting. During May it was decided that it was unwise to place the hydrogen generator within range of enemy guns and the plant was transferred to the tug *Rescue*. Later, in 1916, she was further modified, having a clear 92ft x 30ft opening in the deck forward so that an inflated balloon could be safely stowed below deck. Four other merchant ships were converted in a generally similar fashion but the later ones benefited from experience.[29]

Attempts to tow kite balloons at fleet speed showed a number of difficult problems. The strain on the tow rope was great, it sloped considerably and the vibration caused rapid wear on both cable and envelope. The cable had to have an insulated core for the telephone. The balloon became unstable when close to the water, making landing very dangerous. Above all, sickness of

26. There were innumerable design changes and the initial concept may even have been for a seaplane carrier. See N Friedman, *British Carrier Aviation* (London 1988), pp63 et seq.

27. Mostly taking account of guns already in store (see Friedman, *British Carrier Aviation*, p73).

28. The transverse balance is very difficult in an asymmetric ship. I had to attempt it in the 'Tribal' class frigates with their unusual machinery layout.

29. *Hector, Canning, Menelaus, City of Oxford*. See *Records of Warship Construction during the War 1914-1918*. DNC Department, for a very detailed account.

The balloon ship *Menelaus* manoeuvring her kite balloon. (Imperial War Museum: SP1928)

the observers was a major problem. Trials using *Engadine* and *Campania* gradually reduced these problems and by the summer of 1916 fitting in the fleet began with the battleship *Hercules*. By the war's end eighteen battleships, three battlecruisers and seven light cruisers had been fitted to operate balloons. The balloons were inflated ashore, taken to the ship on a lighter and towed at any convenient height. When needed to operate, the balloon would be hauled down to the quarterdeck for the observer to board.

From May 1917 balloons were fitted to destroyers, sloops etc, to spot for submarines and mines, the destroyer *Patriot* scoring the first balloon-assisted submarine sinking in July 1917. By the end of the war balloons were operated from thirty-eight destroyers, sixty-five sloops, twenty-six P boats, four armed boarding

Kite balloons were also operated from some destroyers after 1917. (Courtesy Ross Gillett)

Barham. Flying-off platforms are visible on the roof of B and X turrets. She would probably have carried one two-seater and one single-seater aircraft. The Grand Fleet battleships and cruisers carried 103 aircraft at the end of the war. (Author's collection)

vessels, two river gunboats and six other vessels, together with eleven USN ships. The fitting and operation of balloons from 180 ships was a great achievement.

Aeroplanes in the Fleet

Both aviation pioneers and admirals felt the need for fighting ships to carry their own aircraft as well as those borne in carriers. Initially, thoughts turned to seaplanes but it was soon realised that sea state limited the times when they could take off from the water, and even when it was possible, the ships would be hampered by the slow launch and recovery of seaplanes. Furthermore, the weight and drag of floats meant that a launching platform on board would need to be very long. Trials in the summer of 1911 with an aeroplane flying off *Vindex* and a seaplane from *Campania* showed the advantage of the aeroplane, which also had the advantage of speed and height climbing once airborne.

In June 1917 a platform was built above the forward gun of the cruiser *Yarmouth*, giving a 20ft run and trials showed that it was practicable, though there was some interference with the forward gun.[30] Soon afterwards, a Pup took off from this platform and shot down a shadowing Zeppelin. Encouraged by this success, three other cruisers were so fitted and *Yarmouth*'s platform altered so that one ship in each Grand Fleet cruiser squadron had a plane. However, these fixed platforms meant the ship had to steam into the wind for take-off. Therefore, in 1917 a scheme was developed for a revolving platform on the forecastle which could be turned into the relative wind. Trials in *Sydney* in November were very successful and a number of ships were fitted with similar platforms, including some which had previously had fixed platforms. The later light cruisers, however, with superfiring guns on the forecastle, could not have this style of platform. It was decided to try a revolving platform abaft the funnels and train as near the wind as possible. To everyone's surprise, it was found possible to take off with the wind up to 20° off the axis.

In 1918 a design was prepared to incorporate a hangar in the bridge structure of 'C' and 'D' class cruisers with a short platform over the gun. This was not found satisfactory as it interfered both with the bridge layout and gun arcs and the ship had to steam into the wind for take-off. Two 'Ds' and one 'C' completed with hangars, but they were little used.

It was thought at first that it would not be possible to fit platforms to capital ships as they could not be expected to turn out of line for a take-off, ruling out fixed platforms. No interference with gunfire was acceptable. However, it was realised that a platform on the roof of a turret could be rotated into the relative wind and would not interfere with the working of the guns. A platform was fitted to B turret of *Repulse* and in October 1917 a Pup successfully took off. A week later a take-off was made from the after turret. It was then decided that all battlecruisers should have a fighter for anti-Zeppelin work.

Early trials with two-seater aircraft were unsatisfactory, but on 4 April 1918 a successful trial was made from *Australia*. This led to the decision that battlecruisers should carry a two-seater forward and a fighter aft. When it was seen that these arrangements did not interfere with the working of the guns it was decided to fit battleships with similar platforms. By the end of the war the eleven battlecruisers had eleven fighters and six two seaters.[31] The battleships had forty-nine fighters and seventeen two-seaters with sixteen more in light cruisers;[32] it is said that there was a total of 103 planes with the Grand Fleet. Some other ships had aircraft including monitors, so that the total at sea was about 150, excluding the carriers.

In 1916 a steam hopper was purchased for trials of an aircraft catapult and named *Slinger*. Several successful launches were made off the Isle of Grain, but work was abandoned and *Slinger* sold in 1919 since the simple launching platform appeared then to be all that was needed.

Seaplane towing lighters

At the end of September 1916 Commander Porte suggested that the effective range of his Large America flying boats could be extended by carrying them out into the North Sea on lighters capable of being towed behind a destroyer at speeds of up to 25kts. There was to be a large ballast tank aft which would submerge the stern and allow the flying boat, which weighed 4½ tons, to be winched in or out of the sea. The first form tried had a straight flare to a knuckle but it threw up too much water. A modified form with concave flare suggested by Edmund Froude at the Admiralty Experiment Works cured the problem. Four prototypes were built by Thornycroft at Chiswick and trials of the first in June 1917 were very successful.[33] In later trials the lighter was successfully towed at speeds up to 32kts in calm water and twenty more were ordered, later increased to fifty, from the Government yard at Richborough (fourteen cancelled when the war ended).

Seaplane lighter particulars

Displacement: 24 tons (*c*30 tons loaded)
Length: 58ft
Beam: 16ft
Maximum draught (without flying boat): 3ft

In the summer of 1918 it was decided to fit twelve of these lighters with a wooden flying-off platform for Camel fighters. This was very successful (one Zeppelin destroyed).

In 1917 two 60ft lighters were ordered in the form of floating docks to house the big H8 flying boats. They could be towed in calm water to ports with no facilities for such aircraft. Twelve more were ordered later housing additional accommodation and equipment, which brought the length up to 70ft.

The end of the RNAS

The RNAS was a victim of its own success. By 1918 it had some 103 airships,[34] 2000 aeroplanes, 650 seaplanes, 150 flying boats and 120 balloons, with 100 shore bases and 55,000 men. The carriers have been described but there were two more building and further plans. The RNAS operated a considerable number of squadrons on the Western Front and it was thought, probably unjustly, that they had a near-monopoly of the best aircraft builders.[35] The RNAS was also tasked with protecting the UK from air raids in which it had not been very successful.

A committee was set up in 1917 under General Smuts to consider the future of air power and they recommended that the RNAS be combined with the RFC to form the RAF. Most of the best RNAS officers transferred to the new service, taking their skill and enthusiasm with them, leaving the Navy short of flying experience for a generation. The formation of the RAF may – or may not – have been justified, but the way in which it was done was certainly wrong and left the Navy without proper air support up to, and during, the Second World War.

Britain leads the world

Drawings of all British carriers were passed to the USN either through Stanley Goodall RCNC, our man in Washington, or Constructor McBride, the USN representative in London. Goodall wrote a lengthy paper outlining British views in 1917.

> The provision of a ship of this type for the US Navy is entirely a matter for those responsible for directing policy, but British experience in the present war shows that such a type of ship is essential for the British Navy. Air fighting has become a feature of naval operations, and tactical movements of a fleet before an engagement opens will most probably be governed by information obtained from air scouts . . . A series of fights between opposing aircraft will most likely be a preliminary to a fleet action. A fleet should therefore be attended by reconnaissance machines and fighting machines . . . an armament of four 4in AA guns is insufficient, and a larger number of heavier guns – preferably 6in – should be carried, together with one or two AA guns. Although such a ship should not by any means be regarded as a fighting ship, it should be sufficiently powerfully armoured to be able to brush aside light vessels of the enemy, so that its planes can be flown off in comparatively advanced positions.
>
> A torpedo armament of about 12 upper deck torpedo tubes should be provided [as in *Eagle* and *Furious* at early design stage] [36] . . . Torpedo protection is considered essential, as the ship would be a valuable unit operating most probably in the vicinity of enemy submarines. Side protection should be as good as that of light cruisers . . . the speed proposed – namely 30 knots – is considered a minimum. It should be equal to that of scouting forces with which the ship would work, and in view of the 35 knot speed of the US battlecruisers and scout cruisers, it is for consideration whether a higher speed than 30 knots should not be provided . . .

Goodall was able to help the Bureau of Construction and Repair with the preliminary studies for a new carrier of 22,000 tons, which would lead to the conversion of the battlecruisers *Lexington* and *Saratoga*. The first Japanese carrier, *Hosho*, was based on drawings of *Argus* sent to Admiral Iida in 1918 whilst the conversions of *Akagi* and *Kaga* were based on *Furious*. Drawings of *Eagle* were passed to France (via Cdr Boris) in 1919 and formed the basis for the *Bearn*.

30. Most of the trials mentioned in this section were carried out by Flight-Commander Rutland, the only flyer at Jutland.

31. Including *Courageous* and *Glorious*.

32. Numbers were continually varying, particularly in cruisers, where the installation of an extra 6in gun might mean the loss of the platform. See *Records of Naval Construction*.

33. One of these survives (1997) on the Thames as a lighter and will probably be moved to the Fleet Air Arm Museum.

34. Though outside the scope of this book, it should be noted that the RN built 225 airships during the war. After the war, the RAF scrapped the cheap and effective non-rigid airships and pursued the expensive failure of the rigid craft. See Patrick Abbott, *The British Airship at War 1914-18* (Lavenham 1989).

35. Sopwith was the best once the Royal Aircraft Factory closed and he built for the RFC as well.

36. Goodall was even to suggest a heavy torpedo armament in the early studies which led to the Second World War light fleet carriers.

J 5 after her transfer to the
Royal Australian Navy. Note the
4in gun, a later modification.
The 'J' class were an attempt to
produce a fast diesel submarine
but even with three shafts they
could only make 19½kts. (WSS)

THE SUBMARINE DEVELOPMENT COM-
MITTEE of 1915[1] considered six types of submarine which they thought might be required:
(1) Coastal; (2) Patrol; (3) Fleet; (4) Cruiser; (5)
Minelaying; and (6) Monitor. They thought that existing
designs for coastal ('F' and 'V'), patrol ('E') and
minelaying (Modified 'E') boats were satisfactory and
should be continued. Since there were hardly any
enemy merchant ships at sea, there was no need for a
cruiser submarine at that time. The fleet submarine
requirement developed into the 'J' and 'K' classes, discussed below, and the monitor, indirectly, into the 'M'
class.

Fleet submarines

The 'J' class

The C-in-C, Grand Fleet believed (false) reports that
the Germans had built submarines with a surface speed
of 22kts and which could accompany the High Seas
Fleet at sea, and wanted similar vessels. In the light of
other work, Vickers were reluctant to attempt the development of an entirely new engine of much greater
power. They suggested a 12-cylinder variant of the 8-
cylinder diesel engine of the 'E' class, developing
1200bhp. DNC designed a three-shaft submarine, but
the expected surface speed was only 19½kts. The elec-

In *J 7*, the last of the class, the
control room was moved
further aft and, with it, the
conning tower. The reason for
this change is not known.
(Imperial War Museum:
SP3094)

tric motors for submerged propulsion were fitted on the wing shafts only. A hull form, based on that of a light cruiser, was developed by Edmund Froude at Haslar. This form (known as UR), also used in the 'K' class, remains even today the best form ever tested for its speed-length ratio.

The bow had to be raised to permit high speed in bad weather but once this was done the class performed well. They mounted four bow and two broadside torpedo tubes, all 18in. A new mechanism which linked the bow door and the outer, fairing shutter was fitted and used in all later submarines. However, they had no clear role; they were too slow to operate with the fleet and unnecessarily fast, big and expensive for patrol submarines. Five were completed to the original design and one to a modified design. The five survivors were transferred to Australia at the end of the war and were soon disposed of in post-war economies. Several were scuttled in Port Phillip Bay, Melbourne, where their remains may still be seen.

The 'K' class

In the spring of 1913, the DNC had prepared the design of a large, fast, steam-driven submarine of 1700 tons, length 338ft and a speed of 24kts.[2] After consideration it was decided to await results of *Nautilus* and *Swordfish* before moving to an even bigger and faster submarine with steam propulsion. In 1915, when it was apparent that the 'J' class would fall well short of the desired performance, this design was re-examined in comparison with a Vickers design. The Admiralty design was selected and passed to Vickers for working drawings to be prepared and twenty-one boats were ordered in August 1915 at a cost of £340,000 each (four later cancelled).

During development a number of important changes were made; the torpedoes were changed from 21in to 18in to speed production. They completed with four bow tubes, two on either beam and a twin revolving unit in the superstructure for use at night (this was soon removed as it was too close to the water and often damaged). They were given two 4in[3] and one 3in AA gun, and an 800bhp diesel generator[4] was fitted. These changes brought the displacement to 1980 tons (surfaced), 2566 tons (submerged).

They were a partial double-hull design with a design reserve of buoyancy of 32.5 per cent. The steam machinery had a far heavier fuel consumption than diesels – at full power the steam plant burnt 1.25lbs/shp/hr compared with 0.43lbs/shp/hr for diesels. To improve endurance the two amidships ballast tanks either side were fitted to carry about 100 tons of oil.[5] Running on the surface with these tanks full cost about ½kt of speed due to the increased draught. There were eight bulkheads (nine compartments) tested to 35lbs/in^2 (70ft).

It was clear from the start that there would be problems with this class of which their sheer size would be the most obvious. Their great length made control difficult and this was accentuated by the flat surface of much of the casing and superstructure. If the boat developed a bow-down angle, water forces acting on this flat surface would tend to increase the angle. The safe diving depth was thought to be 200ft but it could not be calculated with precision. However, with a length of 339ft even a 10° angle would cause a 59ft difference in depth between bow and stern (30° would give 170ft difference).

Telemotor systems were in their infancy, yet the size of the 'K' class boats meant they had to have a large number of trimming and diving tanks, all hydraulically operated from the control room; there were problems in early boats with oil that went waxy at low temperatures. The large openings for the funnels had a double closure; the trunk from the pressure hull to the top of the superstructure was watertight with a hatch top and bottom. The mechanism for swinging-down the funnels was similar to that used by Scotts in the *Swordfish* and was probably designed by them.[6]

1. Members were the Third Sea Lord, Chief of Staff, DNO, Commodore (S), DNC and Mr A W Johns RCNC.

2. This design was quite detailed and model tests had been run at AEW, Haslar (Form UR).

3. The DNC history says that *K 17* was intended to mount two 5.5in. Campbell, based on Priddy's Hard records, says that eleven 5.5in were allocated for *K 15* onwards. *K 17* was the only boat to carry this gun and she carried one only, initially No 38 changed after 3 weeks to No 46 which was mounted when she sank.

4. The original proposal was for this engine to drive a third shaft but it was realised that it was more economical to use it through electric motors on the main shaft.

5. External fuel tanks of rivetted construction are always prone to leak.

6. A N Harrison, *The Development of H M Submarines from Holland No 1 to Porpoise 1930* (BR 3043). HMSO (for DNC), 1979. (Later referenced as Harrison, BR 3043)

The size and length (330ft) of the steam-driven 'K' class is clear in this picture of *K 2*. (Imperial War Museum: SP2765)

The 'K' class's freeboard
forward was inadequate as
shown in this photo of *K 3* at
sea in only moderate weather.
The forward gun was
frequently unusable and the
bridge windows were
damaged. (Imperial War
Museum: SP2737)

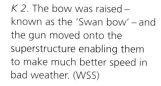

K 3 was the first to complete in May 1916 (just before Jutland) and was formally commissioned in August. Her trials showed that she achieved all the performance requirements, but revealed a number of problems, of which the most serious was the excessive temperature in the boiler room, later reduced by bigger fans but remaining a problem. Steaming into a head sea she broke the glass windows of the wheelhouse and damaged the structure. Thicker glass was a palliative but experience in service showed that seaworthiness on the surface was a more fundamental problem.

The freeboard at the bow was too low and when steaming fast into a head sea, water pressure would force the bow down, making matters worse. The cure was to fit a large buoyancy space called the swan bow.[7] It was also necessary to raise the forward gun onto the superstructure. There was an even more embarrassing and potentially dangerous problem in that seawater could get down the funnels and put the boiler fires out, though this seems to have happened most often in following seas. The oil fuel was mainly stowed internally in tanks which were automatically compensated with sea water admitted to minimise the change of displacement as fuel was burnt. This exposed the tank structure

K 2. The bow was raised –
known as the 'Swan bow' – and
the gun moved onto the
superstructure enabling them
to make much better speed in
bad weather. (WSS)

to sea pressure and there were many complaints that rivets were loosened in the crown, allowing oil to leak into the mess decks.[8]

The 'K' class had an unfortunate record of disasters, sometimes exaggerated. These will be examined to see to what extent these were due to their design.

K 1 was lost following collision with *K 4* in 1917.
K 4 was sunk in collision off May Island in January 1918.
K 5 was lost from unknown causes on exercises in 1921.
K 13 was lost on trials in the Gareloch during 1917 when an intake failed to shut.
K 15 was lost in Portsmouth in 1921.
K 17 was sunk in collision off May Island in January 1918.

The loss of *K 1* and the two off May Island may be seen as a likely consequence of operating in close company with long, unmanoeuvrable boats which were low in the water and not easy to see. There is a suspicion, but no proof, that *K 5* sank due to loss of control and exceeding her safe depth. There is evidence that the hull in the region of the control room collapsed. The loss of *K 13* was not only notorious but the accident which occured had almost been expected. It is still not clear how she managed to dive with a boiler room intake valve open; the engineer officer was suspicious of this valve and a main object of the fatal dive was to check it, but there seems to have been no attempt to ensure it really was shut before diving. There were many minor accidents such as electrical fires, flash-backs etc.

There are two distinct aspects to the discussion of the 'K' class: was the requirement for a fleet submarine sensible? and was the technical solution correct? Most modern writers and submarine staff officers would think that the requirement was wrong[9] but there was a strong body of supporters at the time.[10] Even as late as 1929 the *Thames* class were influenced by the same

operational concept and subject to the same limitations of British diesel technology. Given the requirement to operate with the fleet, there was, in 1915, no alternative to steam turbine machinery and most of the real problems were then inevitable. It would seem that more thought should have been given to the risk of collision with routes kept well separated to avoid disasters like May Island. Co-ordinated torpedo attacks were subject to the same difficulties as discussed under destroyers in Chapter 8.

Control theory hardly existed in 1915, was developed in the aircraft world in the 1920s and 1930s and, though there was awareness of its application to submarines from 1930 at least, it was not really in a state to be used for submarines until after the Second World War. In these circumstances, it is perhaps surprising that the 'Ks' handled as well as they did. There was always a desire to reduce the silhouette of all types of torpedo vessels and inadequate freeboard was a frequent consequence.

In general the complex operation of preparing a 'K' class submarine for diving was well thought-through. It was usually taken at a deliberate pace with a time to dive of about 5 minutes. This allowed time for the captain to walk along the superstructure and check that the funnels were securely housed. The fastest time claimed was 3 min 25 sec by *K 8*.

Harrison quotes a number of comments on the behaviour of the three 'Ks' which took part in the 1925 manoeuvres, together with the later *K 26*.

Hull structure weak, said to be a consequence of relative old age on rushed wartime construction.
Torpedo tube bow doors weak; an old complaint.
External fuel tank arrangements poor.

Poor habitability.
Unreliable generators.
18in tubes when most submarines had 21in.
K 12 had a 36ft periscope which made depth keeping in a seaway much easier than in the boats with a 30ft periscope.

Four much improved 'Ks' were ordered in October 1917, but three were cancelled and only *K 26* was completed, in a leisurely fashion, in 1923. She had six 21in bow tubes, retaining the 18in beam tubes. Her casing was 3ft higher, on which were mounted three 4in guns and the extra height almost cured the problem of water in the boiler room. She had much more internal ballast and more oil carried externally. The re-arrangement of ballast tanks enabled her to dive faster; Keyes quotes 3 min 12sec to 80ft.[11] The increased displacement led to a ½kt loss of speed. She seems to have been a great improvement over the early classes and remained in service until 1931. The earlier 'Ks' went at the same time, as their size bought up too much of the Treaty allocation of submarine tonnage.

Before the war, it was customary to build the first of a new class of submarine at least a year ahead of the follow-on boats so that any problems could be identified and cured for the later ones. In the light of the novelty of the 'Ks', one or two only should have been ordered initially and, with experience, later boats, if any, could have been much better on the style of *K 26*. The author is generally opposed to prototypes which are all too often an excuse for procrastination, but it could be justified for such a novel submarine. Plans for an even larger, 30kt steam submarine were prepared but it was not ordered.

K 26 was a much improved design eliminating most of the problems of the earlier 'Ks'. (WSS)

7. As in the earlier 'J' class and later in the 'A' class at the end of the Second World War.

8. D Everitt, *The K Boats* (London 1963), p76.

9. R Compton-Hall, *Monsters and Midgets* (Poole 1985). We were briefly shipmates in *Tabard* in 1951.

10. Had they completed only a few months earlier and a flotilla met the High Seas Fleet on 1 June 1916 the verdict could have been very different.

11. Sir Roger Keyes, *Naval Memoirs* (London 1934).

The 'H' classes

The background to the purchase of these submarines is extremely complicated[12] and can only be outlined here. Fisher was worried about the slow delivery rate of new submarines and was delighted when Charles M Schwab of Bethlehem Steel offered to build twenty in the USA. The price was to be $500,000 each and the first four would be delivered in 5½ months. President Wilson objected that it infringed US neutrality and after various discussions it was decided that the first ten boats would be built in the Canadian Vickers yard at Montreal. To satisfy US law the hulls had to be erected outside the USA, there was to be no fabrication beyond the preliminary stage within the USA and materials exported must

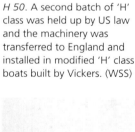

H 50. A second batch of 'H' class was held up by US law and the machinery was transferred to England and installed in modified 'H' class boats built by Vickers. (WSS)

require additional work. This revised schedule brought the price to $600,000, about double the cost of an 'E' class. Schwab and his company did well out of this since the cost to the USN of a similar boat was $491,000.[13]

The contract was signed in December 1914, the first keel was laid in January 1915, launched in April and all ten sailed for the UK that summer. The remaining ten were to be built in the USA and a stricter interpretation of the law meant that none reached the RN.[14] They were similar to the USN *Seawolf* class (nine boats) and others were built for Russia and Italy, while Holland acquired the British *H 6* which grounded off the Texel in 1916. Altogether seventy-two similar boats were built.

They were conventional single-hull boats, well designed and built, of much the same size as the 'F' and

'V' classes. The engines were much admired, powerful for their size and reliable. They were the first RN submarines to enter service with a battery tank; remote from the conning tower, this greatly reduced the chance of seawater entering the battery and generating chlorine. Their nominal diving depth was 200ft but the basis for calculation is not known. They carried four 18in torpedo tubes in the bow.

Though rather small, they were well liked and in January 1917 Vickers were asked to build twelve improved versions, and in June a further twenty-two were ordered from various builders. Many were cancelled and only a total of twenty-two of the thirty-four ordered were completed. The main engines, motors and other fittings for the first batch came from the USA, probably already assembled for the second ten of the original order. The later boats had British-built replicas of this machinery. They were a bit longer and the submerged displacement went up from 434 to 503 tons. The main difference was that the British built 'Hs' had four 21in torpedo tubes. Some survived into the Second World War. As with all single-hull designs, surface stability was marginal. In particular, they were unstable with the battery removed and hence changing the battery whilst afloat required very careful ballasting!

The 'R' class

In March 1917 DNC submitted a design for a small submarine with high underwater speed as a submarine hunter. This was then not approved but later in the year Commodore (S) suggested that the design be completed and it was then approved and twelve boats were ordered in October. The final design had one H class engine,[15] which gave them a surface speed of 9.5kts. A 1200hp motor drove a single screw at the extreme aft end giving a design speed of 15kts submerged. Measurement of submerged speed was very difficult and was read off the log, calibrated on the surface. Raising the periscope reduced speed by about 1kt.[16] Reports clearly state that 15kts was achieved on trial at the '1 hour rate' of battery discharge and give 12.5kts at 1.8 hours as the operational speed.

Control was going to be a problem; the safe depth was 250ft and with a 30° bow-down angle would be exceeded in 20 seconds. Even at 10° it would only take 57 seconds to exceed 250ft. The initial design appears to have had hydroplanes amidships as well as fore and aft. The centre set would not have been very effective and were never fitted. Two bow ballast tanks were fitted right forward and when these were blown, the ship had a considerable trim by the stern. This was used on the surface to stop the bow plunging, but could have given a rapid change of trim when submerged.

The 'R' class were single-hull boats with a considerable reserve of buoyancy – 23 per cent. They had six 18in bow tubes, quite big enough to sink a submarine. There was an array of five hydrophones forward which, it was hoped, would enable an attack to be carried out fully submerged. Unfortunately, the only time an 'R' class boat carried out an attack against an enemy submarine, the torpedo failed. There was a normal stowage for a single spare torpedo (not carried in peacetime) and, at the expense of considerable discomfort to the crew, six reloads could be carried.

R 3. The 'R' class was proposed by the DNC as a submarine hunter with a submerged speed of 15kts. They entered service too near the end of the war for the success of the concept to be demonstrated and were scrapped soon after the end of the war. (WSS)

12. E C Fisher, 'The Subterfuge Submarines', *Warship International* 3/1977.

13. J D Perkins, 'Canadian Vickers-Built H Class Submarines', *WARSHIP* 47-49 (1988).

14. Six were sold to Chile and two went to Canada after the war. Two, *H 11* and *H 12,* nominally joined the RN in 1918

15. Possibly accounting for some of the 'H' class cancellations.

16. *R 3* only reached 10.5kts on her first trial but improved to 13.8kts when her bottom was cleaned. Ships cover 292.

The 'M' class were given a 12in gun for use in destroying merchant ships. The three boats which completed took part in numerous exercises and seem to have been quite successful. *M 3* herself (shown here) was converted to a minelayer in 1927, developing the gear for the later *Porpoise* class. She was the only one of the class not to be sunk. (WSS)

M 2 was converted to carry a small seaplane – a Parnall Peto – the flying crew receiving both submarine and flying pay! She was lost off Portland in 1933 and her remains have been used to train sonar operators in detecting bottomed submarines. (The aircraft in this picture may have been added in.) (Author's collection)

Most of the class were scrapped in 1923. The reason for this early disposal is not known – possibly the control problems were more difficult than realised.[17] Most likely, they fell foul of the idea of the day that the submarine would never again be a serious threat. This mistaken idea was partly the result of undue faith in Asdic; there was an unspoken view that the 1917 U-boat threat had been defeated without Asdic, so with it, victory should be easy. Also, in part, there was an even less justifiable belief that submarines would fight according to Treaty rules.

The 'M' Class – Monitor?

The 1915 Development Committee, discussed earlier, had envisaged a 'monitor' submarine with one or two large guns for coastal bombardment and the driving force was that the Germans might develop such a submarine leaving the British at a disadvantage. Initially, DNC was asked to produce two studies, one with a single 12in gun, the other with one, or preferably two, 7.5in.[18] Commodore (S) Hall thought that the difference between the 7.5in and 6in gun was so small that the

cruiser type with 6in guns could do both jobs. However, he thought that the 12in gun would overcome many of the problems of torpedo attack. The torpedo was not very fast in relation to the speed of warships and hence errors in course or speed estimates would lead to a miss. He said 'No case is known of a ship-of-war being torpedoed when under way at a range outside 1000 yards.' It would also of course be possible to carry many more 12in rounds than torpedoes. Though the 'Ms' were often referred to as 'monitors' (helped by the coincidence of their class initial letter) it is clear that their role had changed to that of a gun-armed anti-shipping submarine before a detailed design started.

Four boats were ordered in 1916,[19] contractually replacing orders for *K 18-21*. They were an entirely different design though it is possible that some material ordered for the 'Ks' went into them. All mounted a 12in/40 calibre, Mk IX taken from the spares held for the *Formidable* class. It could elevate to 20°, depress 5° and train 15° either way. There was also a 3in AA on a rather clumsy disappearing mounting; *M 1* and *2* had four 18in bow tubes, the others had 21in tubes and were 10ft longer in consequence (*M 4* was not completed). There does not seem to have been any trial of the effectiveness of a 12in shell against a merchant ship though a single hit above the waterline would be unlikely to sink a well-built ship.

Perhaps surprisingly, they handled well and could dive in 90 seconds. The so-called 'dip-chick' firing procedure was practised frequently, in which the submarine would approach the surface until the muzzle was about 6ft out of water; the muzzle door would be opened, the gun fired under periscope control (usually at a range of 1200yds making a hit almost certain) and the boat would go under again. The record exposure time is said to have been 35 seconds though 75 seconds was more usual.[20] The gun could only be reloaded on the surface which took about 3 minutes. Even though the breech mechanism was exposed to seawater, there seem to have been few problems. The firing tube did leak occasionally which usually mean the gun muzzle blew off as the exit of the shell was impeded.

The three 'Ms' remained in service after the war and took part in numerous exercises. *M 1* was lost in a collision in 1925. *M 2* was given a pressure-tight hangar in place of the gun and carried a small seaplane. She was lost whilst surfacing in 1933.[21] *M 3* was converted into a minelayer with stowage for 100 mines, testing the gear for the *Porpoise* class, and was scrapped in 1932 when the trials were successfully completed.

The 'L' class – return to sanity

The 'L' class began as 'Improved Es' – in fact, *L 1* and *L 2* were ordered as *E 57* and *58*. By 1916 the 'E' class design was 6 years old and there were many wartime lessons to be incorporated. Experiments with double hulls, steam etc, were abandoned and the well-proven saddle tank design was chosen. The main change in the first group of eight boats was increased surface speed using the 12-cylinder Vickers engine developed for the 'J' class. They achieved their design surface speed of 17kts on trial and the earlier boats reached 11kts submerged. Later boats were about ½kt slower due to the drag of a fixed bridge screen 5½ft high.

Harrison quotes some figures for speed in the 1930s which were about ½kt slower than on the original trials. This was almost certainly due to the increasing roughness of the hull as paint ripples and rust pits increased. When docked, they would be brushed and hand-

17. The cynical believe they were scrapped because the casing was too small for the crew to man the side entering harbour.

18. Submarine administration, training and construction. Naval Historical Branch.

19. R Gardiner (ed), *Conway's All the World's Fighting Ships 1906–21* (London 1985), p92.

20. M H Brice, *M Class Submarines* (London 1983), p7.

21. It has been suggested that the hydraulic capacity of the 'Ms' was inadequate, leading to failure of doors or hatches to close in *M 2*.

The 'L' class were originally designed as improved 'Es' but the changes were so great that they were re-classified as a new class. They were very successful. This photo of *L 4* shows the original, low, gun position. (Author's collection)

L 6 had her gun raised which became standard for the class. (WSS)

scraped before re-painting but this would not produce a fair surface and the increasing roughness would certainly be enough to cause the loss of speed. Ten microns of roughness adds about 1 per cent to the power required for a given speed.

The first eight boats had four 18in bow tubes and one 18in on either beam. The gun armament of the earlier boats varied but from *L 12* onwards a 4in gun was mounted at bridge level with its own access trunk. Earlier boats were modified similarly. The idea was to engage surfaced enemy submarines outside torpedo range with a gun well above water even in the low buoyancy condition.

Needless to say, these changes made the 'Ls' bigger than the 'Es'. *L 9* and later boats were further modified and larger still. The main change was in fitting four 21in bow tubes in place of the 18in. An extra bulkhead was fitted between the tube space and the torpedo room. The beam 18in tubes were retained (these were removed between the wars in surviving boats). The beam tubes were omitted in those equipped as minelayers – *L 14* and *17* with sixteen tubes and *L 24-27* with fourteen tubes.

Even before the first 'L' class boat went to sea a further improved design was started. Six of the *L 50* design were ordered in January/February 1917 and a further nineteen in April. Many were cancelled at the end of the war and only seven completed. This group had six 21in bow tubes and none on the beam. They had a 4in gun either end of the bridge, each with its access trunk. The stern lines were modified to give better propeller immersion and it was hoped that they would also make 17kts . Early trials were very disappointing – *c*12.4kts – but by refining appendage shape[22] and fitting new propellers, *L 71* reached 14kts.

'L' class submarines

Class	E 9	L 1-8	L 9	L 50
Length oa (ft-in)	181-0	231-1	238-7	235-0
Displacement (tons, surface)	667	891	894	960
Displacement (tons, submerged)	807	1074	1089	1150

All groups of the 'L' class had a diving depth of 250ft, quoted as 150ft from 1925. The test depth was 100ft (see below).

Some technical aspects[23]

The success of a submarine design depends on the correct design of detail aspects to a much greater extent than in the case of a surface ship. In this section a few of these aspects will be considered in a little more detail.

Diving depth

In the earlier years of this period the modes of failure of a pressure hull, loaded externally, were not clearly understood and a confused nomenclature resulted. By the end of the war, there was a fairly good, subjective appreciation of the problem though only very simple calculations were possible.[24]

In later years, three values of 'Diving Depth' were considered and, though they were not defined clearly in the early years, one can see a growing realisation of their significance.

COLLAPSE DEPTH: The design figure at which water pressure would cause the hull to fail assuming that all the plates had been rolled to the specified thickness and there were no manufacturing defects. Calculations were only possible on the strength of the plating between frames and though it was recognised that the frames could buckle, it was hoped that this was avoided by using heavy frames. Many early designs had numerous discontinuities or steps in the pressure hull which would have weakened it.

OPERATIONAL DEPTH: This was the maximum depth permitted in normal operation.[25] It seems to have been introduced in 1925 when, for example, the quoted diving depth of the 'Ls' became 150ft instead of the earlier figure of 250ft. It allowed a margin of safety over the collapse depth for errors in the design calculation and for building defects and also for accidental depth excursions. In later years the operational depth was taken as about half the collapse depth. The operational depth would be reduced in older boats if surveys showed serious corrosion.

TEST DEPTH: In the period under discussion, the test dive was usually to about two-thirds of the operational depth.

There does not seem to have been any very clear definition of the point to which 'Depth' was measured. The gauge was roughly at eye level in the control room and this was the accepted base. At some date, this was formalised with depth measured to the axis of the boat, changed only with the nuclear programme to keel depth.

A formula used for calculating the stress in cylindrical boilers was:-

$$\text{Stress} = \frac{\text{Pressure x Radius}}{\text{Plating Thickness}}$$

This can be used for external loads provided the cylinder does not buckle and is truly circular. It was the only tool available to early designers and they made good use of it. Realising that the calculated values it gave were only approximate, they used it to calculate the stress in boats which (accidentally) had made an abnormally deep dive. This figure could be used, with caution, as the limiting value for new designs. This formula is surprisingly accurate for modern designs.

Harrison lists a few of the extreme depths recorded by early submarines.

Boat	Depth (ft)
B 1	95
E 40	318
G?	170
L 2	300[26]

L 2 was on patrol when she encountered three USN destroyers who took her for a U-boat. She dived to 90ft to avoid them but depth charges caused leaks and she sank to 300ft. She blew tanks and, on surfacing, was hit by a 3in shell at 1000yds which did not penetrate. 'The three American destroyers apologised'.[27]

Until the end of the First World War, the quoted diving depth seems to have been a calculated safe depth using the boiler formula with some factor of safety. Captains were generally ordered not to exceed half that depth. There do not seem to have been any cases of loss from structural failure, with the possible exception of *K 5*, though one cannot be absolutely sure since some boats disappeared during the war without trace. With all the uncertainty of structural design there must have been a touch of luck but the main reason was a wise degree of caution in sizing unknown components such as frames making the boats heavy but safe. There is little reliable information on diving times, but the early boats were slow by Second World War standards. The 'Ls' were said to reach periscope depth from full surface buoyancy in 1½ minutes which was probably better than earlier classes.

Hydroplanes

The Hollands had planes aft only, then called Submerged Diving Rudders, which moved through 60° from hard rise to hard dive. Initially they were worked by a compressed-air motor but this was unsatisfactory and hand operation was used. The 'A', 'B' and 'C' classes had a similar arrangement. In the 'B' and 'C' classes a balance weight was arranged so that if the control shaft broke, the planes would move into the horizontal position.

Control using planes aft is quite satisfactory at higher speeds but not at the low speeds which were all that these boats were capable of. To rise or dive the boat had to be put at a trim angle; they could not move up or down in a horizontal orientation. In 1905 approval was given to fit planes on the fore side of the conning tower of the later 'As' and the work was carried out after completion. A few 'Bs' and all 'Cs' were similarly equipped. In 1907 A 3 was fitted with bow planes for trial which appears to have been successful and it seems that most boats which had not already received conning tower planes were fitted with bow planes. All these planes were hand worked through rods and gearing – A 3's gear took twenty-three turns of the handwheel in the control room to move from hard over to hard over. Bow planes are very vulnerable to damage in heavy seas and from impact with floating objects. Heavy guards were fitted but damage still occurred. The 'D' class had submerged bow planes, rather further aft than in the earlier boats and electric motors were provided to operate both bow and stern planes though hand operation was still possible.

Scott's 'S' class had Italian-designed folding planes forward which were unreliable and gave them a bad reputation. On the other hand, the Scotts' developed hydraulic operation of the planes in *Swordfish* was very successful and adopted in all later submarines including

22. The appendages – hydroplanes, guards, rudders etc - contribute much to the resistance of a submarine on the surface. Submerged the bridge, casing gun etc make an even bigger contribution. At the end of the Second World War, the resistance of the 'S' class was halved by removing or streamlining these appendages.

23. D K Brown, 'The Technology of Submarine Design', *Interdisciplinary Sciences Review* 3/1990.

24. D K Brown, 'Submarine Pressure Hull Design and Diving Depths Between the War'. *Warship International*, 3/1987.

25. There was a long-standing tradition of commanding officers going about 10 per cent below the permitted operational depth on the first dive to instil confidence. Since this custom was well known, it was allowed for in the factor of safety.

26. For much of the inter-war period this dive was the basis for diving depth calculations.

27. A W Johns, 5 March 1918; held in d'Eyncourt papers, DEY31. National Maritime Museum.

The three 'S' class were built by Scotts to a Laurenti FIAT design. They were transferred to Italy on completion in 1915. (Imperial War Museum: SP22)

the last of the 'E' class. The drag of submerged planes and guards is very high and it was intended to fit housing bow planes in the 'Gs'. The failure of the 'S' class planes caused this to be abandoned at the cost of 1-1½kts of speed on the surface.

The question of bow planes was reviewed for the even faster 'J' class. Consideration was given to a horizontal propeller but trials in an 'A' class boat showed this was impractical, as were jets driven by a pump. In the end, both the 'Js' and 'Hs' had housing planes forward and there do not seem to have been any problems. The 'H' class had folding forward planes.

Main engines

The first twelve 'A' class boats all had 16-cylinder Wolseley petrol engines but these were steadily developed from 350bhp in *A 1* to 600bhp from *A 5* onwards. The 'Bs' and the 'Cs' up to *C 18* had the same design of engine but built by Vickers; from *C 19* onwards the number of cylinders was reduced to twelve but still delivering the same 600bhp.

The first British submarine diesel for the 'D' class was a 6-cylinder Vickers engine. It was the only diesel design of the period; the 'E' class had the same cylinder design with 8 cylinders and the 'J' and 'L' classes had 12 cylinders. The basic design was refined but unchanged.

Submarine diesels

Class	Cylinders	Wt (lbs/shp)	Consumption (lbs/bhp/hr)
'D'	6	73	0.54
'E'	8	65	0.47
'J', 'L'	12		0.45

It was intended to try a variety of engines from different manufacturers (mainly German) in the 'G 'class, but the war prevented this.

Torpedo firing

Firing a torpedo from a submerged submarine is a complicated process. The torpedo is normally kept in a dry tube and when preparing to fire the tube must be flooded. This needs about half a ton of water for a 21in tube and must be taken from an inboard tank to preserve the trim. This is called the 'Water Round Torpedo (WRT) Tank'. The torpedo is slightly heavier than water and when it is fired some water must be admitted from the sea to prevent the bow coming up. Before re-loading, the tube must be drained into an inboard tank.

The torpedo was blown out of the tube by compressed air. In this era the pressure was 250lbs/in² which was too high, producing a big air bubble which could be seen from the target vessel and the shock swung the depth-keeping pendulum back so that the torpedo ran deep for a considerable distance. The torpedo was not a very accurate weapon, particularly against fast-moving, manoeuvring targets. Compton-Hall quotes figures (from N Lambert) showing German submarines scored 12 per cent hits against British warships but 52 per cent against merchant ships.[28] British submarines averaged some 15 per cent hits, mainly against warships. A crude fire control device was developed in the form of a slide rule called ISWAS (Where it IS based on where it WAS – still used as a backup even after the Second World War).

Radio communications

Even the Hollands had a radio receiver but transmitters were not fitted in submarines until 1912 when it was approved to fit Type 10 (3kW) to 'Ds', 'Es' and some 'Cs'. This was a Poulson arc set with a theoretical transmission range of 250-300 miles and could receive from shore stations at up to 600 miles. It was not very reliable and required a mast or masts to be raised. Later boats had valve sets which were more reliable and had greater range. By the end of the war some boats had the SA set which could receive with the boat at shallow submergence – bridge bulwark level with the sea. The Fessenden sound oscillator permitted communication between submerged submarines at up to 30-40 miles. Pigeons were carried in the early boats and were reliable and could fly at 30mph – if not over-fed. Compton-Hall quotes a message sent from Terschelling at 0400hrs which reached the Admiralty 12 hours later.

Miscellaneous

A submarine contains a remarkable variety of technologies, many of which have no other application and far too numerous and complicated for more than a mention in this brief account. There were problems with magnetic compasses even in surface ships and these were much more difficult in submarines. The compass was outside on the bridge and had to be surrounded by a heavy brass structure.[29] A small, upside-down periscope enabled the helmsman to see it – with difficulty. Gyro compasses were introduced in *Swordfish* and in the 'E' class. These early Sperry units were unreliable and the wise officer of the watch compared them frequently with the slightly less unreliable, though inaccurate, magnetic compass.[30]

Permanent bridge screens (as opposed to canvas dodgers) were fitted from 1917. Whilst greatly improving life for bridge personnel, they were heavy and added considerably to submerged resistance, reducing speed by about ½kt.

Though the RN were probably the first to fit periscopes, they were soon overtaken by superior units from other countries. Keyes' team purchased a number of French and German periscopes in 1911 and, though they seem not to have been used, the British manufacturer (Sir Howard Grubb) was inspired to greater efforts.

Other topics which can only be listed but all of which presented their own problems included air bottles, compressors, LP blowers, batteries and their ventilation.[31] A crude escape chamber was fitted in some of the 'C' class in 1908 and by 1911 a breathing helmet was issued.

How good were they?

Of course there were problems with these submarines; almost every aspect of their technology was novel as were their tactics. Every other navy had problems but only the USN and the German navy were suitable for comparison and the USN had no direct war experience. The best comparison with German submarines is in a paper to the INA by Arthur Johns in 1920.[32] Johns began with a factual description of the main types of German submarine. He emphasised the rising cost per ton which rose from 4000 marks per ton in 1914 to 9000 in 1918 (it is not clear how much of this is due to inflation). Johns says this is about double the figure for British boats but exchange rates in wartime are almost impossible to evaluate. However, the building time of 800-ton submarines increased from 24 months to 30 months. The big cruisers took about double the time to build of a standard U-boat.

All U-boats were double-hull style over most of the surface. However, the top section was usually free flooding and the bottom omitted so that the difference from the British saddle tank was not great. It was noted that the captain controlled the boat from the conning tower, not the control room in the main hull as in the RN. This gave greater submergence for the same length of periscope at the expense of less team contact, a dilemma never resolved.

Johns points out that far from possessing the exceptional speed rumoured for U-boats they were actually rather slow for their power, probably due to large and poorly-aligned appendages. Stability was marginal and some classes required girdling. Captured boats were tried after the war and were thought to be good sea boats, dry and manoeuvring well, but British officers thought their own boats handled better under water.

Since Johns had designed most of the British boats, one may be suspicious of his impartiality but his views were not disputed by RN operators or by overseas designers. On the contrary, every speaker in the discussion paid tribute to Johns. Constructor Commander E S Lands USN, already an experienced submarine designer and destined to become a leading designer between the wars said:

> Boat for boat I consider the *L 50* class of the British design to be the equal if not the superior of the U-boat. If the engines of the two were traded, the British boat would completely outclass the German boat. The British boats are better designs so far as the design of submarines is concerned . . . For fleet purposes the British 'K' class are superior to the UAs . . .'[33]

Other speakers expanded on these points. The DNC, d'Eyncourt, said that the German engines delivered 300hp per cylinder whilst British engines had only 100hp. Rear-Admiral Dent, head of the submarine service, paid the users' tribute to Johns and his designs. He said that 'during the war we built the largest submarine, the fastest submarine on the surface,[34] the fastest submarine submerged, the submarine with the heaviest gun armament and the submarine with the heaviest torpedo armament.' The only great advantage possessed by the U-boats was plenty of targets.

28. R Compton-Hall, *Submarines and the War at Sea 1914-18* (London 1991).

29. To preserve stability, heavy structure high up had to be balanced by ballast low down so that the total added weight was very considerable.

30. H K Oram, *Ready for Sea* (London 1974), p207.

31. It is interesting that many of these are still seen as problems!

32. A W Johns, 'German Submarines', *Trans INA* (1920).

33. G E Weir, *Building American Submarines 1914–1940* (Washington 1991).

34. Though he was referring to the 'K' class, it is arguable that the 'Js' were the fastest diesel boat.

Minesweepers, sloops and patrol vessels

The 'Flower' class sloops

There is very little published information on the RN work on minesweeping that began as a result of the Russo-Japanese War, but many hints show that such work was extensive, effective and generally implemented. By January 1908, Fisher could tell a subcommittee of the Committee for Imperial Defence that mines could easily be cleared, but he would not explain the technique as this would 'throw away one of the deepest secrets' possessed by the Navy.[1] That year the conversion began of thirteen torpedo gunboats (TGB) of the *Alarm* and *Sharpshooter* classes to carry the new sweeping gear,[2] which was a wire sweep between two ships using kites to depress the wire. In 1913 there were six TGB engaged full-time in training for sweeping and four more on fishery protection. They were described as old, slow, with very limited coal stowage and only one had wireless. It was proposed to build up to a second squadron of six minesweeping TGB and fit all twelve with radio.[3]

In 1909 four trawlers were purchased for conversion to minesweepers and renamed *Spider*, *Seaflower*, *Sparrow* and *Seamew*. In 1911 a special section of the RNR was organised as an auxiliary minesweeping service to operate requisitioned trawlers. The crews were volunteer fishermen under a Captain-in-Charge of Minesweepers and divided into seven coastal areas coming under the Admiral of Patrols. During the crisis of 1913 the captain reported that eighty-two trawlers could be equipped immediately. When war broke out the system worked well and by 1 September 1914 some 250 trawlers, drifters etc were on M/S or A/S duties.[4] It is said that one trawler, with half its crew, was lost for every five mines swept.[5]

In 1908 a committee recommended the building of four purpose-designed minesweepers per year to a total of sixteen, with about double the speed of a trawler. Since sweeping was inevitably hazardous, the size of both the ship and its crew should be as small as possible to minimise the effects of the inevitable losses.[6] The target was about 600 tons, a maximum draught of 10ft, a speed of 16kts and good seakeeping. There was to be a crew of three officers and seventeen men[7] and no armament. The water tube boilers should be fitted for dual firing, supplying steam to a triple-expansion engine, a single propeller being preferred to lessen the risk of tangling a mine cable. Fuel for 1200 miles was required.

The general requirement was summarised as 'Inexpensive, Seaworthy, Handy, Speed (17 knots, 21 desirable)'

DNC responded with a range of seven options,[8] the extremes being:

Design	Dispt (tons)	ihp	Speed (kts)	Cost, (£1000)
A1	575	1100	14	30
D	900	2-3000	16-17	55

Length varied from 155-220ft and beam from 26-30ft with a draught of less than 10ft.

Ships based on the Coast Guard vessels *Safeguard* and *Watchful* were also considered. DNC thought that 600 tons was the minimum for reasonable seakeeping and had adopted heavyweight engines in the light of the demanding load when sweeping. To make 16kts would mean both hull and machinery of light weight which would be unsuitable, costly and limit the number of yards which could build them. DNC's preferred option was 600 tons, cost £32,000, 14kts continuous, 15kts for 8 hours. He also objected to unarmed vessels. It was hoped to start the first small batch in 1910-11, building up to a force of between sixteen and eighteen ships (six in each of the Home, Channel and Atlantic fleets), but they were first postponed and then it was decided not to build new minesweepers. It was hoped that the TGB would be sufficient in numbers for roles in which speed was needed and that trawlers could do the rest.

However, the TGBs had limited endurance and some were showing their age. In 1911 and in 1913 minesweepers were reconsidered but no action was taken. Early in 1914 it was decided that something should be done and DNC produced a sketch design. The requirement this time was 16kts continuous with water tube boilers and single screw, triple-expansion engine. Endurance should be 1000 miles at 10kts and it should have the smallest possible crew. There should be two small guns if these could be manned without increasing the total number of men needed. But, again, building was not approved. It was realised that many small, fast ships would be needed in wartime for auxiliary purposes but it was hoped that commercial vessels could be requisitioned. Unfortunately, no one had checked to see that such ships existed, and they did not.

Therefore, instructions were given on 25 September 1914 to proceed with a new design which was to capable

---

1. R F Mackay, *Fisher of Kilverstone* (Oxford, 1973), p378, quoting Cab 16/3.

2. Photos show *Seagull* with an A frame over the stern and *Speedy* with a somewhat similar device, which may be a derrick.

3. Ships cover 351.

4. Admiralty confidence in the Navy's ability to force the Dardanelles may have been founded on Fisher's belief that sweeping had made the mine ineffective. Why were the torpedo gunboats not used? – their greater power could have overcome the current problem

5. K McBride, 'The First Flowers', *WARSHIP 1989*.

6. Almost exactly the approach which led to the Second World War *Bangor* class.

7. Narbeth pointed out that the machinery alone would need at least sixteen men and up to thirty-six in the more powerful options.

8. It would seem that all these designs were prepared by J H Narbeth who took over the auxiliary ships section in 1907 having failed to win promotion in the battleship section. Probably of constructor rank at this time. Chief Constructor by 1916. He sounded rather angry over the incompatible requirements! J H Narbeth, '50 Years of Naval Progress', *Shipbuilder* (Oct-Dec 1927).

9. Narbeth wrote *Lady Grey* but it is possible that he meant *Earl Grey* whose clipper bow featured in the first studies.

10. J H Narbeth, 'A Naval Architect's Practical Experience in the Behaviour of Ships', *Trans INA* (London 1941).

11. A bow protection device 'Skipjack' type was fitted in the earlier ships but it was clumsy and not very effective so it was removed.

12. Narbeth refers to a 'good flare' which it was for the day. I would probably have given more.

13. They could carry up to 50 tons of deck cargo or 700 men.

14. Apparently in the mistaken belief that German destroyers had only two 14pdr. It is unlikely that a 12pdr would penetrate the pressure hull of a submarine. It was approved to replace one 12pdr by a 4in but it is uncertain how many were altered.

of minesweeping, anti-submarine work, towing and acting as a fast messenger. The resulting design was described as a 'New *Seagull*', presumably the TGB of that name being the type ship, though Narbeth writes that he was influenced by the *Lady Grey*,[9] built at Barrow for the Canadian Government. The general style was liked but it was decided to adopt more merchant ship practice so that it could be built in shipyards unused to warship work; in particular, cylindrical boilers were to be fitted. This considerably increased the size of the ship to 1210 tons, 250ft x 33ft x 11ft 7in with two-thirds coal and the complement was now 60-70. Even so, the First Lord (Churchill) objected to spending £2.4 million on forty such ships, each costing more than a submarine.

The ships of the *Acacia* class were handsome with a fine form.[10] Initial studies showed a clipper bow to work a bow mine catcher.[11] The sides were heavily flared[12] to a short forecastle in an attempt to keep them dry and they were said to be good seaboats, dry and comfortable except for quick motions in a heavy sea. Abaft the forecastle, the upper deck had bulwarks with a shelter deck overhead – this open deck was found useful for transporting army horses![13]

There were a number of clever features intended to protect ships engaged in hazardous service. There was a triple bottom forward against mines and the magazine was above water, aft with protective plating 1½in thick. There were cross bunkers as well as side bunkers and in dangerous waters the latter would be closed off to give some protection. They did well in surviving major damage, though losses were heavy – nine (plus one French) out of seventy-two of the original design and nine out of forty of the later convoy sloops. The first twenty-four ships mounted two 12pdr guns,[14] but later ships were fitted with two elderly 4.7in (a few got 4in). They were all fitted for sweeping and, in addition, had a towing winch, hook and beam. A later batch (*Arabis* class) were increased in length by 5ft to accommodate 4-cylinder, triple expansion engines and hence reduce vibration.

Dahlia, one of the first batch of 'Flower' class sloops, with steadying sails set. (Imperial War Museum: SP1249)

Many had the original three-bladed propeller changed to a four-blader to reduce vibration further. Metacentric height was about 2ft in the legend condition for the earlier ships; the convoy sloops were a little less at about 1.75ft.

The main features of the ship were scaled from existing ships. Hull weight scaled from different ships came out as:

Ship	Hull weight (tons)
Halcyon	739
Sharpshooter	578
Safeguard	683
Adamant	758
'L' class destroyer	462

Narbeth took 630 tons and used an average height of the centre of gravity as 0.729 of the depth. The scaling of

Berberis of the later *Arabis* group of 'Flowers'. They mounted 4.7in guns and were a little bigger than the earlier groups. (Imperial War Museum: SP766)

Heather of the *Aubrietia* class. The last 'Flowers' were given profiles resembling small merchant ships in the hope of deceiving submarine commanders. Individual builders were asked to use ships which they had designed as the basis for the warships, known as convoy sloops. (WSS)

horse power (ehp) used some surprising ships but it is the ratio of speed to square root of the length which matters. Ehp and length for a 900-ton ship based on:

Ship	Length (ft)	ehp @ 16kts	ehp @ 17kts	Type
Surprise	216	760	1040	Despatch Vessel
Dreadnought	180	950	1300	Battleship
Invincible	198	770	1080	Battlecruiser
Sentinel	243	650	810	Cruiser

The advantage of length was clear and the *Sentinel* form was selected, but reduced to 210ft for ease of building.

Clever as was the design, the real achievement was in production. There were seventy-four 'Flower' class sloops built for the RN together with eight more for France. It was then decided that when serving as convoy escorts their warship-like appearance warned U-boats off and a further forty (plus one French[15]) were built to look more like merchant ships (Convoy Sloops). Twenty-two builders were involved, most of whom had never worked for the Admiralty. Swan Hunters sold sets

Harebell of the *Anchusa* class of convoy sloops. (WSS)

of building drawings to the smaller companies at £200 a set! Many fittings were ordered in bulk by the Admiralty to save time and effort in purchasing small quantities and to ease replacement in service. Most of the oversight was left to Lloyd's Register but C W J Hopkins, Narbeth's assistant, was the travelling troubleshooter. The original intention was to reduce the amount of wood, but the small yards were short of sheet metal workers and timber had to be accepted.

The shortest building time was 17 weeks by Barclay Curle with *Foxglove*, almost equalled by Swan Hunter with *Acacia*, but 19-21 weeks seems to have been more usual.[16] They lasted well and some gave good service between the wars, and a few were still listed during the later war, though mainly on harbour duties.[17]

The appearance of the convoy sloops varied considerably and was loosely based on merchant ships of that size built previously in the shipyard concerned. Some builders had several styles. The first batch had three concealed 12pdr guns but later ships generally had two 4in and one or two 12pdrs. Most had A/S howitzers and three ships had revolving torpedo tubes forward. The disguise made it difficult to arrange accommodation and they were uncomfortable.

Minelaying

In May 1905 Fisher set up a committee to decide on the number of mines required for war. They decided on 10,000 of which 3000 were to be laid off the Elbe, Weser and Jade. An initial order was placed for 10,000 of the naval spherical type–which subsequently proved almost useless. In 1906 the old *Apollo* class cruiser *Iphigenia* was converted into a minelayer, followed by six of her sister-ships.[18] Enthusiasm then waned, presumably because of the assumed effectiveness of sweeping. By 1914 there were 4000 mines available and though trials of foreign, Herz horn mines had been carried out, none had been ordered. It is likely that there was no direct decision to abandon minelaying but other material was higher priority.

Anti-submarine warfare

Though this book is about the ships, some, all too brief, mention must be made of the methods and weapons used against submarines. In Chapter 6 it was shown that the principal reason for the purchase of the Holland class submarines was to gain experience in anti-submarine warfare (ASW). Their first year was, sensibly, devoted to training but in December 1903 C-in-C Portsmouth suggested that exercises in ASW should begin. Such exercises began in March 1904 but were abandoned when *A 1* was accidentally rammed by a passing merchant ship. Probably all that was learnt was that, once submerged, a submarine was invisible.

Ideas had been put forward for hydrophones[19] and for induction detectors but no useful equipment was produced. Light nets with indicator buoys had some

success in narrow channels but were no use in the open sea. By 1910, the Hollands were obsolete and were expended in trials. Tins of guncotton with a time fuse were not very effective. A 6in gun fired at *Holland 2*, submerged, eventually sank her when her windows broke. Various types of towed explosive sweep did a little better. The final version had nine charges, suspended from twelve floats; it could be deployed in 3-4 minutes and towed at 12-15kts. Many other ingenious ideas were tried but without success. In all these pre-war trials it was assumed that submarines would only be used against warships.

By 1916 the depth charge had been introduced but was only available in very small numbers. The type D had a charge of 300lbs TNT and the D* had 120lbs. The D* was used at shallow settings when the attacking ship might be damaged by a D but it was soon dropped. Jellicoe says that the D was lethal at 14ft from the target and would probably force a submarine to surface if it exploded 28ft away.[20] Even at 60ft it had an important morale effect.[21] The outfit of depth charges for a destroyer in 1917 was only two D and two D* depth charges but they were scarce and many ships did not have their full allowance. The chance of dropping a single charge within lethal distance, without Asdic, was very remote. Even in the Second World War the chance of success in a single attack, with ten charges dropped under guidance from Asdic, was only 3.7 per cent. It is surprising that depth charges did so well (see following table).[22]

U-Boat Sinkings[23]

Type of vessel

	1914-16	1917	1918	Total
Warships	2	0	1	3
Patrols	1	5	1	7
Decoy gunfire	5	6	0	11
Merchant ships	0	3	4	7
Escorts	0	6	10	16
Mines	10	20	18	48
Accidents	7	10	2	19
Unknown	7	2	10	19
Total	46	63	69	178

By cause (Including losses due to German mines and torpedoes, and excluding other accidents and unknown from above).

	1914-16	1917	1918	Total
Ramming	3	10	6	19
Gunfire	10	6	4	20
Sweep	2	0	1	3
Depth charge	2	6	22	30
Torpedo	6	7	7	20
Mines	13	26	19	58

15. It has been said that this ship was smaller than the original on which it was based and small men were picked for the crew to maintain the illusion!

16. Sir E T d'Eyncourt, 'Naval Construction during the war', *Trans INA* (1919).

17. At least two convoy sloops were still in existence in 1997 (*Chrysanthemum*, *President*, ex-*Saxifrage*).

18. Mackay, *Fisher of Kilverstone*, p377.

19. One of the early pioneers in underwater acoustics was Professor Boncastle of the University of Virginia, a graduate of the 1st School of Naval Architecture.

20. Jellicoe, *The Crisis of the Naval War* (London 1920).

21. Jellicoe is probably pessimistic; a Second World War depth charge had the same weight of explosive and was thought lethal against the much stronger U-boats of that war at 20ft, disabling at 40ft.

22. W Hackmann, *Seek and Strike* (London 1984).

23. Based on R M Grant, *U Boats Destroyed* (London 1964).

Note the rapid increase in sinking by mines in 1917 when an effective mine became available; the reduction in 1918 was probably because submarines were avoiding mined areas. Depth charges were becoming the main killer by 1918.

From 1915 much effort was put into the development of hydrophones. By 1917 sets were available which could, sometimes, hear a submarine 1-2 miles away provided the listening vessel was stationary but could not give a direction. By the end of the year, much improved, directional equipment was available which could be used whilst the hunter was under way. The first kill using a hydrophone was claimed in December 1917. It was soon realised that training in both tactics and in the operation of the new equipment was important.

None of these sensors or weapons had any great influence on the design of ships. Most contacts were visual and number of ships was the all-important factor, and for this reason the emphasis in this chapter is on production rather than technical development.

Admiralty organisation – The Deputy Controller for Auxiliary Shipbuilding[24]

By early 1917 it was generally realised that production of ships, particularly merchant ships, was too slow. Too many skilled workers had been taken by the army, particularly the younger men, and there was, inevitably, a shortage of steel. Warship work tended to have priority claim on available resources, leading to a shortage of merchant shipping just when sinkings by U-boats were increasing dramatically.

In May 1917 the First Lord, Sir Eric Carson, proposed a new organisation with Sir Eric Geddes as Controller, responsible for production and repair of both warships (including armament) and merchant ships. Warship design was to remain with DNC under the Third Sea Lord. There was to be a Deputy Controller for Auxiliary Shipbuilding (DAS) and a Royal Engineer, Major-General A S Collard, CB, was appointed. He seems to have had some responsibility for the design of smaller warships, including the '24' class sloops and later 'Hunts'.

There seems to have been much ill-feeling between the new organisation and the traditional departments – DAS vessels are omitted from the DNC history even when designed by DNC. Jellicoe suggests that the new team did very little to increase output of new ships. For example, the output of merchant ships in 1917 was 1,163,474 tons, and an optimistic forecast by Geddes suggested 2-3 million in 1918, but the actual figure was 1,534,110 tons. On the other hand, it seems that repair work was speeded up considerably.

The '24' class sloops

The next design of sloops placed the emphasis on anti-submarine warfare. They were known as the '24' class since there were intended to be twenty-four ships, though two were cancelled. Ordered between December 1916 and April 1917, they mounted two 4in guns and had a speed of 17kts with a displacement of 1320 tons. Though they had a higher freeboard than the 'Flowers' they had the reputation of being bad seaboats.[25] They were disposed of soon after the war or converted to auxiliary duties. Their building coincided with the reorganisation of the Admiralty, described above, and they were built under the Deputy Controller for Auxiliary Shipbuilding.

Spearmint of the '24' class sloops; so called because there were intended to be 24 ships in the class though two were cancelled. They do not seem to have been very successful. Their profile was symmetrical, fore and aft, to confuse submarines and the position of mast and funnel was reversed in some ships. (WSS)

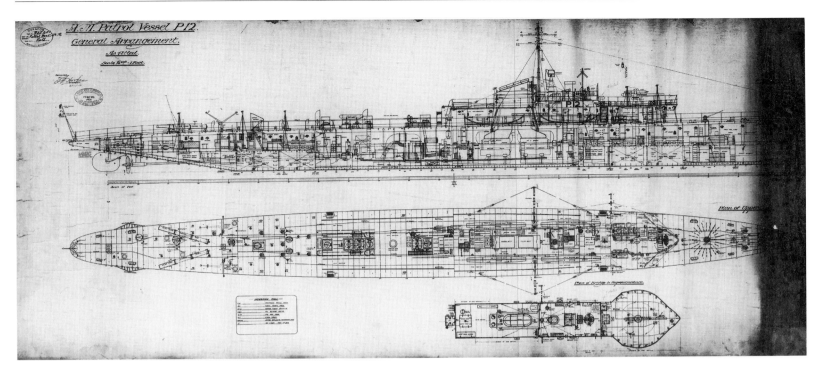

P-boats

The concept was for a small cheap destroyer which could be built quickly. At the suggestion of A W Watson, a young constructor,[26] they were given a very low freeboard (6ft 3in amidships, discussed later) for low visibility which made them look rather like a surfaced submarine; an illusion carefully fostered in the arrangement of the small superstructure and funnel. They also had a shallow draught (8ft) to make them more difficult to torpedo. Mild steel was used rather than high tensile as rivet holes could be punched as opposed to drilling, saving time and cost. They displaced just over 600 tons, had a speed of 22kts on trial[27] from twin shaft geared turbines (330 rpm) and were cut up aft with a big rudder to give a turning circle of only 840ft.

Twenty-four P-boats were ordered in March 1915, mainly from firms not used to warship building; oversight was by the two main classification societies, Lloyd's Register and British Corporation. Most were built on a cost plus profit basis, the price paid being around £104,000. They took anything from 9 to 18 months to build. Thirty more were ordered later of

The P boats were a novel design by a young constructor, A W Watson, for a small and cheap anti-submarine vessel. Their profile was made to resemble a submarine. (National Maritime Museum, London: 305401)

24. Jellicoe, *The Crisis of the Naval War*.

25. It is said that their problem was heavy rolling and a poor GM which does not make sense since excessive rolling is usually associated with high GM.

26. As assistant director, he was to be in charge of escort vessel design in the Second World War.

27. Design figures 20kts from 3800shp, developed 4000shp on trial. Even so, the design estimate was poor.

P 37. This class were well liked in service and were said to be good sea boats despite their low freeboard. (Imperial War Museum: Q66840)

PC 69. Some later P boats were given a merchant ship profile as with the convoy sloops. Their greater freeboard kept them dry. (WSS)

which ten were given the appearance of a small merchant ship. These were numbered in the same sequence but as PC boats (originally PQ series). Later still, ten more PC boats were ordered with increased beam and other changes.

Watson hoped, as Reed had with his breastwork monitors,[28] that seas washing over the low deck would reduce both roll and pitch motions. Rather surprisingly, early reports from sea were favourable, most of the complaints being of spray thrown up by the anchors. This was partially cured by stowing the anchors on billboards and covering the hawse pipes. Their bilge keels were a mere 9in deep. However, there was unanimous agreement that the PC boats, with a high forecastle and bridge, were much better. Watson himself attended the trials of *P 24*, reported that she was designed for 20kts with 50 tons of coal and, with 3500shp, made 21¾kts.[29] Behaviour was very satisfactory with no vibration. Going astern there was no water on the (low) deck, the

spoon shaped stern lifting. She steered 'rapidly'. Driving into a head sea there was no pitching and the after deck was dry; the anchors and propeller guards made spray.

Though the design was hurried, the actual weights agreed well with the estimates;

Weights	Design	Actual
Equipment	35	32.1
Armament	14	11.5
Machinery	190	158.4
Eng Store	10	5
Oil	50	50
Hull	275	254
Total	574	512

The intended armament was one 4in gun forward, a pom-pom and two fixed 14in torpedo tubes. There were several schemes to increase this and a second 4in was approved but not fitted. A single revolving 18in tube was discussed in place of the 14in but again this was not fitted. Admiral Bacon of the Dover Patrol was against any such change; the original armament was perfectly satisfactory against UB and UC boats and there was no way in which a P-boat could fight a destroyer. He found their shallow draught very useful in the Straits of Dover.[30]

'KIL' class patrol gunboats etc

By early 1915 it was apparent that more, and hence cheaper, escort and patrol vessels were needed. The first attempt was the 'Z whaler'. Though DNC was responsible for the design, it was based on a Russian ship built by Smith's Dock and took the form of a whaler with shallow draught. Fifteen were built, but their seakeeping was poor and no more were ordered.[31]

A somewhat similar requirement in 1917 for a 'fast trawler' led to designs by six builders. Eventually,

Cachalot was one of a group of fifteen ships built by Smiths Dock based on whale catchers. Their seakeeping was thought to be inferior to that of trawlers of the same size and no more were built. (WSS)

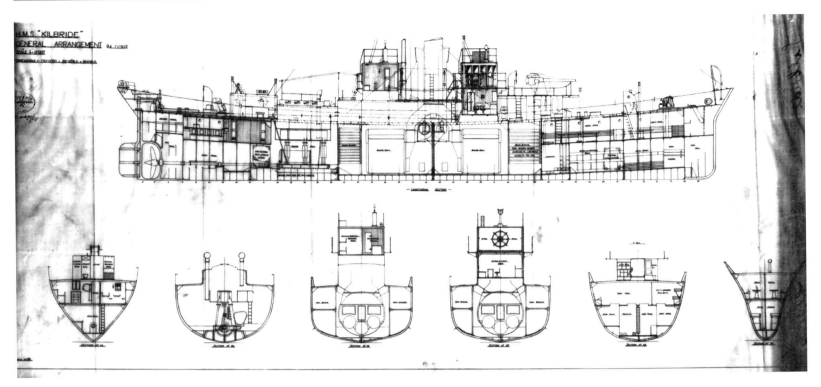

approval was given for eighty-five 'KIL' class trawlers of Smith's Dock design (thirty of these were cancelled in March 1918).[32] They were conventional ships of 895 tons with a speed of 13kts and a single 4in gun. They cost £18-20,000 for the hull and £19,700 for the machinery. Only a few completed by the Armistice.

Three main classes of trawlers ('Mersey', 'Castle' and 'Strath' classes) were built during the war, all based on fishing vessels. 250 were ordered in November 1916, 150 in 1917 and 140 in 1918. Very brief particulars follow. (Figures in brackets are numbers completed without armament for post-war mine clearance)

Trawlers

Class	Dspt (fl) (tons)	Length pp (ft-in)	No Comp.
'Mersey'	665	138-6	69 (8)
'Castle'	547	125	127 (18)
'Strath'	429	115	89 (14)

The 'KILs' were designed by Smiths Dock, winners of a competition for a 'better' trawler. Eighty-five were ordered but many were cancelled and many more went straight on the sales list. (National Maritime Museum, London: 388362)

28. Brown, *Warrior to Dreadnought*, pp56-7.

29. D'Eyncourt papers, DEY 33. National Maritime Museum.

30. After the war it was found that their draught was insufficient for satisfactory Asdic operation.

31. C Ritchie, *Q Ships* (Lavenham 1985), p38.

32. The parallel with the Second World War corvettes, also intended as 'better' trawlers and also designed by Smith's Dock is interesting.

Kilbeccan was one of the few of her class completing with armament. (WSS)

Lingfield was a paddle minesweeper based on a design by Ailsa. Their performance in rough seas was disappointing as the changes of immersion of the wheels as they rolled caused them to yaw. This quarter view shows the minesweeping gear fitted to most classes with a gallows over the stern and a big winch on the quarterdeck. (WSS)

Paddle minesweepers

In May 1915 the Admiral in charge of minesweeping reported that requisitioned paddle steamers were more effective than trawlers, particularly when shallow draught was required. They needed a smaller crew and were cheaper to build than a shallow-draught screw ship. Reports from sea said that *Glen Usk*, built by Ailsa, was the best starting point. A sketch design was prepared by Narbeth in the Admiralty and passed to Ailsa to develop as the *Ascot* class.

Considerable attention was paid to subdivision; there

Gavotte, a 'Dance' class shallow-draught minesweeper with propellers in tunnels. (WSS)

were two boiler rooms, either side of the engine room and there were eleven main watertight compartments. The side plating was thickened and carried up to the upper deck, increasing the reserve of buoyancy. Later, several watertight doors were blanked off and in the later, improved ships access was by hatch from the upper deck.

On trial, they made 14.5-15.4kts with 1400-1600ihp on 740-800 tons. The paddles turned at 53-57rpm. This was an excellent performance, comparable with that from an optimum screw and on their shallow draught, the propeller performance would have been less than optimum. One of the problems with paddles is that the thrust varies rapidly with depth of immersion and hence with a heel due to wind and drag of sweep wire on the same side (or when rolling) it was difficult to hold a course and there was a considerable loss of speed. In the new ships a tank of 10 tons capacity was fitted in either sponson which could correct a 5° heel.

They were intended to carry two seaplanes for anti-Zeppelin work but only two ships were so fitted and, though the trials were satisfactory, they were not used in this way. Twenty-four ships were ordered to the original design in late 1915 to early 1916 whilst eight slightly enlarged ships were ordered in 1917. Eight more were planned in 1918 but not started. They cost about £55,000 each.[33]

Ten shallow draught minesweepers were acquired in 1917 from the War Office (and four more in 1919). They had been built as tugs for use in Mesopotamia and had twin screws in tunnels with a draught of only 3ft 9in. The price paid was about £4500 per ship.

Twin-screw minesweepers – the 'Hunt' class

In 1916 it was realised that the paddle sweepers were unsatisfactory in bad weather and also were at risk from mines under the paddles.[34] A new design of twin screw, shallow draught sweeper was prepared. Presumably the change to twin screws was to reduce draught. They were built to merchant ship standards under Lloyd's and British Corporation survey except that the high-speed triple-expansion engines (250rpm) were to Admiralty standard and the water tube boilers were supplied by the Admiralty.[35] They had paravanes carried aft as well as the A sweep.

Twenty ships were built to the original design at an average cost of £65,000, the apparently high price being largely an effect of wartime inflation which had probably doubled pre-war costs by this date. Favourable reports on the first to complete (*Muskerry*) led to an order for 56 slightly larger ships. Later reports suggest that seakeeping was not as good as the sloops or P boats. Several of these ships served in the Second World War and apart from their coal burning machinery were thought to be very good minesweepers.[36]

Patrol vessels, sloops and minesweepers; a comparison

It was hoped, initially, that the original 'Flower' class design would meet all requirements for small ships in minesweeping and anti-submarine work. It was inevitable that, as weapons and tactics developed, and to make best use of the capacity and skills of smaller shipyards, a range of designs would be needed. Even so, one may wonder if too many different types were built.

Tedworth of the first group of 'Hunt' class minesweepers. They were very successful and several, including *Tedworth*, served in the Second World War. (WSS)

33. Two returned to the RN in the Second World War as auxiliary AA ships.

34. One can only wonder why the later paddle minesweepers were built.

35. Mainly built by major warship builders.

36. The *Bangor* class of the Second World War were proposed as updated 'Hunts'.

Sloop and minesweeper builders

Builder	Flower	Convoy	24	P	PC	KIL	Paddle	Hunt
Ailsa							5	10
Ardrossan							1	5
Armstrong		8						
Ayrshire							4	5
Barclay Curle	12	8	6	1	2			
Bartram				2				
Blyth	1	3	2					
Bow McLachlan	3							8
Caird					2	2		
Clyde SB							2	7
Cochrane						7		
Connell	4			1	1			
Cook, Welton & Gemmell						4		
Henderson	4							
Dundee SB							3	3
Dunlop Bremner	3						1	6
Earle	3							
Eltringham				2	2			6
Fairfield								4
Ferguson							1	
Fleming & Ferguson								6
G Brown						3		
Goole							1	
Gray				4			1	
Greenock and Grangemouth	5	4	4					
H & W, Govan				2	1			
Hall Russell						4		
Hamilton	2	2		4		4	1	
Harkness				2	1			
Inglis				3			1	4
Instow								4
Irvine	2	3						
Lobnitz	6	3					10	
McMillan	5						2	2
Murdoch & Murray							2	5
Napier & Miller	3			1				6
Northumberland				2				
Osbourne Graham			3					
Redhead				3				
Rennoldson	1							2
Richardson Duck	1	1						
Ropner	1	1						
Russell				1				
Scott	3							
Simons	3	2						14
Smiths Dock						37		
Swan Hunter	6	2	7					
Thompson				2				
Tyne Iron				2	1			
White				5	6			
Workman Clarke	2	2		3	4			

Monitors[37]

As soon as the land front in Europe reached the Channel coast, the need for heavily-armed, shallow-draught ships to support the army became apparent. The opportunity to acquire a coastal attack capability quickly came when Charles M Schwab, President of Bethlehem Steel, visited the UK in November 1914. Amongst the items he had for sale were four twin 14in turrets, intended for the Greek battlecruiser *Salamis*, then building in Germany. Someone, possibly Churchill, chose the type name 'Monitor' for new ships, in the mistaken idea that it resembled Ericsson's *Monitor* of the American Civil War.

A very simple design study was prepared by a constructor, A M Worthington, and developed by his assistant, C S Lillicrap.[38] The width of the main hull was to be about 60ft with anti-torpedo bulges, newly developed by d'Eyncourt, outside, bringing the total beam to 90ft, the largest for which a reasonable number of docks were available. The form was a raft with blunt pointed ends, very different from any recent warship. It was not appreciated that the flow of water past such a form is below the bottom rather than along the sides and the after cut up was far too abrupt. The resulting severe eddies increased the resistance of the hull and also reduced the efficiency of the propellers, already low because the shallow draught limited their diameter. This problem was revealed when the lines were sent to Edmund Froude at the Haslar tank but the first ship was laid down and it was too late to change.

In consequence, the best these ships could do was about 6½kts rather than the 10kts hoped for. The four ships (*Abercrombie*, *Havelock*, *Raglan* and *Roberts*) did good work at the Dardanelles, limited only by shortage of ammunition (for the sinking of *Raglan*, see Chapter 11). Their 14in guns had an elevation of 15° giving a range of 19,900 yards, too short for work off the Belgian coast in the latter part of the war.

The 12in gun monitors – Lord Clive class

On 11 December 1914, Churchill proposed eight more monitors using spare 13.5 and 15in guns. It turned out that though there were guns, there were no turrets available. The *Majestic* class battleships had retired from active service and their 35 calibre 12in were examined. As designed these turrets had only 13½° elevation giving a range of 13,700yds but Elswick were able to confirm that it would not be difficult to increase the elevation to 30° with a range of over 21,000yds.

Though Churchill wanted diesel engines, there were no designs of sufficient power and both hull and machinery were very similar to the 14in ships. Construction of these simple ships was rapid; *Prince Rupert* was laid down by Hamilton on 12 January 1915, launched on 20 May and then towed up to Clydebank where her turret (ex-*Victorious*) was installed. She then returned to Greenock where her machinery was installed, completing for trials on 1 July, 24 weeks from laying down. The others were not much slower.

With a similar form to the earlier ships, they were slow (7-8kts). There were teething problems with the increased elevation of the 12in guns, but these were soon overcome, though the aged mountings continued to give trouble. They were soon outranged by German batteries on the Belgian coast. When *Furious* became an aircraft carrier, her two 18in guns and the spare became available and were mounted aft in *Lord Clive* and *General Wolfe* (*Prince Eugene* should have had the spare gun but the war ended before it could be installed). The fixed mount had an elevation of 45° giving a range of 36,500 yards. *Wolfe* opened fire on a bridge on 28 September 1918 at a range of 36,000yds, probably the greatest range at which an RN ship has fired. She fired forty-four rounds in two hours (2min 38sec between rounds) and another eight later in the day, out of her outfit of sixty shells. After the war, *Lord Clive* was given three 15in guns fixed to starboard to test the interference between them before a triple turret was agreed for the new capital ships. No problems were found during trials off Shoeburyness in early 1921.

15in guns and diesels

Since the battlecruisers *Repulse* and *Renown* used only six of the eight twin 15in turrets intended for the 1914 battleships, Churchill and Fisher decided to build two more monitors using these turrets, *Marshal Soult* and *Marshal Ney*. Unfortunately, as it was to prove, there were two sets of diesel engines available. They had been built for two Admiralty tankers to test the suitability of this type of machinery for surface ships. Even more

unfortunately, d'Eyncourt and Lillicrap ignored Froude's model tests and gave these two ships the same poor form as the earlier ships. *Marshal Ney* was first to complete and was almost useless, as she was slow (6kts), her engines were very unreliable and she did not steer. Her engines were of MAN design, built by J S White. The second ship, *Marshal Soult* had engines designed and built by Vickers which were reliable, quiet, free of vibration, but this ship, too, was slow. *Ney* was soon paid off but *Soult* continued to give useful service, becoming a training ship after the war and was finally scrapped in 1946.

Four more 15in monitors were ordered in May 1915 using the turrets in hand for *Royal Oak* but these were cancelled by the new Board in June as the delay to *Royal*

Roberts was one of the first group of four monitors armed with a twin 14in turret by Bethlehem Steel. Note the seaplane – a Short 166. (Author's collection)

37. I L Buxton, *Big Gun Monitors* (Tynemouth 1978). Probably the finest ship 'type' history ever written. It is almost impertinent for anyone else to write of monitors but, for completeness, the story must be summarised here.

38. Lillicrap was to become DNC in 1944.

General Wolfe was originally armed with a twin 12in turret from the pre-dreadnought *Victorious*, modified to give extra elevation and range. She was later given the single 18in from *Furious*, seen here, fixed to fire to starboard. On 28 September 1918 she fired on a bridge at 36,000yds, the greatest range at which any RN ship has fired. (WSS)

Oak was unacceptable. When the failure of the *Marshals* was recognised, it was decided to put their turrets into new hulls (later it was decided to retain *Soult* and a 15in turret ordered for *Furious* was substituted). Machinery of 6000ihp and a much improved form developed at Haslar for the cancelled group ensured that they would easily make the required speed of 12kts; in fact, they made 13-14kts on trial.

Erebus and *Terror* operated successfully off the Belgian coast, firing at about 27,000yds. By May 1917 they seem to have made Ostend dockyard untenable. They had an improved design of bulge which was to prove its value. The outer space was 9ft wide and air filled, the inner was 4ft deep filled with 70 steel tubes each 9in in diameter and sealed at the ends. The inner skin was 1½in of HT steel. The top of the bulge was

18in above the design waterline making it suitable as an embarkation platform for boats.

The Germans had introduced remote-controlled explosive motor boats in the spring of 1917, with a speed of 30kts, a 700kg (1540lb) charge and a control cable 30 miles long. They were controlled from a shore station acting on radio spotting from a seaplane. On 28 October 1917 *Erebus* was hit on the bulge amidships by one of these boats (number FL12). Fifty feet of the outer bulge was destroyed but the inner skin was barely dented and she was back in service in about three weeks. On the night of 18/19 October *Terror* was hit by three 17.7in torpedoes. Two hit right forward, the other 80ft further aft where the bulge was just starting. Repairs took 10 weeks.

Smaller monitors

At the beginning of the war, Vickers had just completed three river monitors armed with two 6in guns, but the customer, Brazil, could not afford to pay for them. Just before war started the Admiralty purchased these ships, renaming them *Humber, Severn* and *Mersey*. Though they did good service,[39] their flat bottom and draught of 4ft 9in made them unsuitable for work in the open sea. At the end of 1914, the Admiralty purchased two Norwegian coast defence ships building at Elswick (*Gorgon* and *Glatton*). They were given bulges and their two single 9.4in were re-lined to 9.2in and given 40° elevation. With 8crh heads they could reach to 39,000yds.

In early 1915, Fisher was keen to build even more coastal attack ships and looked at the availability of medium calibre guns and mountings. There were four 9.2in Mk X and ten of the older Mk VI, which were to arm the fourteen *M 15* class monitors.

The monitor *Terror* firing on the Belgian coast. (Courtesy Julian Mannering)

9.2in guns, 1915

	Calibre	Range (yds) at		Rounds/ per min
		15°	*30°*	
Mk VI	31	11,000	16,300	3½
Mk X	46	15,400	22,000	*c*1

M 21 was one of a class of smaller monitors and is seen firing her 9.2in gun. (Imperial War Museum: SP2031)

As usual, Fisher wanted diesel engines and there were twelve Bolinder semi-diesels of 320bhp each, sufficient for six ships. Two more got four smaller Bolinders, one a paraffin set, and the remainder received steam engines. Though the Bolinder was a well tried and reliable engine in merchant service, running at constant speed, it was less successful in a warship operating pattern with frequent changes of speed. Under these conditions there would be a build-up of unburnt fuel in the funnel which would catch fire. Four of these ships with Mk VI guns went to Dover but their guns lacked range and were soon removed, being replaced by smaller guns for use against destroyers. The Mediterranean ships proved quite useful but all were too lively with a GM of 6ft and, initially, no bilge keels.

Five similar ships (*M 29* class) mounting modern 6in guns intended for the lower casemates of the *Queen Elizabeth*s were also built.[40] As Buxton explains in detail, it was thought that, compared with the 9.2in monitors, displacement should vary in the same way as armament weight. Since the outfit of two 6in weighed 18 per cent less than the 9.2in, the estimated displacement was 340 tons with a draught of 4ft. Unfortunately, the size of these ships was determined by upper deck layout and the size of hull needed to arrange two 6in was about the same as that for a single 9.2in. They com-pleted with a displacement of 580 tons and a draught of about 6½ft. The 6in gun had a range of 14,700yds at 17½° elevation and the ships proved useful in the latter stages of the Dardanelles operation. They cost £25,000, excluding guns.

River gunboats

In February 1915 the Admiralty ordered two classes of shallow-draft ship which for disinformation purposes were described as 'China gunboats'. In fact the larger ships (the 'Insect' class) were intended for use on the Danube, the smaller (the 'Fly' class) for the Tigris. Both classes were designed by Yarrows who built all the smaller ships.

The twelve 'Fly' class gunboats (plus four more ordered later) were built in sections, dismantled for

39. *Mersey* and *Humber* destroyed the cruiser *Konigsberg* in the Rufiji river in 1915.

40. The guns were not those actually removed but spares off the production line.

The later, small monitors, like *M 29*, completed with two 6in guns. *M 33* (*Medusa*) is still afloat. (WSS)

Eastern Theatre. They make an interesting comparison with the 6in monitors, both with two 6in and a few lighter guns.

Comparison between 'Insect' and M 29 classes

	Monitor	*'Insect'*
Displacement (tons)	580	645
Length (ft-in)	177-3	237-6
Beam (ft)	31	20
Draught (ft)	6.5	4
Speed (kts)	9	14

All design is a compromise; both were reasonably satisfactory, the 'Insects' the more so. The monitors were ship-shaped for sea going, while the 'Insects' were river boats though they were used at sea.

Both classes of river gunboat had a propeller ('Fly') or propellers ('Insect') in tunnels with Yarrow's patented flap. The diameter of the propeller was greater than the draught and hence the top of the screw turned in a tunnel cut into the bottom of the hull. In early versions the roof of the tunnel sloped down to form a seal at the transom so that, under way, the air at the top of the tunnel would be driven out. This proved inefficient as the propeller slipstream impinging on the slope created a lot of drag. In 1892, Alfred Yarrow devised a hinged flap which would drop down at rest and be lifted by the slip stream when moving, much reducing the drag.

Cockchafer, an 'Insect' class river gunboat, mounting two 6in guns on a draught of only 4ft. (WSS)

Greenfly of the smaller 'Fly' class of river gunboat. They mounted a single 4in gun and could float in 2ft of water – it is claimed that river pilots would sometimes wade ahead of them! This photo, out of the water, clearly shows her shallow draught. (Author's collection)

transit and re-assembled in Abadan. They mounted a single 4in and smaller guns, had a speed of 9½kts and could float in 2ft of water.[41] The first entered service on the Tigris in November 1915, a remarkable production feat.

The twelve 'Insect' class were much bigger ships mounting two 6in and two 12pdr on a draught of only 4ft. They were very successful ships serving in many areas during the war though they only reached the Danube after the Armistice.[42] Between the wars they served mainly in China and some came back to play an important role in the Mediterranean in the Second World War.[43] They were even modernised for the Far

Coastal motor boats[44]

Early in 1915 three lieutenants of the Harwich Force thought of using small, fast motor boats to torpedo German ships at anchor. Tentative approval was given and a number of firms were approached of which only Thornycroft responded to the draft Staff Requirement.[45] The initial requirement was for a boat weighing not more than 4¼ tons, including an 18in torpedo, so that it could be carried a ship's ordinary 30ft motor boat davits, and capable of 30kts. Thornycroft had built a successful racing launch *Miranda IV* with a stepped, planing hull form before the war and this formed the basis for the new craft. The weight limit did not permit a conventional torpedo tube and it was eventually decided to push the torpedo out over the stern, tail first. The boat, with a speed about equal to that of the torpedo, would turn quickly out of the way. Trials by *Vernon* showed that this seemingly wild scheme actually worked.

The first Coastal Motor Boat (*CMB 1*) was ordered from Thornycroft's Hampton-on-Thames yard in late 1915; *CMB 2-12* were ordered in January 1916 and *CMB 13* a little later and all were complete by mid-August 1916. A typical weight breakdown was: hull 2.19 tons, machinery 0.78 tons and load 1.04 tons, total

Coastal Motor Boat 65A. A
55ft boat designed and built by
Thornycroft. The letter A
designates a Thornycroft 500hp
engine giving a speed of
35¼kts. (Author's collection)

4 tons. Most had a 12-cylinder Thornycroft V12 petrol engine giving 250bhp and a speed of 33-34kts.[46] Forty-four more similar boats were ordered later (seventeen cancelled at the war's end).[47] Six other boat builders were involved in the work though the majority were built by Thorncroft. Most of these later boats had Green (V12, 275bhp) or FIAT (*CMB 40-61* V8, 250bhp) engines giving a slightly higher speed.

Thornycroft anticipated a request for a bigger (55ft), non-hoisting craft carrying two 18in torpedoes and *CMB 14* was started without an order, which, however, followed in May 1916. Five more were ordered in April 1917, fifty in May and twelve in December. Thornycroft built twenty-seven, and forty-three were built by six sub-contractors.[48] There was another order for thirty-two boats about August 1918 which was cancelled in November. There were a very considerable number of different types of engine designated by a letter(s) after the CMB number.[49] All exceeded 30kts and many reached 40kts on trial under ideal conditions. Though the original design was for two torpedoes, many boats completed with one torpedo and two depth charges (a 'D' as the second letter officially indicates two torpedoes but some without a D also had two!).

Twelve 70ft boats were ordered in February 1918 primarily to lay magnetic mines.[50] The war came to an end before they were complete and a few were used for experiments, two surviving to be recommissioned in the Second World War.[51] They carried four mines but with only two 350bhp engines they only made about 30kts. An experimental pair of Y24 engines were fitted in *102* giving 36.6kts laden and 41.9kts light.

41. It is said (*Yarrows 1865-1977*. Glasgow, 1977 – company history) that the local pilots would wade ahead of the vessel in shallow water!

42. For their adventures there, see M Williams, *Captain Gilbert Roberts RN* (London 1979).

43. A C Hampshire, *Armed with Stings* (London 1958).

44. This section is largely based on the research of Geoff Hudson, historian of the Light Coastal Forces Association and a friend of mine from schooldays.

45. K C Barnaby, *100 Years of Specialised Shipbuilding and Engineering* (London 1964) (largely based on a company booklet 'A Short History of the Revival of the Small Torpedo Boat during the Great War', London, 1918).

46. Some had V8 engines and a speed of about 25kts.

47. There are conflicting figures given. The most reliable (by Hudson) gives as completed: 1-13, 40-61, 112, 121-123 and 17 cancelled.

48. In addition, *CMB 113CK* was built by Cox and King, direct order, and was probably designed by them. The builder of *CMB 120F* is unknown but she was not ordered through Thornycroft.

49. Letters given in *Conway's All the World's Fighting Ships 1906-1921* (London 1985), p100.

50. T Burton, 'The Origins of the Magnetic Mine', *WARSHIP 5* (1978).

51. *102* was a target until 1940, *103* and *104* were commissioned.

A total of 580 motor launches
like *ML 397* were built by the
Electric Boat Company, and
assembled by Canadian Vickers.
They were effective AS vessels
in inshore waters particularly
when fitted with hydrophones
and depth charges. (WSS)

The MLs were shipped across the Atlantic, as in the load on SS *Statesman*. (Author's collection)

About the only time these craft were used in the way intended was in 1919 when, in June *CMB 4*[52] sank the Bolshevik cruiser *Oleg* at Kronstadt during the British intervention in Russia; in a later attack in August eight boats set out. Although one broke down, a depot ship and two battleships were hit,[53] for the loss of three CMB. The writing was on the wall for fast attack craft when on 11 August 1918 six CMBs were caught by German seaplanes off the Dutch coast. Three were sunk and the other three driven into Dutch waters where they were interned.

Motor launches

The armed merchant cruiser *Virginian* mounted eight 6in guns. Coal was arranged to give some protection to the top of the machinery. (RINA)

Fifty motor launches were ordered from the Electric Boat Company in the USA[54] in April 1915 and a further 500 two months later followed by 30 in July 1917. To evade US neutrality laws the order was placed through Canadian Vickers who carried out some final assembly at Montreal and Quebec. The first batch were 75ft in length and the remainder 80ft with a speed of 19 knots. The whole fleet of 580 launches was built in 488 working days and shipped across the Atlantic in 130 transports. They were very useful for inshore A/S work, particularly when fitted with hydrophones and depth charges. Several survive as houseboats.

X-lighters

In February 1915 an urgent requirement was stated for a shallow-draft, self-propelled lighter to land troops, guns and horses over a shelving beach. The design was

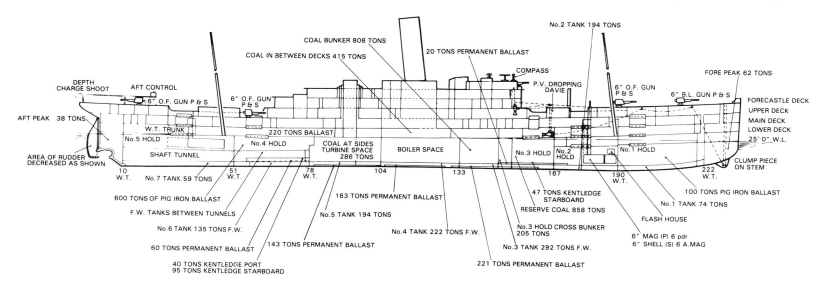

completed in four days for a craft 105ft 6in long and a draught light of 3ft 6in, deep 6ft 6in (1ft stern trim in each case) with corresponding displacements of 160 and 310 tons. They were powered by any diesel available, mostly Bolinder with power ranging from 40 to 90bhp and giving speeds of 5-7kts.

The hold was 60ft long with a full length hatch 8ft wide with a ramp 7ft wide at the fore end. Two hundred were ordered and the first were completed 10 weeks later, 50 per cent by the end of March and almost all by the end of August. Twenty more of a modified – smaller – design were ordered in February 1916 together with twenty-five similar dumb lighters. The X-lighter was regarded as very successful and used for a variety of tasks until well after the Second World War.[55]

Armed Merchant Cruisers

Some preparations had been made before the war to convert selected liners into Armed Merchant Cruisers (AMC).[56] In most cases these consisted merely of selecting positions for guns, magazines etc and preparing an outline of the work which would be needed, but the two biggest Cunard liners had had gun supports installed whilst building as a condition of the subsidy they received. Most of these preparations were of little value, however, as it was soon found that big, fast Atlantic liners were too short on endurance and were too large a target to be useful AMC, whilst they were much more

valuable as transports.

However, by August 1914 thirteen liners were being given a very basic conversion to cruisers. Typically, the conversion took 8 days; for example, in that time *Otranto* had received eight elderly 4.7in guns which required supports and necessitated cutting away some structure to improve arcs of fire. Magazines, a sick bay, and simple signalling arrangements were added, while much flammable material such as furniture and partitions was removed. A small amount of ½in plate and coal was arranged to give some protection and 200 tons of ballast was installed. The labour employed was:

Another, similar armed merchant cruiser, *Victorian*. Most such ships were employed as the 10th cruiser squadron on the Northern Blockade. (WSS)

52. Preserved at the Imperial War Museum outstation, Duxford.

53. *Shipping Wonders of the World* (London 1936), p534. Also: A Agar *Baltic Episode* (London 1963).

54. It is said that the order was suggested by a Mr Henry R Sutphen, *Shipping Wonders of the World*, p1123.

55. One is said to have been used as a Q ship.

56. D K Brown. 'Armed Merchant Ships – A Historical Review'. RINA Conference – *Merchant Ships to War* (London 1987).

The 'Q' ship *Bendish* cleared for action. She was built as the *Arvonian* and in November 1917 she was transferred to the USN as their first Q ship, *Santee*. She was armed with three 4in and three 12pdr guns, and four 18in torpedo tubes. She was torpedoed in Bantry Bay while working up and required extensive repairs returning to the RN as *Bendish* and working from Gibraltar in 1918. (Author's collection)

Shipwrights	45 for 4 days, 14 for 4 more days
Boilermakers[57]	70
Shore part & bosun	20
Joiners	30, reducing to 12
Electricians	3-4
Plumbers	2-4

Together with an unrecorded number in shore workshops.

These early conversions were intended to fight German armed merchant raiders. In the most famous such duel, *Carmania* (eight 4.7in) sank the German *Cap Trafalgar* (two 105mm) on 14 September 1914 but was herself left very seriously on fire, showing the vulnerability of such ships. The AMC were of much greater value on the Northern Patrol between Scotland and Scandinavia where the older, regular cruisers had proved to lack seaworthiness.[58] Medium-sized passenger/cargo ships of about 18,000 tons were found most suitable. Up till the end of 1917 when the Patrol virtually ceased these ships had intercepted 8905 ships (and 4205 fishing vessels) of which 1816 had been sent into port. The cost was high; there were never more than twenty-five AMC in the squadron but ten were sunk.

Q ships[59]

In 1915 a large proportion of attacks on merchant ships were carried out by surfaced submarines and the camoflagued 'Q ship' was conceived which would, at the last moment, drop its disguise, hoist the White Ensign and open fire with guns, concealed until then. This was a perfectly legal tactic and was quite successful to begin with, but once German submarines became aware of it, their attacks became more cautious and submerged attack, without warning, became the norm. Altogether eleven U-boats were sunk by Q ships together with two more sunk by submarines working with a decoy ship (8 per cent of total sinkings). There were 271 ships listed as Q Ships (but this includes the convoy sloops and PC boats) of which 39 were sunk. There was little design work involved but their conversion added to the load on shipyards.

There was one purpose-built Q ship, *Hyderabad*, designed and built by Thornycroft.[60] She was designed with very shallow draught (6ft 8in) with the hope that a torpedo would run under the keel. She was also very well subdivided with eleven bulkheads. Brief particulars of this little known ship are:

Hyderabad

Displacement (tons): 739 deep
Length (ft): 240 wl
Breadth (ft): 36
Depth (ft): 9
Armament: 1-4in (amidships), 2-12pdrs (fore and aft), 4 Sutton Armstrong A/S bomb throwers, 2 depth charge throwers (range 180yds), 2 18in torpedo tubes (4 torpedoes). All these weapons were concealed and could be brought into action in under 7 seconds. (The crews lived close to their guns.)

She made 9kts at a trial draught of 3ft 8in. There were two propellers on each of the two shafts running in tunnels. 135 tons of coal was burnt at 10/11 tons/day at full power. The rake of the funnel and masts could be varied to aid disguise.

57. In a commercial yard all metal work – plating – was done by boilermakers.

58. E K Chatterton, *The Big Blockade* (London 1920).

59. C I A Ritchie, *Q-Ships* (Lavenham 1985).

60. Ships cover 400, Maritime Museum. See also Ritchie for photos.

There was such a range of vessels built during the war that not every one can be mentioned in the text. This is a boom vessel, later gate vessel, to defend booms from attack (two 12pdr), to illuminate with its searchlight and to work gates in the boom. They were 270 tons, 100ft long and were unpowered. Several, including *BV 5*, served in the Second World War. (Author's collection)

Action Damage and the Experience of War | *Eleven*

'Ships are built to fight and must be able to take blows as well as to inflict them.'

(Admiral of the Fleet Lord Chatfield)

CHATFIELD WAS Beatty's Flag Captain in *Lion* at Jutland and held strong views on the need for protection. However, the purpose of a warship is to destroy the enemy or at least to 'frustrate their knavish tricks';[1] survival is only an important means to that end. This chapter concentrates on the ability of ships to withstand enemy weapons – 'Battleworthiness' as it is sometimes called – but destroying the enemy is more important.

The statistics of losses 1914–18[2]

Ship Category	Torp	Gun	Mine	Exp	Wreck	Collision
Battleship			1	1		
Battlecruiser		3				
Pre-Dreadnought	6		4	1	(1)	
Cruiser	10	6	2	1	1	
Destroyer	10	12	19		8	14

One aspect which is apparent from the table and which will not be discussed in detail is the large number of ships, particularly the smaller ones, lost by collision or grounding (see photo of *Laverock* in Chapter 5). A con-tributory factor to these accidents was that there was no gyro compass in most ships and a magnetic compass could be affected by movement of ferrous materials nearby.[3]

Considering the very large number of ships in service, the number lost is very small, particularly in the light of the major submarine threat. Unfortunately, there does not seem to be any overall record of ships damaged and hence only selected damage examples can be considered.

Gunfire damage

Capital ships

The battlecruiser *Tiger* was one of the most heavily hit ships at Jutland, and one of the best documented, and her experience will be considered in some detail before attempting to generalise. All hits were by 11in shells from *Moltke* except that at 1635hrs which was from *Seydlitz*.[4]

1550hrs Hit cable holder, passed through ½in forecastle deck and burst in sick bay, 8ft from impact, severe local damage but no serious effects.

1551hrs Hit starboard side of shelter deck between second and third funnels. Extensive damage to structure but not serious.

1553hrs Passed through ⁷⁄₁₆in side plating below forecastle and burst on 8in armour of A barbette. Armour holed to depth of 2½in and driven in 6in but turret operation not affected.

Invincible exploding at Jutland. The centre magazine (P and Q) has exploded. The forward magazine, A, appears to have a rapid burning – deflagration – whilst there is a low order explosion in Y. There is another photo taken a fraction of a second later which shows the circular blob in front of the compass platform has moved. It is wreckage and not a fault on the film. (Imperial War Museum: SP2468)

1. From the little-known second verse of the National Anthem.

2. Taken from Jane's 1919; may not be entirely accurate.

3. I am indebted to Rear-Admiral R O Morris, former Hydrographer, for this point.

4. These hits are discussed in more detail in J Campbell. *Jutland: An Analysis of the Fighting* (London 1986).

Damage to *Tiger's* Q turret suffered at Jutland. Despite this direct hit the guns were only out of action for a short time. (Courtesy John Roberts)

1553hrs	Pierced 5in belt just abaft A barbette making a hole 13½ x 12¼in and burst 4ft further in making a hole 10ft x 4ft in the main deck.
1553hrs?	Dented 5in armour by conning tower.
1554hrs	At 13,500yds range, descending at 220° , hit the 3¼in roof of Q turret and burst on impact. There was a hole 3ft 3in x 4ft 8in and eight casualties. Various damage put both guns out of action for a short time but they were soon back in action.
1554hrs	Hit 9in barbette armour of X turret near its junction with the 3in armour and the 1in upper deck. A piece of 9in armour 27in x 16in was broken off, the 3in armour was dented some 3in and the upper deck holed. The shell entered the revolving structure about 3ft below the turret and partially exploded, killing one man. The turret was out of action for 7 minutes but was then able to continue, firing 75 rounds during the battle.[5]
1555hrs	Pierced 6in belt just below upper deck, abreast Q turret, making a hole about 12½in diameter and burst 22ft from impact, 8ft from the 6in hoist. Two charges in the top of the hoist were set on fire but the flash did not pass down the hoist. Twelve killed. The after 6in magazine was flooded, probably unnecessarily. There was extensive local damage.

1605hrs	Hit ½in forecastle deck 107ft from bow and burst 22ft from impact.
1620hrs?	Hit 6in armour about 30ft abaft Q which was set in 3in.
1620hrs?	Hit 9in armour just aft of forward engine room. which was set in 4in.
1620hrs?	Through middle funnel. May have been a ricochet.
1635hrs	Passed through side scuttle below forecastle and burst 17ft inboard causing extensive damage.
Early	Ricochet, hit waterline armour 35ft forward of stern and dented it over area 5ft x 2ft to a maximum of 6in with minor flooding.
1658hrs	Probably ricochet through after funnel. (Note accidental damage put one gun out of action for the rest of the day.)
1815hrs+	5.9in shell holed hull abaft X barbette.

Despite these fifteen hits by 11in shells, *Tiger* remained fully capable of continuing the fight though with only six main armament guns for much of the time. It is notable how much of a ship of that era could be damaged without impairing her fighting capability. Conversely, other hits on barbettes and by the 6in hoist could have had much more serious consequences.

Other British battleships which sustained a large number of hits at Jutland are listed below, together with German ships for comparison. Since German armour had only to resist the inferior British shells the comparison means little.[6]

Hits on capital ships at Jutland

British		German	
Ship	*Hits*	*Ship*	*Hits*
Lion	13	*Lutzow*	24
P Royal	9	*Derfflinger*	21
Q Mary	7	*Seydlitz*	22
Warspite[7]	15	*Konig*	10

At the Battle of the Falklands on 8 December 1914, *Invincible* was hit by twelve 8.2in, six 5.9in and four unidentified shells without serious consequences even though, fired at long range, these shells fell steeply.[8] The older, but very well protected, pre-dreadnought *Agamemnon* was hit some twenty-six times during the Dardanelles campaign with mainly trivial damage, though one shell exploded very close to a magazine.

At Dogger Bank *Lion* was hit by sixteen 11in or 12in (mostly 11in) and one 8.3in shell with four hits below the normal waterline on the port side and one to starboard, damaging a total of 1500sq ft of bottom plating. Beatty pointed out that *Lion* was firing 55° forward of the beam and the angle of descent would be about 20°, making impact very oblique.[9] Even so, a 5in plate was

5. At 1811hrs it was discovered that the turret was misaligned by 19° from the director so that most shots from it would have gone wide.

6. The author would suggest as a very rough rule of thumb that it takes twenty large hits to disable a battleship. This seems to fit all twentieth-century wars.

7. Accounts vary as to the number of hits on *Warspite* (eg Gordon). I think Campbell is correct at least in respect of heavy shell hits.

8. N J M Campbell, *Battlecruisers* (London 1978), p40.

9. Letter of 19 Feb 1917 in ADM 137/3837.

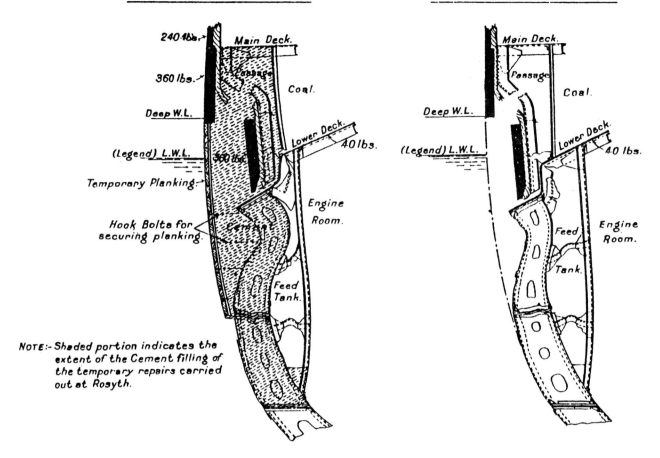

SECTION AT 210 STATION.

240 lbs.
Main Deck.
360 lbs.
Passage
Coal.
Deep W.L.
Lower Deck.
(Legend) L.W.L.
360 lbs.
40 lbs.
Temporary Planking.
Engine Room.
Hook Bolts for securing planking.
Feed Tank.

NOTE:- Shaded portion indicates the extent of the Cement filling of the temporary repairs carried out at Rosyth.

SECTION AT 208 STATION.

Main Deck.
Passage
Coal.
Deep W.L.
Lower Deck.
(Legend) L.W.L.
40 lbs.
Feed Tank.
Engine Room.

Damage to HMS *Lion* at Dogger Bank.

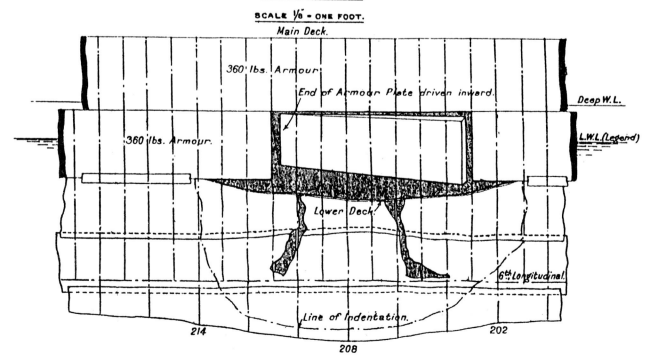

PART PROFILE.

SCALE ⅛″ = ONE FOOT.

Main Deck.
360 lbs. Armour.
End of Armour Plate driven inward.
Deep W.L.
360 lbs. Armour.
L.W.L. (Legend)
Lower Deck.
6th Longitudinal.
Line of Indentation.
214
208
202

penetrated by an 11in shell and a 6in plate by a 12in. A contributory factor was that the battle was fought in shallow water in which the height of the wave pattern generated by the ship is exaggerated with a high bow crest and the trough amidships falling below the bottom of the belt.[10] The worst damage was caused when the aft end of a 9in plate was driven in, flooding the feed tank and leading to a loss of power. It was found that the inboard edge of the plate had a very sharp corner which had cut into the framing.[11] This incident shows how lack of attention to a minor detail can have serious consequences in action. (It will be argued in the final chapter that there were too many errors of detail in the Watts' era, possibly due to insufficient staff.) *Tiger* suffered damage to the roof of Q turret. Magazine explosions will be considered separately.

One cannot help but note how few hits there were on the main belt. The few hits that there were seem to confirm that the armour was rather more effective than in pre-war trials, something noted in earlier wars such as the Russo-Japanese. There was only one hit at Jutland on belt armour thicker than 9in, by *Von Der Tann* (11in guns) on a plate of *Barham* which tapered from 13in to 8in and this did not penetrate. Since the range was about 17,000yds it is unlikely that an 11in shell would penetrate even 8in armour.

There were four hits on 9in armour, that on *Tiger*'s belt having little effect probably because of the long range. *Princess Royal* was hit by a 12in shell on X barbette at 13,000yds. A piece of armour was broken off and the shell was deflected through the 1in deck, bursting 8ft from impact. As listed above, *Tiger*'s X barbette was penetrated at about 13,500yds by an 11in shell. The

hit on *Lion*'s Q turret struck at the junction with the 3¼in roof and close to the port. Of thinner plates, there were three recorded hits on 7-8in ; one 12in shell penetrated, one 11in holed but did not penetrate and one 11in had little effect. Two 12in pierced *Princess Royal*'s 6in side, bursting well behind.

It is not possible to see any great advantage in the thicker German belts since they were attacked by inferior shells, but the thinner British armour did well against German shell. In general, this was true of thinner armour which, even if holed, would keep most of the effects of the explosion outboard, seeming to justify the thin upper and end belts used in both British and German ships. There were seventeen hits on German armour 10in or more in thickness of which one 15in shell penetrated *Derfflinger*'s 10¼in barbette. Four other hits holed the armour but the effect of the explosion was outside. Another seventeen shells hit 6-9in armour of which one 15in penetrated *Moltke*'s 8in upper belt and burst inside. Two 13.5in 1400lb CPC penetrated *Konig* at 12,600yds and burst inside.

After Jutland, two constructors, Payne and Goodall, carried out a study of the damaged ships attempting to deduce the cause in the cases of those lost.[12] They dismissed the idea that shell penetrated the 'lower protective deck and exploded either in the magazine or so close to it as to ignite the contents. This is not substantiated by a detailed examination of all the reports that have been received, and in the ships that returned from the engagement there is no known case of an enemy shell travelling so far down before bursting and only one case [that of *Barham*] where a shell which burst a short distance beyond the point of penetration sent a

10. When a new ship model test tank was built at Haslar between the wars, it was given a false bottom so that shallow-water effects could be studied. The bottom was raised manually and a large number of sailors had to be borrowed from the barracks when it was moved!

11. Records of Warship Construction during the War 1914-18. DNC Department.

12. DNC Memo S 02136/1916 of 19 Dec 1916. Only a fragment of this report has survived.

13. See Campbell, *Jutland*, p290 for details.

14. German claims are fifteen heavy and six 5.9in shells.

fragment so far into the ship'. They also said that there were very few cases of fragments penetrating over the much larger area of the machinery spaces. With hindsight, this report is probably correct in saying that it is unlikely that any protective deck was hit by an intact shell. At the ranges of Jutland, it is unlikely that a shell descended at more than 20° to the horizontal and German shells typically burst between 16 and 24ft from first impact with structure. The report is slightly ingenuous in that it fails to make it clear that the splinter in *Barham* was the substantial nose-cone of a shell which finished in a magazine. It would certainly have ignited any cordite which it contacted. Overall, one may consider that the protective decks as installed were just adequate but the *Edinburgh* trials showed that a thicker deck was highly desirable to keep out large splinters.

The argument that shells would explode before reaching the protective deck did not apply to turret roofs which had to withstand the direct impact of shells. Examination of a deck plan (*Orion*) shows that 17 per cent of the plan area of a battleship was occupied by turrets. There were two hits on roofs at Jutland: *Tiger*, discussed earlier, and *Malaya*, whose X turret was hit on the 4¼in roof at about 20° incidence. The roof was bulged and a very small hole made (*Tiger* had also been hit on the roof of Q turret at Dogger Bank). *Invincible* was hit on Q turret as was *Queen Mary*. There are indications that the frames were inadequate to withstand the impact. (Note the 1907 trials of turret roofs and the strengthening introduced in *Indefatigable*.) There were

two hits on German turret roofs; the Y turret of both *Derfflinger* and *Seydlitz*. In the latter case the roof was bowed but without serious damage. The shell that hit *Derfflinger* penetrated and burst inside causing a serious propellant fire.

Armoured cruisers

There are few lessons from damage to big, armoured cruisers, since they were old, both in years and in concept, and usually sank against overwhelming force. *Good Hope* and *Monmouth* sank at Coronel, both badly on fire. Fire aboard ship was not common in the First World War and there is a suspicion, without proof, that cordite was burning and *Good Hope* finally exploded.

At Jutland, *Defence* was hit aft leading to an explosion in the 9.2in magazine. The flame spread along the ammunition passage to each 7.5in gun in turn, followed by the forward 9.2in magazine which exploded. *Warrior* was hit by about fifteen heavy shells and six 5.9in. The most interesting hit penetrated the 6in belt, then a 2in bulkhead and the ¾in deck, exploding in the port engine room and flooding both engine rooms, ensuring that *Warrior* sank slowly and upright.[13] (See later section for the danger of longitudinal bulkheads.) *Black Prince* was hit by a large number of shells.[14] She seems to have been badly on fire and exploded before sinking.

Light cruisers

In contrast to the bigger cruisers, light cruisers withstood very severe damage without loss. *Chester* was hit

Damage suffered by *Chester* at Jutland. There were heavy casualties among her gun crews because there was a gap between the gunshields and the deck. (Author's collection)

Destroyers were tough; *Magic* floating well without a bow after being mined. (Courtesy John Roberts)

Spitfire after colliding with the battleship *Nassau*. The damage to bridge and funnels was caused by blast from *Nassau's* guns. Only after the war was it discovered that she had rammed a battleship! (Author's collection)

by about seventeen 5.9in, *Dublin* by five 5.9in and eight 4.1in and *Southampton* by one 11in, two 5.9in and eighteen 4.1in at Jutland whilst other cruisers suffered lesser damage. Campbell estimates that the side plating on light cruisers (generally 2in over 1in hull) was struck by four 5.9in, eight 4.1in and three unidentified shells, mostly at very short range. Of these two 4.1in penetrated, four 5.9in and one 4.1in holed the side without penetrating and the rest were resisted. On the other hand, casualties were very heavy due, partly to open-backed gun shields which did not fit closely enough to the deck to prevent leg injuries.[15] *Arethusa* at Heligoland Bight (28 August 1914) was hit by several 4.1in shells on her 3in HT belt without penetration. Some damage was caused to the feed tanks, high in the ship, behind the belt.

At Coronel, *Glasgow* was hit at long range by three shells, falling at a considerable angle, near the waterline but the protective deck prevented serious damage. The DNC account suggests that a light belt would have been more effective.[16]

With the exception of *Wiesbaden* at Jutland, German light cruisers suffered few hits from gunfire. She was disabled by a 12in from one of the 3rd BCS at about 1800 and was then hit by a large number of shells – though far fewer than claimed by the many ships firing on her. Campbell's estimate is fifteen heavy shells, six 9.2in or 7.5in and a number of smaller shells, together with one torpedo right aft.

Destroyers

Destroyers could withstand a great deal of damage before sinking but were often disabled by hits in their steam machinery. Of the British destroyers sunk at Jutland, *Nomad* and *Nestor* were first disabled by machinery damage, as was *Shark*. In at least three cases ammunition exploded. Of the survivors, *Onslow* was most seriously damaged with three 5.9in and two 4.1in hits. She was disabled and towed home as was *Acasta* (hit by two 5.9in). *Spitfire* was in collision with a German battleship, *Nassau*, and was hit by an 11in shell but her damage, though spectacular, was mainly superficial. German destroyers showed similar characteristics.

Details are incomplete for many of these ships but it looks as though several were disabled by loss of feed water and it should have been possible to provide more than one tank. Full 'unit' machinery (alternating boiler and engine rooms) would have added greatly to the size and cost and in such small ships might not have been very effective.

Underwater damage

The loss of Audacious

The battleship *Audacious* struck a mine off Tory Island at 0845hrs on 27 October 1914. The mine exploded under the port wing engine room, about 5-10ft forward of the after transverse engine room (ER) bulkhead where there was no protective bulkhead; there was little or no column of water thrown up which suggests the explosion occurred well under the bottom – one report says 16ft. The crew were just going to battle practice and many doors and hatches were open but it was claimed that all were closed before water reached them.

The compartments flooded immediately were the port ER, port aux M/C, WTC below and outside these rooms and X shell room. The centre ER, X turret cooler space (lower deck), junior officers' bathroom, medical distributing centre, bathroom flat and spaces abaft Y turret on the middle and main deck gradually flooded. Initial heel was about 10-15° but by flooding double bottoms and bunkers starboard, it was reduced by 0945hrs when she was rolling from 0-9° port. With full power on the starboard engine she made about 9kts. Water began to enter the starboard ER and by 1000hrs that engine was stopped. Non-essential crew were removed by 1400hrs, leaving 250 men aboard. She had been taken in tow by the liner *Olympic* but without helm, steering was erratic and the line parted at least twice. The steam valves between the port and centre ER were difficult to close and were not really tight until about 0945hrs when there was 5ft of water in the centre. The longitudinal bulkhead was undamaged where it could be seen above water but it was suspected that there was damage to the lower boundary (this is very likely). In no case was any bulkhead observed to weaken due to static head. The centre ER was abandoned soon after 1000hrs, the water was over the turbine by 1100hrs and 3-4ft below the middle deck at 1600hrs. At 1700hrs there was a further evacuation of all but 50 men and she was finally abandoned at 1815hrs. All the 50-ton pumps abaft the ER were in operation but could not cope. Attempts were made to use the circulators as bilge pumps but without success due to rapid rise.

Reasons given for spread of flooding were:

Junior officers' bathroom door only hand tight, leaked into flat.
Leak from auxiliary M/C to cooler space through holes in longitudinal bulkhead behind a link box.
Main deck hatch outside gunroom not properly closed.
Valve rod glands defective.
Water flowed into the main deck space abaft Y turret through soil pipe of Captain's head (possibly damaged in explosion).

As the ship went lower in the water, seas washed across the quarterdeck which dislodged the accommodation ladder and a whaler. These carried away some mushroom tops and damaged others and also hatch clips. This led to extensive and rapid flooding of the after end and contributed to her ultimate loss.

There was a heavy swell all day which would have caused the undamaged ship to roll about 5°. At 1100hrs she was rolling badly, hanging with the port side of the upper deck just under water before returning. At 1600hrs the mean waterline was 1ft below the upper deck aft and 4ft forward and rolling was violent. At 2045hrs the upper deck was under water, the ship heeled to 120°, hung there and capsized. She floated upside down till 2100hrs when a magazine (probably B) exploded throwing flames and debris some 300ft into the air. She was 45° bow up at the time. There were two smaller explosions. It was suggested that a shell had fallen from the racks, burst and ignited the cordite (probably Lyddite HE, Mk 15 fuse).

Three engine rooms abreast does not allow room for protection and the real danger is with two out of three flooded causing both loss of stability and asymmetric flooding. It sounds as if the explosion was under the bottom which would add to the damage. Watertightness had not been properly inspected or tested and there was poor damage control. The immersion of the quarterdeck would cause further, serious loss of stability leading to capsize.

Mining of Inflexible

One may see somewhat similar aspects in the mining of *Inflexible* at the Dardanelles, on 18 March 1915. During the attack on the Dardanelles, *Inflexible* suffered first from shell fire and was then mined. Early in the attack she was hit by a 5.9in howitzer shell on P turret which put the left gun out of action and damaged the plates protecting the apron between the guns. A few minutes later a 4in shell burst on the yard 10ft above the foretop killing or wounding most of those within.[17] At 1047hrs there was a heavy explosion alongside driving in the plating, 6ft below the waterline, port, between frames 191 and 205. At 1100hrs a 9.4in shell struck the foremast level with the flying bridge making a hole 3ft x 2ft and setting fire to the navigator's sea cabin. The fire destroyed all cables and voice pipes and there was heavy smoke, threatening the wounded in the foretop. The ship withdrew and, head to wind, the fire was soon extinguished.

Soon after 1400hrs, she was at revs for 8kts, 4kts over the ground, when she hit a mine, probably with a 220lbs charge.[18] The shock extinguished all electric lights and nearly all oil lamps, completely wrecking the starboard side of the torpedo flat and compartments below; the crew of A magazine and shell room were thrown off their feet and the turret was felt to lift. The hole in the starboard bow was irregular and variously reported as 15ft square (DNC) or 30 x 26ft (*JNE*).[19] Damage was centred on Frame 41, extending from 35-35. Two transverse bulkheads were ruptured.

The protective bulkhead and deck confined the damage and protected the magazines. A locker full of flares caught fire. Temperature in the engine room rose to 140° F as fans failed but speed was increased to 12kts and she was escorted to Tenedos. Draughts had increased from 30ft 3in forward, 30ft 8in aft to 35ft 6in and 29ft respectively, corresponding to an inflow of 1600 tons of water. She left Tenedos on 27 March for Mudros leaving for Malta on 6 April. Permanent repairs took place at Gibraltar from 21 April-15 June including much other work.

Audacious sinking after striking a mine laid by the converted liner, *Berlin*, on 27 October 1914. As she finally capsized there was a massive explosion thought to be due to fused shells falling out of the racks. (WSS)

15. *Southampton* 29 killed, 60 wounded; *Chester* 29 and 49.

16. Records of Warship Construction

17. The remedial action was to provide thicker floors to the tops as it was thought more likely that shells would burst below.

18. Private letter of 26 June 1997 from Rear-Admiral Mehmet Celayir refers to this.

19. It is difficult and almost meaningless to attempt to distinguish between 'hole' and the badly distorted structure adjoining. Examination of photos suggest five strakes high – say 15-18ft – and over 20ft long.

The pre-dreadnought battleship *Majestic* sinking after being torpedoed of the Dardanelles by *U 21* on 27 May 1915. (WSS)

Torpedo damage

The torpedo hit on the battleship *Marlborough* at Jutland is well documented.[20] Soon after she came into action she was hit, at 1854hrs, by a torpedo from the already disabled *Wiesbaden*. The torpedo hit about 25ft below the waterline abreast the starboard diesel generator room, outboard of the 6in magazine which was abaft B 15in magazine. The side plating, mainly 30lb, and the framing was destroyed over a length of 28ft and for a height of about half that. The side and bottom was badly distorted over a length of 70ft from the keel to the bottom of the armour. This illustrates some factors common to most contact torpedo hits in both world wars: the hole is twice as long as it is high and damage in both directions extends over about twice the dimensions of

the hole. The diesel generator room was wrecked and flooded immediately as did the space above. The forward, starboard boiler room began to flood, mainly through a 'watertight' door into the bunkers but also through the forward transverse bulkhead. Water rose rapidly in the boiler room at first and fires were put out in four of the six boilers; as water rose further, the others were extinguished. Damaged decks and bulkheads were shored up and the ship's powerful pumps[21] gradually reduced the amount of water, the level falling below the floor plates by 1930hrs. The ship had heeled to a maximum of 7-8° to starboard but she could maintain her place in the battleline at 17kts firing in all 162 rounds of 13.5in despite accidental damage to one gun, and problems in the hydraulic line and some difficulty in loading the shells. The 1½in magazine bulkhead about 25ft inboard from the explosion was very successful with no flooding into B magazine and very slight into the 6in magazine and shell room. About 0100hrs the next day the flooding began to increase rapidly,[22] perhaps due to the worsening weather, and, after transferring the Admiral, she made for the Humber at 14kts, reaching port under her own power 37 hours after having been hit.

The damage was much more extensive than in pre-war tests with *Hood* using 280lbs of wet gun cotton at a depth of 12ft. Campbell suggests the torpedo warhead was 440lbs of Hexanite at 25ft depth.[23] Repairs took 6 weeks and required 291 tons of new steel as well as much other needing straightening.

There are a number of common features in these three examples. The damage was more severe than expected from pre-war trials due partly to the introduction of more powerful explosives and, in the case of *Marlborough*, a larger charge. Though two of the three survived, they were both in some difficulty. The thick protective bulkhead over the magazine functioned well in *Inflexible* and *Marlborough*, particularly in the latter as it was far inboard. However, in some classes, it was not continuous over the citadel.

It was hard to prevent the spread of flooding; too many systems – ventilation, soil pipes etc – did not have stop valves at the bulkheads. The electrical system was not sufficiently divided; when *Inflexible* was mined all power was lost and the machinery space fans stopped. A break in the steam pipe to the capstan allowed salt water to reach the condensers. Many of these problems arose because these systems were not designed as such but left to the shipyard to fit in as best they could. Leaks from bunkers to boiler room through doors was a well-known hazard and it is difficult to see how anyone could have done better. There was some leakage through bulkheads due to damaged riveted seams. Some of this may have been caused by rivets overstressed when installed and they may also have been brittle (as in the *Titanic*). A damaged riveted seam is very difficult to make watertight; the recommended procedure was to hammer in wedge-shaped slivers of wood but it is very easy to open the split further if hammering is too vigorous.

Damage to pre-dreadnoughts

The table below lists underwater damage to British battleships earlier than *Dreadnought*.

Damage to pre-dreadnoughts 1914-18

Ship	Weapon	Cause of sinking
Majestic	Torpedo	Capsize
Ocean	Mine	15° list
Goliath	Torpedo	Capsize
Formidable	Torpedo	Capsize
Irresistible	Mine	Sank upright
Cornwallis	Torpedo	Capsize
Russell	Mine	Severe heel
King Edward VII	Mine	Capsize
Britannia	Torpedo	Capsize
Triumph	Torpedo	Capsize

Other fatal damage

Bulwark	Magazine explosion	
Montague	Grounded	

Of the ten ships sunk by underwater explosion, seven capsized, two were abandoned with severe heel and one sank with 6-7° list. In many cases there was a rapid initial heel, 8° seeming typical, which sometimes increased steadily to capsize but, more often, the ships would hang for a considerable time at this angle. There would then be a lurch and further rapid heel to capsize. This could be spread of flooding to a new compartment (possibly associated with bulkhead failure) or free surface high up destroying stability. Heel was often reduced by dramatic counterflooding. In some cases the ammunition passage was identified as spreading flooding.

Almost certainly, these losses can be attributed to the off-centre flooding due to a centreline bulkhead in the machinery spaces; something which Reed had warned against in 1871. The *Irresistible*, which sank with a small list only is, in fact, the clinching evidence as reports say that the centreline bulkhead between the engine rooms was damaged in the explosion.

A very crude calculation, based on *Canopus*, suggests the following figures for heel:

Space flooded	Angle of heel (°)
Engine room	9.6
Boiler room	6.8
Both	16.6

It is assumed that the coal bunkers are flooded but the coal remains in place preserving ⅝ buoyancy and water

plane inertia (stability). There are frequent references to shoring-up bulkheads in damaged ships which suggests the 'lurch' often referred to, could be the failure of a bulkhead (see water testing of bulkheads in Appendix 4)

Armoured cruisers had similar problems, if not worse. Torpedoed in way of machinery spaces, the centreline bulkhead would guarantee capsize. The *Hogue*, *Aboukir* and *Cressy* all capsized after being torpedoed on 21 September 1914. On the other hand, light cruisers stood up remarkably well to torpedo hits. *Nottingham* was hit by two torpedoes from *U 52* at about 0530hrs on 19 August 1916.[24] All lights went out and all boiler fires were extinguished. At 0645hrs she was hit by another torpedo on the opposite side, sinking at 0710hrs. *Falmouth* was hit by two torpedoes from *U 66* at 1645hrs on 19 August 1916.[25] During the night she was making slow progress under her own power and was taken in tow early the next morning. Unfortunately, she came into the sights of *U 63* which scored two more hits at noon. Even so, she floated for eight more hours, sinking five miles off Flamborough Head. One may also note *Conquest*, mined in June 1918 abreast the forward engine room which was flooded together with the after boiler room and an oil tank. She had a list of 10° and the freeboard amidships was only 12in but she reached port. These ships did not have centreline bulkheads, their transverse bulkheads were closely spaced and had few penetrations.

Destroyers of this period were still very small ships and were only likely to survive a mine or torpedo if the explosion was at an end. *Nubian* had her bow blown off in October 1916 and *Zulu* lost her stern to a mine the following month. The surviving pieces were joined together to form the *Zubian* despite a 3½in difference in beam![26] *Valkyrie* did survive a mine or torpedo explosion abreast the forward boiler room, but she was a bigger ship – and, even then, lucky.

Bulge protection

At the outbreak of war, the DNC, d'Eyncourt, devised a scheme of underwater protection in which a bulge was built onto the hull of a ship, extending 15ft from the side.[27] (See sketch). The bulge had an air-filled outer space while the inboard space was free-flooding. The idea was that a torpedo should explode well clear of the original hull and that the initial explosion would be partially dissipated in the air space while the water-filled space would stop fragments. Transverse bulkheads were fitted about 20ft apart to limit the spread of flooding and to stiffen the structure.

Without any trials, bulges were fitted to four old cruisers of the *Edgar* class, intended for shore bombardment. Work commenced in December 1914 and the first two completed 3½ months later; trials showed a 4kt loss of speed, though handling and seakeeping were said to be unaffected. *Grafton* was the first of these ships to be torpedoed, on 11 June 1917. She was hit on the port

20. Campbell, *Jutland*, pp179-81, and Records of Warship Construction.

21. She had a capacity of 675 tons/hour using the ash expellers.

22. The pump suctions became blocked but were cleared by a diver.

23. Campbell is probably right in the light of what is known of German torpedoes but the DNC history suggests that the damage was more consistent with 400lbs guncotton.

24. *Naval Operations* (Official History) Vol IV, p35

25. Ibid, p45

26. She later sank *UC 50*.

27. D'Eyncourt was unusually generous in giving praise to his staff for successful innovation. For that reason, he may be believed when he claims personal credit for the invention of bulges.

d'Eyncourt's original bulge system as applied to an *Edgar* class cruiser.

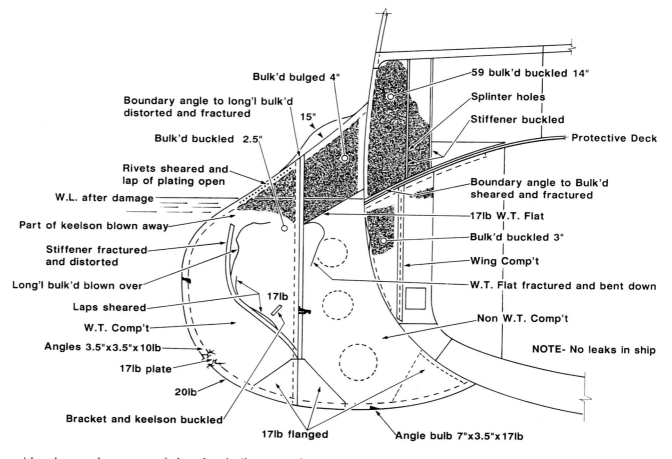

Bulk'd bulged 4"

Boundary angle to long'l bulk'd distorted and fractured

15"

Bulk'd buckled 2.5"

Rivets sheared and lap of plating open

W.L. after damage

Part of keelson blown away

Stiffener fractured and distorted

Long'l bulk'd blown over

Laps sheared

W.T. Comp't

Angles 3.5"x3.5"x10lb

17lb plate

20lb

Bracket and keelson buckled

17lb

17lb flanged

59 bulk'd buckled 14"

Splinter holes

Stiffener buckled

Protective Deck

Boundary angle to Bulk'd sheared and fractured

17lb W.T. Flat

Bulk'd buckled 3"

Wing Comp't

W.T. Flat fractured and bent down

Non W.T. Comp't

NOTE- No leaks in ship

Angle bulb 7"x3.5"x17lb

side, abreast the centre of the after boiler room by a shallow-running torpedo which exploded on the top of the bulge. Serious damage was confined to the bulge though there were a few penetrations of the original hull plating. She had no difficulty in reaching Malta under her own power. Her sister-ship, *Edgar*, was torpedoed in April 1918, the explosion being abreast the engine room, at mid height of the bulge and on a transverse bulkhead. The hole in the outer skin of the bulge was 24ft long and 12ft high; the lower section of the longitudinal bulkhead was torn away and damage to transverse bulkheads flooded 62ft of the bulge. However, damage to the thin plating of the elderly hull was only very slight with a number of dents, up to 4½in deep over an area of some 300sq ft. There was some slight leakage round shaken rivets, but this was easily controlled by pumping.

Many monitors were also fitted with bulges; *Terror* was hit by three torpedoes well forward where the bulge was less deep but damage to the main hull was slight. Her sister ship, *Erebus*, was hit by a radio-controlled explosive motor boat carrying a very large charge. Some 50ft of bulge was destroyed but there was only slight damage to the hull.

From the autumn of 1914 bulges were incorporated in the design of all new classes of large ship.[28] *Ramillies* had shallow (7ft 3in) bulges fitted before completion which reduced her speed by about a knot.

More experiments

At the suggestion of Professor Hopkinson, a series of model tests were carried out at Cambridge (1/10 scale) and Portsmouth (¼ scale) to see if models could accurately reproduce the effects of full-scale explosions. It was deduced that if the size of the model was $1/n$ then a charge of $1/n^3$ would reproduce the effects accurately enough for most purposes.[29] Later work suggested that small charges were about 25 per cent less effective than larger ones. This led to the test of a half section of a merchant ship (¼ scale) at Portsmouth which suggested a bulge 10ft deep would protect against a 350lb charge (however, it should be noted that 440lb charges were already in service)

Other experiments tried various ways of protecting the inner hull plating. First a timber layer equivalent to 12in thick was tried, but this was found to be worse than useless. Much more success was achieved with layers of sealed steel tubes and experiments suggested that, using these, the depth of the bulge could be halved. A test section – The Chatham Float – was built at Chatham; 80ft long, 31ft 6in deep and 31ft 6in wide, representing a section of a battleship. The shell plating was 40lbs and there was a bulge 7ft 6in deep. A 400lb charge was exploded against the bulge making a hole about 15ft in diameter in the outer plating. The tubes were squashed flat but the hull was hardly damaged except for a few leaky rivetted

28. *Repulse, Glorious, Hood, Raleigh* and sisters.

29. Much later work would show that it was very difficult to represent joints, rivetted or welded, in models. These tests were comparative and enabled rapid progress to be made but full scale tests were still needed.

30. D'Eyncourt manuscripts DEY. National Maritime Museum

31. S Ball, 'HMS *Bulwark*', *Warship International* 4/1984.

32. ADM 178/123 dated 17 Dec 1915

seams. There were also detachable bulges fitted to the *Redoubtable* (ex-*Revenge*) and *City of Oxford* (dummy battleship). D'Eyncourt was extremely proud of this work and in his papers there is the draft of a letter to the Prime Minister complaining that not enough had been done to fit bulges and suggesting that the Board needed a technical officer (himself).[30]

Ammunition explosions

During the First World War there were a considerable number of disastrous ammunition explosions in British warships, some accidental and others initiated by enemy weapons. There were also a smaller number of serious propellant fires which did not lead to a major explosion.

Accidental magazine explosions in RN ships 1914-18

Name	Ship type	Date
Bulwark	Pre-dreadnought	26 Nov 1914
Natal	Armoured cruiser	30 Dec 1916
Vanguard	Dreadnought	9 Jul 1917
Glatton	Monitor	16 Sep 1918

In addition, *Audacious* exploded after capsizing, probably as fused shell fell out of the racks. The minelayer *Princess Irene* was lost in 1915 due to explosion of her mines, but this was unrelated to cordite.

Bulwark was moored near Sheerness when, at 0753hrs on 26 November 1914, she was totally destroyed by a series of explosions.[31] The first explosion was in the region of the after turret and was followed almost immediately by one or two more with a cloud of black and yellow smoke. The damage was so great that there could be no conclusive proof of the cause. Suspicion rested on about thirty aging (up to 13 years old) 6in charges stowed at the fore end of the ammunition passage, some resting on a hot bulkhead (some charges are said to have been at 70°F for a long time). It is thought that some of these may have caught fire, the heat then detonating some or all of the 275 6in and 178 12pdr shells stowed in the same passage. Ammunition was being re-stowed and it is probable that all hatches to the magazines and shell rooms were open. This incident is interesting as the evidence points to the explosion of both shells and charges.

At the court of inquiry into the destruction of the *Natal* at Cromarty on 30 December 1915, it was said that there was a small explosion first, followed after some 4 seconds by a much larger explosion.[32] After about 3 minutes the ship was listing heavily and capsized after a further 2 minutes. The inquiry was told that both Mk I and MD cordite would deteriorate, the rate depending on the quality of the ingredients, care in manufacture and the thermal history whilst in storage. The 'heat test' was a good guide but depended on sub-

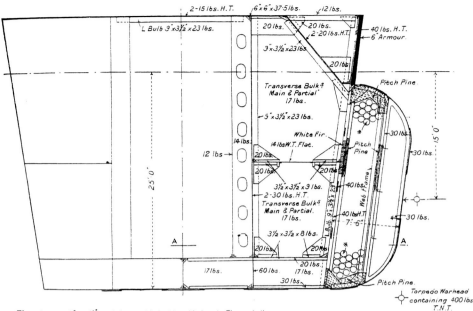

SECTION THRO. AA.

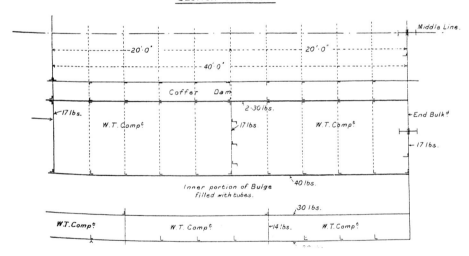

jective judgement of colour. Over 5 minutes was satisfactory; older cordite was labelled 'First Use' and should be expended in practice within 12 months, but it appeared that some 'first use' material in *Natal* had been so labelled up to 20 months ago. The inquiry concluded that 'certain inferior cordite not having been expended, appears to have been overlooked', there was therefore the risk of spontaneous ignition of any one of 'several lots on board with a very questionable history' and that the Cordite Regulations should be re-examined.

Magazine explosions in action

The evidence on the loss of ships from magazine explosions in action is incomplete and largely circumstantial. The sequence of events in *Lion* at Jutland, where the ship barely escaped the fate of *Queen Mary*,

The Chatham float was a large pontoon used to test full-size torpedo protection.

Accidental explosions in ships of other navies

Ship	Nationality	Date	Notes
Karlsruhe	German	4 Nov 1914	Possibly initiated by coal explosion
Benedetto Brin	Italian	27 Sep 1915	Possibly sabotage*
Leonardo da Vinci	Italian	2 Aug 1916	Possibly sabotage*
Imperatritsa Maria	Russian	21 Oct 1916	BN powder
Tsukuba	Japanese	14 Jan 1917	Blamed on inadequate security, possibly sabotage*
Kawachi	Japanese	12 Jul 1918	No evidence of cause*

*In none of these cases is the evidence of sabotage very strong.

Indefatigable and *Invincible*, is fairly well documented and will be described in some detail as it throws light on what may have happened in other ships.[33]

She was hit on Q turret by a 12in SAP shell from *Lutzow* at 1600hrs when the range was 16,500yds.[34] The shell descending at 20° to the horizontal, hitting the right upper corner of the left gun port where the 9in face plate met the 3¼in roof. A piece of the 9in plate was broken off and driven into the turret and the shell exploded 3ft from impact over the centre of the left-hand gun, killing or wounding everyone in the gun-house. The front roof plate was blown off, landing upside down 12ft away. The centre face plate was also

blown off, landing 15ft away. The left-hand gun was damaged beyond repair as was most but not all of the machinery. A fire was started which it was thought was extinguished from above.

The right-hand gun was in the act of loading and the dying loading number pulled a lever which sent the gun cage to a position 4ft above the working chamber. The left-hand cage was in the working chamber and loaded. Both waiting positions in the working chamber were loaded while both central cages were down and loaded and both magazine hoppers were loaded. Two or three minutes after the hit the Chief Gunner (Grant) visited Q magazine and gave orders for the magazine doors to be closed and later for the magazine to be flooded.

At 1628hrs Grant was approaching the middle deck hatch to the handing room when a large sheet of flame came up it. It is assumed that the smouldering fire in the gunhouse had spread to the eight charges in the working chamber and ignited them. They burnt very violently, the flames reaching as high as the mast head. Despite the fact that the missing roof plate vented much of the pressure, the doors to the magazine were severely buckled. It is probable that the magazine was already flooded by that time in which case the water pressure would have given support to the doors. Later tests showed that such doors were not flash-tight under severe loading and it is

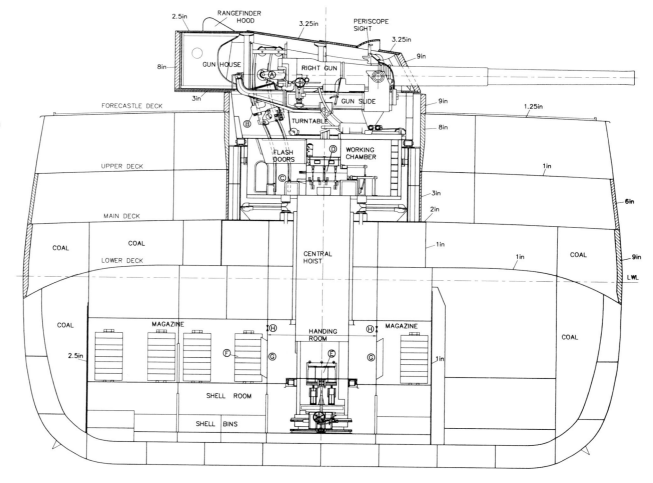

Midship section of hull and Q turret of HMS *Lion*, looking aft. The loading apparatus is shown as it was when this turret was hit at Jutland.

Key
A Breech of right gun (open)
B Right gun loading cage (shown approximately 4ft above working chamber)
C Position of gun loading cage in working chamber (left cage in this position and loaded)
D Waiting position for ammunition before transfer to gun loading cage (both left and right positions loaded)
E Cordite hoppers in handing room (both right and left positions loaded, together with central hoists which were down and loaded)
F Cordite cases in magazine
G Magazine doors
H Vent plates to magazine

likely that the magazine would have exploded had it not been flooded. The delay between the hit and the cordite fire in the trunk is important since the rise of pressure is so rapid once cordite begins to burn that it is impossible to flood. However, in *Lion*, the missing section of turret roof would have allowed good venting. It is important to note that eight full charges[35] could burn violently without explosion. (It will later be argued that this is strong evidence that gunpowder igniters were not a prime cause of explosion.)

It may be significant that Grant had had all the cordite in *Lion* changed the previous year. He had found that charges had been taken out of their cases in preparation for action and replaced in the wrong case, bearing a different date.[36] He also reduced the number of charges out of their case without reducing the rate of fire.

The battleship *Malaya* had a major cordite fire in her battery in which a considerable number of 6in, bagged, cartridges burnt violently, without exploding[37] (see Chapter 3). An interesting and possibly significant event was the sinking of the monitor *Raglan*. She had an American 14in turret with nitrocellulose propellant charges and was attacked by the *Goeben* and *Breslau* off Imbros (Dardanelles) on 20 January 1918. An 11in shell from *Goeben* penetrated the 8in barbette armour below the turret and ignited several charges. Though these burnt vigorously, there was no explosion.[38] She finally sank, after extensive damage, when the (British) 12pdr magazine blew up. One incident is not conclusive but even in the Second World War it would seem that USN propellant was safer. The smaller monitor *M 28* was sunk at the same time due to an explosion of her 9.2in magazine.

For obvious reasons, survivors from the ships lost due to magazine explosions at Jutland were few and such accounts as exist are incomplete and confused. Brief notes follow (based on Campbell) outlining the known facts.

Indefatigable was fired on by *Von der Tann* (range *c*16,000yds) and blew up shortly after 1600hrs. A photograph taken shortly before the final explosion shows her sinking by the stern, listing to port with the after part of the hull up to the middle funnel under water. Accounts of the final explosion(s) differ. It is most likely that X magazine exploded but Admiral Pakenham in *New Zealand* says that she blew up from forward after a hit near A turret. Some German accounts refer to two or three explosions (see note under *Invincible* below).

Queen Mary was initially under fire from *Seydlitz* (range *c*16,000yds) who scored about four hits up to 1615hrs, probably starting a fire in the after 4in battery. About 1621hrs *Derfflinger* scored a hit on the right side of Q turret putting the right-hand gun out of action. Five minutes later, there was a hit forward and either A or B (or both) magazine blew up breaking the forward end of the ship near the foremast. Hydraulic pressure

failed in the remaining turrets and Q and X turrets were wrecked with a cordite fire in Q working chamber. There may have been a further hit on Q turret at this time. The remains of the aft end listed heavily and, as the heel increased, there was a further major explosion (perhaps shells breaking loose as in *Audacious*?). An Anglo-German team inspected the wreck in 1991. The after end lies upside down and intact (except that the propellers have been stolen).

One of the survivors from the *Invincible*, the gunnery officer Commander Dannreuter, was in the foretop and says that a shell hit Q turret and burst inside, blowing the roof off. A tremendous explosion followed almost immediately as Q (and presumably P) magazine blew up. Two good photos exist, taken about ⅛ second apart, showing smoke, flame and wreckage flung high above the mast heads. There is a high-velocity jet of flame coming out of A turret containing wreckage and, apparently, further flame and smoke from X turret. The 1991 expedition found a large hole in the starboard side abreast X magazine and a considerable number of unexploded charges on the sea bed.[39] A reasonable interpretation would seem to be that P and Q magazines exploded and that the flash and possibly hot fragments flew fore and aft in the hull to A and X magazines. It is likely that A magazine burnt violently but did not explode whilst there was a low-order explosion in X magazine. A well-informed guess would be that the multiple explosions in *Indefatigable* and *Queen Mary* had a similar cause.

The armoured cruiser *Defence* was hit around the after 9.2in turret and an explosion was seen to travel forward along the magazine passage supplying the 7.5in turrets, each of which exploded in turn from aft. A somewhat similar event occurred in *Blücher* at Dogger Bank though with only fire rather than explosion. Evidence from other ships which blew up is too scanty to be of any value.

Hits on turrets

As well as the hits on the turrets of *Queen Mary* and *Invincible*, described above, there were one on *Lion* (also described) and one each on the roofs of *Malaya* X and *Tiger* Q. There were four hits on barbettes. In all the turret hits the armour was displaced or holed, but only in *Lion* and in *Tiger* X did the shell burst inside and the latter did not function properly.

Post-Jutland investigations

As mentioned earlier, soon after the battle, DNC sent S Payne and S V Goodall to inspect damaged ships and, if possible, deduce possible explanations for the loss of other ships. This report suggests that the cause was 'the method adopted in the transportation of the charges to the guns, whereby these charges which were not in non-inflammable cases had an open course from magazine to the gun'. They also thought that there were too many

33. Campbell, *Jutland,* pp64-67

34. Many of these ranges and times are approximate but I see no point in writing 'about' each time unless there is some special point of importance.

35. Sixteen half charges, thirty-two gunpowder igniters.

36. A Grant, *Through the Hawse Pipe*, Draft Memoirs, IWM 66/28311. Quoted by N Lambert.

37. The battery was a fairly open space and there would not have been much pressure build-up.

38. Beatty in a letter of 14 July 1917 (ADM 1/8463/176) suggests that the USN made great improvements after minor propellant fires in *Missouri* (1904) and *Kearsage*. No details have been found.

39. After the accidental explosions in *Natal* and *Vanguard* intact and even partially burnt charges were found on neighbouring ships.

Prince of Wales in post-war trials of flash tightness (July 1919). Two full 15in charges have just exploded in the supply trunk. (Author's collection)

charges exposed between the magazine and gun. (The young constructor, V G Shepheard – later Sir Victor, DNC – was damage control officer in *Agincourt* and has told this writer of his horror over the number of uncovered charges in the trunk and working chamber – particularly in the Marines' turret.)

DNO, replying to a letter of Beatty's, blamed overenthusiastic haste in supply of charges to the guns.[40] 'Magazine doors were left open, lids were off the powder cases and all cages were loaded. German nitroglycerine was very similar to MD. Cordite in the open or lightly confined will burn; *Lion* did not explode.' DNO said that magazines would be below shell rooms in new design ships and also that the igniters were little more likely to explode than the cordite.[41]

In 1913 the USN Bureau of Ordnance wished to carry out trials on British MD cordite but this plan was abandoned on cost grounds. After Jutland the Board arranged for some British 6in charges to be sent to the Naval Proving Ground, Indian Head, 'to determine the relative inflammability and fierceness of burning' of British and US propellants.[42] In their report of 11 January 1918 the conclusion was that 'cordite burns very fiercely, even when unconfined . . . nitrocellulose is consumed slowly and quietly under similar conditions . . . also *bare* cordite Mk 1 ignites about twice as readily as as *bare* charges of nitrocellulose powder.'[43] (See *Raglan* fire earlier in this chapter.)

Combining remarks by DNC and DNO, the Controller, Tudor, wrote a number of minutes putting the blame squarely on ships' staff for having too many exposed charges and generally slack procedures, encouraged by senior officers to whom rate of fire was everything. When Jellicoe became First Sea Lord he ordered Tudor to retract these criticisms of senior officers and also supressed the DNC report. He put the blame entirely on inadequate armour and physical protection against flash.[44]

Within days of the return from Jutland, Whale Island issued sketches of measures to prevent the spread of flash. By the spring of 1917 fearnought and leather screens had been installed and better working practices introduced. Handing rooms had been fitted to the secondary armament supply and their cartridges were carried in leather Clarkson cases. A trial was arranged in the fore turret of the old battleship *Vengeance* which was quite similar to modern designs and had been given all the latest modifications. The first series in August 1917 showed that the improvements had been successful resisting the flash from two full charges set off in the handing room. Later that month, a further trial with two 15in charges showed that the doors were still too weak and could distort sufficiently for flash to enter the magazine. A further trial in July 1919 using the *Prince of Wales* showed that this problem had been overcome.

There were a number of other tests at Whale Island in which a flash-tight scuttle was developed and proven. It was found that molten lead dripping from burning cables could ignite charges and such cables were removed from magazines. (It was noted the *Lion*'s cables were so burnt.)

Vanguard

The battleship *Vanguard* blew up at anchor at 1120pm on 9 July 1917 and the enquiry was told that there was a white glare between the foremast and A turret with a small explosion followed by two much heavier explosions also with a white glare.[45] After hearing all the evidence, the court decided that the main explosions were in either P or Q magazine, or both.

The ammunition had been landed and examined when the ship was in dockyard in December 1916. There was both Mk I and MD cordite. Early MD may have been nitrated for less than 2½ hours which would lead to more rapid deterioration. The Ordnance Stores Officer refused to answer when asked if overage, deteriorated cordite was less stable than new material.[46] As discussed earlier, the life of cordite could vary considerably but typically, that of Mk I was 12 years as was MD nitrated for over 2½ hours. MD with a shorter nitrating time should last 8 years.

Dr C A Parker suggests that the high nitroglycerine content of Mk 1 cordite may have been a factor.[47] The presence of impurities during manufacture, aging or high temperature (or both) would release liquid nitroglycerine which is very easily detonated. This could explain the eventual detonation of the large mass in the Plumstead trial (Chapter 2). No fire/explosion tests were carried out on aging or deteriorated cordite, possible as a result of Jellicoe's cover-up refered to above.

It was noted that the cooling in the magazines was not uniform and some bays were much hotter than others; the temperature readings were not a reliable guide to maximum temperature. There was a potential hazard in running electrical leads through magazines. It was learnt that empty coal bags were stowed adjacent to the magazine and spontaneous combustion, though unlikely, could not be ruled out.

The inquiry showed that cordite regulations had not been strictly followed and that there was a considerable quantity of Mark I cordite on board, some of it long past its safe date. As a result a large quantity of old cordite was removed from the magazines of the Grand Fleet.[48]

There are two points to be considered here. The 'Best By' date of the older cordite was probably a very safe figure and moderate extensions would not necessarily be dangerous. On the other hand, neglect of temperature control would much accelerate decomposition. No tests were carried out then or later to see if over-age cordite was more susceptible to flash; rightly, the concern was to get rid of it. However, it seems to stand to reason that material tending towards spontaneous detonation would be more easily detonated by flash and there was a lot of such over-age material in the magazines at Jutland.

There is also evidence that quality control at the manufacturer had been poor.[49] From April 1917 clean cotton sliver was to be used in place of cotton waste for the manufacture of nitrocellulose. Nitrating time was increased and inspection improved.

German experience

This will be considered only briefly; for further information see Campbell. The only explosion in action was that of the pre-Dreadnought *Pommern* which was almost certainly caused by her 6.7in shells. There were a considerable number of propellant fires, some of them very serious but they did not lead to explosions. *Goeben* had sixteen 5.9in cartridges burn in November 1914 and the flash entered the magazine but did not cause an explosion.

At Dogger Bank between thirty-five and forty 8.2in charges burnt in the ammunition passage of *Blücher*. At the same battle, *Seydlitz* was hit on the barbette of her after turret and a piece of armour detached by the explosion ignited a charge. In all sixty-two 11in charges burnt without exploding.

At Jutland there were five hits on German turrets and five more on barbettes. Most failed to penetrate but two that did caused serious fires in *Derfflinger*'s X and Y turrets, due in part to there being too many charges in transit. There were less serious fires in *Seydlitz*'s X and *Lutzow*'s A turrets. There were three fires in the secondary ammunition of *Konig* and others in *Seydlitz*, *Moltke* and *Schleswig-Holstein*, of which one below water in *Konig*'s 5.9in magazine was potentially very serious.

The majority of German propellant at Jutland was RPC/12, a solventless mixture of nitrocellulose and nitroglycerine with a stabiliser. Post-war tests are said to show that it was no more resistant to flash than British MD. These tests seem to have been conducted on single charges and all the evidence is that small quantities of cordite would only burn under these conditions. The solventless material was far less likely to have impurities which would lead to decomposition. At least the rear 75 per cent of German charges were contained in a brass case which protected the single igniter.

Other explosions

A ready-use locker exploded on the flotilla leader *Tipperary* and there were minor ammunition explosions in two other destroyers with cased charges. There seem to have been no explosions in British magazines due to underwater explosions, contrary to experience in the Second World War. This may be that there were very few torpedo or mine explosions close to magazines! The sloop *Rosemary* was hit by a torpedo under her magazine (which contained 4.7in separate ammunition). The magazine was badly damaged but shells and charges were scattered without exploding.

Some tentative conclusions

It is unlikely that it will ever be possible to explain in full why so many British[50] magazines exploded and few, if any, German. In the following paragraphs I will, with the blessing of hindsight, examine each aspect of ammunition safety and consider what contribution it might have made to disaster. It has been said that one mistake can cause an accident but it needs two or more mistakes to cause a disaster. It seems quite probable that magazine explosions had more than a single cause.

It can be argued that turret (and barbette) armour was

40. ADM 1/8463/176.

41. This surely suggests that the cordite was very dangerous?

42. Records of the Bureau of Ordnance, Doc 27809, National Archives, Washington; per I McCallum.

43. Comparative burning tests of Cordite and Nitrocellulose Powders. (Unfortunately no tests were carried out with German RPC12.)

44. This paragrah is a summary of the detailed views given by Dr N Lambert in 'Our Bloody Ships or Our Bloody System and the Loss of the Battle Cruisers', *Journal of Military History* (January 1998).

45. ADM 116/1615A.

46. One may draw one of two conclusions from his silence. Firstly that it was known to be dangerous and this was to be concealed or, more likely, that no tests had been made and it was not known if old cordite was dangerous. It is surprising that this point was not pursued.

47. Private communication via RN Cordite Association.

48. The figure of 6000 tons is given in the Technical History (MoD Library) and quoted by both Campbell and Roberts , but it seems very high and may be a misprint.

49. M R Bowditch, *Cordite-Poole* MOD PE 1983.

50. Also Japanese and Italian who also used the same method of cordite manufacture and picric acid in shells.

inadequate in both British and German ships. The roof, and in particular its supports, was vulnerable (see the 1907 trials in Chapter 2). Even the inferior British shells were able to cause fires in German turrets. It may be important that turret armour was the responsibility of the DNO whilst DNC was responsible for other armour. It is always unwise to have divided responsibility of this sort, however capable the departments concerned.

Deck armour was quite thin in both navies and intended only to keep out splinters, since it was believed that shells would burst before reaching the deck. By and large, this view seems to have been justified as there is no evidence that a shell passed through the deck of any ship, although there was a small chance of a big splinter piercing the deck as happened in *Barham* at Jutland. It does not seem that any of the losses were caused by penetration of the side armour though this cannot be ruled out in the case of *Defence*. *Invincible*'s side armour was vulnerable at the range concerned, but evidence makes it clear that a hit on Q turret was the cause of her loss.

Penetration of a turret or barbette will expose charges to flash and hot splinters (experience in the Second World War showed that the propellant then used was much more easily ignited by splinters than by flash). There does not seem to have been very much difference between British and German charges in this initial ignition (confirming post-war tests). One burning charge could ignite neighbouring charges as in *Lion* but *Seydlitz* at Dogger Bank and *Derfflinger* at Jutland showed that German charges could burn in this way without exploding. Both navies had far too many charges exposed between magazine and gun though the Germans did try to limit this after *Seydlitz* at Dogger Bank.[51]

Two very tentative conclusions may be drawn from the burning of these charges though the evidence in support is not very strong. The exposed gunpowder igniters on British charges are often seen as the primary cause of magazine explosions yet at least eight full charges (thirty-two igniters) burnt in *Lion* without exploding and probably even more in *Malaya*'s battery fire. The way in which German charges ignited suggests that their brass case was not as effective as usually believed in protecting them. Explosions in British destroyer ready-use lockers also suggest that brass cases made little difference.

The 1917 tests on *Vengeance* showed that the flash doors, even in good order, were not strong enough to resist severe pressure. Post-war examination of German ships showed that in 1918 they were barely up to 1916 British flash-tightness. There is also plenty of subjective evidence that doors were left open or even removed to improve the rate of fire in both navies. It would seem that flash could reach the magazines of any ship yet many British ships exploded and few others did.

Factors which probably contributed to explosions in British ships were:

Poor quality control in manufacture in the manufacture of cordite.
Retention of over-age material which would be less stable. (Grant's replacement of *Lion*'s material may have been important.)
Exposed igniters (but see *Lion* which suggests this made little difference).

It was then be necessary to have a source of ignition – flash or hot splinter – and a large quantity of charges in a confined space. In *Lion* the gases vented through the missing turret roof, but one would have therefore expected *Invincible*'s gases to vent through Q turret's missing roof.

One must turn back to the only large scale test, that of 1897 at Plumstead. British cordite, which would burn in small quantities, detonated in a large pile. This test was presumably with Mark I cordite but the *Vanguard* inquiry showed there was plenty of Mark I remaining in the Grand Fleet. The German RPC/12 was generally similar to British Second World War cordite and there were a number of explosions in British magazines during that war (*Hood*, *Barham* and others). It seems likely that the pressure rise[52] associated with a large quantity was a major factor in the disastrous explosions.[53] It is very likely that over-age cordite was more susceptible to such effects.

There is another common factor in the navies which were prone to ammunition explosions; the use of picric acid in shells. The safe navies did not use this filling. It is quite possible to explain[54] the major explosions, both accidental and in action, as starting with a cordite fire which would cause the detonation of a number of Lyddite shells which, in turn would explode the magazines.[55] The fires in *Lion* and *Malaya* and, possibly, *Raglan* and *Glatton*, involved lyddite-filled shells which did not explode.

There were a considerable number of trials of different aspects of the ship and, in particular, of ammunition supply. Most related to proposals for new design ships and will be covered in a later volume but some apply to ships of the war period and these will be discussed here.

Post-war trials

The Admiralty did not rest on its laurels when the fighting stopped. There were many technical developments in hand and work on most continued albeit at reduced pace. Some of the most important related to protection against shells, torpedoes and bombs and it is convenient to consider these as the sequel to the lessons of the war itself.

During the autumn of 1919 the new type of 15in shell was fired against plates arranged to represent *Hood*'s protection.[56] The weakness was that the upper 7in belt could easily be penetrated and the shell, which would explode about 40ft from impact, was still capable of

51. See N Lambert (n44).

52. There was an interesting discusion in 1926 concerning the 16in charges for *Nelson*. Tests in 1918 with a 12in charge had shown that a double silk bag greatly increased resistance to flash. The new tests in 1926 did not confirm this result and the difference was thought to be that in the later test the charge was partially confined allowing *pressure to rise*. Monthly record of important papers dealt with by the DNO. March 1926, page 3247. (MoD Library)

53. Note that Hiram Maxim believed that nitrocellulose and cordite were equally liable to explode in large quantities.

54. This explanation is due to Iain McCallum. It does seem to make a clearer distinction between navies which suffered explosions and those which did not. Nose-fused Lyddite-filled HE were seen as a particular risk and were withdrawn after Jutland.

55. Most reports describe a series of explosions and the picture of *Invincible* blowing up appears to show a major explosion amidships (P and Q magazines), a low-order explosion in X magazine (confirmed by 1991 video pictures) and very rapid burning (deflagration) in A turret

56. R A Burt, *British Battleships 1919* (London 1993), pp30.

57. Ibid, p335.

58. J Campbell, 'Washington's Cherry Trees', Part I. *WARSHIP* 1 (January 1977).

59. Probably filled Trotyl.

60. Burt, *British Battleships 1919*, p336.

61. R A Burt, *British Battleships of World War I* (London, 1986), p142.

penetrating the deck and magazine roof. The main deck over the magazine was increased to 3in which was thought to be the best that could be done with this old-fashioned ship, already grossly overweight.

The salvaged German battleship *Baden* was used for firing trials on 29 September 1921.[57] Thirty-one 15in shells were fired by the monitors *Erebus* and *Terror*,[58] the range was about 500yds but the charge was adjusted to give striking velocities of 1550 or 1380ft/sec, equivalent to ranges of 15,500 or 21,800yds respectively. At 1550ft/sec a 14in turret face plate was penetrated by APC at 18½° to the normal. The 14in conning tower resisted a hit at 30°. Another shell went through the 10in upper belt at 14½° to the normal and burst 38ft later against the funnel casing having gone through a 1.2in bulkhead and a ½in deck on the way.

Three 15in APC rounds were fired through 7in battery armour, at least one of which hit and nearly penetrated the 7⅞in barbette beyond. CPC shells[59] were fired against the decks and caused very severe blast damage. It seems to have been concluded that the new generation of shells would penetrate thick armour and the new fuses would explode them about 40ft beyond the point of impact. The filling, Shellite in the APC, Trotyl in CPC, would explode violently causing severe damage. This conclusion at least contributed to the adoption of the 'all or nothing' system of protection in the new *Nelson* class battleships. These and other tests showed that the German armour was almost identical in performance to British plates.

Some plates from *Baden* were fitted in the *Superb*[60]

for further tests on 2 May 1922. The plates and supporting structure were similar to that envisaged for the 'G 3' battlecruisers with a 14in belt which the shells would strike at 34° and a 7¼in deck over ¼in plating which was struck at 59°. Both deck and side protection was fired on with 15in shells fired from *Terror*. The range was 500yds but the charge was adjusted to give a striking velocity equivalent to battle range. Some of the deck plates were 290lb (7¾in) and it was thought that there might be difficulties in providing adequate support. However, the supports proved satisfactory except for some failures in welded joints. Two inert-filled APC hit the deck and only scooped the surface of the armour, though the beams below were seriously damaged. The 14in belt was hit by two APC at 1350ft/sec which broke up with little effect on the plate, though damage was caused when the bottom of one plate moved 15in inboard at its lower end.

Monarch was fired on both by cruisers and battleships on 21 January 1925.[61] Her protective deck was penetrated by fragments of 6in shell from the cruisers. APC 13.5in shells, filled with shellite, were capable of penetrating the 11in barbette and supporting structure before exploding. Some experimental shells with a TNT filling and a gaine worked well causing very severe blast damage. Several of these trials involved tests with bombs which will be described in a later volume.

It is clear that the new shells in the magazines of the Grand Fleet in 1918 could penetrate any side or deck armour then in use and burst reliably and violently many feet from impact.

Twelve

Warship Design from the Armistice to Washington

Capital ship design before Washington

When the war ended it was clear that many of the existing British battleships and battlecruisers, armed with 12in guns and worn out by the strains of wartime steaming, were too weak to oppose the new generation of big USN and Japanese ships. New ships would have to incorporate both the lessons of the war itself and those of later trials of shells and protection. It was also certain that a much more powerful gun than the 15in would be needed. The last three ships of the *Hood* class were soon cancelled and the Admiralty hoped to order three battleships and one battlecruiser in 1920-21 and a battleship and three battlecruisers in the following year,[1] although it seems most unlikely that the Government would have funded such a programme in full. Though the designs for battleships and battlecruisers were quite distinct, there was a considerable interaction between them, particularly in layout, and hence they will be considered together.

A Post War Questions Committee was set up under Vice-Admiral R F Phillimore and reported in March 1920. They recommended a battleship of 35,000 tons mounting five twin or four triple turrets with 'powerful' guns and a speed of 23kts. It should have a secondary armament in four twin turrets each side. The battlecruiser should have four twin turrets and a speed of 33kts. There seems to have been no technical input into this report and its pipe dreams had little influence.

The choice of armament and protection was much more important although, in fact, there was little real choice of gun.[2] The 15in 42cal Mk I was a very good gun but was too small in the light of the USN and Japanese 16in and the strong possibility of even larger weapons. The 18in 40cal mounted in *Furious* and two monitors was satisfactory but thought to be too short and some experimental 18in 45cal guns were started. It was fairly clear that the 18in would be the preferred weapon for the battleships and that a reasonable outfit could be mounted in a ship of about 50,000 tons, but the battlecruiser would have to be a good deal bigger. In order to keep the size down a smaller gun was developed, first a 16.5in 45cal, later changed to a 16in 45cal. Three 15in guns were installed in the monitor *Lord Clive* in an improvised mounting to study possible interference between the shells if all three guns were fired simultaneously. As a result, triple mounts were thought acceptable though there was still a preference for four twin mounts. Some trials, which later proved misleading, suggested that heavier shells were less effective due to

1. This was soon changed to four battlecruisers in the first year and four battleships in the following year.

2. For a more detailed account of the gun question, see J Campbell, 'Washington's Cherry Trees', *WARSHIP* 1 (Jan 1977).

3. The term 'baseline design' is more modern but there is no doubt that d'Eyncourt and his staff used the same approach.

4. The exact timing of the designs in this period is unclear; Haslar tested a model of the 'New Battlecruiser' in January 1920.

5. There is no firm evidence to confirm the last two sentences but they seem very likely in the light of the author's experience in preliminary design.

Superb at Malta in 1919. Wartime alterations to fire control and searchlights have led to a much more cluttered superstructure. However, the 12in gun Dreadnoughts were obsolescent by the end of the war and much inferior to US and Japanese ships under construction. (Author's collection)

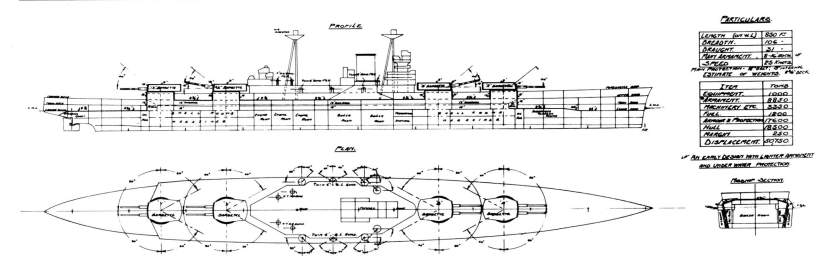

PARTICULARS.	
LENGTH (ON W.L)	850 FT
BREADTH.	106 ″
DRAUGHT.	31 ″
MAIN ARMAMENT.	8-16 50CAL 4
SPEED	25 KNOTS
MAIN PROTECTION: A″ BELT, 5″ INTERNAL	
ESTIMATE OF WEIGHTS. 6½″ DECK	

ITEM	TONS
EQUIPMENT.	1000
ARMAMENT.	8850
MACHINERY ETC.	5550
FUEL	1800
ARMOUR & PROTECTION	17600
HULL	18500
MARGIN	250
DISPLACEMENT.	50750

AN EARLY DESIGN WITH LIGHTER ARMAMENT AND UNDER WATER PROTECTION.

MIDSHIP SECTION.

their length and the new guns were designed to fire rather light shells.

There was an important correspondence between d'Eyncourt and the DNO, F C Dreyer, in May 1920. They agreed that three levels of protection should be investigated.

Against 18in attack throughout.
Against 18in for the magazines, 15in elsewhere.
Against 15in throughout.

Compared with the third, lowest level, the first ship would be 7000 tons heavier and 2kts slower whilst the intermediate would be 5000 tons heavier and 1kt slower. It was later decided to use the USN 16in, 2100lb shell, with a striking velocity of 1500ft/sec, as the standard though it had no better penetration than the British 15in.

Baseline designs

It was clear from the start that a wide range of options would have to be considered before any decision could be made and hence it was necessary to define one or two baseline designs in fair detail from which others could be scaled.[3] Since it is easier and generally more accurate to scale up than down, the baseline studies should be near the bottom of the range.[4] Existing docks limited the length to about 850ft and, more important, the beam to 106ft and, even then, there were few docks of this size.

The two baseline designs of June 1920 mounted four twin or three triple 18in and had a speed of 25-26kts. It was soon decided that battleship designs were to be designated by letters advancing from 'L' with figures 2 for twin turrets and 3 for triples. Battlecruisers were designated in reverse order from 'K' backwards. These first studies were based on the 1914 'U 4' with all four turrets on the same level so that only the end turrets had axial fire. It is probable that this strange style was adopted to lower the centre of gravity and hence obtain adequate stability even with the restricted beam. It is also possible that d'Eyncourt and Attwood were trying to emphasise the difficulty of designing a satisfactory ship with 18in guns and corresponding protection on such limited dimensions.[5]

The protection consisted of an 18in belt, inclined at

Design 'L' with twin turrets. Note that all turrets were at the same level.

Design 'L' with triple turrets, still on the same level.

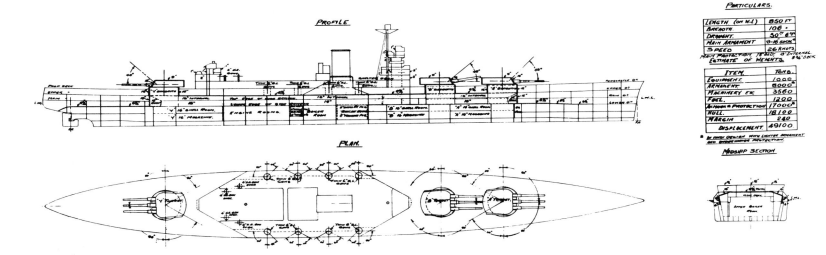

PARTICULARS.	
LENGTH (ON W.L)	850 FT
BREADTH.	106 ″
DRAUGHT.	30″ 6″″
MAIN ARMAMENT	9-18 50CAL
SPEED	26 KNOTS
MAIN PROTECTION: 18″ BELT, 5″ INTERNAL	
ESTIMATE OF WEIGHTS. 6½″ DECK	

ITEM	TONS
EQUIPMENT.	1000
ARMAMENT.	8000
MACHINERY ETC	3580
FUEL.	1200
ARMOUR & PROTECTION	17000
HULL	18100
MARGIN	240
DISPLACEMENT.	49100

AN EARLY DESIGN WITH LIGHTER ARMAMENT AND UNDERWATER PROTECTION.

MIDSHIP SECTION.

Pre-Washington capital ship designs

Design	L x B x T (ft)	Dspt (tons)	Armt	shp = kts	Belt (ins) @ slope (°)	Deck (in)
Battleships						
'L' twin	850 x 106 x 31	50,750	8-18	70,000=25	18@10	8¾
'L' triple	850 x 106 x 30.5	49,100	9-18	70,000=26	18@10	8¾
'L 2'	850 x 106 x 33.5	52,100	8-18	70,000=25	15@25	8¾
'M 2'	805 x 106 x 33	48,750	8-18	56000=23	15@25	8-9
'M 3'	765 x 106 x 23	46,000	9-18	56,000=23.5	15@25	8-9
'N 3'	815 x 106 x 33	48,000	9-18	56,000=23	15@18	8
B'cruisers						
'K 2'	875 x 106 x 33.5	53,100	8-18	144,000=30	12@25	6-7
'K 3'	875 x 106 x 33	52,000	9-18	144,000=30	12@25	6-7
'I 3'	915 x 108 x 33	51,750	9-18	180,000=32½	12@25	7-8
'H 3a'	850 x 105 x 33	52,000	6-18	180,000=33½	14@25	8-9
'G 3' initial	850 x 106 x 33	46,500	9-16.5	180,000=33	14@25	8-9
'G 3' final	850 x 106 x 32.5	48,400	9-16	160,000=32	14@18	8-4

10°, over a length of 495ft, with 5ft above the load water-line and 3ft below. The armour deck was at upper deck level (No 2 in modern terms) with the edges, 13in thick, sloped down to the top of the belt. The torpedo protection was 12ft deep with an outer, air-filled space and an inner, liquid-filled one. There was a double bottom, 7ft deep, as some protection against attack from below. Magnetic, ground mines had been used in 1918 and a prototype acoustic mine was under development.

Both the 'L' designs had a stem shaped like that of *Hood* and the same long, pointed stern. Someone, probably d'Eyncourt, suggested that this long stern was only kissing the water and that there might not be a very big penalty if it were cut off square. Model tests were carried out at Haslar during March 1920 with a model of the new battlecruiser, 'AR'.[6] The stern was to be cut off in a square transom, first at 30ft abaft the after perpendicular (then defined as the rudder stock) then at 15ft and 7½ft abaft, and finally at the rudder. To everyone's surprise, the first three forms had resistance curves indistinguishable from the original and even the final, extreme version showed only a slight penalty.[7] The new Superintendent, S Payne, who had taken over from Froude in 1919,[8] indulged in an orgy of stern-cropping and it was soon found that a transom was beneficial at higher speed/length ratios but there was a penalty at moderate speeds. The broad transom can also be very helpful in preserving damaged stability. In the ships under discussion, the transom gave the performance of a hull form some 20ft longer.

Later designs, which are fully described by Campbell, can only be outlined except when radical new features were introduced. The preliminary 'L' design was developed into 'L 2' with four twin 18in turrets and 'L 3' with three triple 18in.[9] They both had a flush-decked hull, a broad transom and a solid tower bridge with a single mast and funnel behind but the traditional conning

tower was omitted. The inner turrets were now super-firing over the end mounts. The belt was reduced to 15in but, being sloped at 25° it was probably as effective as the originally planned thickness.

The 'L' design was also translated into the battlecruisers 'K 2' (eight 18in) and 'K 3' (nine 18in) with speeds of 29-30kts. Their armour was much thinner than that of the battleships at 11in belt and 6in deck.[10] They had two funnels and the machinery occupied 250ft of their length compared with 152ft for the battleship. Discussion of the 'Ls' and 'Ks' seems to have led to the contradictory conclusions that both were too big, that the belt of the 'Ls' was too short and that the 'Ks' needed more protection and a 33kt speed to match the USS *Lexington*.

Engines aft

The next pair of battleship designs ('M') showed a dramatic change of style with the machinery aft and all the heavy guns forward. This change coincided with Stanley Goodall's return to the design section as Attwood's deputy after his work in Washington.[11] Attwood, himself, was an innovative designer and, joined by an even more innovative assistant, dramatic changes were to be expected.[12] The object of this change of style was to reduce the length of the main armoured citadel, saving on both belt and deck armour. There were, inevitably, problems; the safe firing arcs of the after turret ('M3') was given as from 60° off the bow to 75° forward of the stern. However, blast effects from a triple 18in turret would have been very severe and, in practice, only a much smaller arc on either beam could have been used.[13]

There was another less obvious problem; by its very nature the shorter belt protected a smaller proportion of the waterplane and, hence if the unarmoured ends were riddled there would be a considerable loss of stability. The metacentre would fall due to the loss of waterplane area and the freeboard to the armoured deck would be reduced. In the designs then being developed, these difficult problems were made worse as the sloping belt was set back from the side, allowing the torpedo protection to vent outboard. These problems were overcome.[14] The USN designers in the Bureau of Construction and Repair had a rigid rule for length of belt as a fraction of ship length and their studies of *Nelson* (reverse engineering) showed that the design was impossible by their rules.[15] However, the benefits were considerable:

Armour: 'L' and 'M' designs

Design	Lgth of belt (ft)	Wt of armour (tons)	% of dspt
'L 2'	470	18,850	37.1
'L 3'	445	17,800	36.3
'M 2'	440	17,310	33.2
'M 3'	401	16,060	31.4

6. Note the inconsistency in dates.

7. D K Brown, 'The Transom Stern in the RN', *WARSHIP* 5 (1978).

8. Edmund Froude became Superintendent in 1887 on the death of his father, William, and retired on health grounds in 1919. See my forthcoming biography of the Froudes, Mauve publications.

9. Model tests Sept 1920, drawings dated October.

10. The combined weight of armour and machinery was virtually the same in battleship and battlecruiser.

11. D K Brown, 'Stanley Goodall', *WARSHIP 1997-8* (1997).

12. Two or more bright people within a team interact producing much more than either would alone.

13. Firing trials in *Nelson* showed that her triple 16in turret caused severe damage to the bridge if fired abaft the beam.

14. *Nelson*, RN College, Greenwich notes.

15. N Friedman, *U S Battleships* (Annapolis 1985), p209.

15. Ibid.

16. It may have been difficult to fit in the gear boxes with the engine room aft. I designed a frigate with small blisters in the side to accommodate the corners of the large gear boxes!

17. Triple 6in were to be considered.

18. Though the use of tubes is not mentioned for earlier designs, it is probable that they were intended since they were fitted in *Hood*.

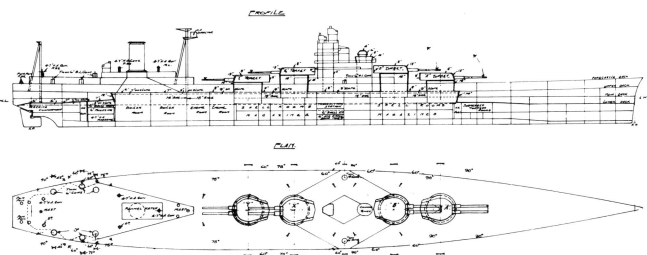

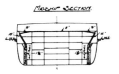

Or, putting it another way, the weight of 'M 2's armour was only 92 per cent of that of 'L 2' and 'M 3's was 90 per cent of 'L 3' – a saving of 1500-1800 tons. Note also the saving in length of belt and hence weight by having three triple turrets instead of four twins.

The 'Ms' were twin-shaft ships with the engine rooms forward of the boiler rooms, presumably to reduce shaft rake.[16] Surprisingly, the more powerful, four-shaft battlecruisers ('I 3') had the engine rooms abaft the boilers. These designs were submitted in December 1920 and 'M 3' was selected as the basis for future battleships. It was intended to improve the ammunition supply to the eight twin 6in turrets[17] and to do away with the slope to the armour bulkheads at the ends of the citadel.

The battlecruisers were more difficult: 'J 3' was a fairly conventional design with two triple 15in turrets forward and one aft. 'I 3' had the same layout as 'M 3' and nine 18in guns. She was a very long ship at 915ft and could not have docked at either Portsmouth or Rosyth. The space between the internal belt and the ship's side

was filled with sealed steel tubes which it was hoped would retain some buoyancy and stability after a torpedo hit and might function as a de-capping layer for APC shells.[18] This ship was thought to be too big and three smaller variants of 'H 3' were prepared.

'H 3a' was virtually 'I 3' with X turret omitted leaving her with two triple 18in superfiring forward, and as the deleted turret had only a very limited arc of fire, the loss of capability was not very great. 'H 3b' had one triple 18in forward of the bridge in the raised B position and one between bridge and funnel, also raised. 'H 3c' was similar except that both turrets were lowered.

'H' battlecruiser designs

Design	Dspt (tons)	Speed (kts)
'H 3a'	44,500	33.5
'H 3b'	45,000	33.25
'H 3c'	43,750	33.75

The first engines aft design, the battleship 'M 2'. It is probably no coincidence that it appeared soon after Stanley Goodall's return to the battleship section. The head of section, E L Attwood was also an innovator.

'M 3' with triple turrets.

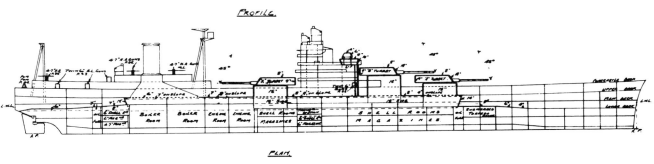

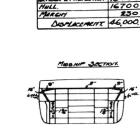

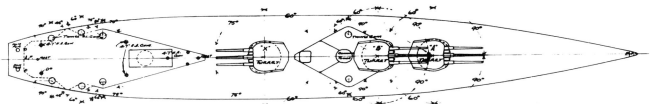

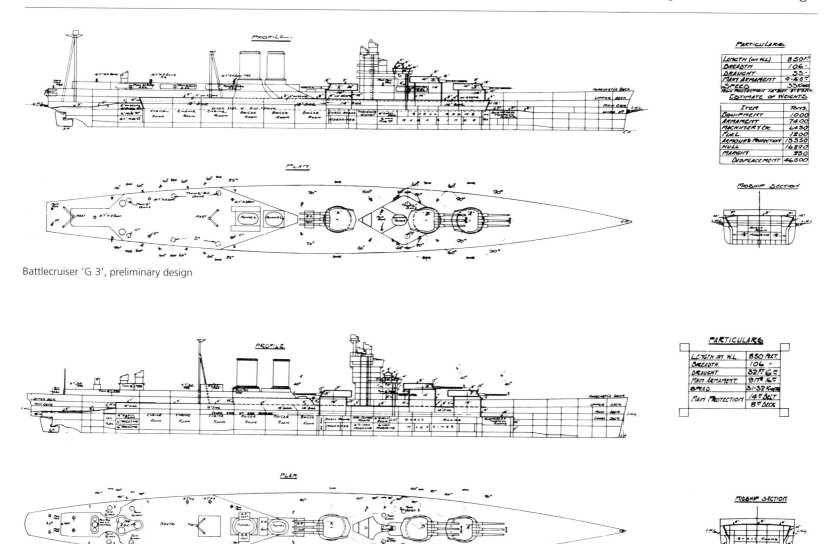

Battlecruiser 'G 3', preliminary design

Battlecruiser 'G 3', final design

Battlecruiser 'G 3'

In the next battlecruiser design, 'G 3', the 18in gun was replaced by the 16.5in, changed to 16in in January 1921. (DNC pointed out that there would be little change needed to fit twin 18in in place of the triple 16in.) She carried three triple turrets in the same configuration as 'M 3' and there were two funnels on her long after superstructure. The 'G 3' design was much admired, then and now, was developed and even ordered, and must be considered in a little more detail.[19]

The original design only had a 3in deck over the machinery and this was increased to 4in. Over the main magazines and as far aft as the middle boiler room the deck was 8in with 9in slopes and it was 7in over the after 6in magazine and half way along the after engine-room. Deck armour is costly in weight and these changes added 1125 tons, but savings elsewhere reduced the total increase in displacement to 710 tons. Consideration was given to increasing the torpedo protection to resist 1000lb charges instead of 750lb but the consequent

increase in ship size was thought excessive.

The secondary armament was reduced to twelve 6in as part of the savings described above but was later restored to sixteen guns. The twin 6in was originally expected to weigh 48¾ tons but this figure was soon increased to 60 tons and the turrets eventually installed in *Nelson* weighed in at 77 tons! The anti-aircraft armament was increased to six single 4.7in and there were to be four 8-barrel pom-poms; a very heavy armament for the day. Two beam-mounted 24.5in torpedo tubes were intended with six torpedoes each (to be increased to eight in war), and an oxygen enrichment plant was fitted. DNC argued against the torpedo armament but was overruled. It is interesting that the staff read the lessons of the war as justifying both torpedo tubes and the heavy secondary armament, the opposite to the views given in Chapter 3. It would have been possible to carry aircraft on B and X turrets but no decision had been made when the ships were cancelled.

The Engineer-in-Chief complained that the boiler rooms were too small and, even though some more space n a

was found by extending the engine rooms right out to the torpedo holding bulkhead, he could only provide 160,000shp which might just have given 32kts. Even so, the lines aft had to be distorted, probably to accommodate the gear boxes, which led to a penalty of 7½ per cent on power, later reduced to 4 per cent by modifications suggested at Haslar. A new plant of 180,000shp would add 25ft to the length and only increase speed by ½kt which was not thought worthwhile.

There is a well known story of a bet, preserved in the Ship's Cover.

'Speed expected at full power. If any of these ships obtain an official mean speed of 32 knots over the measured mile – no matter what the shp developed – I will pay DNC £1. If none of these ships obtain this speed DNC will pay me £5.' Signed S V Goodall, witnessed C M Carter.

This lighthearted note illustrates the excitement and pure fun[20] of preliminary design as well as the strong difference of opinion within the team.

The ship had to be designed with a high initial metacentric height in order to retain stability with spaces outside the citadel riddled.

Stability of 'G3'

Condition	Light	Legend	Deep	Extra Deep
Intact				
Dspt (tons)	46,830	48,400	53,910	56,540
GM (ft)	4.9	5.6	7.9	8.5
Angle Max GZ (°)	34	35	36	36
Range (°)	61	63	72	74
Riddled				
GM		4.1		6.5
Angle Max GZ (°)		13		10
Range (°)		27		21

For such extensive damage, the riddled figures appear reasonable satisfactory. Such calculations are very time-consuming which is presumably the reason why only two damaged conditions were worked out. Four ships were ordered in October-November 1921 but were suspended in November and cancelled in February 1922 as a result of the Washington Treaty.[21]

Similar development of the 'M 3' battleship design led in November 1921 to the sketch design of the 'N 3', 50ft longer than 'M 3' but generally similar. During the Treaty negotiations a 35,000-ton battleship, 'O 3', was designed and submitted on 1 November 1921 which was to emerge as *Nelson*, discussed later. Of all these capital ships, only the original 'Ls', 'G 3' and 'O 3' were tested as models at Haslar.[22]

Conclusions

Compared with pre-war designs, all these capital ships were much bigger. Both the armament weight and that of protection (particularly the deck) had roughly doubled only partially offset by lighter machinery (on the basis of shp/ton).

Comparison of weights, *Royal Sovereign* v 'M 3'

| | *Royal Sovereign* | | 'M 3' | |
	Tons	%	Tons	%
Hull	8630	33.5	16,700	36.3
Equipment	750	2.9	1000	2.1
Armament	4570	17.7	8850	19.2
Protection	8250	32.0	15,400	33.4
Machinery	2550	9.9	2720	5.9
Fuel	900	3.5	1100	2.4
Margin	100	0.4	230	0.5
Legend Dspt	25,750		46,000	

In general, thin armour was abolished, even before the Washington Treaty, as the damage potential of the new APC shell was so much greater and wartime experience was thought to show that large capacity HE shell was a lesser hazard than expected.[23] They were a little faster than pre-war battleships at 23-25kts instead of 21kts but, even so, the proportion of weight devoted to machinery was less because of the belated use of small tube boilers. There were also less obvious features such as the extensive torpedo protection, the heavy and useless secondary armament and the increasing anti-aircraft armament. Based on the experience of war, they were far superior to contemporary ships of other navies.

Comparison of designs from War to Washington

Ship	Navy	Dspt (tons)	Speed (kts)	Main armt	Belt, max (ins)	Deck, max (ins)
'G 3'	RN	48,400	31-32	9-16in	14	8
'N 3'	RN	48,500	23	9-18in	15	8
Lexington	USN	43,500	33.25	8-16in	7½	2
S Dakota	USN	43,200	23	12-16in	13½	6
Amagi	IJN	40,000	30	10-16in	11½	6
Kii	IJN	41,400	29¼	10-16in	11½	6
'I 3'	IJN	47,500	30	8-18in	13.3	5

Some later ships for comparison

Ship	Navy	Dspt (tons)	Speed (kts)	Main armt	Belt, (ins)	Deck, (ins)
Iowa	USN	48,110	32.5	9-16in	12.1	6
Yamato	Japan	62,315	27	9-18.1in	16.1	9.1
Bismarck	Germany	41,700	29	8-15in	12.5	4.75

19. Full particulars are available in articles and books by Campbell, Roberts and Raven and Burt.

20. A few years later, Carter was again working for Goodall, this time on destroyers, and, much later, talking to the author, was to emphasise Goodall's zest for life and sense of fun – he ran the department's concert party.

21. One may surmise that the order was hastened to give a bargaining point in the Treaty negotiations.

22. It would have been quite satisfactory to scale other designs from these few tests backed by the Iso-K data books.

23. The reduction of thin armour probably went too far as thin armour was added to the ends of *Nelson* to protect against bomb splinters.

Rodney in 1934, almost as completed. (Courtesy John Roberts)

The figures below suggest that the 'G 3s' were the equal or better than their contemporaries and even any Second World War ship except, possibly, the much larger *Yamato* – their thin belt would rule out the *Iowa*s. It would have been fascinating to see an ageing 'G 3' take on the *Bismarck*. It is interesting that the RN staff of the early 1920s still saw the battlecruiser as an essential part of the fleet.

Washington Treaty designs to *Nelson*

The Washington Treaty

The Treaty negotiations and their outcome will be dealt with in a later book but the designs for 'Treaty' ships which finally led to *Nelson* and *Rodney* are the end points of post-war capital ship designs and are covered here for completeness. During the first half of 1921

hints were dropped by ministers in both Britain and the USA of a possible conference to discuss limitations on warship building. In July, the USA issued a formal invitation and the main naval powers assembled in Washington in November.[24]

The USA proposed a limit of 35,000 tons on future capital ships and studies were put in hand to see what was possible within this limit. (The UK argued for 43,000 tons in the vain hope of saving two of the 'G 3s'.) By 21 November sketch designs for two battlecruisers had been prepared – it is of interest that the first choice was still for battlecruisers. Their guns were only 15in and, since the USA and Japan were certain to have at least two ships with 16in guns, it was decided on 17 December to look at a 23kt battleship with 16in guns. All these designs had the engines aft but the arrangements of the turrets with respect to the bridge tower varied.[25] There were at least three variants of 'O 3', two with A and B turrets low and X superfiring, ahead of the bridge; in the other variant B turret was raised and the third turret low (as *Nelson* completed). 'P 3' and 'Q 3' had the third turret abaft the bridge. The Haslar model tests of 'O 3' were reported in February 1922 and they must have been carried out before then.[26]

The final version of 'O 3' (*Nelson*) was approved on 6 February 1922 and the legend on 11 September. They were officially ordered on 1 January 1923 having been laid down 3 days earlier. The tender price was about £7.5 million.

Washington designs

Design	L x B x T (ft)	Dspt (tons)	Main armt	shp=kts	Belt (in)*	Deck (in)*
'F 2'	760 x 106 x 28½	35,000	6-15in	112,000=29.5	13	7
'F 3'	740 x 106 x 28½	35,000	9-15in	96,000=28.5	12	7
'O 3'	717 x 104 x 30	35,000	9-16in	45,000=23	14	7½
'P 3' & 'Q 3'	717 x 104 x 30	35,000	9-15in	45,000=23	14	7½
Nelson	710 x 106 x 30	35,000	9-16in	45,000=23	14	6¾

* Protection is maximum thickness over magazines, machinery spaces thinner.

Stability and rolling

All designs of this style, with engines aft and a short citadel, had difficulty in obtaining satisfactory stability characteristics.[27] If the unprotected ends were flooded the armour box had to provide enough stability to keep the ship more or less upright and, to achieve this standard, the stability (metacentric height) undamaged was likely to be much greater than desirable. *Nelson's* belt was 384ft long, only 54 per cent of her overall length.

There was another feature which made the problem worse for *Nelson*; the armour belt was set back from the side so that the torpedo protection spaces could vent outboard. This meant that stability was further reduced if all unarmoured spaces were flooded. In consequence, she had an intact metacentric height (GM) of 9.4ft deep, and 7ft light. Model tests with a GM of 7.5ft suggested a roll period of 14 seconds. Trials at sea indicated periods from 11½ to 13½ seconds.[28] This period implies fairly high roll accelerations which would impair gunnery.

Stability conditions for *Nelson*, intact

Condition	Displacement (tons)	GM	Max. GZ (ft)	at°
Light	34,521	7.0	4.2	37.5
Deep	39,245	9.4	6.0	38.5
Extra deep	42,774	10.2	6.0	38

Calculations were made to show the effect of flooding on draught and freeboard. In the worst case it was assumed that the ends were open to the sea above the lower deck as were the side spaces outside the armour. Spaces above the armour deck were riddled and gutted but bulge compartments were intact. In this condition the metacentric height was very small as was the range of stability in all loading conditions.[29] For such extreme damage this result seems satisfactory.

Flooding five bulge compartments and spaces outside the armour would cause a heel of 11½° (deep), and 15°(light). Flooding the whole of the fore end would give a trim of about 25ft with a freeboard of 5.8ft whilst flooding the aft end would give about the same trim by the stern with a worst freeboard of 6.8ft.

Protection

The main armour belt was 13ft deep, 14in thick over the main magazines and control positions, and 13in over machinery and the 6in magazines. The belt was sloped at 18° to the vertical and was inboard. The individual plates were as large as possible and the butts were keyed, further strengthened by heavy bars behind the butt.[30] The upper edge of the belt was supported by the armour deck and the lower edge was supported by a heavy steel casting, itself supported off the torpedo protection. The deck was 6¾in over the main magazines, 3¾in aft, both over ½in deck plating. Firing trials against *Baden* and

Superb showed that the magazines were safe against all shells at battle range whilst there was only a slight risk to the machinery.

The turrets had 16in face plates, 11in front side and 9in rear and there was a heavily armoured conning tower.[31] The boiler rooms were aft of the engines which kept the large openings for uptakes and downtakes as far from the magazines as possible. These large openings were protected by 8-9in rings between the main and middle deck. However, weight had run out when the protection of the secondary armament was considered and it could only be given 1in splinter plating.

The torpedo protection consisted of an outer air-filled space and an inner space, usually water-filled.[32] The inner space held 2870 tons of water which increased the draught by 23in and reduced speed by ⅓kt. The total depth was 12ft with the holding bulkhead made of two thicknesses of ¾in D quality steel, rivetted together. Inboard of this bulkhead there was either a coffer dam or a non-vital compartment. Initially, the air spaces were intended to vent outboard through circular plates, lightly bolted in place. These were found to be ineffective and were sealed. It was intended that this protection should resist a 750lb charge[33] and a full-scale section was made and tested against a 1000lb charge. This made a very large hole in the outer plating but leakage through the holding bulkhead was very slight.

Neither of these ship was hit by shells (*Rodney* was only hit by a few splinters from *Bismarck*) and the torpedo which hit *Nelson* in September 1941 exploded well forward of the protection where it caused major damage. *Nelson* had also been mined early in the war with the explosion forward of A turret. Damage and casualties were severe and she was out of action for 7 months. *Rodney* was hit by an 1100lb armour-piercing bomb which hit just forward of the funnel. It broke up in the armour deck with a partial detonation, and damage and casualties were slight. Post-war trials with new 2000lb AP bombs against *Nelson* showed that such bombs could penetrate the thick deck and burst with delay below – but only if dropped from 5000ft or more, and even against a stationary, undefended ship in good weather hits were rare at this height.[34]

They were the most heavily protected ships of their day and even later were only surpassed (possibly) by the much larger *Yamato*. Little improvement could be attempted within Treaty limits, though *Nelson* did receive some 100-120lb NC plate on the lower deck forward during the war.

Weight saving

After the design was approved it was decided to use the new, stronger D quality steel in the hull. It had an ultimate tensile strength of 37-44 tons/in² compared with 26-30 tons/in² for mild steel. The saving is not pro rata to strength since many members would fail by buckling at lower stresses and need the greater thickness. This

24. UK, USA, Japan, France, Italy (Australia and New Zealand attended as part of the British team).25. Burt, *British Battleships 1919-1939*, p328. For sketches.

26. Preliminary results would have been reported by phone.

27. See Friedman, *U S Battleships*, pp209-10 for US bewilderment over the *Nelson* design.

28. Roll periods are not easy to measure at sea.

29. Book of Calculations, Maritime Museum.

30. Presumably a reaction to *Lion's* damage at Dogger Bank.

31. Something which could well have been omitted in the pursuit of weight saving – it weighed 222 tons.

32. The Washington Treaty definition of 'standard' displacement excluded liquids. Both the USN and RN were using water-filled spaces in torpedo protection and wished to conceal this!

33. It was claimed that she could withstand four torpedoes with such charges.

34. Burt, *British Battleships 1919-1939*, p363.

permitted the use of thinner plates and sections with an estimated weight saving of 1500-2000 tons.

Design stresses (tons/in²)

	Keel	Deck
Sagging	7.5 T	5.9 C
Hogging	5.4 C	8.3 T

C = Compressive, T = Tension

I have been told that the overseers at the building yards were given delegated authority to reject fittings which they considered overweight. After launch, the displacement was reconsidered and in January 1926 the figure corresponding to the legend outfit was only 33,000 tons. The 16in shell outfit was increased to 100 rounds per gun bringing the displacement to 33,600 tons. This was embarrassing since the extra weight could have been used in the design stage. *Nelson* finally completed at 33,580 tons and *Rodney* at 33,785 tons.

Armament

The 16in guns and their triple mounts had a number of problems which took a considerable time to cure. The gun was designed to fire a light, 2048lb, projectile at a muzzle velocity of 2670ft/sec. On first firing it was found that this high velocity made barrel wear excessive with a loss of 1.5ft/sec of muzzle velocity between each round and a barrel life of only 180 rounds, and consequently the charge was reduced from 525lbs to 510lbs improving life to 200 rounds. Much later, a modified rifling was introduced improving accuracy.

Charges and shells were brought to the gunhouse in the vertical position in flash-tight hoists with flash-tight scuttles top and bottom so that the charge was exposed

Inside a 16in gunhouse of *Rodney*. There were considerable problems initially with the triple turrets of the *Nelson* class battleships. (Courtesy John Roberts)

only as it crossed the handing room and while actually entering the gun. There was a very large number of safety interlocks which made loading slow. It was necessary to fire the centre gun in a different salvo from the outer guns but the guns had to be loaded together so that the practical interval between rounds was about 65 seconds. And there were other problems including damaged rollers. However, in sinking the *Bismarck*, *Rodney* fired 375 rounds, including a considerable number of broadsides, with only a few problems. She fired salvoes at 1.6 per minute and broadsides at 1.1 per minute.[35]

There were problems with the 6in secondary armament as well. They were intended to fire 7-8 rounds per minute but 4 was the best achieved on completion. In the *Bismarck* action, *Rodney* was able to fire at 5.9 rounds per minute at close range, suggesting that most of these problems had been overcome by 1941. She had six 4.7in AA guns (it was intended that four 8-barrel

pom-poms be fitted but these were not available until much later) and two 24.5in torpedo tubes (10 torpedoes). The torpedoes were short to ease the problem of transporting them through the ship to the bow tubes. They ran on enriched air and had a charge of 743lbs.

Blast damage

The blast from a 16in gun was very severe and during trials in *Nelson* the bridge structure was damaged when the after turret fired abaft the beam. *Rodney* was given additional stiffening and a young constructor, H S Pengelly, reported that the blast on the bridge was acceptable. Years later (*c*1954), Pengelly, then Deputy Director, told the author of another blast trial in which A turret was to fire forward at depression. Pengelly was on the deck below, in line with the muzzles, measuring the deflection of the deck above. When the gun fired, he and his team saw a vivid red flash around them and the

35. J Roberts, 'The Final Action', *WARSHIP* 28 (Oct 1983).

Inside the training engine space of one of *Rodney*'s 16in turrets (taken in 1943). (Courtesy John Roberts)

Rodney as completed. Note the three twin 6in either side. Weight considerations meant that these turrets could only be given 1in splinter protection. (Courtesy John Roberts)

Rodney firing off Normandy in 1944. The blast from her 16in guns could cause serious damage to the ship. (Imperial War Museum: A23961)

trial was suspended. Weeks later a doctor found the explanation, noting that the 'flash' had caused no burning. It had in fact been the result of concussion of the eyeball!

Rodney suffered a great deal of blast damage when firing on *Bismarck*. The upper deck was badly distorted, wood planking ripped and many fittings dislodged. Even below deck, pillars and girders were bent or broken.[36] Periscopes in A turret were bent and broken by blast from B turret and there was damage to the 6in tur-

rets. The bridge had few problems as there had not been much firing abaft the beam during the action. It seems likely that in the quest for weight saving, the structure was not quite strong enough.

Costs of Nelson and Rodney[37]

The cost figures for *Nelson* and *Rodney* are of interest not only in their own right but also because they formed the basis for the estimated costs of the *King George V* class which proved so seriously in error. The tables which follow break down the total in different ways.

Costs for *Nelson* and *Rodney* (£)

Ship	Nelson	Rodney
Hull	1,130,000	1,215,000
Dockyard stores	67,875	67,875
Armour	1,431,000	1,431,000
Machinery	453,896	452,759
Gun mounts & TT	2,300,244	2,300,244
Armament	831,695	831,695
Armament stores	672,000	672,000
Incidentals	100,000	100,000
TOTAL	6,986,710	7,070,573

Notes: The cost of machinery is divided into main and auxiliary – £348,095/£105,801 for *Nelson*; £348,801/£103,958 for *Rodney*.

Gun mountings divide into £2,280,000 for the mountings them-selves, £4625 for torpedo tubes, £5706 air conditioning, air bottles & misc £9913.

Armament divides into £519,000 guns + £219,000 reserves, the remainder being torpedoes and spares. Armament stores covers £270,000 for shells + £402,000 reserves.

The corresponding figures for group weights (tons) are as follows, including Bates' figures for actual weights.

Group weights (tons)

Group	Design wt	Actual wt
Hull	14,250	14,568 inc 1300 protection, 118 equipt
Machinery	2420	2329
Armament	6950	
Armour	10,250	8750
Equipment	1050	
TOTAL	30,050	Zero oil, Board Margin

There follows a very detailed breakdown of the ship-builders costs.

Shipbuilder's costs (£)

	Nelson	Rodney
	Armstrong	C Laird
Hull	1,130,000	1,215,000
Main machinery	348,695	348,801
Distilling machinery	7553	7553
Steering gear	7175	7175
Steering engines	1820	1820
Steering wheels etc	2350	2350
2 Diesel generators	19,569	22,773
4 Turbo generators	18,810	16,861
Refrig M/C	9500	9500
Capstan forward	10,525	10,525
Capstan aft	1919	1919
Elec Boat hoists	6147	6147
Engine turning motors	378	378
Sub Total	1,564,442	1,650,803
Spare boiler tubes	1475	1464
Spare outboard prop shaft	150	256
2 spare props	—	4952
Spare gearing	8380	8350
Jigs and gauges	450	—
Lifting gear for props	9000	1945
TOTAL	1,583,897	1,667,760

Finally, Bates gives an as completed breakdown, includ-ing additional items such as establishment charges. Where corresponding items can be identified, the differ-ence from the original estimate is not great.

Labour costs (£)

	Nelson	Rodney
Dockyard Labour	18,045	15,815
Dockyard material	159,376	162,071
Hull & fittings	1,171,400	1,248,956
Armour	1,431,054	1,436,781
Machinery	514,657	516,883
Gun Mountings etc	2,415,058	2,406,083
Boats	28,946	23,723
TOTAL Direct	5,738,536	5,810,312
Establishment Charges	225,679	232,465
Guns & Ordnance stores	1,418,000	1,418,000
TOTAL	7,382,215	7,460,777

It is very difficult to say what is the actual, full cost of a ship.

The cruiser-minelayer *Adventure*

At the end of the First World War a need was seen for a fast, surface minelayer.[38] Converted merchant ships[39] were, in general, either too slow or, if fast cross-channel steamers, limited in range or capacity.[40] Tentative requirements were issued on 5 July 1920, following a meeting, of which the most important aspects were:

250 mines, more if possible.
Speed and endurance similar to recent light cruisers.
Low freeboard consistent with a drop of 12ft or less from the mining deck to the waterline.

Later papers emphasise that she was needed to develop modern minelaying techniques and might be the proto-type for a squadron of minelayers, tentatively planned for the Home Fleet.[41] It is clear that she was not intend-ed for offensive laying in enemy waters, as were the much later fast minelayers; her role was probably more related to a Northern Barrage type of operation. DNC (d'Eyncourt) responded on 25 September 1920 with a design prepared by C Lillicrap, the head of the cruiser section and, himself, a future DNC.

Displacement: 6800 tons
Dimensions (ft): 495 x 58 x 15 (mean)
No armour, shallow bulge – as *Raleigh*
Armament: 8-3in AA, 280 broad gauge mines on four rails, two traps, 10ft 6in drop
Machinery: as 'D' Class, 40,000shp = 28kts at half oil.
Endurance: 6000 miles at 14kts with 1600 tons oil
Cost: £1,250,000

It was suggested that three *Chatham* class could be con-verted for minelaying, with oil firing, for the same cost

36. Burt, *British Battleships 1919-1939*, p332.

37. These figures come from the papers of E R Bates, later transferred to the National Maritme Museum. They are not easy to read but the figures seem generally consistent.

38. Unfortunately the Ships Cover and Book of Calculations are missing and the background of this fascinating ship is unclear. This note is based on PRO papers in ADM 1/9228 and 167/64 by courtesy of G Moore

39. J S Cowie, *Mines, Minelayers and Minelaying* (Oxford 1949), p108.

40. The Vancouver ferries *Princess Irene* and *Princess Margaret* were exceptions.

41. S Roskill, *Naval Policy between the Wars* (London 1968), Vol I, p106.

The cruiser-minelayer *Adventure*, the first post-war design. Taken after her original transom stern had been rebuilt. The diesel engines exhausted up the narrow third funnel close behind the second. Her high freeboard, flush deck and bridge probably contributed to the *Kent* design. (Author's collection)

but it was generally felt that a modern prototype was a better investment. There was a desire to carry more mines and DNC came up with a proposal to carry an extra seventy mines on the lower deck aft. These would have to be raised to the mining deck by lift, an operation which could not start until the mines on the deck above had all been laid. This proposal degraded the subdivision aft and a suggestion of using the lower deck forward would have been even worse. By December 1920, DNC had managed to increase the stowage on the mine deck to 300 and the lower deck stowage proposal was abandoned.

The argument for four traps was pressed hard. It was argued mines could be dropped at 12-second intervals from each trap and the normal spacing should be 150ft. With two traps the ship would have to slow to 15kts at 150ft spacing but a speed of 20kts, the limit from wave effects on the mines, was desirable and needed four traps. Consideration was also being given to reducing the spacing of mines to 100ft, making four traps even more essential. DNC explained that the original design had the traps arranged abaft of, and outside the tips of, the propellers. However, in December, he proposed a square-cut stern with four traps.

I am suspicious of this justification of a transom stern. The Admiralty Experiment Works were very enthusiastic over transoms at that date and had reported preliminary tests for the minelayer in June 1920 and a final report in October. A transom stern would have given *Adventure* about a ½kt increase in top speed. I suspect DNC wanted a transom for trial and used the mine trap

argument to justify it.[42]

The gunnery division had second thoughts on the armament and asked for six 4in AA and one or two multiple pom-poms with director control. DNC said this was possible but the guns would add about 40 tons and the director with a tripod mast still more. After a further meeting the armament was decided as four 4.7in AA and two multiple pom-poms. In March 1921 a joint paper by DNC and the E-in-C (G G Goodlow) made a more radical proposal, to fit a diesel cruising plant. It was pointed out that there had been no tests of diesel engines since 1913 and the UK was well behind developments in such machinery. A new Admiralty diesel, designed by the Admiralty Engineering Laboratory, West Drayton, was to be tried in the submarine *X 1* and it was proposed to try a Vickers design in *Adventure* for comparison. It was pointed out that endurance would go up from 5000 to 11,000 miles at 13kts and there would be a great economy in fuel used. Fitting diesels would involve lengthening the ship by 24ft and increasing headroom by 4ft. It would preclude any possibility of reserve mine stowage on the lower deck. However, the engines should be regarded as an experimental, peacetime outfit only; in wartime they could be removed quickly and the space used for stowing mines. (They were, in fact, removed in 1943.) The main problem was that the ship would have to stop for one to two hours to change from steam to diesel or back again!

There was considerable discussion of this proposal both on paper and at a meeting chaired by Controller on 8 March and most were enthusiastic. It is interesting

The cruiser *Enterprise* was completed post-war with a new design of bridge, foreshadowing that of the later 'County' class cruisers. (WSS)

that neither the proposal docket nor the discussion gave the cost.[43] A formal submission for Board approval was made on 25 April 1921 and approved soon after. It was noted that the displacement was now just over 7000 tons with dimensions of 550ft x 59ft x 15ft 3in which reduced the speed to 27¾kts.

Adventure was finally laid down in November 1922. She was the first post-war cruiser type ship and d'Eyncourt and the head of the cruiser section, Charles Lillicrap, tried out a number of new ideas. The decision to provide a covered mine deck made it almost inevitable that she would be flush-decked with a high freeboard, a style which may have influenced the 'County' class cruisers. The bridge arrangement clearly foreshadowed that of the 'Counties' (as did that of *Enterprise*). She had a patch of 2in protection over the machinery (but none over the mines!) and a 1in deck over and also had a minute bulge.

The transom stern was not a success as the severe eddies behind the stern caused the mines when dropped to bounce back into the stern, knocking off their horns. In 1932 she was rebuilt with a conventional stern. It is a pity that a valuable idea like the transom should have been misapplied in its first application as, in consequence, transoms were not used again until the *Fiji* class cruisers of 1939.[44]

The diesel-electric cruising plant was not very satisfactory either, the ship's commissioning being delayed after launch in June 1924 until the end of 1925 due to difficulty in the manufacture of this plant.[45] It was heavy and took a good deal of space, and was removed

in 1943. There were two Vickers 8-cylinder, 4-stroke engines of 2300bhp each driving three phase alternators rated at 1650kw, continuous, and 2120kw for 6 hours. The propulsion motors were of 4-pole induction type and were coupled to the two shafts via the main gearboxes. A repeat *Adventure* was planned for 1924-25 but, not surprisingly, would not have had the diesels.

D'Eyncourt seems to have had a personal enthusiasm for diesel propulsion and in 1925 he persuaded Armstrongs to carry out two studies for diesel-engined cruisers. Both were to be driven by four Armstrong Sulzer engines of 440bhp each. A 5700-ton ship would have mounted two twin 8in turrets and had a speed of 25kts whilst a 5120-ton ship could have reached 25½kts and mounted three twin 6in – not very attractive. Interest in diesel propulsion died when the Washington Treaty definition of standard displacement excluded oil fuel making fuel economy seem less important.

The cruiser submarine *X 1*

The 1915 Submarine Committee had seen a possible requirement for a 'cruiser' submarine but did not consider it urgent. After the war, the navies of the Allied powers all built big submarines with a heavy gun armament in the belief that the German cruiser submarines had been successful. In fact they were demanding in resources, both to build and to operate, and scored no more successes than standard boats. The post-war submarines were no more successful and only Japan built such boats in any numbers.

42. Some early studies for the *Kent* also featured a transom.

43. An incomplete and not very clear cost breakdown for *Adventure* is contained in the E R Bates' papers. An entry under machinery – contract – for £55,907 probably referes to the diesel machinery.

44. D K Brown, 'The Transom Stern', *WARSHIP 5* (1978).

45. E R Bates papers, now in the Maritime Museum.

The cruiser submarine *X 1*. Many navies built similar submarines soon after the war but none were successful. *X 1* had unreliable machinery. (WSS)

Cruiser submarines

Navy	Submarine	Launched	Guns	Sub. Dspt (tons)
German	*U 139*	1917	2-5.9in	2500
RN	*X 1*	1923	4-5.2in	3600
Japan	*I 1*	1924	2-5.5in	2790
USN	*V 4, 5, 6*	1927	2-6in	4000
France	*Surcouf*	1929	2-8in	4300

At the end of 1920 the RN decided to build a large, experimental submarine to study the submerged handling of very large submarines and the feasibility and value of a heavy gun armament. Provision was made for such a submarine, *X 1*, in the 1921-22 Estimates and she was laid down on 2 November 1921.[46] A W Johns was still in charge of submarine design and he produced a double hull design with a reserve of buoyancy of 18 per cent. The pressure hull was 1in thick and had a diameter of 19ft 7½in. The diving depth is said to have been 400ft, once the torpedo tube doors (ex 'L' class, designed for 200ft) had been strengthened.

Most of her problems lay in the engines. The two main engines were 8-cylinder Admiralty design, built by Chatham Dockyard, which, it was hoped, would deliver 3000bhp each (2750bhp seems to have been the best they achieved). There were also two auxiliary engines, 6-cylinder, MAN (ex-*U 126*) which were supposed to be 1200bhp but delivered 1100bhp at best. It is said that she reached 19.5kts on one trial but in 1930 her speed was given as 18.6kts and, unofficially, 12½kts was

the limit of reliability. Several sets of propellers were tried and she broke both propeller shafts soon after entering service. Most of her fuel was stowed externally and the rivetted tanks soon leaked, disclosing her position.

The gunnery arrangements worked well, though the aim of sinking a destroyer at 6000yds was thought unlikely. The complete gunnery team numbered 58 out of a total crew of 109. The guns were 5.2in Mk I QF firing a 70lb shell. When teething troubles had been overcome, they could fire at six rounds per minute.

After completing in 1925 she went to the Mediterranean, returning in 1930 and was paid off, being scrapped in 1936. On the good side, her submerged handling was excellent and the guns did all that was possible. Because of her unreliable machinery, she was never able to show her full potential, but the cruiser submarine was anyway a blind alley. Funds were very scarce in 1921 and it is surprising that so much effort was devoted to such a submarine – particularly when the UK was still pressing for the abolition of submarines.

Revolution manque[47]

Developments in protection and magazine safety have already been discussed, together with the numerous full-scale trials such as those involving *Prince of Wales* and *Superb*. Protection in another sense led to the 4.7in AA gun and to the multiple pom-pom. This was tried as a six-barrelled lash-up in the cruiser *Dragon* in 1921. The mock-up of the eight-barrel mount was approved in 1923 but the Treasury refused to make funds available.[48] It was a very advanced weapon by the standards of 1923 but was already obsolescent by the time it came into general use in the mid 1930s.

A number of new carriers were planned in 1923 but postponed until more experience was gained. In itself, this delay was not unreasonable but it went on too long until the 1934 *Ark Royal*. RAF Coastal Command was grossly neglected and what little funds were available went into flying boats instead of landplanes such as the Kangaroo. Primitive guided missiles – radio-controlled aircraft – such as the 'RAE 1921 Target' and the Larynx were built and tried. Considerable effort was put into developing torpedoes with up to 57 per cent oxygen in the Mark VII. There were real problems and this, too, died. Despite building the specialist minelayer *Adventure*, little effort went into mines and magnetic mines, which were used in 1918-19, and the prototype acoustic mine were forgotten.

There were many promising ideas in anti-submarine warfare (ASW). Asdic (active sonar) was tried in *P 59* in 1919 and on a good day could detect a submerged submarine at up to 3000yds. Unfortunately, this was seen as a better alternative to hydrophones (passive sonar) and further development of listening devices stopped. The ideas of quiet propulsion using water jets died in consequence. It is likely that the success of Asdic led to a line of thought such as – we beat the U boat in 1917-18 without asdic; with it, the submarine is no longer a threat. Therefore, the ASW submarines of the 'R' class were paid off and few convoy escorts were built.

Machinery made one step forward with the introduction of superheat and then stopped. When the war ended, the all-welded ship was seen as near. In fact, Cammell Laird built the all-welded merchant ship *Fullagar* in 1921 but it was many years until the first all-welded British warship, the minesweeper *Seagull*, appeared. Part of the reason was the introduction of the high tensile strength D quality steel. For its day it was a good steel and its strength made possible weight savings which helped to meet Treaty limits, but it was not really suitable for welding.[49] The use of longitudinal framing in destroyers pioneered by Denny in the *Ardent* was forgotten, though it would have been much more suitable with welded construction. The loss of executive status by engineer officers in 1925 with the insulting removal of the 'curl' from their stripes is an indication of the low esteem in which technology was held.

Why did so many of these promising developments die about 1923? The obvious answer is lack of money, but few of them were very costly and money was not all that short in the 1920s. Admiral Louis le Bailly suggests that the Board of Admiralty of the day was very hostile to technology.[50] There were other difficulties; many temporary officers and civilian scientists had left the Admiralty whilst the formation of the RAF had taken air-minded officers from the Navy (they were probably technically progressive in other aspects as well). It is most likely that all these factors combined in a climate which was devoted to economy and well-proven solutions rather than technical advance.

46. D K Brown, 'X1 – Cruiser Submarine', *WARSHIP 23* (July 1982). (Based on Harrison BR 3043 and *Records of Warship Construction*, notes from J Maber and I Grant.)

47. D K Brown, 'Revolution Manque', *WARSHIP 1993*.

48. This is probably the only real case of Treasury obstruction between the wars.

49. I am sure bigger savings could have been made using welding and mild steel.

50. Sir Louis le Bailly, *From Fisher to the Falklands* (London 1991).

Thirteen

The Achievement: the Right Ships and the Right Fleet

Hood in 1931. Note the catapult on the quarterdeck – it is lucky that it carried a seaplane as it was usually awash at sea! (Author's collection)

FOR THE ROYAL NAVY before the First World War, the perceived threat from the German navy lay in their capital ships. It was thought that they could force a battle by choosing the right time when the High Seas Fleet was at full strength whilst the Grand Fleet was weakened by normal maintenance and, possibly, attrition from mines and submarines. This was a real possibility during 1914 and early 1915 but became less likely once the ten battleships of the *Queen Elizabeth* and *Royal Sovereign* classes entered service with their 15in armament.

It followed therefore that Britain had to build more capital ships than Germany and they had to be 'better', ship for ship. The diagrams on page 14 show that numerical superiority was achieved, almost to the 160 per cent of declared intent. Ship to ship comparisons are much more difficult as there are so many extraneous factors to be considered. British battleships and battlecruisers usually mounted heavier guns than German ships of the same date, offset by thinner side armour. Other things being equal, the RN surely made the right choice since the chance of the bigger shell penetrating thick armour should have been about the same as that of the smaller shell penetrating thinner armour whilst the big shell would do far more damage when it burst after penetrating. But unfortunately, this was not so: British armour-piercing shells had weak casings which would break at the shoulder on oblique impact, and the Lyddite filling would detonate on hitting thick armour which concealed the fact that the Krupp-designed fuse did not always function. There was little to choose

between the navies in the thickness of the protective deck. In both, it was barely able to stop splinters and was certainly inadequate to stop a plunging shell. The German propellant was far less likely to explode than British charges.

The armour disposition of battleships up to the *Queen Elizabeth* may be seen as satisfactory. With hindsight, there may have been too much thin armour, but this was a considered judgement based on the effect of high-capacity HE shells. Had British armour-piercing shells not been so poor, less attention might have been given to the effects of high capacity shells. d'Eyncourt's decision to raise the armour deck in the *Royal Sovereigns* is probably correct but he was wrong in reducing the metacentric height so dramatically.[1] Protection to the magazines was weak in the battlecruisers because it was thought, mistakenly, that cordite MD did not present a serious explosion hazard.

The number of guns which could fire on the broadside was generally similar, as the wing turrets of the first two classes of German Dreadnoughts were wasteful of space and weight. The upper deck layout of the British 12in Dreadnoughts was badly constrained by blast effects through the sighting hoods, preventing the introduction of superfiring turrets. The German guns had a higher muzzle velocity but the lighter shell lost speed more quickly and at longer range there was little to choose in accuracy. The RN had a substantial advantage in fire control instrumentation but seemed incapable of capitalising on it, partly because of the use of 9ft base rangefinders and inadequate practice firing at long range.

The first eight German Dreadnought battleships had triple-expansion engines with penalties on weight and, in particular, ability to run at full power for long periods. On the British side, the persistent use of large tube boilers absorbed a lot of space and weight without any conspicuous gain in reliability. Both navies had problems with condenser tubes, the Germans suffering slightly more.

Departmental warfare was – and is – a fact of life and the author, a naval architect, may be seen as biased but it is a fact that the majority of problems with the capital ships – of shells, propellants, blast and sighting hoods (and hence upper deck layout and masts) and of turret armour – were the responsibility of the DNO, at first Jellicoe who, a little later became Controller and still responsible for the work of DNO. DNC Department made a number of errors in detail mainly in failing to ensure that subdivision remained intact after damage. This was partly due to overwork[2] but Sir Phillip Watts does not seem to have had an eye for detail.

The paragraphs above make it clear that there was no scope for saving in the number or of the individual cost of capital ships. There was certainly no prospect of winning more funds for the Navy from Parliament. Of the total funds allocated to navies, British capital ships absorbed 65 per cent, German 72 per cent. It follows that other categories of warships had to share a small proportion of the total. British cruiser building was off to a slow start due to Fisher's view that nothing was

needed between the battlecruiser and the destroyer. The comparatively slow and very lightly armed Scouts were developed into the excellent 'C' class. To some extent, the way in which they were used was as super-destroyers and Fisher's super-*Swift* might very easily have evolved into something quite similar. The 'Cs' were still small ships and seakeeping was an important topic with successive classes having longer forecastles with the bridge further aft, guns mounted higher and increased freeboard. The 4in gun proved too small to disable a destroyer quickly but the 6in was rather long and heavy for hand elevation and training, whilst its 100lb shell was certainly too heavy for hand loading in a seaway. The Coventry Ordnance Works 5.5in gun mounted in *Chester* would probably have been better in these respects.

War on the trade routes had been expected, with the use by the Germans of regular and auxiliary cruisers, operating under the Prize Rules. British countermeasures began with the elimination of German radio and cable stations which made it difficult for raiders to find victims or evade their hunters. Actual destruction of raiders proved difficult (eg *Dresden, Emden, Karlsruhe*) and there was a serious shortage of the bigger cruisers with long endurance. The *Hawkins* class[3] were built for this role and clearly were seen as very suitable since the post war 'Counties' and their foreign rivals were derived from this class.

Unrestricted submarine warfare was unthinkable

1. The consequences of losing protection from coal bunkers above the deck in oil-burning battleships does not seem to have been thought through. That the reduction of stability was wrong was recognised quickly and when bulges were fitted, they were arranged to improve GM.

2. D K Brown, *A Century of Naval Construction*, p92.

3. As discussed, the author does not think that a hand-worked 7.5in was an appropriate weapon to stop a raider. The rapid-fire 8in of the 'Counties' went to the opposite extreme. Perhaps *Effingham* as rebuilt with all 6in, three firing forward, would have been the right answer for the first war.

The cruiser *Hawkins* during the Second World War. In this aerial view very few changes are visible. (Author's collection)

before the war. There were those who thought that submarines could operate legally against trade, keeping within the Prize Rules. The difficulties of working to the rules were clear and most saw this as negating any submarine threat to trade. Few, on either side, realised that unworkable 'rules' get broken in war, particularly by the losing side. In consequence, no specialist escorts were built before the war. The resulting scarcity of AS ships was exacerbated by the near fatal delay in introducing convoys. Some effort had been put into the techniques of locating and sinking a submerged submarine but none of these were within sight of a solution.

Minesweeping was in a slightly better position following the lessons of the Russo-Japanese War. An effective sweep had been designed and proved, a number of fast torpedo gunboats had been converted to use it, and stocks had been assembled for a large number of trawler conversions for which reserve crews had been trained. Shortage of funds meant that none of the pre-war designs for fleet minesweepers were built. It would have been wise to have built a small prototype batch (say four) to iron out any problems. It was not fully appreciated how many ships were needed to deal with the mine threat though, in partial justification, it was thought that minelaying would be in accordance with international law, with laying only in declared fields.

The evolution of the British destroyer had led to a very successful design in the 'M' class, further developed in the 'R' and 'S 'classes. Their heavy gun armament even gave them an initial advantage over most German ships in torpedo attack, though the 4in was still a little on the light side. Turbines, oil fuel and, later, gearing gave them further advantages. Seakeeping was improved by increasing freeboard, lengthening the forecastle and moving the bridge aft. The bigger 'V' and 'W' classes were extremely successful and were the basis of post-war development in Britain and other countries.

The Royal Navy had the largest number of submarines of any navy at the outbreak of war, something all too often forgotten.[4] The latest design in 1914, the 'E' class, was amongst the best and further developed in the 'L' class. RN boats had good auxiliary equipment such as hydraulic systems,[5] many of which were pioneered by Scotts in the unsuccessful steam submarine *Swordfish*. There was too much effort put into building many different types of submarine instead of concentrating on a very few good types.[6] The different small foreign types building at the start of the war were failures though a well-meaning attempt to break the Vickers monopoly.

The real problem lay in the engines; the original Vickers diesel was adequate when introduced but soon obsolescent with only about 100bhp per cylinder. More power was obtained by adding cylinders or increasing the number of engines, both costly in weight and space. Even so, the 'Ls' were excellent boats and formed the starting point for the post-war 'O' class. The problem

with engines was recognised before the war and a number of alternative designs were to have been tried in the 'G' class but the war put an end to any hope of experiment. The achievements of British submarines were splendid, working in very dangerous waters – the Dardanelles, Baltic, Heligoland Bight – with few targets.

The Royal Navy and the Admiralty were very quick to realise the importance of aviation at sea. Shore-based air – airships, flying boats and landplanes – lies outside the scope of this book but further demolishes the myth of the reactionary, battleship admiral.[7] Putting aircraft to sea involved a considerable number of problems in ship design. *Ark Royal* was an excellent start as a seaplane carrier, a theme developed in other ships during the war. *Argus* was the first true aircraft carrier, the only one anywhere to complete during the war. The early use of wind tunnels to solve airflow problems is noteworthy, as is the attention paid to reducing the risk of fire. The different problems of operating planes from battleships and cruisers – even towed lighters – were also successfully solved.

The resistance of all classes of ship to damage from shellfire was very good, provided the magazine did not blow up. There were detail errors, such as the failure of the supports to *Lion*'s armour, probably due to overwork in DNC department. There were very few hits on the main belt and it may be that too much weight was put into this feature. With hindsight, based on the design of totally unarmoured ships, it is clear that greater duplication of systems would have provided better protection to overall fighting capacity than armour, giving some justification to Fisher's battlecruiser philosophy. The steam plant of destroyers was easily disabled by action damage and there seems to have been no easy solution. They were very small ships and the use of a unit system of machinery would have led to a very considerable increase in size and would not have been all that effective in a small ship.[8]

Magazine explosions seem to have been due to the propellant rather than anything else. The flash precautions[9] in pre-war designs were as good as those in any other navy and were not seriously inadequate. Responsibility for protection of the ship lay with the DNC but protection of the turret and its internals lay with DNO. Division of responsibility is never wise as there is always the risk that each thinks the other is carrying out the vital work when it is actually neglected by both. As a well-known saying puts it 'Disaster strikes down departmental boundaries'.

Resistance to underwater attack was not as good as it should have been. *Audacious*, *Marlborough* and *Inflexible* all failed in some way. Pre-war trials – the *Belleisle*, *Ridsdale* and *Hood* – had shown what was needed. Progressive leakage is bound to more of a problem in a ship stitched together with rivets than in a welded unit. What protection there was, was too often interrupted for wing turrets etc. Centreline bulkheads cap-

4. It is sometimes claimed that most RN boats were small and obsolete. This could be said of most other navies though slightly less in the case of Germany due to their late start.

5. The leading company in submarine hydraulic systems, McTaggart Scott, received a large award after the war from the Royal Commission on Awards to Inventors which was used to build a new office block which was in use till well after the Second World War.

6. The diversion of effort in a multitude of designs is probably the biggest error in the 'K' class submarine story.

7. See R D Layman, *Naval Aviation in the First World War* (London 1997).

8. This problem was to recur in the Second World War with the steam driven steam gunboats. See G Moore, 'Steam Gunboats', *WARSHIP 1998* (To be published – Conway).

9. Also the responsibility of the DNO.

10. D K Brown, *A Century of Naval Construction*, Ch 4.

sized many older ships and some later ones. The very high resistance to torpedoes shown by light cruisers was largely due to their lack of longitudinal bulkheads.

The greatest achievement lay in the vast number of ships designed and built by and under the supervision of 125 members of the Royal Corps of Naval Constructors (plus 76 temporary constructors).[10] Battleships were built in the Royal Dockyards at Portsmouth and Devonport and in eight commercial yards. Two more Dockyards and four more commercial yards built cruisers and seventeen shipyards built destroyers.

Numbers of ships completed during the War

Category	Numbers
Battleships and battlecruisers	18
Cruisers	39
Monitors and coastal defence ships	40
Destroyers	283
Submarines	146
Aircraft and seaplane carriers	8
TOTAL	534
Sloops, P and PC	187
Gunboats, trawlers etc	412
Minesweepers	99
River gunboats	28
Repair and depot ships	10
CMB	83
Others	160
TOTAL minor vessels	979
GRAND TOTAL	1513

This vast programme involved many shipyards but these were supported by marine engine works, gear cutting, gun and armour founders etc.

The lessons of the war were reflected in the post-war plans. There was an abundance of good light cruisers and destroyers and there is no evidence of any new design work in these categories. As discussed in the previous chapter, the battlefleet was a different story, ageing, worn by wartime steaming and with many ships armed only with 12in guns, they were no match for the larger ships building in the USA and Japan.

In view of the public attacks, then and more recently, on the whole concept of the battlecruiser, it may seem surprising that the Admiralty saw the need for the type to continue and, in placing orders for the four 'G 3s', gave it priority over the battleship. The new battlecruisers were much more heavily protected than earlier ships and, since they also carried a heavy armament at high speed, they were going to be big and expensive. It is unclear as to whether the orders for the 'G 3s' were realistic or whether they were just seen as bargaining chips for the naval limitation treaty which was seen as inevitable. It is most likely that the Admiralty hoped that they would be built but would be cancelled only if rival powers made major concessions.

It is strange that the first ship ordered after the war should be the minelayer *Adventure*, but she was an important test-bed for new ideas, even though neither the transom stern nor the diesel engine were successful in this application. All of the major navies perceived a role for the big cruiser submarine but none, including the British *X 1*, were successful.

The Washington Treaty and its effects will be considered in a future book but, though painful, it can be seen as a success for the Royal Navy. It achieved parity with the USN at an affordable price which would stand it in good stead in the lean years to come.

The Royal Navy emerged victorious from the war with technological leads in many areas. The larger ships forming the enormous wartime fleet were small, worn out and built to outdated concepts; a new fleet was needed.

The cruiser *Caroline* as a reserve training ship. She is the only major ship described in this book still afloat. The bridge, mast and funnels are not original. Minor vessels which survive include the monitor *M 33* (*Medusa*), CMBs *4* and *102* (Imperial War Museum, Duxford) and at least two MLs as houseboats. (Author's collection)

Appendices

Appendix 1

Views on the All-Big-Gun Battleship

Two highly classified papers, with limited circulation, were prepared in 1906, setting out the views of senior staff of the Admiralty in support of the all-big-gun battleship.[1] They were probably in the nature of briefing papers so that readers would have the facts readily available to defend such ships. These papers were largely written by Jellicoe, the Director of Naval Ordnance (DNO), with contributions by Phillip Watts, DNC, and by the Controller and the arguments will be summarised below.

The papers begin by saying that the aspects most often criticised in *Dreadnought* and *Invincible* were the all-12in armament, the speed and, as a result of these, the size and cost. The authors say that it is taken for granted that a battleship shall have a primary armament of four 12in guns which can be supplemented by more 12in or a secondary armament of 9.2in or 6in guns. A simple comparison is made of the weight of shell fired by two guns hitting a battle practice target in 10 minutes.[2]

Battle practice target – 10 minutes

Two guns	Weight of shell hitting (lbs)	Ratio
6in	840	1
9.2in	2812	3.3
12in	4250	5

The great superiority of the 12in is immediately obvious, to a considerable extent, due to the much higher percentage of hits scored at longer range. Critics had confused the high rate of fire of the smaller gun with rate of hitting.

The damage inflicted on an enemy ship depends on the number of hits and on the damage caused by individual hits. Rate of hitting depends on rate of fire, the dangerous space at each range and the probability of hitting. Damage will depend on penetration and the destructive power of the shell. The high rates of fire achieved for a short time in the gunlayers' competition was much reduced over a longer period and at longer range when spotting fall of shot was necessary. The rates achieved in battle practice were thought realistic and were quite similar to that realised in the Russo-Japanese war.

Rates of fire (rounds per minute)

Gun	Gunlayers'	Battle Practice
6in	12	4
9.2in	5	2
12in	2	1

Even then, the rates of fire for the 6in were thought to be too high since control of a battery would be increasingly difficult for ranges over 2000yds. There is an interesting aside here: 'It may be assumed that in future battleships [1906] 6in guns will not again be mounted singly on the main deck, but if introduced again would be mounted in twin turrets on the upper deck. To repeat the mistake of mounting these guns as heretofore after the experience we have gained would be a very retro-

Dreadnought, proudly flying an Admiral's flag. (Author's collection)

grade action'. This lesson was forgotten and 6in batteries were re-introduced in the *Iron Dukes* with all the hazards discussed in Chapter 3.

The paper then considers the chance of hitting at short, moderately long and long range (3000, 6000 and 9000yds). It is, perhaps, a weakness that in this paper of 1906 9000yds is seen as long range. The next table shows the danger space for various guns at these ranges.[3]

Danger space (yds)

Range (yds)	3000	6000	9000
6in	266	73	31
9.2in	385	132	57
12in	370	144	66

This shows that the chance of a hit from a 6in is much less than that for the bigger guns. The paper then goes on to compare the actual percentage of hits achieved in battle practice from the various guns and then estimate the weight of shell hitting at the different ranges.

	Battle Practice	Estimated		
	% Hits	Wt hitting in 10 min (lbs)		
Range (yds)	6000	3000	6000	9000
6in	15	3000	1200	500
9.2in	25	4400	3500	1650
12in	37	11,165	6600	2885

The superiority of the big gun is seen to increase rapidly as range is increased was to some extent supported by the lessons of the Russo-Japanese war, particularly the Battle of the Yellow Sea. It was often argued by critics that visibility in the North Sea would not often permit these longer ranges to be used which seems a rather exaggerated viewpoint.

A more sensible objection is that it may be possible to mount several smaller guns within the weight and space budgets of the bigger mount so the paper continues by comparing the weight of shell hitting per ton of turret weight.

Gun	Wt turret (tons)	Weight of shell hitting per ton of turret (lbs)		
Range (yds)		3000	6000	9000
6in	136	32	8.5	3.7
9.2in	447	25	8.5	3.7
12in	890	18	7.0	3.2

At the shorter range the smaller gun has a big advantage but by 9000yds there is little in it and at longer ranges the big gun resumes its advantage. This simple comparison neglects the extra men who would be needed to crew the more numerous small guns. There would also be a problem in arranging all these guns on the upper deck, clear of blast from each other and limiting blast on bridges, boats etc. The paper (surely Phillip Watts) reads 'while consideration of weight alone might allow more guns those of space forbid any large increase in numbers, if they are to be used with effect, unless the ship is lengthened abnormally, so as to space them well apart'. This is a most interesting–and somewhat surprising–passage, which is further discussed in Chapter 3. This section of the paper then goes into a detailed examination of arcs of fire which, to some extent gives further support to the all-big-gun ship.

Consideration is then given to the effects of a hit, looking first at the penetration of armour. The table below shows the penetration of KC armour in inches by APC shell at normal impact.

Penetration (in)

Range (yds)	3000	6000	9000
6in	5.0	3.0	Less than 3
9.2in	9.7	7.7	5.3*
12in	13.5	10.75	7.7

*The original paper gives 7.3in, clearly a misprint.

As discussed later, these figures greatly exaggerate the capability of British shells. However, it is clear that the 6in is useless against the armoured portion of an enemy ship. It was argued by critics that an enemy could be disabled by hits on unarmoured areas such as control tops, boats, gun ports, exposed personnel etc. The experience of the Russo-Japanese war was that damage to lightly-protected areas was mainly due to large-calibre, high-capacity shells and, even so, was rarely disabling. Experience in the First World War (Chapter 11) largely confirmed this view; only one of the fairly numerous hits by 5.9in shells on British battleships at Jutland caused any serious damage.

Bigger shells do more damage when they burst; Jellicoe said that 'the effect of shell from different natures of gun may be taken as proportional to the square of the weight of the bursting charge'.[4] This seems a fairly good rule of thumb though it does not distinguish between blast and splinter effect nor on what is hit –people, systems or structure.

These two papers have been quoted at length since they provide a valid defence against most of the criticisms of the all-big-gun *Dreadnought* battleship and there was very little opposition within the Admiralty. Most of the arguments apply to the battlecruiser but there were many who would have preferred the 9.2in gun for that type of ship (see Chapter 4). The balance between quality and quantity will be different in a cruiser from that of the battle line.

1. 'The Building Programme of the British Navy'. Tweedmouth Papers, MoD Library. Very Secret. 12 Copies, and 'HM Ships *Dreadnought* and *Invincible*'. Strictly Secret. 25 Copies.

2. The rate of fire and percentage of hits were taken as the average achieved in the 1905 battle practice at just under 6000yds.

3. This is not clearly defined but appears to be the horizontal distance shadowed by a ship allowing for the angle of descent of the shell.

4. And the bursting charge is proportional to the cube of the bore!

Speedy, a Thornycroft Special. The extra beam, needed to fit the bigger boilers, made it possible to raise the forward gun. (Author's collection)

Appendix 2

Thornycroft and Yarrow 'Specials' of the First World War

Before and during the First World War (and very occasionally after), Thornycroft and Yarrow were allowed to design and build destroyers, loosely based on current Admiralty designs, but with considerable higher trial speed. Some writers and even seamen have argued that all destroyers should have been to such 'advanced' design and even seen the improved performance of these 'Specials' as a criticism of Admiralty designers. Such criticism was strongly resented within the Admiralty but, even with hindsight, the Admiralty case seems valid.[1] They believed that the high performance achieved depended on a quality of workmanship which could not be matched in other yards building destroyers and hence the Admiralty designs were more conservative and could be built in many shipyards.

In March 1940, the Controller, (Fraser) again asked DNC and E-in-C if there was anything which could be learnt from the earlier Specials. By this time the dust had settled and the technical departments had more recent research findings which explained the real advantages of the Specials – and some unsuspected dangers – whilst fully justifying the contemporary Admiralty position.

Hull design

The DNC, Goodall, replied on 21 March 1940, bringing out the point that, not only did Thornycroft and Yarrow design practice differ from the Admiralty but there were major differences in approach between the two companies. Yarrow's hull and machinery weights were well below Admiralty practice which they – and

the Admiralty – thought justified by their superior workmanship, and this light weight accounted for much of the improved performance. It was, however, noted that their stability was marginal. Even in 1940 it was notable that Yarrow's machinery was the lightest of a class even when nominally of the same design. Thornycroft were less concerned with weight saving but used more powerful machinery leading to a wider ship, needed to accommodate the bigger boilers. This increased beam gave them more stability and enabled them to increase freeboard, to raise the forward gun (in some classes) and, in the 'V' and 'Ws', to increase the height of the second funnel, reducing the smoke problems found in earlier classes. The overall length of the machinery spaces was the same as in the Admiralty design but the engine room was one frame space less, making it a little cramped.

There are few figures for the weight saving actually achieved by Yarrow. *Miranda* (1914) was said to have a hull 50 tons lighter than the 368 tons of the Admiralty design. She ran trials at 850 tons instead of the 990 tons typical of other builders. *Truculent* was said to have been 130 tons lighter overall than a standard ship of the class. There is no doubt that the displacement on trials of Yarrow ships was much less than for other builders. Only part of this was due to lighter construction; they ran trials with the ship as light as possible to get the highest speed. A rule of thumb used then was that 10 tons reduction in weight gave an extra 0.2kt on the mile. Those who built to Admiralty design had only to demonstrate that the contract power had been developed; they had no incentive to try for a high trial speed.

There was some discussion in 1940 as to whether the light construction of the Yarrow ships had led to early corrosion failure. Here was no clear evidence either way, but the general view was that corrosion had not led to early scrapping. It was possible that the poorer stability of the Yarrow ships had contributed to their early disposal but the concept of the earlier classes, 'Ms' and 'Rs', which included most surviving Yarrow ships, was outdated by the 1930s and it was not obvious that their ships were singled out.

Machinery design

The Specials went faster on trial because they developed more power. Both firms designed their turbines to accept more steam generated by boilers which, on trial, were forced to a much greater extent than envisaged in Admiralty practice.

Machinery particulars

Class	shp	lbs/shp	Remarks, rpm
'K' & 'L' Adm	24,500	34	Direct drive
Miranda (Yarrow)	25,000	34	Direct, 650, superheated
'M' Adm	25,000	31	Direct, 450
'R' & 'V' Adm	39,000	34	Geared, 350
Radiant (Thornycroft)	29,000	30.5	Geared, 450
Viceroy (Thornycroft)	30,000	33.5	Geared, 370
Ambuscade (Yarrow)	33,000	30.5	Geared, 430
Amazon (Thornycroft)	39,000	31	Geared, 430
'A' & 'B' Adm	34,000	34	Geared, 450
'J' Adm	40,000	30	Geared, 350

It is notable that the Specials tended to higher rpm which was favourable for top speed (lighter transmission) at the cost of higher fuel consumption.

The nominal powers listed above were much exceeded on trial and the Engineer-in-Chief (1940), Engineer Vice-Admiral Sir George Preece, noted that from more recent experience '. . . the use of the high rates adopted by Yarrow and Thornycroft for the burst of speed on the measured mile must have been attended by considerable risk and could only have been achieved under the condition of an absolutely clean boiler.' By 1940, all service boilers could be forced, quite safely, to even higher rates.

Machinery on trial

Ship	Dspt, trial (tons)	shp	Speed (kts)
Tyrian (Yarrow)	850	30,650	39.72
Radiant (Thornycroft)	—	30,000	39.08
Teazer (Yarrow)	839	34,327	40.41
Adm	c 1100	28,000	33.00

The E-in-C minuted that 'These figures are very interesting and one wonders how they got away with it since so far as my memory serves me they are above those which Engineer Admiral Dight found were safe for an ordinary boiler without augment.' Many components were very highly stressed, *eg* the torsional stresses in the shafts were all well above normal practice as was the loading on the propeller. Failure under these conditions would occur after repeated loads as fatigue cracking. Since the Specials were usually in company with other boats, they very rarely used extreme power and that is 'how they got away with it'.

The Yarrow 'Special' *Oak* (foreground). The hull and machinery were lighter than in the Admiralty design *Acheron* class which made her faster – and more expensive. (Author's collection)

'Clever Running of Trials'

Some care is needed in comparing trials data. Only measured-mile figures can be trusted and these must be the mean of at least four runs in alternate directions. Some books quote the 'fastest' run but, as this will be with wind and tide helping, it is a meaningless figure. To be of value, comparisons must be at similar loading. Since there was no advantage in very high speed to the builders of the Admiralty design ships, their trials were usually run at 'normal' load, quite close to deep. Yarrows, in particular, ran at very light displacement of which only part was due to their skill in light weight construction. Displacement made a big difference; *Tyrian* with 25,000shp was 2.5kts faster at 845 tons than at 873 tons.

The effect of shallow water is very complicated but ships of the size and speed of those under discussion will go faster in shallow water than in deep. The shallow St Catherine's mile, used by Thornycroft, was said to increase speed by 1.35kts over deep water. (The *Tobago* trial suggested it was more like 0.75kts.) Note that there was no deception; both the firm and the Admiralty were well aware of the difference.[2]

Goodall noted that both firms ran their trials very 'cleverly'. As usual, he is using words very precisely; he is not suggesting that the firms' procedures were in any way improper but that they were clever in squeezing out every fraction of a knot. One example was Yarrow's practice of having an engineer on deck to watch the colour of the smoke. A pale grey denoted correct combustion and would be signalled to the boiler room by ringing a gong.

Speed in service is always hard to measure, which is why speed trials are run in idealised conditions. There are indications that the Thornycroft leaders were nearly a knot faster than the Admiralty ships but this could be due to differences in fouling.

Cost

It is surprising that, in the 1940 discussions, no one considered the cost difference between the Specials and the standard ships. Wartime records are incomplete and there were many reasons why cost – or at least the price paid – should differ. Figures for the 'M' class just before the war were:

Ship	Cost (£)	%
Average, 6 Adm ships	111,833	100
Mastiff (Thornycroft)	124,585	112
Miranda (Yarrow)	132,646	119

Less reliable figures for the wartime 'R' class are:

Ship	Cost (£)	%	
Admiralty	159-166,000	100	Based on £162,000
Thornycroft	171,000	106	
Yarrow	178,000	110	

The value of speed

The *Shakespeare* class flotilla leaders were designed by Thornycroft subject to a penalty clause should they fail to meet the required speed. They were expected to reach 36kts for 4 hours with a penalty of £500 per ¼kt, increasing to £1500 per ¼kt below 34.5kts and £2500 below that. There were also heavy penalties for excessive draught and for low metacentric height (GM) with rejection if the GM was less than 18in.

The cost and price of speed

Early destroyers and a few later ones were designed by their builders to meet a required performance and it was usual to include a penalty clause in the contract should the requirement not be met. Less often, there was a bonus for exceeding the specified speed. To some extent, such penalties may be seen as a measure of the value placed on speed. Some typical penalties are listed below.[3]

Penalty on speed

Ship	Date	Penalty/kt (£x1000)	Total Cost (£x1000)	Penalty %of total
'27 Knotter'	1895	1.0	42	2.4
'River'	1904	2.0	78	2.6
'Tribal'	1904	2.0	78	2.6
'*Beagle*'	1910	4.5	110	4.0
'K' Specials	1912	2.0	110	1.8
Shakespeare	1918	2.0	275	0.7
Brecon	1941	6.0	300	2.0

Conclusions

The Special builders did all that was asked of them by the Admiralty. Their ships were fine examples of contemporary skill and workmanship but few, if any, actions of the war showed a need for very high speed. DNC liked the extra beam and hence enhanced stability of the Thornycroft ships and, with hindsight, one would value most highly the greater freeboard and raised guns of their destroyers. The machinery was very highly stressed and that there were no accidents was probably because full power was used very rarely – and a touch of luck.

2. It looked good in advertisements.

3. D K Brown, *The Price of Speed* (Unpublished Memo, University College, London, 1970).

Appendix 3
Rivetting

All the ships in this book were of rivetted construction.[1] Few readers[2] will be aware of the problems associated with this form of construction outlined in this brief appendix.[3] Rivetted construction inevitably involved extra weight as plates had to be overlapped or strapped to join them, whilst beams and frames had to have an extra flange so that they could be rivetted to the plating. In calculating the weight of hull structure the following percentage additions were made to the weight of plates and frames.

Lapped joints	11
Butt straps	5
Liners	6
Rivet heads	2-3

A close-up of rivetted detail on *Caroline*. Note the butt straps (centre) with four rows of rivets either side. This photo, taken by the author in 1998, shows the excellent condition of the ship. (Author's collection)

Holes

Any hole will weaken the plate and a continuous row of holes, as in a rivetted joint, will lead to a serious loss of strength. The strength of a joint was not equated to that of the intact plate since the plate was weakened at every frame space by a row of rivets. The plate (or butt strap) could tear along the line of holes or the rivet could tear its way to the plate edge or the whole set of rivets on one side could shear. There were well-known codes of practice to overcome these problems but they usually involved extra weight and were labour intensive.

The quickest and cheapest means of making rivet holes was punching, usually with a machine which would punch a number of holes in each operation. However, the steel round the hole was made brittle by the operation of punching, starting small cracks which would spread later.[4] The act of hammering a hot rivet helped to make the steel less brittle but it was laid down that holes in important structure – inner and outer bottoms etc – should either be drilled or punched ⅛in small and reamed out to size, removing the affected material. High tensile steel was always drilled.

Rivets

Figure 1 opposite shows the types of rivet used in warship work. A is the most common type, called the pan head. It has a slightly tapered neck intended to fill a punched hole which will always be slightly conical. D, E and F show the hammered points which go with a pan head. D is the countersunk point needed in the outer bottom, under water; note that the hole has to be drilled out with a countersinking drill. E is used for most internal work with F where an attractive appearance is wanted. B is a snap head rivet, usually associated with a snap point as at G using a hydraulic rivetting machine. If a flush surface is needed on both sides, a countersunk head such as C will be needed with a point as H. The double conical shape pulled the plates together very hard as the hot rivet cooled and contracted and this type of rivetting was always used for oil-tight work.[5]

If one side is inaccessible, as when connecting shell plating to the stem forging, a tapped rivet is needed. If the joint is permanent L is used and the projection shown dotted is chipped off. If the plate is portable M or N is used. Behind armour, there is a risk of injury since rivet heads may be thrown off by the impact of a projectile. In manned spaces, the inside of the frames is closed in by a steel lining secured by screw rivets (K).

The general rule was that the diameter of the rivet should be ¼in greater than the thickness of the plate. However, it was hard to knock up rivets bigger than 1⅛in and plates thicker than 30lbs were avoided if possible by using two thicknesses of thinner plate.[6]

Joints, laps and butts

F and G in Figure 2 show plates which are lapped; one over the other. Thin plates were fastened with a single row of rivets (F) but thicker plates needed a double or even a triple row. The width of a single lap was 3½ rivet diameters and that of a double lap was 6 diameters. Experience was to show that the strains of bad weather would lead to leaks in single rivetted joints, particularly on the forecastle of destroyers, making the mess deck even more unpleasant. A lapped joint would tend to twist if pulled in tension, weakening it and leading to leaks. Underwater explosions would distort the structure causing rivetted joints to open up, allowing flooding to spread. Such leaks were very difficult to stop; the only possible method was to hammer in small wooden wedges but it was all too easy to hammer too hard and

1. There was a considerable effort put into welding during the war but its use was almost entirely confined to emergency repair (see Chapter 12).

2. The author drove at least three rivets as an apprentice!

3. This appendix is mainly based on E L Attwood, *WARSHIPS, A Textbook* (London 1910).

4. Some tests reported by Wildish suggest a 22 per cent loss of strength.

5. In 1923 it was proposed to sheath a sloop (with copper over wood) for Persian Gulf service. DNC pointed out that it would have to burn coal as the bolts to the sheathing could not be made oil-tight.

6. R N Newton, *Practical Construction of Warships* (London 1941).

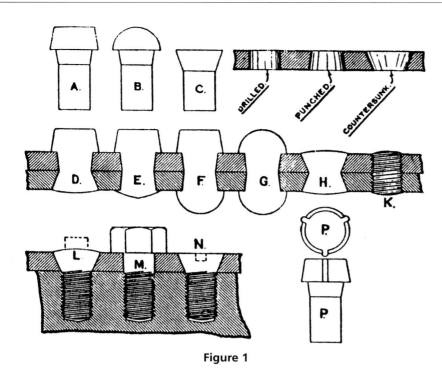

Figure 1

strapped with a short piece of angle, usually with three rivets each side of the joint. Plates meeting at right angles – deck to side – had to be connected by angle bars. It was the need for laps and joining angles which made rivetted structure heavier than the later welded construction (weakening the steel by holes also contributed).

Spacing

The spacing of rivets, centre to centre, was called the pitch. For watertight work the pitch would be 4-5 diameters and for oil tight it would be less than 4. Non watertight work did not require caulking and the pitch could be increased to 7-8. At least two and preferably more intact strakes had to pass between two butt joints within the same frame space.

Caulking

In a watertight lapped joint the edge, which would usually be planed, of one plate would be split using a chisel and the lower part forced hard against the adjoining plate (Figure 2). For a butt joint, both edges would be planed, both plates would then be split close to the joint and the pieces forced together with a special hollow tool.[8]

Strength

In the overall strength calculation, $\frac{1}{7}$th of the steel in tension was deducted from the effective area to allow for the weakening caused by rivet holes.[9] Biles' analysis of the *Wolf* trial[10] showed that this was not strictly necessary but the practice continued for the sake of consistency.

7. Not always; in explosion tests after the Second World War on the cruiser *Orion*, cracks crossed many seams. It is also certain that cracks spread across joints in the break-up of the *Titanic*.

8. N J McDermaid, *Shipyard Practice* (London 1911). Shows an assortment of caulking tools.

9. D K Brown, 'British Warship Design Methods', *Warship International*, 1/95

10. D K Brown, *Warrior to Dreadnought*, pp184-5.

further open the leak. On the other hand, brittle cracks would usually stop at a rivetted joint.[7]

Where a flush joint is needed, a butt strap was used, single, double, treble or quadruple (A, B, C and D; 6½, 11½, 16½ & 21½ diameters wide respectively). In some cases double butt straps were used, half on each side of the main plates. In non-watertight work, where great strength was needed, the spacing of the rivets in the outer row might be increased, reducing the loss of strength in the plate. This was not usually possible in watertight work as the widely-spaced rivets did not permit proper caulking. Angle bars and other sections would be

Riveters

A hand rivetting squad would consist of two men with hammers – one left-handed – and one 'holder up' behind the plate using a special tool to hold the red hot rivet in place. The heater 'boy' – of any age – had to ensure that sufficient rivets of the types and sizes needed were always ready. Pneumatic tools both for rivetting and caulking were coming in in this period but were not yet common. Big hydraulic riveting machines were used where space permitted. Rivets were always tapped with a small hammer to check that they were firm; failures were replaced though in non-vital work a defective rivet could be caulked.

Rivetted construction was straightforward but it was very labour intensive; there might be up to 1000-2000 steel workers on a battleship. The structure could be held in place by bolts in a few rivet holes aided by wooden ribbands if necessary. A considerable number of bolts were needed in watertight work to ensure that the plates were in close contact before rivetting began.

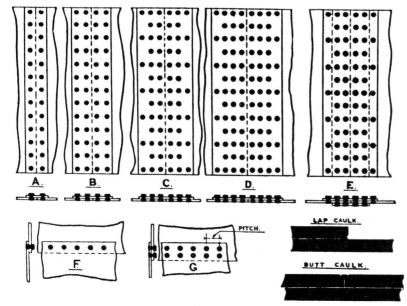

Figure 2

The Stability of a Flooded Ship

The stability of a partially-flooded ship was a very tricky subject and comprehensive calculations were not possible before the introduction of the computer. If a small compartment is completely filled to the deck head with water the problem becomes fairly simple. The added weight of the water could be calculated – 35ft³ of sea water weighs 1 ton – and the ordinary hydrostatic curves for the ship then used to calculate the heel and trim.

Even in this simple case there are complications; the contents of the compartment occupy some of the space and hence the volume of water entering is less than the empty volume of the compartment. Permeability is the percentage of the space which can be flooded.

Permeability, typical figures

Watertight compartment	97%*
Accommodation spaces	95%
Machinery spaces	80%
Magazines	70%
Cargo holds, stores	60%
Full coal bunker	38%

* 3% is deducted for the space occupied by frames, stiffeners etc

The case of loose water in a compartment which is not open to the sea can also be dealt with fairly easily. The loose water will slop from side to side due to any heel or roll and this may be allowed for by taking its weight at a 'virtual' centre of gravity above the upright, real position by a distance equal to i/V, where i is the second moment of area (see Appendix 5) and V is the new immersed volume of the ship.[1] Note that this approach is only valid for small heel angles; it is not true that a few inches of water will capsize a RO-RO ferry. It will cause a small heel but only if water is still entering will this heel increase rapidly.

If a large space occupying the full beam of the ship and extending above the waterline is open to the sea, calculations become very difficult as the amount of water in the compartment will vary with heel and trim which are themselves dependent on the amount of water in the space. The most direct approach is to recalculate the hydrostatic particulars for the 'new' ship bounded by the undamaged bulkheads at either end of the flooded compartments. This was quite a lengthy task.

Finding the new waterline was a matter of 'trial and error' (mostly the latter) and would have taken quite a long while. Without a computer, it would be possible only to consider flooding near amidships so that any change of trim would be small and could be neglected. If the change of trim is sufficient to immerse the deck at either end (usually aft as in the sinking of *Audacious*),

hand calculation is virtually impossible. (The author did such calculations for the 'Tribal' class in 1955, without a computer. For this very simple ship, it took about three months.) Because immersion of a low quarterdeck with associated loss of waterplane inertia causes such a serious loss of stability, damage aft of amidships is usually the most serious case – and could not be studied with any accuracy.

The problem gets even worse for a large compartment extending only part of the beam as the heel will be so large that approximations based on metacentric height are no longer valid. However, such approximations had to be used for lack of anything better. The error is not too great for one engine room flooded – heel about 7 or 8° – but will be greater if more than one space is flooded, as in a torpedo hit. There is a particular problem with wing compartments abreast a large central space. The heel due to flooding one wing compartment will be quite small and can be estimated using simple methods. A torpedo or mine will flood one wing compartment and the central one (and very probably the adjoining compartments, fore and aft) reducing the stability considerably. With reduced stability, the heel produced by the buoyancy of the undamaged wing space will be very large.

There are other problems; the final case, with the ship floating at a new, damaged waterline may not be the worst case but without the computer there was no way of looking further at transient stages. If the undamaged stability is thought to be inadequate in the design stage, the problem can be resolved by a small increase in beam which will raise the metacentre but much of the benefit of the extra beam is lost if big compartments amidships are flooded. It is probable that many of these points were appreciated by the beginning of the century but unlikely that the true magnitude was recognised. Students calculated the effect of flooding on geometrical shapes which may have helped their understanding.[2] It was possible to investigate the effect of flooding using models.[3] Such models are extremely expensive if the detail is fully reproduced and misleading if it is not. Models can also be a very useful training aid for both designers and seamen but there is no evidence of any being made after the *Inflexible* of 1876 whose model was used to train constructors up to the Second World War.

Testing

Watertight bulkheads are of no value unless they remain watertight after damage and to ensure that they could take the load at least some were tested under full load - some 2500 tons acting on the full area of a main bulk-

1. For a rectangular space, length l and breadth b, the value of the second moment, i, is l.b³/12.

2. This exercise was so boring that most students 'switched off' and learnt little or nothing.

3. A very large model of the *Inflexible* was made and tested, both in calm water and waves – D K Brown, *Warrior to Dreadnought*, p65.

head. The collision bulkhead was tested by alternately filling the compartments either side to a height 12ft above the normal waterline. One engine room and one boiler room would be filled to a height 5ft above the load waterline. Deflections would be carefully measured. Other bulkheads would be tested by playing a high pressure hose on them. Despite this, there are many accounts of bulkheads leaking or requiring shoring after damage. The most likely cause would be deflection of the shell at the periphery of the bulkhead, shearing rivets in the boundary angle.

Appendix 5
Second Moment of Area and Moment of Inertia

There are some effects in rotating things and in the bending of beams and girders which involve the way in which area or mass is distributed about the axis of rotation.

For instance, when a ship heels, buoyancy is lost on the side coming out of the water and gained on the other side. For a given angle of heel, the amount of buoyancy lost or gained at each element (say square metre) of the ship's waterplane is proportional to the distance of each element of that area from the axis about which the ship is heeling. Further, the moments of each of these amounts of buoyancy about that axis is also proportional to its distance from that axis. Thus the total effect helping to right the ship is proportional to the sum of the squares of the distance of each element of the area of the waterplane from the axis about which the ship is heeling. That sum is called the Second Moment of Area of the waterplane about that axis. (For a symmetrical ship it will be the longitudinal centreline.) It is obtained by multiplying each small element of area (dA) by the square of its distance (y) from the axis and summing all these elements (y^2.dA) together – written mathematically as $\int y^2$.dA

The distribution of the mass of an object, say a gun, affects the forces and their moments which have to be applied in order to elevate or train it when on a ship which is rolling and pitching. It is not easy; try and keep a long and heavy stick pointing at a 'target' from a jolting vehicle over rough ground. In this case the critical factor is the distance of the mass from the axis; a short stick is easier to point than a long one. The moments of the forces which have to be applied are, in similar manner to the previous paragraph, proportional to $\int y^2$.dM where elements of mass, dM, replace those of area and is called the moment of inertia.[1]

When a beam is bent by a load on it, or when a ship's hull is similarly bent as its support changes in waves, the bending is resisted by the structure. On the top of the beam – upper deck – material may be stretched while the bottom – keel – will be compressed. At the axis of bending, known as the neutral axis, the stress will be zero and elsewhere it will be tensile or compressive and its magnitude will depend on the distance from the axis which is the axis of a kind of rotation. Again, as with the example of heel above, the further each element of the structure is from the neutral axis the more effective it is in resisting bending. The cumulative effect is similarly proportional to the sum of the areas of the elements, dA, multiplied by the square of the distance from the axis which again leads to the Second Moment of Area – $\int y^2$.dA.

The significance of all this lies in the square sign; very roughly, the height of the metacentre depends on the square of its beam, the bending strength of the hull on the square of the depth and the difficulty in pointing a gun on the square of its length.

There are many complications; notably it is often difficult to find out where the axis lies. With a computer it is all done at the push of a key, in days gone by, a lengthy spell of boring arithmetic was required.

1. The term moment of inertia is often used, incorrectly, for second moment of area – yes, I do it too!

Review of Principal Sources

While the main references are listed below, many others will be found in the footnotes which deal with specific points.

Parliamentary Papers
Mainly useful for Naval Estimates. Security meant that there were no great committee studies of the Navy as in the nineteenth century.

Other PRO Documents
The reports of the shell and projectile Committees and the enquiries into the explosions in *Natal* and *Vanguard* are of particular value in exposing the faults of both shells and propellant. Referenced in detail in Chapter 11.

Ship's Covers
Those for the bigger ships have been thoroughly explored by other writers such as Burt, McBride and Roberts but there are many gems in those for smaller classes.

Records of Warship Construction during the War.
DNC Department (Undated). Originally confidential, this two-volume work forms an excellent factual account of warship designs of the period. Copies are held in some specialised libraries.

d'Eyncourt papers, National Maritime Museum.
A great fund of little-used material, His papers are identified as DEY followed by a file number. There is also a book containing brief note and, usually, sketches of all design studies of the d'Eyncourt era. (Referenced as MS93/011). Also the E R Bates papers.

Tweedmouth Papers, Admiralty Library.
Two invaluable papers justifying the 'all-big-gun ship'. See Chapter 1.

Published Sources

Transactions of the Institution of Naval Architects (*Trans INA*, London)
Particularly d'Eyncourt, 'Naval Construction during the War'. (1919) and 'Notes on some Features of German Warship Construction', (1921). Goodall, 'The ex German Battleship *Baden*' (1921), A W Johns, 'German Submarines'. (1920)
In all these papers the discussion is important.

E L Attwood, *Warships, a Text Book* (London 1910)
A clear and accurate account of the technology of the day. Attwood was head of the battleship section during and after World War I and was much respected. A key source. Also – *The Modern Warship*. (Cambridge 1913). A short version of his earlier book for the non-technical reader with some new material.

Admiral Sir R H Bacon, *The Life of Lord Fisher of Kilverstone* (London 1929)
A useful source but Bacon seems to have relied on memory too often.

Vice-Admiral Sir L le Bailly, *From Fisher to the Falklands* (London 1991)
A personal view of naval engineering, mainly between the wars.

G Bennet, *Charlie B* (London 1968)
This book on Lord Charles Beresford is a useful corrective to worship of Fisher.

G Bennett, *Naval Battles of the First World War* (London 1968)

D K Brown, *A Century of Naval Construction* (London 1983)
The centenary history of the Royal Corps of Naval Constructors.
Also *Warrior to Dreadnought* (London 1997). The predecessor of this book.

R A Burt, *British Battleships of World War One* (London 1986) and *British Battleships 1919-1939* (London 1993)
A careful and detailed account of the ships and their career. Many unusual photographs.

I L Buxton, *Big Gun Monitors* (Tynemouth 1978)
A detailed and fascinating account of monitors of both world wars covering design, building and operations.

J Campbell, *Jutland: An Analysis of the Fighting* (London 1986), and also *Naval Weapons of World War II* (London 1985)
Jutland includes very detailed accounts of the damage sustained by both British and German ships. Many weapons of the First World War survived to fight again and are included in the Second World War book.

Sir E T d'Eyncourt, *A Shipbuilder's Yarn* (London 1948)
Some background material but disappointing.

N Friedman, *U S Battleships.* (Annapolis 1985) and *British Carrier Aviation* (London 1988)

R Gardiner (ed), *Conway's All the World's Fighting Ships, 1905-1921* (London 1985)
Complete tabulated data of all ships of the era with short but excellent descriptions.

J Goldrick, *The Kings Ships were at Sea* (Annapolis 1984)
The opening months of the First World War in home waters.

A Gordon, *The Rules of the Game* (London 1996)
An interesting approach to the nature of command in the era.

R M Grant, *U-Boats Destroyed*. (London 1964)

D Griffiths, *Steam at Sea* (London 1997)
The history of the marine steam engine.

W Hackmann, *Seek and Strike* (London 1984)
The development of anti-submarine weapons and sensors.

A N Harrison, *The Development of H M Submarines* (BR 3043) (London 1979) Harrison was involved in submarine design and refit during his career before retiring as DNC. A mass of factual material but little background on why they were designed as they were.

Vice-Admiral Sir Arthur Hezlett, *The Electron and Sea Power* (London 1975)
A most useful and interesting book on naval applications of electricity.

W Hovgaard, *Modern History of Warships* (London 1920, Re-print London 1971) Very good descriptions of warships of the day. He worked with S V Goodall in Washington at the end of the war and presented a copy of his book to Goodall. (Now in the possession of Dr Peter Brooks.)

Admiral J Jellicoe. *The Grand Fleet 1914-16* (London, 1919) There are interesting passages on both reliability and endurance. Not always reliable on technical matters but essential reading.

I Johnston, *Beardmore Built* (Clydebank 1993)
An excellent account of the brief life of this great company – and of the men who worked there.

B Kent, *Signal!* (Clanfield 1993)
An interesting history of naval signals.

R D Layman, *To Ascend from a Floating Base* (Cranbury NJ 1979)
The attempts by navies to fly. A fascinating account. Also *Naval Aviation in the First World War: Its Impact and Influence* (London 1996).

R F Mackay, *Fisher of Kilverstone* (Oxford 1973)
The best biography of this controversial person. (Or does he merely match my own prejudices?)

F Manning, *Life of Sir William White* (London 1923)
Commissioned by Lady White after her husband's death but not unduly prejudiced. Quotes many official papers which appear no longer to exist.

E J March, *British Destroyers* (London 1966)
Based entirely on ships' covers. Full of errors and omissions but has some useful material.

H K Oram, *Ready for Sea* (London 1974)
An exciting autobiography with fascinating accounts of life in First World War submarines. Later, Oram was a survivor of *Thetis*.

Oscar Parkes, *British Battleships* (London 1956)
Though the battleship is not quite such a dominant feature of *Designing the Grand Fleet* as it was in *Warrior to Dreadnought*, Parkes is still a key source. The book is unreferenced and it is not possible to identify the source of all his detailed comments.

A Preston, *V and W Class Destroyers* (London 1971)
A well-researched account of these fine ships.

P Pugh, *The Cost of Seapower* (London 1986)
Financial provision is a little studied aspect of seapower but essential as this book makes clear.

A Raven and J Roberts, *British Cruisers of World War II* (London, 1980)
A very careful study of all significant sources and very enjoyable, too. And the same authors' *British Battleships of World War II* (London 1976).

C I A Ritchie, *Q Ships* (Lavenham 1985)
Describes the ships and their operations in great detail.

J Roberts, *Battlecruisers* (London 1997)
A fine account of this much maligned category.

E C Smith, *A Short History of Naval and Marine Engineering* (Cambridge 1937). Originally written as a series of articles and there are gaps but where a topic is covered, it is excellent.

J Sumida, *In Defence of Naval Supremacy* (Boston, Mass. 1989)
Essential reading for the political and economic background. Also fire control.

Articles in *Warship*, quarterly and annual, together with those in *Warship International*.

Glossary and Abbreviations

AA: anti-aircraft
Adm: Admiralty
AEW: Admiralty Experiment Works. See Haslar. R E (Edmund) Froude was the Superintendent from 1879 to 1919.
AFES: Admiralty Fuel Experiment Station
AP, APC: See Shells
A/S: Anti-submarine

BCS: Battlecruiser Squadron
BL: breech-loader
BR: boiler room
BTU: British Thermal Unit. The heat required to raise the temperature of 1lb of water through 1°F

°C: Temperature Degrees Celsius (In the era covered in this book it would be read as degrees Centigrade)
c: circa
cal: calibre (of gun) eg 12in. Calibre is then used as a unit of length eg 45 cal gun – length of barrel 45 times the bore
C-in-C: Commander-in-Chief
Circ: (as in circ M) refers to Froude's 'circular' notation
CMB: Coastal Motor Boat
crh: calibre radius head – the longitudinal radius of the head of the shell expressed in units of its calibre (diameter)
CT: conning tower
cu: cubic
cwt: hundredweight = 112lbs
cyl: cylinder

deg: degree
dia: diameter
DNC: Director of Naval Construction (Watts followed by d'Eyncourt). Also used for his department.
DNO: Director of Naval Ordnance
dspt: displacement (tons)
downflooding angle:
       angle of heel at which water would pour into permanent openings. Righting moments (GZ) beyond this angle are meaningless.
drt: draught

(E):   Engineer officer (eg Captain (E))
E-in-C: Engineer-in-Chief
ehp: estimated horsepower. The horsepower needed to tow a bare hull through the water at a given speed
equipt: equipment
ER :   engine room

F: freeboard
°F: temperature degrees Fahrenheit
ft: feet
ft/sec: feet per second

gaine: a small charge of sensitive explosive to boost the effect of the fuse when the main charge is insensitive (eg TNT).
GM: metacentric height
GNP: Gross National Product

GZ: Righting lever; a measure of stability at larger angles. (The angle of heel at which the maximum GZ occurs is important)

Haslar: site of AEW, often used as its title
heater (torpedo):
       One in which fuel is burnt in the compressed air to increase the energy of the gases entering the engine.
hog: Where the ship is supported amidships by a wave crest and the ends tend to droop.
HP: high pressure (cylinder or turbine)
hp: horsepower
HT: high tensile (steel)

ihp: indicated horse power; the potential power available in the cylinder
IJN: Imperial Japanese Navy
in: inch(es)
INA: Institution of Naval Architects
Inclining (Experiment): Weights are moved across the deck and the angle of heel   measured. The value of the metacentric height and hence the position of the centre of gravity can be estimated

JNE: Journal of Naval Engineering

KC, KNC:
       Krupp Cemented/non-cemented armour
kt(s): knot(s)

lb: pound weight. Also used as a measure of plate thickness - a one 1in plate weighs 40lb per square foot, ¼in 10lbs.
lbs/in²: pounds per square inch
ld: laid down
LP: low pressure (cylinder)
lyddite: high explosive – picric acid

machy, M/C:
       machinery
min(s): minute(s)
MoD: Ministry of Defence
Moment of Inertia :
       See Second Moment of Area and Appendix 5
MS: mild steel
M/S: minesweeper(s)
MV: muzzle velocity

nm: nautical mile (knot)
normal (impact):
       at right angles to the surface struck

OPV: Offshore Patrol Vessel

QF: quick-firing gun, ie firing ammunition where shell and propellant are combined.

pdr: pounder, eg 12pdr gun
pp: (length) between perpendiculars. Note that until after the Second World War, the after perpendicular was the rudder stock.

RCNC:	Royal Corps of Naval Constructors	shp:	shaft horsepower (delivered at the tail shaft)
RFC:	Royal Flying Corps	sq rt:	Square Root
RML:	rifled muzzle-loader		
RN:	Royal Navy	T:	Draught
RNAS:	Royal Naval Air Service	TBD:	Torpedo Boat Destroyer
rpg:	rounds per gun	TGB:	Torpedo Gunboat
RPI:	Retail Price Index	TNT:	trinitrotoluene (high explosive)
rpm:	revolutions per minute	*Trans*	*INA*:
RU:	ready use (ammunition)		*Transactions of the Institution of Naval Architects*
		TT:	torpedo tube(s)
sag:	Where the ship is supported at the ends by wave crests and the middle tends to droop in the trough.	USN:	United States Navy
SAP:	See Shells		
sec:	second(s)	V:	speed (knots)
Second Moment of Area:			
	See Appendix 5	wl:	waterline (length)
Shells	APC: Armour-Piercing Capped	wt:	weight
	AP: Armour-Piercing	WTC:	watertight compartment
	SAP: Semi Armour-Piercing	WSS:	World Ship Society
	CPC: Common Pointed Capped		
	HE: High Explosive. (High Capacity)	yds:	yards

Index

Page references in *italics* refer to
illustrations and those in **bold** to
tables.
For individual ships see under Ships.
All ships are British Royal Navy
unless otherwise stated.

Abbreviations
Adm = Admiral; Cdr = Commander;
Fr = France; GB = British merchant
ship; Ger = Germany; Jpn = Japan;
Lt = Lieutenant; R/A = Rear-Admiral;
Rus = Russia; sub = submarine;
USA = United States of America;
USN = United States Navy;
V/A = Vice-Admiral

1917 Plan 114-5

'A' class (subs) 80, *80*
accommodation 51, *52-3*
aesthetics 105
Ailsa 144
aircraft carrier 111, *115*
aircraft platforms 122
Argo 47
Armed Merchant Cruiser (AMC)
    153-4
armour disposition 47, **99**, 58, 170,
    175, 179
armour plate, KC 7, 18, 19, 32, 47, 55
armour plate, KNC 31, 47
armoured cruisers 60-61
Armstrong 84, 113
Atlantic cruisers 64, 66, *67*, **67**
Attwood, E L 48, 51, *51*, 94, 173

'B' class (subs) 80, *80*
Bacon, Adm Sir R H 46, 55, 79, 142
balloons 120, *121*
Barclay Curle 139
Barrow-in-Furness 78, 80
battlecruisers (general) 58, 100
battleships 53-54, **54**
Bauer, Wilhelm 78
Beardmore 75, 117
Beardmore 1912 design 75, *76*
Beatty, Adm of the Fleet 95, 96, 114,
    120, 155
Beaulieu river 31
Beresford, Lord Charles 79
Berry, W 65-6
Bethlehem Steel 128
bilge keel **93**
Blanche Nouvelle (BN) 34
blast damage 19, 181
Boiler Committee 94
Boiler Formula 133

boilers 25
Bolinder diesel 149
Bridgeman, Sir Francis 41, 58
British Corporation 141
Brown-Curtis turbine 7, 20, 64
Bruhn method 71
budgets 12
builders (sloops etc) **146**
building time 13
bulge protection 163-4, *164*
bulkhead, longitudinal 27
Bureau of Construction and Repair 94

'C' class (cruiser) 65, 101
'C' class (subs) 80, *80*
Cammell Laird 113
Carson, Sir Eric 140
Chatfield, Adm of the Fleet Lord 165
Chatham 80, 83
Chatham Float 98, 164, *165*
Churchill, Winston 22, 65, 88, 137,
    146, 147
Clarkson case 168
coastal motor boat (CMB) 150-152
Cody, S F 74
Collard, Major General A S 140
'condenseritis' 93-4
control top 59
Cordite 33, 168-170, 188
cost **61, 182-3, 186, 196**
cruiser submarines **186**
Curtis pusher 74
Curtis turbine *see* Brown Curtis

'D' class (sub) 82-3
d'Eyncourt, Sir Eustace Tennyson 48,
    49, 53, 57, 60, 67, *88*, 92, 98, 135,
    146-7, 163, 165, 185, 188
Dardanelles 55
de Laval turbine 20
Denny 70-1
depth charge 139
Deputy Controller for Auxiliary
    Shipbuilding (DAS) 140
design methods 17
Dewar 33
diesels 71, 83, 134, **134**, 184, 185
Dippy 71
diving depth 132-133, **133**
Dixon, Sir Robert 7
Dogger Bank 58
double hull 85, 115
Dreyer, F C 47, 96, 173
Dumaresq 37, 46
Dunning, Cdr E H 113
Durston, Sir John 7

'E' class (sub) 83, 103, 114
Electric Boat Company 79, 84, 152

Ely, Eugene P 74
endurance **109**
Estimates **13, 15**
Explosives Committee 33

Föttinger, Dr 25, 66
Falklands 101
Fessenden underwater signalling 83
FIAT 84-86, 151
fire control 19, 37, 46-47
Fisher, Lord 11, 16, 22-23, 31, 36, 55,
    58, 63, 96, 113, 136, 147, 189
flare 73
Flotilla defence 58
Flotilla leader 106
'Flower' class 136-38, 145
Flush decker 111
'Fly' class 149-50
Freeboard 66, 89, 90, *91*, **105**
Froude, Edmund 17, 80, 123-4, 146-47
Froude, William 16, *17*
Fusion design 55

'G' class 85
'G3' battlecruiser 175-77
Garret, Rev G W 78
Gaudin, Edward, Eng R/A 94
Geddes, Sir Eric 140
German construction **15**
GM *see* metacentric height
Goodall, Stanley V 24, 49, 50, 65, 66,
    94-95, 123, 158, 167, 174, 176, 194,
    196
Goodwin, Sir George 7
Gordon formula 71
Grant, A 166-67
Green engine 151
Gunnery Manual 27-29
guns 37

'H' class (sub) 128-29
Hall, Commodore (S) 130
Hall, Reginald 59
Hampton on Thames 150
Hannaford, C 71, 107
Hardcastle, Eng Lt 68-9
Harrison, A N 80, 126, 131, 133
Haslar (AEW) *18, 21 80*, 80, 144, 146,
    174, 184
heave *90*
Heligoland Bight 101
Henderson gyro 96
Hexanite 162
Holland, J P 79-80
Holmes, Lt R A 115
Hopkins C J W 76, 139
Hopkinson, Professor 164
Hornsby-Acroyd 81
'Hunt' class minesweepers 145

hydraulic transmission 25, 56
hydroplanes 133-34

'Insect' class 149-50
Iso K Book 19
ISWAS 134

'J' class (sub) 124
Jellicoe, Adm Sir John 11, 18-9, 36, 42,
    46, 53, 92, 94, 140, 189, 192
Johns, A W (later Sir Arthur) 135

'K' class (sub) 125-27
Kerr, Admiral Mark 42
Keyes, Roger 12, 84, 127
'KIL' class 142
knuckle 105

'L' class 131-32, **132**
Lands, E S USN 135
Laubeuf 84
Laurenti 84
Layman, R D 74
Lillicrap, C S 146-47, 183
Lloyd's Register 139, 141
longitudinal framing 70-71
losses **155**
Lyddite 26, 28, 32-34, 170

'M' class (sub) 130-31
'M' class (destroyer) 68, 73, **73**
'M' class monitors *see* monitors
Madden, Adm Charles 90
magazines 33-34, 165, **165-166**, 190
Malone, Cdr L 'Estrange 76
MAN Diesel 86, 147
Marconi 16
Maxim, Sir Hiram 34
May, Admiral Sir William 11
May Island 125
McBride, L B 51, 123
McKenna, Reginald 13, 42
metacentric height 48-49, 65
Michell 24
mines 27, 151
minesweeping 136
Moment of Inertia 200
monitors 146-149
Moore, Rear Admiral 75
motions 88-93
Motor Launch (ML) 152

Narbeth J H 76, 117, 137, 144
nausea 91
Naval Necessities 55
nitrocellulose 33, 168, 169
nitroglycerine 33, 169
Nobel 33
Nordenfelt 78

oil burners 21
oil fuel 21-22, 37, 68
Oram, E-in-C, Sir H 7, 23, 72
Oram, H K 82

P Boats 141, *141*
paddle minesweepers 144-45
Pakenham, Capt W C 27
Parsons 7, 20, 23, 24, 49, 64, 158, 167, 173
Payne, Stephen 60
PC Boats 142
penetration 32, 37, 193, **193**
Pengelly, H S 181
Perkins R 38
periscopes 79
permeability **199**
Perret, J R 88
Pethwick, P L 71
Phillimore, V/A R F 172
pitch *90*
Plumstead 4, 169, 170
Porte, Cdr 123
Portland 31
post war capital ships 172-83
Post War Questions Committee 172
pre-Dreadnought (damage) 163
Preece, V/A Sir George (E-in-C) 195
Projectile Committee 29, 96
propeller 19

Q Ships 154-55

'R' class (sub) 129-30
'R' class (destroyer) 73, **92**, 190
radio 134-35
Reed, Sir Edward 7, 88
Retail Price Index **6**, 14, **15**
Revolution manque 186-87
Rice, Isaac 79
'River' class **68**, 89, **92**
river gunboat 149
rivetting 49, 197-198, *198*
RNAS 123
Roberts, J 48
roll 48
Rosyth 11, 53
Rusden & Eeles 21
Russo-Japanese War 11, 45, 59, 136, 193
Rutland 120

'S' class (destroyer) 73, 91
'S' class (subs) **92**, *134*, 190
Samson, Lt C R 74
Scapa Flow 89
Schwab, Charles M 128
Schneider 84-85
Schwann, Capt O 113
Scott Russell, John 78
Scotts 84, 190
'Scouts' 61, 106
Sea State 93
seakeeping 88-93, *91*
seaplane lighters 123

Second Moment of Area 200
secondary armament 42-45
Selbourne, Lord 13, 55
Shakespeare class 109, 196
shallow draught minesweepers 145
Shell Committee 96
Shellite 96
shells
    armour piercing 27, 32, 96
    common 28, 32, 96
    Eron, (CPC) 32
    Heclon, (APC) 32
    high explosive, (HE) 27, 31, 96
    Palliser 32
    Rendable (AP) 32
    semi armour piercing (SAP)45
Shepheard, V G 168
Shipbuilding 136, 191
ships
    '24 Class' sloop 140
    A 1 139
    A 3 80
    A 13 78, 81, 83
    Abercrombie 146
    Aboukir 163
    Acacia 137, 139
    Acasta 22, 43, **68**, 70
    Acheron **14**, 20, **68**, 69, **92**, 109
    Acorn **68**, 69, **92**, 109
    Adelaide 64
    Adventure 183-85, *184*, 191
    Africa 47, **74**
    Agamemnon 37, 156
    Agincourt 95, 168
    Akagi (Jpn) 123
    Albemarle 89
    Aquidaban **34**
    Arabis 137
    Ardent 70
    Arethusa 24, 29, 65-66, 101, 105, 160, 190
    Argus 7, 115-118, *116*, *117*, *118*, 123
    Argyll 22
    Ark Royal 76, 77, *77*, 190
    Audacious 49, 160, *161*, 165, 190
    Aurora 65, 104
    Australia 57, 122
    B 8 81
    B 98 (Ger) 92
    Baden (Ger) 23, 49, 50, *50*, 51, 171
    Badger 24
    Bagley 74
    Barham 12, 122, 158-59, 170
    BB 49 (*South Dakota*) (USA) 94
    Beagle **22**, **23**, **68**, 69, **92**, 109
    Bearn (Fr) 123
    Beaver 24
    Bedford 21
    Belleisle 26, 31, 190
    Bellerophon 37, *40*, 46, 47, **47**, 48, **51**, **59**
    Bellona 90
    Ben-my-Chree *111*, 112, 115

Bendish 153
Birkenhead 64
Birmingham **59**, 64
Birmingham (USA) **20**, 74
Bismarck (Ger) 49, 177, 179, 181
Black Prince 22, 44, 159
Blanche 89
Blücher (Ger) 45, 167, 169
Boadicea 61, 89
Borodino (Rus) 34
Breslau (Ger) 167
Brisk 20
Bristol 20, **59**, 62, *62*, 63
Britannia 22
Broke 45, *107*
Bulwark 165
BV5 154
C 4 15
Cachalot 142
Caledon 105
Calliope 24, **24**, 43, 90, 101, 105
Campania *112*, 112-13, 12
Canada 91
Canopus 163
Cap Trafalgar (Ger) 154
Capetown 102
Carmania 154
Caroline 24, *25*, 66, 24, **24**, 101, 105, 190
Castor 102
Cavendish see Vindictive
Centaur **42**, 101, 105
Ceres 102
Challenger **59**
Chameleon 109
Champion 24, **24**
Charmian 23
Chatham **14**, 29
Chester 64, 159, *159*, 189
Chester (USA) **20**
City of Oxford 165
Cleopatra 105
CMB 4 152
CMB 65A *151*
Cockchafer 150
Colossus 37, 38, 44, **47**, **48**
Concord 101, *102*
Conqueror 41
Conte Rosso (It) *see Argus*
Courageous **18**, 37, 96, 97, *97*
Cressy 163
D 4 82
Dahlia 137
Danae 103
Dauntless 102
Decatur (USA) **92**
Defence 42, 45, **59**, 159, 167, 170
Defender 22
Derfflinger (Ger) 58, 158, 167, 169, 170
Despatch 103
Dragon 102, *103*, 186
Dreadnought 7, 10, 13, 19, 27, 32, 36, 37, *38*, 41, 46, 47, 51, 55, 192-3, *192*

Dresden (Ger) 189
Dublin 160
Duke of Edinburgh 22
E 4 83
Eagle 115, *119*, 120, 123
Earl Grey 136
Eclipse 75
Edgar 164
Edinburgh 26, 27, *28*, 33, 49, 64, 96, 159
Emden (Ger) 189
Emerald 104
Empress 111
Empress of India 29, 54
Engadine 111, 112
Enterprise 185
Erebus **18**, 148, 164, 171
Erin 90, 95
Excellent 33
F 2 84
Falmouth 163
Faulknor 92, 106
Ferret 30
Fox 34
Foxglove 139
Fraunlob (Ger) 45
Frobisher 104
Fullagar (GB) 187
Fuji (Jpn) 34
Furious 37, 97, *113*, 113-14, *114*, 116, *118-19*, 123, 148, 17
G 14 86
G 41 44
Gabriel 106
Gavotte *144*
General Wolfe 147, *147*
Glasgow 160
Glatton 147, 170
Glen Usk 144
Glorious 97
Goeben (Ger) 51, 147
Goliath 147
Good Hope 159
Gorgon 147
Grafton 163
Grasshopper 68
Greenfly 150
Grosser Kurfurst (Ger) 94
H 4 150
H 50 150
Hannibal 21
Hardy 70, 72
Harebell *138*, 146
Hawkins 64, 189, *189*
Heather 138
Hercules 41, 90, 121
Hermes (1898) 75, 76, *76*, 77, 112
Hermes (1918) 115, 120
Hero 26
Hibernia 74, *75*, **74**, 89
Hindenburg (Ger) 25
Hindustan **32**
Hogue 163
Holland 4 79
Hood (1891) 31, 162, 190

Hood (1918) 25, 37, 49, 95, 98-100, *98*, *99*, *100*, 170, 172, 173, *188*
Hosho (Jpn) 123
Humber 147
Hyderabad 154
Iena (Fr) **34**
Indefatigable 30, 37, *38*, *55*, 56-57, 159
Inflexible 16, **51**, *55*, 101, 161, 162, 190
Indomitable 46, **51**, *57*
Invincible 37, *38*, 40, **51**, 55, 57, **60**, 101, *155*, 156, 159, 166, 167, 192
Iphigenia 139
Iron Duke **18**, 37, *38*, 41, 42, *43*, 44, 45, **47**, 90, 93, *95*, 166, 167, 193
Irresistible 162
Iwate (Jpn) 34
J 5 124
J 7 124
Javelin 71
K 2 125, *126*
K 3 126
K 13 126
K 26 127, *127*
Königen Louise (Ger) 25
Kaga (Jpn) 123
Kaiserin (Ger) 94
Karlsruhe (Ger) 189
Kearsage (USA) **34**
Kilbecan 143
King Edward VII 16, 22, 29, **32**, **59**
King George V (1911) 37, *40*, 42, 43, **47**, 48, **51**, **59**
King George V (1936) **14**
Kongo (Jpn) 59
Konig (Ger) 45, 155, 169
L 4 131
L 6 132
Lady Grey 136
Laforey 68, 70
Landrail 26
Laverock 70, 155
Lennox 70
Leonidas 24, 25, 70
Lexington (USA) 49, 123
Liberte (Fr) **34**
Lightfoot **92**, 106, 107
Lingfield 144
Lion 37, *38*, 41, *58*, **58**, 58, **59**, 96, 101, 155, 156, *157*, 158, 165, *166*, 167, 168, 190
Liverpool 29, 92
London 74
Lord Clive 147, 172
Lucifer 24, 70
Lutzow (Ger) 44, 46, 166, 169
M 2, M 3 130
M 21 149
M 28 167
M 29 149
Magic 160
Maine (USA) **34**
Majestic 26, **32**, **59**, 146, *162*
Malaya 44, *45*, 159, 167, 170

Manica 120
Manxman 115
Markgraf (Ger) 43
Marlborough 45, 162, 190
Mars 21
Marshal Ney 147
Marshal Soult 147, *148*
Mastiff **92**, 110
Matsushima (Jpn) **34**
Mayfly 74
Medea 73
Melbourne 63
Menelaus 121
Mersey 147
Mikasa (Jpn) **34**
Milne 110
Minos 110
Mississippi (USA) 95
Missouri (USA) **34**
ML397 151
Moltke (Ger) 57, 155, 158, 169
Monarch 171
Monitor (USA) 146
Monmouth **59**, 159
Moorsom 43
Murray 72
Muskerry 145
Nairana 115
Nassau (Ger) 160
Natal 165
Nautilus (Fr) 79
Nautilus 84, 125
Nelson 171, 175, 177, *178*, 179-83, 181
Neptune 27, 29, 37, 38, *38*, 40, **47**, 48, **51**, 90
Nestor 44, 160
New Mexico (USA) 89, 51
New York (USA) 51
New Zealand 57, 167
Nisshin (Jpn) **34**
Nomad 44, 160
Norman 24, 73
Nubian 163
Oak 92, *195*
Oklahoma (USA) 23
Oldenburg (Ger) 44
Olympic (GB) 160
Onslaught 43
Onslow 43
Orion 17, *20*, 29, 37, *38*, 41, 41, **47**, 47, 48, **51**, **59**, *89*, 90, 93, 159
Otranto 153
P 17 13
P 24 142
P 37 141
Pallas 74
Paris (GB) 25
Patriot 121
Pegasus 115
Pegasus (WW2) 77
Penelope 105
Pennsylvania (USA) 49, *50*
Petard 44
Peterel 21

Phaeton 65
Pommern (Ger) 169
Porpoise 44
Posen (Ger) 44
Prince Eugene 147
Prince George 22
Prince of Wales 168, *168*
Prince Rupert 146
Princess Irene 165
Princess Royal 58, 59, *89*, 159
Queen Elizabeth **18**, 18, 23, 31, *36*, 37, 42, 44, **47**, *47*, 48, 49-51, *50*, 98, *188*
Queen Mary 37, 59, 101, 159, 165, 167
R 3 129
Raglan 146, 167, 168, *167*
Raleigh 67
Ramillies **48**, 164
Redoutable 165
Redpole 69, 109
Renown **18**, 37, 47, 96, 97, *97*, 147
Repulse 96, 97, 122, 147
Rescue 120
Resistance 53
Resolution 47
Resurgam I 78
Resurgam II 78
Revenge (1892) 34
Revenge (1913) 90
Rheinland (Ger) 44
Ridsdale 190
Riviera 111, 115
Roberts 146, *147*
Rodney 178-183, *178*, *180*, *181*, 182
Romola 24, 73
Rosemary 169
Royal Oak **48**, 147
Royal Sovereign 37, 42, 47, *47*, 48, 49, *50*, 51, **93**, 95, *188*
S 51 44
Safeguard 136
Salem (USA) **20**
Saratoga (USA) 123
Schleswig-Holstein (Ger) 169
Scott **92**
Seaflower 136
Seamew 136
Seawolf (USA) 128
Severn 147
Seydlitz (Ger) 44, 155, 169-70
Shark 43, 160
Skate 30
Slinger 122
Southampton 45, 64, 160
Sparrow 136
Speedy 194
Spearmint 140
Spider 136
Spiteful 21
Spitfire 160, *160*
St Vincent 37, *38*, 40, **47**, 90
Statesman 152
Steadfast 109

Stonehenge 73
Sultan 21
Superb 171, *172*
Surly 21
Swift **93**
Swordfish 85, 85, 125, 135, 190
Sydney 63, 122
Talisman 73
Tarus 72
TB 047 71
Tedworth 145
Tennessee (USA) 49
Terror 148, *148*, 164, 171
Thunderer 29, *44*
Tiger **18**, 25, 37, 42, **51**, **59**, 60, 97, 101, 155, 156, 158
Tipperary 169
Titanic (GB) 162
Tobago 106
Truculent 194
Tsessarevitch (Rus) 31
Tyrian 196
Umikase (Jpn) 30
V8 (Ger) 44
V28 (Ger) 44
Valentine 107
Valiant 44, **48**, *88*
Vanguard 40, 168
Vengeance 168, 170
Vernon 150
Versatile 92
Vespasian 23
Victorian 153
Victorious 21, 146
Viking **93**
Vindex 115, 115, 122
Vindictive 114, 114, *119*
Virginian 152
Vivien 92, 111
Von der Tann (Ger) 57, 158, 167
Vortigern 108
Warrior 43, **60**, 159
Warspite 43, 158
Watchful 136
Weisbaden (Ger) 45, 160, 162
Westfalen (Ger) 44
Weymouth 63
Wishart 108
Wolf 7
X1 185-86, *186*, 191
Yarmouth 20, 122
Zealandia 11, 89
Zubian 163
Zulu 163
Shoeburyness 30, 147
Short Folder 76
Short Type C 76
slamming *91*
sloops 140
Smith, W E 71, 88
Smiths Dock 142, 143
Sopwith 76
Sopwith Cuckoo 117
space limited 17
Specials (destroyers) 69, 194-6

speed,
    cruising 17, *91*
    top **17**, **104**, 196
Spithead 31
spotting top 41
SSZ airship 113
St Vincent, Lord 78
stability 199-200
structure 49, 50, **180**
subdivision 50
Submarine Development Committee
    124
submarines 78
submerged torpedo tubes 45
Sueter, Capt Murray 75-76, 111,
    114
Sulzer 72, 86
Swan Hunter 138

Taylor, Adm David W USN 94
TBD Committee 93
telemotor 85, 125
Thornycroft 72-73, 109, 123, 150,
    194-6
Thornycroft-Schultz boiler 49
thrust blocks 24
TNT (Trinitrotoluene) 33
torpedo 45-46
torpedo – heater 68-69
torpedo firing **110**, *110*, 134
torpedo gunboat (TGB) 136
'Town' class 63-64
transom stern 184
trawler 143
'Tribal' class **68**
triple expansion 49, 136
Tsushima 36

Tudor, Admiral Sir F C 98, 168
turbines 20, 49
Two Power Standard 10, 13

U-Boat sinkings **139**
underwater protection 31
upper deck layout 37

'V & W' class 73, **92**, 107, 190
'V' class (sub) 82
Vickers 72, 79, 80, 81, 83, 84, 86, 124,
    125, 190
Vickers clock 37, 46

Washington Treaty 172, **177**, 191
Watson, A W 141-42
Watts, Sir Phillip *16*, 18, 23, 36, 42, 47,
    49, 53, 57, 65, 95, 101, 158, 189, 192

weight groups 17, **18**, **137**, **142**, **177**
weight limited 17
wetness 88-93
White, J Samuel 86, 106, 147
White, Sir William 7, 16, 37, 47, 49, 79
Whiting, W H 65, 88
Williamson H A 115, 117
Wilson, Admiral of the Fleet Sir
    Arthur K 75, 79
Wolsey petrol engines 81
Worthington, A M 146

X Lighters 152

Yarrow small tube boiler 94, 100
Yarrows 72, 194-6